¡ADIOS, AMERICA!

¡ADIOS, AMERICA!

THE LEFT'S PLAN TO TURN OUR COUNTRY INTO A THIRD WORLD HELLHOLE

ANN COULTER

Author of 10 *New York Times* Bestsellers

REGNERY
PUBLISHING
A Division of Salem Media Group

Regnery® is a registered trademark of Salem Communications Holding Corporation

Cataloging-in-Publication data on file with the Library of Congress

ISBN 978-1-62157-267-1

Published in the United States by
Regnery Publishing
A Division of Salem Media Group
300 New Jersey Ave NW
Washington, DC 20001
www.Regnery.com

Manufactured in the United States of America

10 9 8 7 6 5 4 3 2 1

Books are available in quantity for promotional or premium use. For information on discounts and terms, please visit our website: www.Regnery.com.

Distributed to the trade by
Perseus Distribution
250 West 57th Street
New York, NY 10107

For M. Stanton Evans

CONTENTS

THE END OF AMERICA
WON'T BE TELEVISED

THIS IS "GOODBYE," AMERICA. ADIOS. PAALAM NA. 再见.
No further warning will be issued.

For forty years, the people have tried to tell politicians they want less immigration, but the politicians won't listen. Every single elite group in America is aligned against the public—the media, ethnic activists, big campaign donors, Wall Street, multimillionaire farmers, and liberal "churches." They all want mass immigration from the Third World to continue. Both political parties connive to grant illegal aliens citizenship and bring in millions more legally, and the media hide the evidence.

Their game plan is: Never allow an honest debate on immigration. On every other important subject, both sides can be heard. The media are against pro-lifers, but it's possible to hear the pro-life side—from churches, pro-life organizations, and the alternative press. The mainstream media neurotically push global warming, but, on the other side, we have the entire conservative media, MIT scientists, and even some lefties, like the late Alexander Cockburn of the *Nation* magazine. There was no difficulty getting both sides of the debate on the Iraq War, Obamacare, the shooting of Michael Brown in Ferguson, and any number of other hot-button issues.

Only in the case of immigration is the public systematically lied to from every major news outlet. The media lie about everything, but immigration constitutes their finest hour of collective lying. They know their ideas on the topic are not popular.

How immigration is changing our country is a lot more important than most of the "news" we hear about endlessly. The media will pound away at Chris Christie's "Bridgegate," apocryphal fraternity rapes, the Augusta National Golf Club's membership policies, "white privilege," four Americans killed in Syria, and the sexual preferences of various Olympic athletes. But getting the truth about immigration is nearly impossible.

The media tell us, for example:

- Polls show the public overwhelmingly supports "comprehensive immigration reform."

No poll shows this. Only polls that lie about what "comprehensive immigra-tion reform" is manage to produce majority support. These are polls about a bill that doesn't exist.

- Immigrants are doing jobs Americans just won't do.

Americans are perfectly happy to do all manner of jobs—they just won't do them for $7.00 an hour. Unions used to care about that, but now they just want political power. Greedy businessmen: What do you think the business climate will be like under a government run by AFSME?

- Amnesty will be fantastic for the economy.

Unless we're talking about the Mexican economy, this is patently ridiculous. Adding another 30 million poor, unskilled, non-taxpaying, welfare-receiving people to America is good only for government workers and employers who refuse to mechanize their operations or pay Americans one dollar more.

- Obama is the "Deporter in Chief"—he's deported more than Bush!

To the contrary, Obama is deporting far fewer illegal aliens than Bush—and that wasn't a high bar. The Obama administration simply changed the definition of "deport" to include "illegal aliens turned away at the border." It's as if a school lowered the definition of "passing grade" from 70 to 40, then bragged about its high graduation rate.

- Hispanics will never vote for Republicans unless they pass amnesty.

First of all, moron Republicans: If they can't vote, they can't vote against you. Voting machines don't register angry glints in people's eyes. Second, Hispanics who are citizens don't care about amnesty! They're already in. They vote 8–2 for the Democrats because they like big government. That's why Obama's Spanish-language ads during the 2012 campaign didn't say word one about amnesty. Instead, he promised Hispanics free healthcare under Obamacare.

- "Comprehensive immigration reform" isn't amnesty.

And abortion isn't "abortion," it's "choice"!

The problems stemming from unchecked immigration are all over the news. You'll just never be told they *are* problems of immigration—children living in poverty, childhood obesity, teen pregnancy, out-of-wedlock births,[1] abysmal high school dropout rates,[2] income inequality, "homegrown" terrorists, massive Medicare frauds, internet crime, identity theft, prison overcrowding, the vast number of uninsured used to justify Obamacare,[3] sex trafficking, the epidemic of child rape, the destruction of our national parks, drunk driving casualties, drug-resistant tuberculosis, measles and other viral outbreaks, bankrupt government pensions, lower reading and math scores, and shorter "Americans."

Are these problems made better or worse by mass immigration from the Third World? The fact that Hispanics have the highest unmarried birthrate in the country—even higher than American blacks—accounts for a raft of social problems that are discussed ad infinitum by the media, but that will never be identified as the consequence of mass immigration.[4]

A nation's immigration policies are at least as important as, say, going to war. But the media have decided that who gets to live in America is none of America's business. The public can't be trusted with the truth. Go back to the kids' table. The grown-ups are deciding this. Anyone who challenges the elite consensus on immigration will be swarmed with blitzkrieg attacks. It can be difficult to discuss America's immigration policies when it's considered racist merely to say, "We liked America the way it was."

There's no sense in arguing about any other political issue. If we lose immigration, we lose everything.

THE ISSUE THAT WON'T GO AWAY: SHOULD DEMOCRATS BE GIVEN 30 MILLION NEW VOTERS?

The media convince people to believe lies by the simple process of repetition: Diversity is a strength! We're a nation of immigrants! It's a crisis to have people living in the shadows! If it doesn't fit, you must acquit! It's like the hypnotic repetitions drilled into infants' sleeping brains 150 times a night, three times a week, in *Brave New World*.

By neurotic perseveration, mass-immigration proponents have completely moved the goalposts. After Reagan's amnesty, no one talked about allowing *new* illegal aliens to stay. The only issue was: When are we going to get started on those promised employer sanctions and securing the southern border? Now we're told we have to both allow new people in and amnesty the illegal immigrants already here. We're getting the exact same arguments that were made for the old amnesty, but this time with attitude: *Wait a minute—you're not seriously telling me that you don't want to give amnesty to the people already here?* To which Republican politicians whimper: *We hope we're not inconveniencing you by not moving more quickly to forgive you for the laws you broke, illegal aliens.*

I don't mean to be obtuse, but why is it a crisis that illegal aliens are "living in the shadows"? I forget. We need to bring in more people who will drive down the wages of our fellow Americans because—why again? It is not a crisis for Americans that other people have come into their country illegally and now find it uncomfortable to be living here breaking the law. It's *supposed* to be uncomfortable to break the law. Perhaps illegal aliens should have considered that before coming.

Americans are being asked to respond to the world's oldest joke: A guy kills his parents, then throws himself on the court's mercy as an orphan. How *did* all these illegal aliens get into "the shadows" in the first place? They weren't kidnapped and dragged across the border. They came here. At most—and this is dubious—it's a crisis for the illegal immigrants. But "living in the shadows" is evidently better than living in Guadalajara, otherwise, there's an easy solution. Living in the shadows doesn't seem to be much of a crisis even for them.

Historically, Democrats have found it fun and profitable to bully Republicans into taking suicidal positions. This latest push for amnesty is approximately the Republicans' fifth mugging. As with all disastrous legislation, Republicans are being told, "We have got to do this yesterday!" *If we don't produce a global warming bill, the American people will have our heads! If we don't pass campaign finance reform tomorrow, the voters will punish us! You're not seriously thinking of blocking a new gun control bill, are you?* It always turns out, no, there's no backlash. The only politician who was ever punished for his position on global warming was Al Gore.

Debate any urgent liberal demand long enough, and the problem usually just goes away.

It's entirely possible that the only Hispanics enraged about amnesty are the ones we see on TV. In polls, a majority of Hispanics answer "Don't know" to the question "Who is the most important Hispanic/ Latino leader in the country today?"[5] Self-appointed Latino spokesmen, claiming to speak for millions, apparently speak for about fifteen people. At least Al Sharpton has a posse of two hundred losers he can drag around with him. Most Hispanics seem completely unaware that they're part of some angry movement led by Jorge Ramos. The notion of Hispanic unity—much less Hispanic-black unity—is pure liberal fantasy. Puerto Ricans and Dominicans hate one another, blacks and Mexicans hate one another, Haitians and African Americans hate one another, and everyone hates the Cubans.[6] Republican elites apparently don't talk to their servants: They're convinced Cuban Marco Rubio will be catnip to Hispanic voters. Yes, remember how Manhattan women flocked to Sarah Palin just because she was a woman? GOP political consultants will never steer you wrong.

The only place a failure to pass amnesty will produce genuine, heartfelt remorse is in the better sections of town, when wives of Wall Street bankers realize that Manuela the nanny will not be able to get taxpayer-subsidized healthcare.

There is simply no reason for Republicans to legalize 30 million people who will vote 8–2 against them. They don't have to be embarrassed about opposing immigration because of how the immigrants vote. The reason Democrats *support* immigration is because of how they vote. Al Gore didn't mind challenging military ballots during the Florida 2000 recount. Obama challenged the petition signatures of every single Democrat running for an Illinois senate seat in 1996, disqualifying all of his opponents and "winning" by being the last man standing.[7] Israel won't allow Palestinians to return to homes they used to live in because of how they'd vote. Palestinians demand a right to return to their pre-1967 homes, but Israel says, quite correctly, that changing Israel's ethnicity would change the idea of Israel.[8] Well, changing America's ethnicity changes the idea of America, too. Show me in a straight line why we can't do what Israel does. Is Israel special? For some of us, America is special, too.

Democrats aren't big on amnestying other lawbreakers. They don't hysterically demand amnesty for accounting cheats or polluters—not even for "the children" of accounting cheats and polluters. Enron executives were hard workers. They loved their families and wanted the best for them, just as I'm sure MS-13 gang members love their families. Think of how the executives' children have suffered—the divorces, the broken families, the prison sentences. Why do we have to punish the children?[9] How many breaks did liberals cut the Amirault family in Massachusetts after they were sent to prison in the child molestation hysteria of the 1980s, even after it was proved they were innocent? Martha Coakley fought like a banshee to keep Gerald Amirault in prison well after the charges were exposed as a fraud. Where was his amnesty? Democrats only care about the children of lawbreakers when it will get them 30 million new voters. Convicted felons are next.

Republicans have no obligation to make a grand forgiving gesture toward lawbreakers, hoping that Hispanics will applaud their sportsmanship. This doesn't require bravery. It requires that Republicans not be idiots. Democrats are just going to have to get 30 million new voters some other way.

STEP ONE: SECURE THE BORDER; STEP TWO: REPEAT STEP ONE

As Reagan's amnesty proves, it's pointless to talk about what to do with the illegal aliens already here until we've secured the border. When the bathtub is overflowing, the very first thing you do is: TURN OFF THE

WATER. You don't debate whether to use a rag or a mop to clean up the water, whether to get a bucket or put a hose out the window, whether to use towels or sponges. The No. 1 priority is: Shut off the water.

Obviously, any amnesty functions as a magnet for more illegal aliens. Nothing shows the bad faith of amnesty advocates with more blinding clarity than their steadfast refusal to seal the border. Ordinary people see this and know they're being lied to.

The "border security" measures of every amnesty bill all employ the same meaningless Washington metric of success. In government, effectiveness is measured not by results, but by how much money is spent. How effective is it? Why, we've tripled the budget! That's what Republican Senator Bob Corker of Tennessee actually said about Rubio's "Gang of Eight" amnesty bill, formally titled "The Border Security, Economic Opportunity, and Immigration Modernization Act of 2013"—which was way better than its original title: "We Surrender."

"The fact is," Corker exclaimed, "we are investing resources in securing our border that have never been invested before."[10] Why, he's so serious about getting in shape, he's taken out three gym memberships! Increasing the pensions of border agents is not a measure of border effectiveness. We're interested in results, not outlays. Even within the meaningless category of "Money Spent," it can be spent in ways that are counterproductive. If the bill includes one dime for ACLU attorneys to process immigration claims, then part of the money we're spending to make the border more secure is going to make it less secure. Rubio's bill gave $150 million to nonprofits to help illegal aliens apply for amnesty.[11]

Most Hispanics are smarter than Marco Rubio. In 2011, 73 percent of California Hispanics said they'd support a candidate who wanted to "secure the border first, stop illegal immigration, and then find a way to address the status of people already here illegally."[12] In a 2014 Univision poll, 58 percent chose "require border security first" over "pass immigration reform."[13]

PEOPLE WHO LIVE IN GATED COMMUNITIES TELL US FENCES DON'T WORK

Americans ought to be suspicious about being incessantly told fences "don't work." It's like being told wheels don't work. The media maniacally repeat this nonsense, hoping to lull people into thinking, *Maybe it is impossible to control the borders.* The *New York Times* explains, for example: "Would-be migrants still find ways over, under, through and around them."[14] *Wheels still find ways to bend, break, or spring leaks.* China built a thirteen-thousand-mile wall several centuries before Christ, and it's still working.

The *Times* gave the game away with this sentimental glop about border fences being "the approach favored by ancient empires: the raising of a wall." The article continued: "The barrier wasn't very likely to overturn the law of supply and demand, but it did serve as a useful symbol of the process of alienation, a closing-off of lives and minds, along the line it traces."[15] Yes, that's precisely the idea! Aren't fences peachy? Tellingly, the *Times* added: "Still, the tattered ideal of a world without borders holds great power." For whom is a "world without borders" an ideal? People who don't much care for America, I gather.

Even Republicans who pretend to want a secure border are always telling us fences won't work. The NEW WAY of stopping tubs from overflowing is to use mops and blow-dryers. Sure, we can always turn the water off, but that won't work because it could always spring a leak. Let's just keep mopping. Responding to an increasingly annoyed public, Congress has repeatedly voted to build a border fence. But somehow, the fence never gets built—and Congress does nothing. In January 2011, Obama's Department of Homeland Security announced that it had "ended the Secure Border Initiative Network" on the grounds that "it did not meet cost-effectiveness and viability standards."[16] And if there is one thing the Obama administration absolutely insists upon, it's cost-effectiveness and viability!

The steadfast refusal of the amnesty crowd to agree to a fence tells us that Americans should not budge on the point. In addition to being the only sane, logical thing to do, demanding a fence forces amnesty proponents to admit that they have no intention of ever sealing the border. The surge of ninety thousand poor Central Americans across the border in 2014 proved that. Obama pretended his hands were tied. *It's the law!* It wasn't the law. So either Obama is stupid or he was deliberately lying, and the smart money is on "deliberately lying." But Democrats—and some Republicans—insisted there was some mysterious "loophole" in the law that prohibited this country from stopping illegal aliens at the border. If politicians really believed that, why didn't they close the loophole?

Instead, amnesty supporters tried a surprise argument: To stop illegals pouring across the border, Congress had to pass amnesty. They were hoping to stun us into silence with the stupidity of their argument. No one was prepared for it. *I'm sorry, Your Honor, we didn't bring our notes on that. We were ready for "It's wrong" or "What about the children?" We weren't expecting: To stop the surge at the border, we need to reward the people surging across it.*

Everyone knows that one amnesty begets more illegal aliens, which begets another amnesty. It's called an "incentive." There's less of an incentive if the gate is locked. First lock the gate, then figure out what to do with the people already here. Any amnesty is an inducement to illegal aliens. If you choose to argue it's not, I refer you to history. This is not the first time Americans have been promised secure borders in return for amnesty. The 1986 Simpson-Mazzoli Act, also known as "The Charlie Brown and Lucy with Football Act," was supposed to end illegal immigration forever: Give us amnesty one time, then: Never again.[17]

As with all laws that combine the bitter with the sweet, such as tax hikes and spending cuts, we got one and not the other. The amnesty came, but the border security never did. Illegal immigration sextupled. There have been a half dozen more amnesties since then, legalizing millions more foreigners who broke our laws.[18] Perhaps we could have trusted Washington's sincerity thirty years ago, but Americans have already been fooled once—then, six more times. They aren't stupid.

The two parts cannot be done simultaneously. A border fence must be started first—and completed first. Only after all the ACLU lawsuits and INS rulings have run their course, and the border is still secure, do we move to Step Two. I happen to think we don't do the amnesty part ever, but it's tendentious even to discuss what to do with illegal aliens already here until we can prevent more from coming. We'll talk about legalization as soon as it's as hard to get into the United States as it used to be to get out of East Germany.

To review:

Step One: Secure the border.

Step Two: Discuss what to do with illegals already here.

AMNESTY IS GOODBYE, AMERICA

Contrary to everything you've heard, the only options are not: Amnesty or deporting 11 million people. There's also the option of letting them stay in the shadows—or *the same thing we've been doing for the last thirty years*. Americans are under no moral obligation to grant amnesty to people who have broken our laws. "The moral thing to do" is usually defined as "following the law." The fact that Democrats want 30 million new voters is not a good enough reason to ignore the law and screw over American workers, as well as legal immigrants already here. How about Republicans try this: *We're not giving you anything—not even half—because there's no reason to do so.*

The demand for amnesty is not going away. Nothing ever gets struck from the Left's "To Do" list. Democrats had been angling for national healthcare since the FDR administration. Conservatives thought they killed it with the ignominious defeat of Hillarycare in 1994, but the very next time Democrats controlled both Congress and the presidency—we got Obamacare. To paraphrase what President Bush used to say about terrorists: The anti-amnesty side has to be perfect every time; the pro-amnesty side only has to win once. And then the country is finished. There won't be any reason to care about politics, anymore. At least I can finally clean out my attic.

Any other bad law can be repealed. *Roe v. Wade* can be overturned. Obamacare can be repealed. Amnesty is forever.

2

TEDDY: WHY NOT
THE THIRD WORLD?

HOW DID IMMIGRANTS BECOME A SPECIAL INTEREST GROUP MORE POWERFUL than Americans? I'm not a high-priced political consultant, but shouldn't politicians be more concerned with what citizens think of them than what foreigners do? It's a measure of how out of whack public dialogue is on immigration that it comes as a startling concept to even ask if our laws should help our country rather than help other countries solve *their* problems. Wouldn't any sane immigration policy be based on the principle that we want to bring in only immigrants who will benefit the people already here? Why not take immigrants who are better than us, instead of immigrants who are worse than us?

A good-for-America immigration policy would not accept people with no job skills. It would not accept immigrants' elderly relatives, arriving in wheelchairs. It would not accept people accused of terrorism by their own countries. It would not accept pregnant women whose premature babies will cost taxpayers $50,000 a pop,[1] before even embarking on a lifetime of government support. It would not accept Somalis who spent their adult lives in a Kenyan refugee camp and then showed up with five children in a Minnesota homeless shelter.[2] An immigration policy that benefits Americans would not result in news items like this one: "After arriving from Kampala, Uganda, Ayan Ahmed and her nine children, ages four to eighteen, spent six months in Phoenix. There, Catholic Charities had lined up a furnished four-bedroom home for the family and a neurologist for Ahmed's eldest son, *who is blind* [emphasis added]."[3]

If our government were in the international charity business, they'd be doing a fantastic job. America takes in half the refugees of the entire world.

In fact, however, taking in refugees is not even in the top hundred jobs we want the government doing. At what point will Americans remind their government that it has a responsibility to us, not to every sad person in the world? We can't solve everyone's problems—and that's not what we're paying taxes for our government to do. Catholic Charities may enjoy taking in immigrant families, so they can feel like the Harriet Tubman of Uganda, but they don't have a right to do it on the taxpayers' dime.[4] It's not "charity" if we have to pay for "their" good works. It's charity if *they* pay. But I notice that we always end up paying, while they go to all the awards dinners at the Ugandan-American Society.

Try calling another country's embassy and asking to immigrate there.

> Consulate: *What do you do?*
> You: Well, I can't read or write, I have no skills, and I've got nine kids. Oh and by the way, if I can't make it in your country, would you mind cutting my family a check once a month?
> Consulate: *Click.*

Other countries must be laughing their heads off at us. Our "family reunification" policies mean that being related to a recent immigrant from Pakistan trumps being a surgeon from Denmark. That's how we got gems like the "Octomom," the unemployed single mother on welfare who had fourteen children in the United States via in vitro fertilization; Dzhokhar and Tamerlan Tsarnaev, who bombed the Boston Marathon, killing three and injuring hundreds, a few years after slitting the throats of three American Jews; and all those "homegrown" terrorists flying from Minnesota to fight with ISIS. Family reunification isn't about admitting the spouses and minor children of immigrants we're dying to get. We're bringing in grandparents, second cousins, and brothers-in-law of Afghan pushcart operators—who then bring in their grandparents, second cousins, and brothers-in-law until we have entire tribes of people, illiterate in their own language, never mind ours, collecting welfare in America. We wouldn't want our immigrants to be illiterate, unskilled, *and* lonesome.

LIVING IN THE SHADOWS—
COLLECTING GOVERNMENT BENEFITS IN BROAD DAYLIGHT

We're told—as if it's good news—that immigrants use welfare only at 18 percent above the native-born rate.[5] No, the fact that any immigrants are on welfare proves we're not taking the right immigrants. It's like saying, *Only 18 percent of our cars burst into flames when you start them.* We don't want *any* cars bursting into flames. These aren't native-born citizens who are poor. Aren't immigrants who immediately go on government assistance, by definition, immigrants we don't want? We can't pay for our own poor people, but now we have to be the welfare ward of the world?

Our government does such a terrific job at choosing who gets to immigrate to America that 52 percent of *legal* immigrant households with children are on government assistance. In all, nearly 60 percent of immigrants—legal and illegal—are on government assistance, compared with 39 percent of native households.[6] Why would any country voluntarily bring in people who have to be supported by the taxpayer?

Immigrants from nineteen of the top twenty-five source countries are more likely to be in poverty than native white Americans, generally far more likely.[7] Immigrants from Mexico and Honduras, for example, have a poverty rate three times higher than white Americans.[8] The only immigrants *less* likely to be in poverty than white Americans are those from Canada, Poland, the United Kingdom, Germany, India, and the Philippines.[9] Needless to say, we take fewer immigrants from these countries than from the neediest immigrant countries. Poland and Germany aren't even in the top ten source countries, and Canada and the United Kingdom *combined* send us fewer immigrants than Mexico does.

Business lobbyists have an irritating habit of dismissing the massive welfare use of immigrants by saying, *Yes, of course, we have to get rid of welfare.* First of all, their cheap labor wouldn't be so cheap if not for all the goodies provided by the U.S. taxpayer, so this is a ruse. The immigrants get a taxpayer subsidy to work for the rich, and the rich get a break on the maid. This cozy deal is funded by the long-suffering middle class.

Second, it would be easier to repeal the law of gravity than to prevent immigrants from accessing welfare. The Republicans' 1996 welfare reform bill barred immigrants from receiving direct welfare payments for a mere five years. That turned out to be the single biggest cost savings of the entire welfare reform. Most people said, *THAT'S NOT ALREADY THE LAW?* But at the *New York Times*, needy immigrants are the most desirable immigrants. The *Times* hysterically attacked the immigration provisions as one of the "cruelest aspects" of welfare reform. Congress immediately restored welfare for immigrants who arrived before the law passed on the grounds that it would be unfair to take welfare away from immigrants who came here *expecting* to live off the American taxpayer. Subsequent Congresses restored welfare for elderly immigrants, immigrants with children, refugees, and immigrants who are hungry, get pregnant, or brought a wife-beater with them.[10]

America should be choosing immigrants like the New England Patriots choose players. They don't have a lottery system for their draft picks. No one guilts them into taking a blind kid with one leg over an All American—much less the blind kid's cousin, to keep him company. But that's America's immigration policy. We're in a seller's market, but instead of taking the top draft picks, we aggressively recruit cripples, illiterates, and the desperately poor. A strange idea has taken hold that it's unfair to get the best immigrants we can. Why should that top model be allowed to date only rich, good-looking guys? She should be forced to date poor, balding losers. Maybe Kate Upton should have a lottery system to decide whom she goes out with.

Proposing an immigration policy that serves America's interests should not require an apology.

THIS IS ON THE KENNEDY HIGHLIGHTS REEL, RIGHT AFTER THE PART WHERE HE KILLS THAT GIRL

It's our current immigration laws that demand an apology. It was Teddy Kennedy's 1965 immigration act that snuffed out the generous quotas for immigrants from the countries that had traditionally populated America— England, Ireland, and Germany[11]—and added "family reunification" policies, allowing recent immigrants to bring in their relatives, and those relatives to bring in *their* relatives, until entire Somali villages have relocated to Minneapolis and Muslim cabdrivers are refusing to transport passengers with dogs or alcohol.[12] America has to take in all the poor people of the world, so that Ted Kennedy could get his face on commemorative plates. I'm sorry the Kennedy family felt awkward in Brahmin Boston, but that isn't enough of a reason to wreck our country.

Kennedy's immigration law was enacted during the magical post-1964 period, when Congress had free rein to push through the craziest left-wing legislation since the New Deal. It was the most destructive period in American history. Anything the Left had ever dreamed of became law, in such profusion that it could have been a test to see if members of Congress were actually reading the bills. The premise of the 1965 immigration act sounds like the bizarre belief of a weird hippie cult: The poor of the world have the right to come to America, and we have to take care of them!

Liberals had tried convincing Americans to vote for them, but that kept ending badly. Except for Lyndon Johnson's aberrational 1964 landslide,

Democrats have not been able to get a majority of white people to vote for them in any presidential election since 1948.[13] Their only hope was to bring in new voters. *Okay, fine. You won't vote for us, America? We tried this the easy way, but you give us no choice. We're going to overwhelm you with new voters from the Third World.* As Democratic consultant Patrick Reddy wrote for the Roper Center in 1998: "The 1965 Immigration Reform Act promoted by President Kennedy, drafted by Attorney General Robert Kennedy, and pushed through the Senate by Ted Kennedy has resulted in a wave of immigration from the Third World that should shift the nation in a more liberal direction within a generation. It will go down as the Kennedy family's greatest gift to the Democratic Party."[14]

Since then, the Democrats' insatiable need for more voters has continued unabated. A year before the 1996 presidential election, the Clinton administration undertook a major initiative to make 1 million immigrants citizens in time to vote. The White House demanded that applications be processed twelve hours a day, seven days a week. Criminal background checks were jettisoned for hundreds of thousands of applicants, resulting in citizenship being granted to at least seventy thousand immigrants with FBI criminal records and ten thousand with felony records.[15] Murderers, robbers, and rapists were all made citizens so that the Democrats would have a million foreign voters on the rolls by Election Day.[16] The *Washington Post* reported—after Clinton was safely reelected—that the citizenship initiative was intended to create "a potent new bloc of Democratic voters." Even the INS had objected to "running a pro-Democrat voter mill."[17] Democrats didn't care. Clinton's reelection was more important than the country.

The mass migration of the poorest of the poor to America is bad for the whole country, but it's fantastic for Democrats. Ask yourself: Which party benefits from illiterate non-English speakers who have absolutely no idea what they're voting for, but can be instructed to learn certain symbols? The foreign poor are prime Democratic constituents because they're easily demagogued into tribal voting. A white person can vote Republican or

Democratic without anyone saying to him, "HOW CAN YOU VOTE AGAINST YOUR RACE?" By contrast, every nonwhite person is required to vote Democrat.[18] Republicans' whispering sweet nothings in Hispanic ears isn't going to change that. Voting Democratic is part of their cultural identity. Race loyalty trumps the melting pot.

Moreover, poor people are never opposed to big government because they're exempt from all the annoying things that government does. They're not worried about taxes: The government is not going to raise any taxes that they pay. They drive unlicensed cars, have no insurance, flee accidents, and couldn't pay a court judgment anyway. The government doesn't want to get in touch with the poor for any reason other than to give them things. So it's lucky, in a way, that Democrats are the party of government workers. Unending immigration means we need rafts of government workers to educate non-English speakers, teach cultural sensitivity classes, arrest criminals, man prisons, clean up parks, distribute food stamps, arrange subsidized housing, and work in hospital emergency rooms to deliver all those premature babies.

MSNBC is constantly crowing about Democrats sweeping every ethnic group. Could we see the party preferences of voters whose great-great-grandparents were born in America? Republicans would win that demographic in a landslide. The American electorate isn't moving to the left—it's shrinking. Democrats figured out they'd never win with Americans, so they implemented an evil, genius plan to change this country by restocking it with voters more favorably disposed to left-wing policies than Americans ever would be. Unfortunately, this scheme was implemented long before I was able to object.

But that's not how the story of the end of America will be written. Rather, it will be: THEN, FINALLY, PROGRESSIVE POLITICS SWEPT THE NATION! THERE WAS RESISTANCE, BUT, IN THE END, THE LEFT'S ARGUMENTS WON. No minds have been changed. Democrats just brought in a new group of voters whose minds don't need to be changed. It's as if the Democrats switched teams at halftime, from the worst team in the NBA to the best. *We've got five NBA All-Stars guarding LeB-ron—Woo hoo! We won!* Don't pat yourselves on the back, Democrats. The country isn't changing—you changed the voters.

Occasionally, Democrats speak openly about what they're doing. In 2002, liberal journalist John Judis and political scientist Ruy Teixeira wrote a book boasting that immigrants, combined with the Democrats' usual disgruntled voters—divorcées and college professors—would give Democrats an insuperable majority within a few decades. Third World immigration, they said, would consummate "George McGovern's revenge"—which up to that point I thought was a particularly nasty lower intestinal condition. A decade later, when Obama won his 2012 reelection, Teixeira gloated that—as he had predicted—ethnic minorities were voting 8–2 for the Democrats, and had grown to nearly one-third of the electorate. "McGovern's revenge only seems sweeter," Teixeira said.[19]

McGovern's revenge also represents the Democrats' switch from a party of blue-collar workers to a party of urban elites—feminists, vegans, drug legalizers, untaxed hedge fund operators, and transgender-rights activists. Back when Democrats still claimed to represent working Americans, they opposed illegal immigration. Since being taken over by the Far Left, all that matters to them is changing the electorate to one that doesn't mind liberal insanity.

PROUD TO BE UN-AMERICAN

It's striking how so many immigration activists don't seem to particularly like this country. They tell us that America is a teeming mass of racist, sexist, homophobic bigots. But then they insist on bringing the rest of the world to live here. As Jesse Mills, an ethnic studies professor at the University of San Diego, put it: "The legacy of race, gender, and class oppression in the United States has transported many Somali refugees from one epic struggle to another."[20] Why are liberals so determined to drag innocent Somalis to this hell on earth?

Immigration is how the Left decided to punish America. The anti-American crowd used to dash off to fight with Communist insurgencies in Third World jungles. But the fun of being self-righteous was sometimes cut short when they ended up in prison, like Lori Berenson, who was arrested for her activities with the Túpac Amaru Revolutionary Movement in Peru. Rather than hating America from abroad, today's radicals can hate it right here at home by bringing the Third World to America! Google *immigrant rights group files suit* and you'll get 20 million hits.

Even after the country had twice elected the angel Obama, only 40 percent of liberals told Pew Research they were "proud to be American"—compared with more than 70 percent of conservatives.[21] Our recent immigrants agree with liberals! They may like the money, the jobs, and the government benefits, but—like liberals—most immigrants have zero emotional attachment to the United States. According to a *Washington Post* poll, a majority of second-generation immigrants from Mexico, Cuba, Haiti, Vietnam, and the West Indies did not refer to themselves as "Americans" and said America was not the best country in the world.[22] They're not the hottest immigrants in the world, so maybe a solution presents itself.

Being openly hostile to America has become a part of ethnic pride. U.S. Representative Luis Gutierrez calls on his own country (technically, the USA) to "stop the deportation of *our people* [emphasis added]!"[23] Don't be thinking that just because he's a member of Congress, sworn to uphold the Constitution, that his first loyalty is to the United States. That's where you always make the same mistake. Gutierrez told *Newsweek* that he has "only one loyalty, and that's to the immigrant community."[24] When demanding special treatment, immigrants are minorities oppressed by America; when they commit crimes or terrorist acts, they're "local man."

Sending undesirable immigrants to an enemy nation is a war tactic, such as, in 1980, when President Jimmy Carter idiotically offered to take any Cubans who wanted to come to America and Fidel Castro responded by emptying Cuba's prisons and mental institutions onto the Mariel boatlift.[25] Today, immigration is again being used as a war technique by America's enemies: Democrats. Instead of Communist dictators conniving to send their headaches to the United States, American liberals are conniving to bring them here—and then hand them voter registration cards. Third World immigration is a win-win for the Left. They can instruct immigrants on hating the country *and* get their housework done at the same time!

It is a striking fact that Communists have managed to infect the working class everywhere in the world—except the United States. Nineteenth-century anarchists hoped to stir up labor unrest with mob violence such as the Haymarket Riot. Stalinists infiltrated labor unions in the 1930s and 1940s. Long-haired student radicals tried to organize blue-collar workers in the sixties. How did that work out? All their efforts fizzled. By 1970, building trades guys were beating up antiwar hippies on Wall Street and storming City Hall to raise the American flag—then being flown at half-staff by Mayor John Lindsay to honor students killed at Kent State University. Blue-collar workers voted overwhelmingly for Reagan, who, along with Nixon, was endorsed by the Teamsters Union.

To its dismay, the American Left is utterly bereft of working-class members—the very proletarian masses they hoped to champion! Instead, their meetings are jammed with college professors and feminists. But you know where liberals have finally found a working class amenable to left-wing politics and violent political demonstrations? Take a look at Latin American politics for your clue.

The immigrants themselves are window dressing for left-wing activists' campaign to destroy America. Foreign names go on the masthead, but left-wing zealots lead the team.[26] Michele Waslin, for years the spokesman for "La Raza"—meaning "a race other than hers"—denounced a legislative proposal to encourage immigrants to learn English and American history, saying "patriotism and traditional American values" are "potentially dangerous to our communities."[27] Leftists have no trouble adopting the persona of an oppressed Third World person. The only identity they have difficulty assuming is: "American."

At least liberals have a clear mission and know what they're fighting for: Their plan is to turn America into another Third World hellhole, where the two parties are the Chuck Schumer Democratic Party and the Nancy Pelosi Democratic Party. Republicans can't think past the next election. They need campaign cash, and their big donors want cheap workers now. We're lucky if we can get Republicans to think past their kids' summer jobs. Karl Rove praises illegal immigration, saying: "I don't want my 17-year-old son to have to pick tomatoes or make beds in Las Vegas."[28] How about one illegal alien gets to stay if Karl Rove goes?

MEXICO HAD ONE-PARTY RULE FOR 70 YEARS . . . AND SO WILL WE

Democrats love the "browning of America" because they need the votes; liberals want it because they seek the destruction of America; and certain business interests support it because they want the cheap labor. They think: *Subsidizing my cheap labor with immigrant workers will cost everybody—and we're part of "everybody"—but the benefits of cheap labor go JUST TO US!*

If businessmen think immigrants are going to be libertarians, they're out of their minds. Look at their home countries! Immigrants have always favored the Democratic Party, but Mexicans can be counted on to develop into a voting bloc that will remain poor and in need of government assistance for generations. Also, it's part of Mexican culture to bloc-vote for useless left-wing parties. Despite scandals, corruption, and economic failure, the Institutional Revolutionary Party ruled Mexico for seventy-one straight years. Seventy-one years! Even African Americans haven't been bloc-voting for the Democrats that long. (The GOP might get black votes again if they stood up for African American jobs by opposing the dump of low-wage immigrant labor on the country. Mitt Romney, who had the toughest position on immigration of any major presidential candidate in generations, won nearly 20 percent of the young black male vote—and that was against the country's first black president.)[29]

What will happen when people who come from countries where tax evasion is a way of life are supposed to pay taxes? What's going to happen when a mostly white senior population is being supported by a mostly brown younger population? Whose taxes will be raised to make up the shortfall? Not the people who don't pay any taxes at all. Employers don't care. They want the cheap labor NOW. American businesses are like sharks: All appetite, no brain. They're willing to screw over everyone in their line of sight to make one more dollar in profit. We're seeing exactly what Lenin is supposed to have said about capitalists: *They will sell us the rope with which to hang them.*[30]

How about asking the employers of immigrant workers to pay the full price of their employees? Immigration is the only area where the rich are allowed to externalize their costs without anyone complaining. If Company A buys Company B in 2015, it will be responsible for Company B's pollution back in 1975. Why shouldn't employers be on the hook when their cheap labor becomes a public charge or commits a crime?

> Dear Smithfield Packing Company:
>
> Please find enclosed an itemized bill for $1,879,003.59 through June 2015. You've been paying your illegal alien workers $8/hour, and that's just not enough to cover the delivery of their premature babies, schools for their children, and law enforcement to process their crimes. We know it's not your fault when your illegal employees have children, access welfare, or commit crimes, but it's not the county's fault either. Luckily, you've got deep pockets—thanks in part to all that cheap foreign labor. Please remit this payment by next Monday or your CEO and board of directors will be criminally prosecuted.

At least mass immigration from the Third World has finally solved the rich's "servant problem." As soon as European immigrants figured out they had other options besides being housemaids in Manhattan, the servant problem arose. It has been a headache for the well-heeled Manhattanite ever since. An immigration policy heavily biased toward the world's poor fixes that. Today, even TV writers and law associates can have veritable retinues of domestics. Upper-middle-class people enjoy not having to make their own beds or pick up the kids from school. And their pools are totally clean—not even a little slime! Instead of just admitting that immigration benefits only a small group of already well-off people, mass-immigration advocates say: If you oppose how we're changing the country, you're against Lupe, the maid. The one-percenters can't grasp that the law of supply and demand means that they're the ones hurting Lupe by bringing in more poor people to compete with her. The rich get all the benefits of cheap servants—and they get to look enlightened at the same time!

Without an immigration moratorium, the country Lupe thought she was moving to won't exist anymore.

I WANTED TO LIVE IN AMERICA

Never in human history has a country simply decided to turn itself into another country like this. No offense to Mexico. Love the food! But Japan doesn't say, "Let's become Sweden!" Finland doesn't say, "Let's be Scotland!" I don't want to live in Japan. I don't want to live in Scotland. I wanted to live in America. So did Lupe. Why don't American elites?

Everyone who supports our current immigration policies does so for his own reason:

- Democrats for the votes;
- Employers for the cheap labor;
- Rich people for the nannies, maids, and gardeners;

- Republicans for the campaign cash; and
- Churches for the taxpayer money.[31]

You will notice that none of these reasons has anything to do with what's good for the country.

An immigration law premised on the idea that America owes the rest of the world would be bad enough. But Third World immigration + massive welfare state + political correctness = *The End of America*. We not only favor immigrants as different from us as possible, but we no longer ask anything of immigrants in terms of assimilation. We can't. That would be "racist."

In 1915, future Supreme Court Justice Louis Brandeis gave a speech on what he called "Americanization Day"—the Fourth of July. He said that the process of newcomers becoming Americans involved not only superficial changes, such as adopting "the clothes, the manners and the customs generally prevailing here" or even the "far more important" acquisition of English.[32] The change, he said, was far more "fundamental":

> [T]he immigrant is not Americanized unless his interests and affections have become deeply rooted here. And we properly demand of the immigrant even more than this. He must be brought into complete harmony with our ideals and aspirations and cooperate with us for their attainment. Only when this has been done will he possess the national consciousness of an American.[33]

And Brandeis was talking exclusively about European immigrants— not Mapuche Indians of Araucanía, with their rich tradition of human sacrifice.[34]

Flash to 2014: The U.S. Court of Appeals for the Ninth Circuit upholds a California school's ban on wearing American flag T-shirts so as not to upset Mexican immigrants celebrating Cinco de Mayo.[35] It is impossible to imagine a prominent American like Louis Brandeis giving a speech today titled: "True Americanism"—unless it were to pay tribute to the important contribution made by Mexicans demonstrating on Cinco de Mayo.

As long as the immigrants were white Europeans, America was allowed to demand that they assimilate, by which it is meant: You adopt our culture. Not: You get to impose your culture on us. But now that our immigrants are overwhelmingly poor brown people, the rules of political correctness require that we submit to their culture. "[W]e have left the time," Martha Farnsworth Riche of the Population Reference Bureau said in 1991, "when the nonwhite, non-Western part of our population could be expected to assimilate to the dominant majority. In the future, the white Western majority will have to do some assimilation of its own."[36]

By 1993, citizenship ceremonies were being conducted in Spanish— presided over by U.S. District Judge Alfredo Marquez—a Carter appointee, naturally. When some Americans complained about Spanish-language swearing-in ceremonies, civil rights advocate Isabel Garcia de Romo accused them of "insulting the American people by making us think that we need to function with only one language and only one culture."[37]

Before 1980, the census didn't even ask about languages other than English spoken at home.[38] By 2010, 60 million people primarily spoke a language other than English. Thirty-seven million people living in America spoke Spanish at home, followed by Chinese, French, Tagalog, Vietnamese, and Korean.[39] Pew Research estimates that by 2050, Hispanics will make up 30 percent of the country and Asians nearly 10 percent, while whites will constitute less than half of the population.

We have some worthy recent immigrants who vote Republican right away and don't require six generations to understand the Democrats. But most don't. Unlike in Brandeis's day, immigrants today are immediately sunk into the warm bath of food stamps, housing assistance, Social Security disability payments, and multilingual ballots and street signs. The whole country can't keep suffering through Obama presidencies just to teach the newcomers a life lesson. We can't wait for every state to become California for the country to see what a white-minority country will be like.

NOWHERE LEFT TO GO

It's not helping to have liberals patronizing immigrants with manifest nonsense about America being "a nation of immigrants!" If U.S. schools still taught U.S. history, this would not come as an exciting surprise, but America is not a nation of immigrants. It's a nation of British and Dutch settlers. We all have a stake in preserving what they created—"we" meaning all of us, except the very rich and the Democratic Party. If America disappears—the America liberals hate and Wall Street is indifferent to—everyone will suffer.

Despite a hegemonic propaganda campaign about all cultures being equal, they aren't. Americans are utterly unprepared for the cultures being imposed on them, and the media cover-up can't hide the truth forever. People notice when their little girls are raped and killed by Mexicans, their Arab shopkeepers commit honor killings, their Hmong neighbors are pimping out little girls and clubbing German shepherd puppies to death, their Indian landlord is importing concubines, and their Chinese acquaintances are murdering their wives out of "humiliation." They notice when Albanians and Russians move in—and suddenly their communities are hotbeds of human trafficking, Medicare fraud, and "crash for cash" auto insurance frauds. They can see when their national parks are closed because Mexicans have dumped trash, set wildfires, planted pot farms, and scrawled graffiti on ancient Indian petroglyphs.

This is a price the elites are happy to pay. Of course, they aren't the ones paying it. The Third World invasion being aggressively hidden by the media will never make it to Park Avenue or Nob Hill. The price is being paid exclusively by ordinary Americans. Almost alone in the world, white, Protestant, Anglo-Saxon America has been a haven for minorities, women, children, plants, and animals. None have fared so well in any other culture. As the lawyer for two Iraqi men charged with child rape in Nebraska said, America's views about women and children "put us in the minority position in the world."[40] Once America is gone, there won't be anyplace left to go.

AMERICA TO THE MEDIA: WHATEVER YOU WANT, JUST DON'T CALL US RACISTS

WITH IMMIGRATION, THE MOST POWERFUL FORCES IN OUR CULTURE ARE ALL on the same page—the Democrats, the rich, Washington lobbyists, Republican consultants, and money-grubbing churches. Even stalwarts on other conservative issues, like the *Wall Street Journal*, are with the Left on mass immigration from the Third World. When it comes to society's rich and powerful, immigration is the great unifier. The only ones opposed to fundamentally transforming this country into some other country are the American people.

IF ONLY OUR BORDERS WERE POLICED AS WELL AS OUR SPEECH

Their goal, therefore, is to prevent Americans from thinking about immigration. Mass-immigration advocates keep banning words, so no one can ever talk about what is being done to the country. They say, *Great, sure, talk about immigration. Here are the ground rules: You're not allowed to use*

31

the words "amnesty," "alien," "illegal," "Third World," or "primitive culture."
They're halfway to banning the word "Mexican." (That's how popular
immigration is!) Any mention of the forbidden words will prompt open-
borders proponents to veer off into a lecture about tolerance and racism.
Oh well, if it's racist, we want no part of it. We didn't realize the New York
Times *had made that finding.*

It's bad enough that illegal immigrants are taking African Americans'
jobs, but they're trying to take black Americans' history, too. As you may
have heard, blacks were brought to America as slaves, freed by Republicans,
then discriminated against for another century—mostly by Democrats—
until Republicans finally got the Democrats to stop. Because of that, blacks
can tell the rest of us to stop using certain words. Immigrants can't. They
don't get to piggyback on the black experience in America. Immigrants:
You're not black. If your ethnic group has been aggrieved, go back and
address the perpetrators. You don't get to make demands on Americans,
and you certainly don't get to control our language. Just because immigration cheerleaders want to avoid a debate doesn't give them the right to label
random words the equivalent of the "N-word."

Amnesty is not "comprehensive immigration reform," "an earned path
to citizenship," or, as Obama calls it, "steps to deal responsibly with the
millions of undocumented immigrants who already live in our country."
It's amnesty. Illegal immigrants broke this nation's laws to be here. Any
law that forgives an illegal act, in whole or part, is an amnesty. What we
mean when we say "illegal alien" is "illegal alien," not "undocumented
migrants," people "staying" here, "Dreamers," "people without papers"—or
"undocumented citizens," as Senator Rand Paul calls them.[1]

In April 2013, the Associated Press formalized existing practice by
banning the phrase "illegal immigrant" from its stylebook. Instead, AP
instructs:

> **illegal immigration** Entering or residing in a country in viola-
> tion of civil or criminal law. Except in direct quotes essential to

the story, use *illegal* only to refer to an action, not a person: *illegal immigration*, but not *illegal immigrant*. Acceptable variations include *living in* or *entering a country illegally* or *without legal permission*.[2]

It's sort of like saying Charles Manson was guilty of "ending people's lives without legal permission." Illegal alien activist groups demanded a ban on the words used to describe them, and the media happily complied. It would be as if child molesters demanded an end to the phrase "child molester." *Please describe only the act of molesting children, but do not label the person.* And don't say "rapist." That will be "people who enter a woman's vagina without permission." Call *the crime* "rape," but don't label *people* "rapists." It's also wrong to use the word "reporter" to describe a person, but unfortunately, we're unable to replace it with "a person who reports the news" because no one does.

There are so many things we can do with "undocumented." Polluters should denounce insinuations that they engaged in illegal dumping. It was *undocumented dumping*. Bush critics will have to start referring to his "undocumented war in Iraq."

WE HAVE ALWAYS BEEN AT WAR WITH EASTASIA

The campaign to ban the phrase "illegal immigrant" was launched in 2010 by an illegal immigrant advocacy group, Race Forward. The group claimed that the term was always considered an "epithet," but had been recently revived by anti-immigration groups intent on "dehumanizing" illegals. This assertion was repeated, without correction, by the *New York Times* in a November 2014 article that objectively reported: "the term 'illegal immigrant' is a tactical term promoted by anti-immigration groups starting in the mid-2000s."[3] Like everything else printed in the *Times* about immigration, this is a lie. The first use of "illegal immigrant" in the Nexis archives is from August 29, 1969—in, of all places, the *New York Times*.

That's as far back as the Nexis archives go. The *Times* alone used the phrase "illegal immigrant" more than three thousand times before 1990—three thousand being the number at which Nexis stops counting. It took approximately sixty seconds to run that search, and I paused for a drink of water. But *Times* reporter Julie Turkewitz blandly repeated the absurd statement that the phrase "illegal immigrant" was popularized by anti-immigration groups in the mid-2000s as a dehumanizing "epithet," without considering whether *Times* readers might remember what happened yesterday.

At least the AP and the *Times* try to shut down debate with words—albeit lies. Illegal immigrants from the Third World prefer to make their point with violence. Any newspaper that dares use the term "illegal alien" can expect to have its offices vandalized, as happened to the *Santa Barbara News-Press*'s offices in January 2015.[4] Local police had been "braced" for an attack on the *News-Press*'s offices because illegal immigrants don't like being called "illegal immigrants" and tend to express themselves with mob protests—in the grand tradition of John Stuart Mill.

WHAT WORDS *CAN* WE USE?

The media also render discussion of anchor babies beyond the pale by banning all words necessary to discuss the phenomenon. Quoting a California nurse who told the *Times* she had delivered "hundreds of anchor babies," the *New York Times* quickly added that she was using "a derisive term to describe children whose parents did not hold citizenship."[5] This is how the *Times* treats all subjects it would frankly prefer that we not discuss. The paper has an auto-key for "partial birth abortion," for example, reading: "a procedure referred to by its opponents as 'partial birth abortion.'" Okay, the *Times* doesn't like that name. What name does the *Times* like? It won't tell us. And what *would* the *Times* call a baby whose birth in America allows all the child's relatives to stay? It's not "birthright citizenship"—that would include legal aliens, who don't need a baby to stay in the country, but whose U.S.-born children are automatically citizens.

The behavior "anchor baby" refers to is the fraud of illegal aliens giving birth at U.S. hospitals, thus anchoring an entire extended family to the United States by virtue of the child's auto-citizenship. There's no logical reason for the whole family to come here, but we get wails of *You're trying to separate us from our American citizen child!* No one ever considers the possibility that the family could also stay together by going back to their own country. This is the way immigration law is abused with "family reunification" policies, also known as "chain migration"—or as the *Times* would put it, "a derisive term" to describe remote villages relocating to America on the basis of a single villager's U.S. citizenship.[6]

JUSTICE BRENNAN'S FOOTNOTE GAVE US ANCHOR BABIES

Anchor babies are "citizens" only because of a phony constitutional principle cooked up by Justice William Brennan in 1982. Just like abortion, sodomy, gay marriage, and unicorns—it's in the Constitution! If Americans want to be generous enough to provide for millions upon millions of illegal aliens, they ought to at least be asked. Instead, the taxpayers are forced to support foreign-born poor through a legal fiction, and are called racists if they ask any questions.

Americans are smugly informed that the Fourteenth Amendment confers U.S. citizenship on anyone who is born in the United States. Liberals act as if this amendment was added to the Constitution in an early burst of multicultural sentiment, so that La Raza could come along a century later and make millions of foreigners citizens without the consent of the people. *Look, we've got to make sure that no matter how people get here, their children will be American citizens.* ARE YOU KIDDING ME? THAT'S NOT ALREADY IN THE CONSTITUTION? Most people are too cowed to ask the obvious question: *Why would Americans have done that?*

They didn't. Automatic citizenship for anyone born in the United States was invented out of whole cloth by Justice William Brennan and slipped into a footnote in a 1982 Supreme Court case. It's so crazy that even Nevada Democratic Senator Harry Reid knows it's crazy. In 1993, Reid introduced a bill that would clearly end citizenship for the children of illegal aliens. As he explained:

> If making it easy to be an illegal alien isn't enough, how about offering a reward for being an illegal immigrant? No sane country would do that, right? Guess again. If you break our laws by entering this country without permission, and give birth to a child, we reward that child with U.S. citizenship and guarantee full access to all public and social services this society provides—and that's a lot of services. Is it any wonder that two-thirds of the babies born at taxpayer expense in county-run hospitals in Los Angeles are born to illegal alien mothers?[7]

Noting that the false promise of citizenship was luring "pregnant alien women to enter the United States illegally," Reid said his bill simply "clarifie[d]" that anyone born in the United States to an illegal alien mother "is not a U.S. citizen."[8] But then Democrats discovered that parents of the anchor babies were voting for them! Suddenly Senator Reid decided it wasn't insane to give citizenship to children born to illegals, after all. To the contrary, it was racist not to do so.

Appellate court judge Richard Posner, the most-cited federal judge, wrote a concurring opinion in a 2003 case for the sole purpose of asking Congress to rethink "awarding citizenship to everyone born in the United States." Justice Brennan's invented constitutional right, he said, was luring "illegal immigrants whose sole motive in immigrating was to confer U.S. citizenship on their as yet unborn children." Referring contemptuously to the idea that citizenship by birth is compelled by the Fourteenth Amendment, he asked Congress to pass a law and "put an end to the nonsense."[9]

ABRAHAM LINCOLN FREED THE MEXICANS

Just so everyone knows the facts, the Fourteenth Amendment was part of the Reconstruction amendments after the Civil War, passed in response to the South's sleazy attempts to deny freed blacks their rights, over which a bloody war had just been fought. To get a constitutional amendment passed, there has to be a mass feeling about a big problem. It isn't a secret trap door put in the Constitution for fun. The sole and exclusive purpose of the Fourteenth Amendment was to stop Democrats from nullifying the entire Civil War by continuing to deny citizenship rights to newly freed slaves.

The idea was not to ensure that every pregnant Mexican who runs across the border would win citizenship for a child born here. *That's weird that women who are eight and a half months pregnant suddenly want to go on an arduous trip to another country. Wouldn't you rather wait until you have the baby? Oh...I see.* Even the former Ku Klux Klanner on the court, Justice Hugo Black, admitted that the sole purpose of the Fourteenth Amendment was to protect freed slaves.[10]

In a widely ridiculed 1898 case, *United States v. Wong Kim Ark*, the Supreme Court ruled that the children born to *legal* immigrants in the United States were citizens. As the dissent, legal commentators, and the *Yale Law Journal* pointed out at the time, the majority opinion had based its ruling on British feudal law, forgetting America had pretty forcefully rejected Britain's ideas about a king.[11] As ridiculous as it was for the *Wong Kim Ark* Court to grant citizenship to the children of *legal* immigrants, that's how the law stood for eighty-four years. And then, out of the blue, during the Reagan administration, Justice Brennan slipped a footnote into a 5–4 decision in *Plyler v. Doe* asserting that "no plausible distinction" could be drawn "between resident aliens whose entry into the United States was lawful, and resident aliens whose entry was unlawful."

I can think of a few "plausible distinctions." For one, there's the lawful versus unlawful part. Also, legal immigrants, in theory, have been looked over by the country's immigration officials and approved for permanent residency. Legal immigrants—all of whom will now have access to taxpayer-funded Obamacare—have been checked for contagious diseases, insanity, mental defects. (Again, this is "in theory.") The *Journal of American Physicians and Surgeons* reports that "many illegal aliens harbor fatal diseases that American medicine fought and vanquished long ago, such as drug-resistant tuberculosis, malaria, leprosy, plague, polio, dengue, and Chagas disease."[12]

Brennan's only authority for the drivel about there being no "plausible distinction" between the children of legal immigrants and illegal aliens was a 1912 book written by Clement L. Bouvé. Bouvé was not a senator, nor an elected official, and certainly not a judge. He was just some guy who wrote a book. So on one hand we have the history, the objective, the plain meaning, the authors' intent, and more than a century of law on the Fourteenth Amendment. On the other hand we have the idle ramblings of Clement, who, I'm guessing, was too cheap to hire an American housekeeper.

AND WHAT A BOON ANCHOR BABIES HAVE BEEN TO AMERICA!

Combine Justice Brennan's footnote with America's ludicrously generous welfare policies, and America may as well have a sign on the border that says: "FREE MONEY." Consider the cost of just one family of illegal immigrants attached to America by its anchor babies.

The Silverios from Stockton, California, are illegal aliens.... Cristobal Silverio came illegally from Oxtotitlan, Mexico, in 1997 and brought his wife Felipa, plus three children aged 19, 12, and 8. Felipa...gave birth to a new daughter, her anchor baby, named Flor. Flor was premature, spent three months in the neonatal incubator, and cost San Joaquin Hospital more than $300,000. Meanwhile, [Felipa's oldest daughter] Lourdes plus her illegal alien husband produced their own anchor baby, Esmeralda. Grandma Felipa created a second anchor baby, Cristian.

Anchor babies are valuable. A disabled anchor baby is more valuable than a healthy one. The two Silverio anchor babies generate $1,000 per month in public welfare funding. Flor gets $600 per month for asthma. Healthy Cristian gets $400. Cristobal and Felipa last year earned $18,000 picking fruit. Flor and Cristian were paid $12,000 for being anchor babies. This illegal alien family's annual income tops $30,000.

Cristobal Silverio, when drunk one Saturday night, crashed his van. Though he had no auto insurance or driver's license, and owed thousands of dollars, he easily bought another van. Stockton Police say that 44 percent of all "hit and runs" are by illegal aliens. If Cris had been seriously injured, the EMTALA-associated entitlement would provide, as it did for the four-year rehabilitation of a quadriplegic neighbor illegal alien. Rehabilitation costs customarily do not fall under the title "emergency care," but partisans clamor to keep paraplegics in America rather than deport them to more primitive facilities south of the border.[13]

In 2003, 70 percent of the 2,300 babies born in Stockton's San Joaquin General Hospital's maternity ward were anchor babies.[14] By 2013, Stockton was bankrupt. Any politician who opposed our insane anchor baby policy would be smugly denounced by the *New York Times*—and wouldn't lose a single vote.

Granting citizenship to the children of illegal aliens has turned American citizenship into a game of Red Rover with the border patrol. The anchor baby foolishness takes this country's immigration policy completely out of Americans' hands and puts it into the hands of foreigners. It would make as much sense to allow Mexican migrant workers to decide when America goes to war.

As Chief Justice Fuller quaintly wrote in *Wong Kim Ark*: "Nobody can deny that the question of citizenship in a nation is of the most vital importance. It is a precious heritage, as well as an inestimable acquisition."[15] Not anymore. Now anyone can get American citizenship. The Somali warlord Hussein Mohammed Aidid was an American citizen. Muhamed Sacirbey, the foreign minister of Bosnia-Herzegovina in the 1990s, was an American citizen. Valdas Adamkus, the president of Lithuania, was an American citizen—and an employee of the U.S. government at the same time. The head of the Estonian army, Aleksander Einseln, was an American citizen. Iraq's ambassador to the United States in 2003, Rend Rahim Francke, was an American citizen.[16] A slew of Islamic terrorists are "American citizens," such as al Qaeda operative Anwar al-Awlaki and his son Abdulrahman al-Awlaki. You can read about the younger al-Awlaki's "mop of curly hair" and "wide, goofy smile" in the *New York Times* op-ed "The Drone That Killed My Grandson" by Nasser al-Awlaki.[17]

The amnesty-pushers have beautiful homes, beachfront property, European vacations, Senate offices, vast portfolios, influence with the Harvard admissions committee, and powerful friends in the media and politics. What do they care about American citizenship? But for most Americans, our most precious possession is citizenship in this amazing country. That endowment is being bartered away by our elites in exchange for votes, for profits, or for campaign dollars.

AMERICA TO POLLSTERS: WE SURRENDER

Although we've been authoritatively informed that a majority of Americans support a "pathway to citizenship," approximately five hundred times in the last two years alone, according to a quick Nexis search,[18] that is a lie. This is part of the media's campaign to convince Americans they're nuts for preferring not to turn America into Mexico. Polls are irrelevant if you lie to the people being polled.

> Poll: Do you support commonsense gun safety or are you against it?

Headline: MAJORITY OF AMERICANS SUPPORT GUN
   CONTROL.
But I hate gun control!
*Too late! You agreed to "commonsense gun safety"—that means
   gun control.*

Similarly, polls purporting to show a majority of Americans supporting a "pathway to citizenship" invariably offer choices that are not on the
table, that no one has proposed, and that do not exist in any piece of legislation. The amnesty option is always loaded up with imaginary hurdles
that illegal aliens will have to clear—learning English, passing citizenship
tests, and paying fines, fees, and "back taxes." The non-amnesty option
always seems to entail rounding up 11 million illegal aliens, putting them
on buses, and deporting them. Neither of those choices describes the position of anyone on either side of the immigration debate. Amnesty proponents have no intention of making illegals jump through any hoops
whatsoever to become citizens, and not a single amnesty opponent has
proposed any program to round up and deport 11 million illegals. Maybe
just one, if you count me.

This is how the Left uses polls to manipulate public opinion, rather
than quantify it. They provide the ingredients for today's political discussion, and you're not allowed to choose any items off the menu.

But can't I be against amnesty without voting for rounding up illegals
at gunpoint?
No! Look at the menu—no substitutions!

BROOKINGS POLL: WOULD YOU PREFER A UNICORN OR A LOCH NESS MONSTER?

Typical is a Brookings Institution poll, asking respondents to choose
one of two imaginary options:

"The best way to solve the country's illegal immigration problem is to secure our borders and arrest and deport all those who
are here illegally."
Or:
"The best way to solve the country's illegal immigration problem is to both secure our borders and provide an earned path
to citizenship for illegal immigrants already in the U.S."

Absolutely no one has proposed that we deport all those who are here
illegally—much less "arrest" them. No one. Mitt Romney had the toughest stance against illegal immigration of any major presidential candidate
since Dwight Eisenhower, and he only suggested encouraging illegal
immigrants to "self-deport," i.e., go back the same way they came. We
didn't "round them up" to get them here, and we don't have to "round
them up" to get them home. As for the Brookings poll's second option—
"both secure our borders and provide an earned path to citizenship"—
there's no "both." There's no border security, ever. And there's no "earned"
path, either. It's no-strings-attached legalization now and vague promises
of border security later.

> Poll: What ice cream flavor do you prefer: Delicious chocolate
>   or three-day-old raw squid?
> Headline: CHOCOLATE AMERICA'S FAVORITE ICE
>   CREAM FLAVOR!

Marco Rubio went on a worldwide tour swearing that his "comprehensive immigration reform" absolutely insisted on "enforcement first." Then
the bill was unveiled and it said:

> *Step One: Everyone who came here illegally is legal.*
> *Step Two: After they're amnestied, they can bring in all their*
>   *relatives.*

So Rubio's plan—approved by a majority of the Senate, including fourteen Republicans*—was: Dessert first, then, we all agree, no more dessert! We'll start the diet tomorrow!

When would the enforcement part of Rubio's "Enforcement First!" plan have kicked in? Answer: Never. As Rubio said on *Fox News Sunday*: "Basically, Homeland Security will have five years to meet that goal. If after five years Homeland Security has not met that number, it will trigger the Border Commission, who will then take over this issue for them."[19] So if the Department of Homeland Security failed to secure the border, ANOTHER GOVERNMENT COMMISSION WOULD BE CREATED! (*That always works*, said the Department of Education.) And if the second commission failed, Rubio would personally write a strongly worded letter. Would the 11 million illegals already legalized lose that status if the border remained wide open? Of course not. Refer to Step One. But the bill sure would have spent a lot of taxpayer money!

WALL STREET JOURNAL POLL: OR HOW ABOUT A SASQUATCH?

In November 2014, a *Wall Street Journal*–NBC News poll asked respondents if they would support "a proposed pathway to citizenship" that: "allowed foreigners who have jobs but are staying illegally in the United States the opportunity to eventually become legal American citizens if they pay a fine, any back taxes, pass a security background check, and take other required steps."[20]

After the word "foreigners," everything in that poll question is pure fantasy.

---

* The GOP senators who voted for Rubio's legalization-first immigration bill: Lamar Alexander (Tennessee), Kelly Ayotte (New Hampshire), Jeffrey Chiesa (New Jersey), Susan Collins (Maine), Bob Corker (Tennessee), Jeff Flake (Arizona), Lindsey Graham (South Carolina), Orrin Hatch (Utah), Dean Heller (Nevada), John Hoeven (North Dakota), Mark Kirk (Illinois), John McCain (Arizona), Lisa Murkowski (Alaska), Marco Rubio (Florida).

Let's start with: "staying illegally in the United States." We're talking about people who sneaked into the country by hiring smugglers, wading through the Rio Grande, and hiding in truck beds. They traveled through remote desert locations in the dead of night, fled from U.S. agents, and stole American IDs. They broke the law and—look me in the eye, illegal aliens—they know they broke the law. But at the *Wall Street Journal*, how they got here is a complete mystery—maybe we dragged them across the border. All we know is, right now, they are "staying" illegally in the United States. Perhaps if what illegals did to get here were not hidden from poll respondents, it would seem less draconian to propose that they go home the same way. The return trip would be a lot easier.

Moreover, all that stuff about jobs, fines, and taxes is utter nonsense. I know it, the *Wall Street Journal* knows it, and the Mexicans hurtling toward our border with the speed of cannonballs know it. But it convinces Americans who aren't paying attention that we're only going to get the most diligent illegals. Not only that, but we're going to make all kinds of money off of amnesty! The last amnesty was loaded up with fines, fees, back taxes, and English lessons for illegal aliens. Let's review how that panned out: English-language requirement—dropped by the INS; fines—dropped by the INS; fees—waived by the INS; back taxes—dropped by the IRS.[21]

Rubio's amnesty didn't even contain the promises of the Reagan amnesty. The only "fee" in Rubio's bill was defined as the actual cost to the government to process an illegal immigrant's application. Who else is supposed to pay that? In fact, however—you will, taxpayer. The bill allowed the INS commissioner to waive the fee for any reason. The INS already waives fees for illegal immigrants who are on government assistance, which is 71 percent of them. We want no delay in legalizing the neediest immigrants!

The alleged fine has enough exceptions to ensure that no one ever pays it. The law provides that any illegal alien currently under the age of twenty-one is exempted, but so are illegal immigrants of any age who merely have a GED and assert that they came to the United States before age sixteen.[22]

As we know from Reagan's amnesty, when nearly 1 million illegal immigrants falsely claimed to have been farmworkers to get amnesty, foreigners who have already broken U.S. laws are not always punctilious about telling the truth to government officials. Under the special agricultural amnesty of the 1986 bill, the INS received nearly one hundred thousand applications from "farmworker" illegal aliens living in the lush, fertile farmland of New York City. Another hundred thousand applications were mailed in directly from Mexico.[23] Some "farmworkers" told agents that cotton was purple or described pulling cherries from the ground. Within the first three years of the agricultural worker amnesty, the government identified 888,637 fraudulent applications, of which it approved more than 800,000.[24] And consider that the age at which someone who is living in the shadows first began living in the shadows is a lot easier to fake than prior farmwork.

True, any wealthy illegal immigrants would be required to pay back taxes. Unfortunately, there are no wealthy illegal immigrants. Half of Americans don't pay income taxes! No illegal immigrant will. That leaves only Social Security taxes. We're always told that we need to amnesty illegals to shore up Social Security. How, exactly, are people who make so little money that they don't pay income taxes going to save Social Security? If we had an adversarial press—or even a curious press—it would ask:

> *Will immigrants be paying in as much as they take out?*
>   No, they won't.
> *So that makes it worse, right?*
>   Why yes, it does. I only hoped you would not ask that
>   question.

Under Rubio's bill, illegal immigrants weren't even required to pay their back Social Security taxes. Instead, the IRS was directed to collect only those taxes already "assessed." Guess how Social Security taxes are assessed against people without valid Social Security cards? They aren't.

Even before the INS commissioner starts waiving payments, illegal aliens owe $0.00 in back taxes.[25] Rubio's bill could have required employers to calculate the Social Security taxes illegal aliens owed, but that idea was expressly rejected by Senate negotiators in early 2013. Amnesty supporters complained that it was just too hard to collect back taxes from illegal aliens. As Senator Jeff Flake explained, "Getting back taxes is incredibly difficult, particularly when someone has paid into a fraudulent Social Security number."[26]

Okay, fine. Then how about dropping poll questions claiming that illegal immigrants will be paying "back taxes"? The *Journal* poll was taken in the fall of 2014—more than a year after the Senate bill had explicitly dropped the possibility of collecting back taxes from illegal aliens. But the question polled not only implied that illegal aliens would pay "back taxes," but claimed that that particular question gave respondents "more details about the proposal." Not any proposal on Planet Earth.

30 MILLION NEEDY IMMIGRANTS, SURPRISINGLY, NOT GOOD FOR THE ECONOMY

Somehow, the idea that the mass importation of poor people is good for the economy has caught on like a runaway train. Everyone agrees!

These claims refer to the size of the entire economy, which inevitably expands the more humans we have living here. So does your household budget if I move in to your extra bedroom. The cost of your electricity, cable TV, water, food, newspaper subscriptions, Netflix subscription, and overdue books will go through the roof. But don't worry, I'll be writing you a check for $250 a month. Unfortunately, I will be eating $400 worth of food every month. So the size of your household GNP has increased, but you aren't ahead of the game. I am ahead of the game. The entire benefit is captured by *moi*.

It's the exact same math with any immigrant to America who does not pay in taxes more than he gets back in government services. That includes not only assistance programs, but also schools, highways, police, hospitals, and so on. Thus, a more detailed breakdown of the costs and benefits shows that college-educated Americans pay an average of $29,000 more in taxes every year than they get back in government services, according to an analysis by the Heritage Foundation's Robert Rector. By contrast, legal immigrants, on average, get back $4,344 more in government services than they pay in taxes. Those with only a high school degree net about $14,642 in government payments, and those without a high school degree collect a whopping $36,993.[27] Contrary to the claims of Senator Chuck Schumer's press secretary, Marco Rubio, making illegal aliens citizens will not result in the U.S. Treasury being deluged with their tax payments. The vast majority of illegal aliens—about 75 percent—have only a high school diploma or less, so legalization means they will immediately begin collecting an average of $14,642–$36,993 per year from the U.S. taxpayer.

Even worse, under Rubio's bill—and Obama's executive action— amnestied illegal aliens immediately collect a windfall directly from the U.S. Treasury in missed earned income tax credits.[28] So the definition for "paying back taxes" under Rubio's bill was: "receiving welfare." Of course, with 71 percent of illegal alien households already on government assistance,[29] "paying back taxes" meant "getting *even more* welfare than you do currently." Illustrating the principle that, in matters of great importance, the difference between evil and stupidity is irrelevant, Marco Rubio stoutly asserted that, under his bill, amnestied illegal immigrants "don't qualify for any federal benefits."[30] A huge majority—71 percent!—were already collecting federal benefits when he said that and were on track to collect a lot more welfare had his bill become law.

Can we retake the *Wall Street Journal*'s poll, but this time inquire about the only pathway to citizenship proposed or passed by either house of Congress? *Would you support a pathway to citizenship for illegal immigrants who knowingly broke this country's laws that would allow them to immediately collect past welfare payments they lost out on while working off the books?*

CALIFORNIA'S FIELD POLL: ELECTROCUTION OR A WARM PUPPY?

When it comes to immigration polls, the Brookings Institution's and *Wall Street Journal's* are two of the more honest ones. California's Field Poll asks respondents if they support "having federal immigration agents round up, detain and deport immigrants found to be living here illegally"; or if they would support a (nonexistent) proposal to "[c]reate a program that would allow illegal immigrants who have been living in the U.S. for a number of years an opportunity to stay in this country and apply for citizenship if they have a job, learned English and paid back taxes."[31]

There's no "program" for allowing illegals an "opportunity" to stay and pay "back taxes." The plan is to legalize illegal aliens immediately, without regard to how long they've been here, much less whether they have a job, speak English, or will ever pay one penny in taxes.

Nonetheless, more poll respondents—46 percent—favored "having federal immigration agents round up, detain and deport immigrants found to be living here illegally" than were opposed to that policy—43 percent.

Polls that neglect to stack the deck with lies on both sides of the equation never come out so well for mass-immigration advocates. The pro-amnesty technology website TechCrunch, for example, forgot to ask about the nonexistent hurdles for illegal immigrants, and asked only about the nonexistent proposal to deport 11 million people. The question polled was: "Do you support or oppose deporting the 11 million undocumented immigrants currently living in the U.S.?" Again: No politician has proposed any program to deport 11 million illegal aliens. So the TechCrunch poll was biased, but only by half. Still, a majority of respondents, 53.4 percent, supported mass deportation, compared with 42 percent opposed. Among Republicans, 74.1 percent chose the deport-11-million option, with only 22.3 percent opposed.

And that's what Americans say after years of relentless media propaganda. Where was the word "amnesty" in the TechCrunch poll? That's what we're talking about, not some imaginary plan to round up illegals and deport them.

With immigration polls, there's never a "no" button. The only question is: Do you want more immigration, or do you want a lot more immigration? There's no place to write in: "How about none?" The people feverishly hiding the truth from the public are perfectly aware that they are completely transforming this country. They cheer the end of America.

4

THE LIE:
THERE'S NO SUCH THING
AS AMERICA

AMERICANS SEEM TO BE UNDER THE MISIMPRESSION THEY DON'T HAVE A
country at all, but rather live in something like the international
waiting room at JFK Airport. America is not a "nation of immigrants," it
is not an "idea," it was never "diverse," and "diversity" is a catastrophe.

If America were an "idea," every country on earth could be America.
Electricity is an idea. The airplane is an idea. Washing with soap is an idea.
That's why other countries have been able to adopt those innovations. No
other country on earth has been able to approximate America—except our
fellow Anglo-Saxon nations.[1] Why is that? We've been dropping enormous
hints to the rest of the world for centuries. America is not a mere landmass—
otherwise, the Indians would have written the Declaration of Independence
and put a man on the moon. Far from discovering America, Indians didn't
even detect America. There *was* no America until the British and Dutch
arrived. They were not "immigrants" because there was no established
society for them to move to. Without the white settlers, what is known as

51

"America" would still be an unnamed continent full of migratory tribes chasing the rear end of a buffalo every time their stomachs growled.

AMERICA'S CRIME OF NON-DIVERSITY

At a swearing-in ceremony for new immigrants in the summer of 2014, the Harvard-educated First Lady Michelle Obama said: "It's amazing that just a few feet from here where I'm standing are the signatures of the fifty-six Founders who put their names on a Declaration that changed the course of history. And like the fifty of you, none of them were born American—they became American." That's if you don't count the forty-eight of fifty-six who were born in America. The other eight—like the rest of them—were either British or Dutch. Fifty-five were Protestant. Only one was Catholic. There's a reason King George called the American Revolution "a Presbyterian war."[2]

The single document in Nexis's news archives to report the First Lady's jaw-droppingly ignorant remark about the signers of America's Declaration of Independence did so in order to proclaim her "correct." Yes, Snopes.com said Mrs. Obama was "correct" in the sense that "the Founding Fathers were not born into a fully formed and established America with its own history, customs, culture, and values, as modern American children are."[3]

That's if you don't count the 85 percent of the Declaration's signers who were born into a fully formed and established America, with its own history, customs, culture, and values. The American colonies had been around for about 150 years at that point. Not only the signers of the Declaration, but the first seventeen presidents, were all born in one of the original thirteen colonies. The eighteenth was Ulysses Grant, who was born in Ohio.

The vast majority of U.S. presidents were exclusively of British or Dutch descent. There has not been a single one without at least some British ancestry. Not one. The few recent presidents with exotic ethnicities were: Teddy Roosevelt and Franklin Roosevelt, who were part French—in addition to British and Dutch; Herbert Hoover, who was Swiss and German—in addition to British; Dwight Eisenhower, who was German and Swiss—in addition to British; Richard Nixon, who was part German—in addition to British; George H. W. and W. Bush, who are also part German—in addition to British and Dutch; and Barack Obama, who is part Kenyan—in addition to British.

No Swedes, no Finns, no Ukrainians, and certainly no Salvadorans or Chinese. The entire British Isles, plus the Netherlands, covers a geographic area smaller than Japan.[4] If 83 percent of American presidents had been exclusively Japanese and 100 percent were at least part Japanese, would we talk about America being a "nation of immigrants"? Every single president, except Kennedy, was a Protestant. (Recent Democratic presidents were, of course, atheists, but all except JFK professed to be Protestants.) Argentina has had a president who was of 100 percent Syrian ethnicity (Carlos Saúl Menem). The prime minister of Belgium was Italian (Elio Di Rupo). Peru has had a Japanese president (Alberto Fujimori). Britain had a Jewish prime minister, all of whose grandparents were born in Italy (Benjamin Disraeli). No one calls these countries "nations of immigrants." America has never had a president who wasn't, at least in part, of British ancestry, but people still babble that we're a nation of immigrants.

For one hundred years before the signing of the Declaration, and one hundred years after, America was extraordinarily un-diverse in ethnicity (British, Dutch, West African, and Germanic), in religious practice (overwhelmingly Protestant, 98 percent Christian), in language (English), and in cultural mores (no wailing at funerals or child rape). Even the few French settlers in colonial America were Protestants—they had fled France under threat of forced conversion to Catholicism. Pre-Revolutionary America allowed the naturalization of Jews—but not Catholics.[5] Curiously, in contemporary America, Hispanic Protestants are majority Republican, while Hispanic Catholics are nearly monolithically Democrat.

Harvard professor Samuel Huntington asks: "Would America be the America it is today if in the 17th and 18th centuries it had been settled not by British Protestants but by French, Spanish, or Portuguese Catholics?" Clearly not: "It would not be America; it would be Quebec, Mexico, or Brazil."[6] Author Richard Brookhiser writes: "The WASP character is the American character.... It is the mold, the template, the archetype, the set of axes along which the crystal has grown. Without the WASP it would be another country altogether."

For its 1976 bicentennial edition, *Time* magazine tried to cover up the Founding Fathers' crime of non-diversity by making them look less WASPy.[7] A photo display of eleven descendants of the Founders included Yukiko Irwin, born and raised in Japan,[8] and an African American probation officer, Elmer Roberts, allegedly descended from Thomas Jefferson's nonexistent sexual relationship with slave Sally Hemings. *Time* wanted to make absolutely clear that the United States was not the product of a bunch of Protestant, Anglo-Saxon men, if that's what you were thinking. Except, the problem is, it was. And the country remained overwhelmingly Anglo-Saxon and Protestant right up until Teddy Kennedy decided to change it.

A NATION OF IMMIGRANTS IS NOT A NATION

Contrary to PC nonsense about America being a "diverse" melting pot, America has never been a "nation of immigrants." Most Americans have always been born here. Even as late as 1990—a quarter century into Teddy Kennedy's scheme to remake the nation—half of the American population traced its roots to the black and white populace of 1790.[9]

Nearly the entire white population of America from 1600 to 1970 came from a geographic area of the world about twice the size of Texas. The entire black population came from an area of West Africa about the size of Florida.

Until Teddy Kennedy struck, America was never less than 99 percent white Western European and West African black.[10] That's "bi-racial," not "diverse." African Americans are every bit as much a part of Anglo-Saxon America as the Anglo-Saxons themselves. Cheap-labor enthusiasts love to insult black workers with fulsome tributes to hardworking immigrants doing jobs that "Americans"—wink, wink—"just won't do," but you cannot understand America without talking about blacks. America is the only country to fight a revolution based on the principle that all men are equal before God, and it is the only country to fight a bloody civil war to end slavery and redeem that promise.

African Americans' contributions to the nation's wars, and especially to its culture, make this country what it is. Blacks served with one of the most important outfits in the American Revolution, John Glover's Marblehead Regiment, which provided the Continental Army with its first naval ship and also stood guard at General George Washington's personal headquarters. In 1775 America, General Glover was perfectly at home with black Americans, who "served aboard vessels in Marblehead's fishing fleet, lived in the same town that he did, and even attended the same church."[11] The Civil War might have ended differently if so many blacks hadn't fled their Confederate masters—including the inspirational abolitionist leader Frederick Douglass—or without free blacks fighting with the Union army. Black Americans fought bravely in both world wars, even in an army kept segregated by part-French FDR.

In addition to fighting its wars and helping shape its history, black Americans have an outsized influence on the nation's style—the Christianity, the slang, the music. For half a century, every rock group in the world aspired to sound like Chuck Berry. No one has ever wanted to sound like a mariachi band. The nation's most pressing social problems—principally illegitimacy—are also disproportionately black problems. Imagine if all the resources lavished on immigrants had gone to American blacks!

Two centuries after the first Europeans settled America, the white population was 80 percent British and 98 percent Protestant.[12] A century after that, the populace was still overwhelmingly English-speaking, British, and Protestant, but, for an exciting change, also included Germans and Scandinavians.[13] The colorful immigrants at the turn of the nineteenth century were wildly different from the original settlers in the sense that they were white people from a different part of Western Europe. For vibrancy,

America had the Puerto Ricans, whom President Woodrow Wilson made citizens in 1917, because Democrats needed bodies to fight World War I and employers needed—guess what? That's correct: Cheap labor. By 1970, fewer than a million Puerto Ricans lived in the United States.[14]

MY, OUR POST—WELFARE STATE IMMIGRANTS HAVE CHANGED!

The entire time it was processing immigrants from 1892 until 1954, Ellis Island received only 12 million immigrants.[15] Please stop weeping about your grandfathers arriving at Ellis Island. It's irritating. And it bears absolutely no relationship to immigration today. Earlier immigrants proved their heartiness by vomiting all the way across the Atlantic Ocean to get here. There was no welfare, and certainly no welcoming committees of ethnic grievance groups.

People weren't allowed to come to America and just hang out. Towns provided for their own infirm and elderly, and they definitely didn't want deadbeats wandering over from the next town. In 1797, for example, Vermont state law required each community to "prevent the poor, resident within their respective towns or places, from strolling into any other town or place." When a new family showed up, the town clerk would promptly investigate, and if it looked as if the newcomers might become a burden, the family would be sent a "warning out" letter, telling them to leave.[16]

About a third of pre-1965 immigrants went home—except British and Jewish immigrants, less than 10 percent of whom returned.[17] Now no one goes home, they go on welfare. Today's immigrants aren't coming here to breathe free, they're coming to live for free. Most of them wouldn't come at all if they had to survive in the work-or-die America that existed when we got all those relatives being wept over. What are Mexico's policies on that? If my money runs out and I have a few kids with my equally non-Mexican boyfriend, do we get free money from Mexican taxpayers? *What about the babies! They didn't do anything wrong!*

Today, any immigrants who didn't come expressly for the welfare have the Ford Foundation to acquaint them with their rights. If the Ford Foundation is busy, there's always the National Council of La Raza, George Soros's Open Society Foundations, the Southern Poverty Law Center, the Migration Policy Institute, the Mexican American Legal Defense and Education Fund, the National Network for Immigrant and Refugee Rights, the National Immigration Law Center, the American Immigration Lawyers Association, the American Bar Association's Commission on Immigration Policy—all working to transfer money from the American taxpayer to poverty-stricken immigrants from primitive cultures. Not only are immigrants taught to live off the American taxpayer, but they are counseled in resentment toward their benefactors. The vast majority of children of Mexican, Filipino, Haitian, Vietnamese, Laotian, and Jamaican immigrants complain about being discriminated against.[18] We take fewer immigrants from Britain than from any of these countries, except Haiti, Laos, and Jamaica—all of which have populations about the same size as, or much smaller than, the city of London.[19]

DARFUR IS THE NATURAL STATE OF THE WORLD

America is not the natural state of the world. The natural state of the world is Darfur. The British Empire spread Anglo-Saxon culture around the globe—Protestant morals, individualism, and the rule of law. Most British colonies rejected those values. Only the ones populated by actual British people—America, Canada, Australia, and New Zealand—managed to hold on to them and, as a result, prospered. The empire's most successful experiment was the United States. Anyone who hesitates for a moment to recognize that some groups have it over other groups in producing free and prosperous nations has been brainwashed beyond reclamation.

The UPI syndicate puts out a weekly almanac column listing important world events that happened on given dates in other years. I happened to come across the one for the week of April 9 and noticed something about the rest of the world. From UPI:

- In 1992, a federal jury in Miami convicted deposed Panamanian dictator Manuel Noriega on cocaine trafficking charges.
- In 1997, a government of unity was launched in Angola, three years after the end of the country's 19-year civil war, with the seating of 70 members of the rebel UNITA party in parliament.
- In 1999, the president of the African nation of Niger was assassinated, reportedly by members of his own guard. A military junta led by the commander of the presidential guards took over.
- In 2000, Peru's President Alberto Fujimori failed to win a first-round election victory, forcing a run-off in May, which he won. However, a vote-fraud scandal forced him to step down later in the year.
- In 2003, the mood in Iraq became exuberant as Iraqis, with help from Americans, toppled a 20-foot statue of Saddam Hussein in Baghdad's Firdos Square.
- In 2004, authorities in Bulgaria said at least 40 people were injured, some seriously, in a toxic gas attack on a police station in Sofia.[20]

While most of the rest of the globe is a cesspool of civil war, revolution, drug dealing, military coups, and assassinations, UPI's almanac entries for America are things like "first American to circumnavigate the globe" (1790) and "William Hunt of New York patented the safety pin" (1847). Immediately following an entry for 1916—"Professional Golfers Association of America was founded"—is this one: "In 1919, Emiliano Zapata, a leader of peasants and indigenous people during the Mexican Revolution, was ambushed and killed in Morelos by government forces." And that particular week was short on Muslim entries, thus avoiding any noteworthy beheadings.

That's how the lists looked until fairly recently, anyway. Lately, the almanac has been acquiring events in America like this one: "In 2006, an estimated 500,000 people protested in Los Angeles against proposed U.S. legislation that would make it a felony to be in the United States illegally." Thanks to our new we-assimilate-to-them strategy, angry immigrants seem to be in a constant state of protest. After Professor Huntington wrote a book warning that America could not survive the cultural onslaught from Latin America, Hispanics responded with a flurry of scholarly papers and academic critiques countering his thesis. Just kidding! They called for national protests against Huntington, his publisher, and Harvard University.[21] These are not the descendants of the Magna Carta.

Edmund Burke, Britain's most eloquent defender of the American Revolution, attributed Americans' love of freedom expressly to the dual facts that they were British and they were Protestants: "First, the people of the colonies are descendants of Englishmen.... They are therefore not only devoted to liberty, but to liberty according to English ideas, and on English principles.... The people are Protestants; and of that kind which is the most adverse to all implicit submission of mind and opinion. This is a persuasion not only favourable to liberty, but built upon it."[22] As Huntington says, all religions come to America and become Protestant. Catholics, for example, were not fully accepted into American society until the church became less "Roman Catholic" and more "American Catholic."

EARLIER IMMIGRANTS WERE CHAMPS AT ASSIMILATION

Obviously, members of other ethnic groups can be great Americans, but that doesn't mean America is an "idea." It means America's distinctively British Protestant culture can be acquired. Earlier immigrants were, as a rule, fantastic assimilators. While WASPs seem embarrassed about their own culture, Jewish Americans have taken to it with gusto. Ralph Lauren is the ne plus ultra celebration of WASP style. Harold Koda, curator of the Costume Institute at the Metropolitan Museum of Art, called Lauren—

born Ralph Lifshitz to Jewish immigrants from Belarus—"the greatest ambassador of American style."[23] The quintessential American garment, blue jeans, was invented by a Jewish immigrant, Levi Strauss. Another tribute to America's British roots is the profusion of American Jews with adopted Anglo-Saxon names like Jon Stewart, David Gregory, Lorne Michaels, and, of course, Ralph Lauren himself.

Hollywood is the only major American industry that was largely built by immigrants. Jewish directors, writers, and producers celebrated their new country with wildly patriotic films such as *The Yankee Clipper*; *Rally 'round the Flag, Boys!*; and *Plymouth Adventure*. A big part of their patriotism was the reverence they exhibited for specifically WASP America. Scores of movies were set in Connecticut—*Christmas in Connecticut*, *Holiday Inn*, *The Talk of the Town*, *Mr. Blandings Builds His Dream House*—as well as in other WASP redoubts such as Newport, Boston, Vermont, and Main Line Philadelphia (*The Philadelphia Story*). Bing Crosby, Cary Grant, Katharine Hepburn, Donna Reed, and Spencer Tracy were all uber-WASP inventions of the Jews. Jewish immigrant Irving Berlin wrote "God Bless America," "White Christmas," "Easter Parade," and "This Is the Army." Try to imagine an immigrant in La Raza doing any of that.

Nearly all immigrants who arrived before Teddy Kennedy's immigration act were like this. America used to get "educated, Westernized" immigrants who "assimilated with relative ease," as Margaret Talbot put it in the *New Republic*, referring specifically to Muslims.[24] Today, instead of educated Lebanese and Iranian Muslims, we're getting Muslim refugees from tribal societies in Afghanistan and Pakistan, thunderstruck by indoor plumbing.

> Stage One: Make it harder for immigrants to assimilate by admitting only those from cultures wildly divergent from ours.
> Stage Two: Stop asking immigrants to assimilate.
> Stage Three: It is hate speech to ask them to assimilate.

It's still possible to meet a Honduran or Bosnian immigrant more completely imbued with Anglo-Saxon values than a tenth-generation American WASP. But they're the exception. To keep bringing in waves of foreigners hostile to the native population in hopes of getting a few good ones is like draining the ocean to find a ring you lost.

DIVERSITY: THAT CULTURE YOU RISKED YOUR LIFE TO FLEE FROM

The companion lie to the "America is a nation of immigrants" lie is "diversity is a strength." Praising diversity is simply part of the PC dogma, a mantra constantly being pounded into our heads. Repeat after me: *Diversity is a strength. Diversity is a strength. Diversity is a strength.* It's like the shrieking radios permanently attached to bright people's ears in the Kurt Vonnegut story "Harrison Bergeron," to prevent them from using their superior intelligence. Contrary to everything you've heard, never in recorded history has diversity been anything but a disaster.

Look at Ireland with its Protestant and Catholic populations, Canada with its French and English populations, Israel with its Jewish and Palestinian populations. Or consider the warring factions in India, Sri Lanka, China, Iraq, Czechoslovakia (until it happily split up), the Balkans, and Chechnya. Also review the festering hotbeds of tribal warfare—I mean the "beautiful mosaic"—in Third World disasters like Afghanistan, Rwanda, and South Central LA. If diversity is their strength, I'd hate to see what their weakness is. The fact that we have to be incessantly told how wonderful diversity is only proves that it's not. It's like listening to a waiter try to palm off the fish "special" on you before it goes bad.

In response to the wanton slaughter of thirteen American troops at Fort Hood by a disgruntled second-generation Muslim immigrant, Army Major Nidal Malik Hasan, Army Chief of Staff General George Casey went on *Meet the Press* and said: "Our diversity, not only in our army but in our country, is a strength."[25] Then a few years later, after two Chechen immigrants bombed the Boston Marathon, former CIA director Michael Hayden told a *Fox News Sunday* panel: "We welcome these kinds of folks coming to the United States." Really? The kind that launch murderous attacks on Americans? Do people even listen to themselves when they spout these bromides, or is it just background music? Saying he was speaking "as the former director of the Central Intelligence Agency," Hayden added: "Immigration to this country contributes to our national security." The 9/11 attacks must have been fantastic for national security!

Hayden also made the strange announcement that America is "required to look like the world." Is that in the CIA charter? I know it's in the Democratic Party's platform and also in the wedding vows of John Kerry and Teresa Heinz. This wasn't some nut from the ACLU. It was a former government official—the head of the CIA. At least it becomes less of a mystery why no one at the CIA saw 9/11 coming.

A few days later on MSNBC, Democratic Congressman Adam Schiff of California responded to Muslim immigrants' bombing the Boston Marathon by saying, "The American-Muslim community is a source of great strength to us...our strength in America has always been our diversity."[26] Do these people have a silicone chip in their brains that makes them say that? *How about a rousing chorus of: "Four legs good, two legs bad!"* This is the sort of brainwashing Americans are relentlessly subjected to, day after day, from every major news outlet. The good news is, even after years of wall-to-wall propaganda, Americans still aren't sold on the idea.

IMMIGRANTS: YOU'RE NOT BLACK

Americans used to talk about "integration." Then one day, out of the blue, the word "integration" got replaced with "diversity"—just like "global warming" suddenly became "climate change"—then "July." Integration was about redressing historic wrongs done to black America. Diversity isn't. Under the diversity regime, everyone gets special rights and privileges, except white men.

Affirmative action, welfare, enterprise zones, minority set-asides—all these used to be justified by the legacy of oppression: It all goes back to the Middle Passage! But now we're talking about social welfare being dispensed in great heaping portions to Hmong, Somalis, and Latin Americans. They arrived circa 1997. So now liberals act as if they never mentioned anything about the redress of historic grievances.

The entire edifice of civil rights and discrimination law was meant to address the black experience in America, not to reward any loser with resentments. The idea was: *Okay, we've got 10 percent of the population that got the short end of the stick for a couple of centuries, so we're spending it all on them.* America altered constitutional provisions about private property and freedom of contract—for blacks. Huge social welfare programs were established—for blacks. Affirmative action policies and racial quotas were developed—for blacks. We agreed to virtually criminalize the use of certain words—for blacks.

Are you seeing the pattern? There's no justification for civil rights laws without blacks. But under the "diversity" regime, parasites from the entire world came in and announced, *Here's a new agenda for the civil rights movement and it doesn't include you, black America.* After pretending to care about black people for approximately six minutes, Democrats ran off and redefined "civil rights" as the right to get an abortion, the right for a lesbian to take a date to her high school prom, and the right of foreigners to vote in America on ballots printed in their native language. And thus ended the brief era of liberals' pretending to care about black people. At least lesbians and the abortion ladies are *American* lesbians and *American* abortion ladies. Without reason, the Left has appropriated the black experience in America and given it away to foreigners. But they'll never pay a price for it, because African Americans still bloc-vote for the Democrats.

It's understandable that the Democrats would want to dump "integration" the first chance they got. Democrats could never accept the fact that "civil rights" was about correcting specific and severe injustices done to

American blacks, principally because they were the ones who had perpetrated the injustices.[27]

But why did Jesse Jackson and the "rainbow coalition" give away blacks' unique claim to America's sympathy to people who never experienced oppression in the United States? Jews are very protective of the Holocaust as a unique event. For fifty years, there's been a raging debate about whether the Turkish slaughter of more than a million Armenians in 1915—another chapter in the glorious history of "diversity"—can be described as a "genocide." It's one thing to adopt quotas and affirmative action as a response to slavery and the Democratic policies of Jim Crow. But to apply these policies to people who have never set foot in this country is insane. We owe you nothing.

LIBERAL RESEARCHER ADMITS THE TRUTH: DIVERSITY SUCKS

Even when Third World immigrants aren't trying to blow up the First World, as in Boston, ethnic "diversity" is all downside. Members of the same ethnic group know each other, care about each other, help each other. Leaving aside the exciting parts of diversity, such as terrorism, civil wars, and ethnic cleansing, the greater the diversity, the higher the transaction costs. Even after almost four centuries together, blacks and whites haven't yet achieved what anyone would regard as perfect harmony.

Robert Putnam, Harvard professor and author of *Bowling Alone*, has spent years studying the effects of ethnic diversity on a community's well-being. It turns out diversity is a train wreck. Contrary to his expectation—and desire!—Putnam's study showed that the greater the ethnic diversity, the less people trusted their neighbors, their local leaders, and even the news. People in diverse communities gave less to charity, voted less, had fewer friends, were more unhappy, and were more likely to describe television as "my most important form of entertainment." It was not, Putnam said, that people in diverse communities trusted people of their own ethnicity more, and other races less. They didn't trust anyone.[28] The difference in neighborliness between an ethnically homogeneous town, such as Bismarck, North Dakota, and a diverse one, such as Los Angeles, Putnam says, is "roughly the same as" the difference in a town with a 7 percent poverty rate compared with a 23 percent poverty rate.[29]

Putnam refused to publish his study for seven years because he didn't like the results. As a "liberal academic whose own values put him squarely in the pro-diversity camp," the *New York Times* said, he had hoped to find another explanation. He reran the numbers, accounting for differences in crime rates, age, income, marital status, home ownership, education, language, mobility, and every other factor under the sun. But no matter how many variables he accounted for, Putnam kept getting the same results: Diversity damages social cohesion.[30] When Putnam finally released his study in 2007, he included an incongruous statement of his personal admiration for diversity—leading critics to complain that he was "straying from data into advocacy," as the *Times* put it.[31] The disadvantages of diversity were in the cold, hard numbers. The advantages were in Putnam's hopes and dreams.

Diversity from immigration harmed social harmony even more than America's traditional black-white racial diversity. "[B]oth 'percent black' and 'percent immigrant,'" Putnam said, have a "significant and independent" negative effect on social capital. But comparing "percent black" with "percent immigrant," he found that the "more consistent and powerful" degradation of social capital came from "percent immigrant."[32]

Leaping out from Putnam's graphs is the fact that wealthy, wildly diverse San Francisco repeatedly comes in dead last in social capital. This is one problem you can't blame on the blacks—that city is 42 percent white, 33 percent Asian, 15 percent Hispanic, 6 percent black (and 100 percent *fabulous*). Notwithstanding all the blather about Asians being the "model minority" and Hispanics being such "hard workers"—compared to you-know-who—people who live in communities dominated by the traditional black and white races trust their neighbors a lot more than they do in places like San Francisco with large immigrant populations.[33]

This is especially noticeable in Southern towns, where black and white Americans have been living together forever. In San Francisco, only 29 percent of people trust their neighbors. By contrast, in each of these three mostly black and white North Carolina towns, more than 40 percent of people trust their neighbors:

- Greensboro: white: 48 percent; black: 40 percent; Hispanic: 8 percent; Asian: 4 percent.
- Winston-Salem: white: 51 percent; black: 35 percent; Hispanic: 15 percent.
- Charlotte: white: 50 percent; black: 35 percent; Hispanic: 13 percent; Asian: 5 percent.[34]

Also unlike San Francisco, people in these towns trust one another without regard to race. In San Francisco, the correlation between "same race" and "trust" is quite high.[35]

There's nothing good about diversity, other than the food, and we don't need 128 million Mexicans for the restaurants.[36] True, America does a better job than most at accommodating a diverse population. We also do a better job at setting compound fractures. But no one goes around mindlessly exclaiming: "Compound fractures are a strength!"

5

THIRTY MILLION MEXICANS

SO DIVERSITY IS NOT A STRENGTH. BUT THE STRANGE THING IS, IT'S NOT EVEN diverse. In *New York Times*–speak, "diversity" simply means "non-white." Most of the time, it means "Mexican."

The first recorded use of "Diversity is a strength," according to Nexis, was on November 16, 1989, and we haven't been able to get rid of it since. The phrase appeared in a *Boston Globe* retrospective about court-ordered busing in Boston in the 1970s—which illustrated the wonders of diversity by inciting race riots.[1] The second use of this grating cliché was in a 1992 *Los Angeles Times* article gassing on about diversity at A. G. Currie Middle School in Tustin, California. The school was celebrating diversity by flying sixty-five flags to represent its students' home countries. Principal Dan Brooks said he planned to turn Currie into a "model multicultural school," adding that although many view diversity as an obstacle, he saw "diversity as a strength."[2] By 2009, the most recent year for which statistics are available, A. G. Currie Middle School was 91 percent Hispanic.[3] There's "multicultural" for you. Nine percent more Mexicans, and it will have achieved perfect "diversity." Compared with other schools in California, A. G. Currie scored a D– in math, a C in language, and a C+ in science, for an overall grade of D+.[4] Diversity is a strength!

About the same time, Hollywood High School was flipping from the storied institute of legend to the high school of the barrio. Or, as CNN put it in a series of rave reviews for the "predominantly Latino" school: "Hollywood High Now a Diverse High School."

Hollywood High alumni include Cher, Carol Burnett, Lon Chaney, James Garner, Linda Evans, John Huston, Judy Garland, Ricky Nelson, Sarah Jessica Parker, John Ritter, Mickey Rooney, Lana Turner, and Fay Wray, among many others. By the mid-2000s, Hollywood High was more than 70 percent Hispanic,[5] and students were less likely to be getting publicity shots than mug shots. Today the school is mostly famous for its stabbings, shootings, child molestations, thefts, and graffiti.[6] Around 1990, a California TV producer trying to enroll a German exchange student in a Los Angeles high school asked the principal at Fairfax High if a foreign exchange student would be better served by Fairfax or Hollywood High. Without looking up, the principal replied, "Well, 90% of my students can speak English, and we haven't had a shooting here in 5 years." As CNN's Suzanne Malveaux said, that's why Hollywood High School is called "Diversity High."[7]

In 2011, the *New York Times* described the angry reaction of Mexicans living in 80 percent Hispanic El Paso to proposals to enforce the border. People in the majority-Mexican town booed when Obama mentioned putting up a fence, viewing efforts to reduce illegal immigration from Mexico as part of a "larger surge of xenophobia."[8] So Hispanics living in a town that's already 80 percent Hispanic denounce limits on how many *more* Hispanics can move in as "xenophobia." You know who doesn't seem to like diversity? Hispanics. Do they fear white Americans, seeing them as "the other," as they say on MSNBC? Why are we letting in immigrants who are racists? At what point will the *New York Times* stop accusing opponents of nonstop immigration from Latin America of "xenophobia"? (That's a rhetorical question. The answer is: "Never.") The *Times* needs to come up with a new word for people who think 80 percent Hispanic is enough, something like "I-Didn't-Want-to-Live-in-Mexico-bia."

DOESN'T MEXICO WANT ANY MEXICANS?

America has already taken in more than one-quarter of Mexico's entire population, according to the Pew Research Center's analysis of census data.[9] The United States has more Hispanics than any other country besides Mexico.[10] Do we have to admit all 120 million Mexicans to prove to the *New York Times* that we're not "nativist"? Eighty percent Mexican wasn't good enough for the Hispanic residents of El Paso. In two states, New Mexico and California, Hispanics have already surpassed whites as the largest ethnic group—and that's just the official count from the U.S. census, which massively undercounts illegal aliens. The Hispanic population, overwhelmingly Mexican,[11] makes up 47 percent of New Mexico, 39 percent of California, 38 percent of Texas, 30 percent of Arizona, and 27 percent of Nevada.[12] Hispanics are also the largest minority group in Colorado, Connecticut, Florida, Idaho, Illinois, Iowa, Kansas, Massachusetts, Nebraska, New Hampshire, New Jersey, New Mexico, New York, Oregon, Rhode Island, Texas, Utah, Washington, and Wyoming.[13]

Is that "diverse" enough, yet?

This is a shockingly rapid transformation. In 1980—back when California was giving us our Republican presidents—it was home to 4.5 million Hispanics.[14] Today, there are officially 14 million.[15] There are more Hispanics in California than there are people in 46 other states.[16] Reagan couldn't get elected in a congressional district there now. And the state is running like a top! According to the county supervisor, Los Angeles alone spends more than $1.6 billion a year on illegal aliens—$600 million for welfare, $550 million for public safety (mostly jail costs), and $500 million for their healthcare.[17] In 1980, Nevada was less than 6.8 percent Hispanic.[18] By 2010, Hispanics had grown an astonishing 386 percent to nearly one-third of the population. Or, as Brookings Institution researchers put it, "the ethnic composition of the state has become considerably more diverse."[19]

Would the media be so thrilled with mass immigration if it were coming from Western Europe? No, the blue-chip immigrant investment is Hispanic—maybe Indian or African. You can't lose with those in *New York Times* World. Tatars are worthless in multicultural terms. They, too, have a distinctive look and unique culture, but it's not going to get you anywhere in America being a Tatar.

Diversity in immigration ought to mean every country on earth sends the same percentage of immigrants. Instead, our immigration policies are producing a *less* diverse country. Before Teddy Kennedy's 1965 immigration act extended "civil rights" to the entire world, immigrants to America were far more varied. Seven countries each provided 5 percent or more of the total number of immigrants each year—Italy, Germany, Canada, the United Kingdom, Poland, the Soviet Union, and Mexico.

By 2000, Mexico was the only country supplying more than 5 percent, accounting for nearly a third of all immigrants to the United States. China came in a distant second, finally surpassing 5 percent in 2010.[20] At the same time, immigrants from Britain, Canada, Germany, Italy, and Poland were cut off—none of these countries was among the top ten immigrant-supplying countries by 2010. Each one accounts for less than 2 percent of all immigration to America.[21] In 1970, there were fewer than 10 million foreign born in the United States, and 75 percent of them were from Europe. By 2010, there were 40 million foreign-born in the United States and only 13 percent were from Europe.[22]

Even the pro-browning-of-America Pew Research Center describes Mexico's domination of American immigration as "one of the largest mass migrations in modern history."[23] From 1890 to 1970, there weren't enough Hispanics in America for the Census Bureau to count.[24] In 1970, there were fewer than a million Mexican immigrants here. Today there are between 25 million and 50 million Mexican immigrants, depending on whose estimate of the illegal population you accept. And that's not including babies born to Mexican illegal immigrants, who are instantly labeled "Americans."

Commenting on this stunning displacement of Americans by Mexicans, the Census Bureau dryly stated: "Paradoxically, as the number of foreign born continued to increase after 1980 and the regions of origins shifted to include more countries in Latin America and Asia, the foreign born became proportionally concentrated into fewer country-of-birth groups."[25] *Paradoxically!*

This isn't "paradoxical"; it's "diabolical." The Democrats never particularly cared for Americans, so they needed to bring in new people. Immigration is the advance wave of left-wing, Third World colonization of America. Democratic vice presidential candidate John Edwards used to claim that there are "two Americas," the rich and the poor. If Democrats have their way, there will be two Latin Americas, both of them poor. You're living in one of them right now.

THERE ARE A LOT MORE THAN 11 MILLION ILLEGAL IMMIGRANTS

Most Americans have no idea of the scale of Third World immigration pouring into the country. This is where numbers can make a difference. Sometimes quantity is quality. So it's significant that Americans are being so aggressively lied to about the number of illegal immigrants in the country. Has it ever seemed strange that there have been exactly 11 million illegals here for the past decade? Did they stop coming? That's hard to believe. President Bush prosecuted border guards for getting too rough with illegals. President Obama encouraged one hundred thousand illegals to surge across the border, then put them on buses to their new homes in the United States, courtesy of the taxpayer.

The reason we are angrily told there are 11 million illegals and you're a racist if you say there is one more than that is that if Americans ever suspected there were 30 million illegal immigrants in the United States, our elected officials would find out what a "crisis" really is.

There were 11 million illegals in the United States as of 2005, according to everyone. Thus, for example, the pro-browning Pew Hispanic Center estimated the number of illegal aliens in the United States to be 11.1 million in March 2005.[26] The Department of Homeland Security put it at 10.5 million in January 2005.[27] Other estimates from the *New York Times*, the Center for Immigration Studies, the Urban Institute, and the Current Population Survey produced similar numbers.[28]

It's been a decade and we're still being told—emphatically—that there are just 11 million illegal immigrants here. Manifestly, 11 million is less a serious estimate and more "the smallest number illegal immigration advocates think they can get away with." The usual impulse of special interest groups is to overestimate their numbers. But with illegal immigration, the number has to be just large enough to hector Republicans about alienating the coming Hispanic majority, but not so high that Americans boil politicians in oil.

The reason all the estimates from Pew, DHS, CIS, the Urban Institute, and the Current Population Survey are nearly identical—11 million!—is that they all use the same census data. To count illegals, analysts subtract the number of legal immigrants (estimated from those who answered census surveys) from the number of foreign-born residents (also estimated from those who answered census surveys). But if the census's figures are wrong, then, obviously, so are the estimates.

THE REAL NUMBER IS 30 MILLION ILLEGALS

There's good reason to believe the census numbers are wrong. In 2005, two Bear Stearns analysts, Robert Justich and Betty Ng, warned clients that there was "significant evidence" that the census undercounted the illegal immigrant population by at least half.[29] They estimated the number at closer to 20 million—and they were advising clients about something important: their money.

Justich and Ng discounted the census data because it relied on illegal aliens answering surveys. As Justich told the *Wall Street Journal*, "The assumption that illegal people will fill out a census form is the most ridiculous concept I have ever heard of."[30] People who have left their families, paid huge sums of money to smugglers, trekked thousands of miles, and broken American law to enter this country don't have much incentive to fill out questionnaires from the U.S. government.

The census tried to account for the reluctance of illegal aliens to answer government surveys by adding 10 percent to their population estimate. Guess where they got 10 percent? From another survey of illegals. In 2001, the University of California asked Mexican-born residents of Los Angeles if they had taken the recent census. Ten percent said "no." But almost 40 percent refused to take that survey.[31]

Citing the work of anthropologist Maxine Margolis, Justich and Ng argued that the nonresponse rate of illegal immigrants might be quite a bit higher than 10 percent. In 1990, Margolis found that the Brazilian consulate counted 100,000 Brazilians living in New York City, while the Brazilian foreign office put the number at 230,000. That same year, the 1990 census reported that only 9,200 Brazilians lived in New York City.[32]

Dispensing with the census's figures, the Bear Stearns analysts looked at remittances from the United States to Mexico. These are electronic money transfers recorded by a nation's central bank—not surveys of people who don't want to answer surveys. The report found that while the number of Mexicans living in the United States was supposed to have grown by only 56 percent from 1995 to 2003, remittances from the United States to Mexico grew by almost 200 percent, even as the median weekly wage increased by just 10 percent. The Bear Stearns report also compared the growth in housing permits and school enrollment with official population figures in various immigrant enclaves. According to the census, for example, the combined population growth of Brunswick, Elizabeth, and Newark, New Jersey, was only 5.6 percent between 1990 and 2003. But housing permits in these towns grew by more than 600 percent, and 80 percent of the new permits were for multiple dwellings.

From these and other calculations, they estimated the illegal population to be 20 million, and that was back in 2005. The very next year—the same year illegal immigration was supposed to have nearly stopped—two Pulitzer Prize–winning investigative journalists, Donald L. Barlett and James B. Steele, undertook their own study for *Time* magazine and concluded that "the number of illegal aliens flooding into the U.S. this year will total 3 million—enough to fill 22,000 Boeing 737-700 airliners, or 60 flights every day for a year. It will be the largest wave since 2001 and roughly triple the number of immigrants who will come to the U.S. by legal means."[33] But according to every major news outlet, America gained fewer than a million illegal immigrants that year, and then miraculously went right back down to 11 million illegals by 2007.

Combining Justich and Ng's conclusion that there were 20 million illegal aliens here in 2005 with the estimate of Pulitzer Prize winners Barlett and Steele that another 3 million illegal immigrants would enter in 2006, plus at least another 3 million illegals coming in every year throughout the following decade—surely a low estimate—would mean there are at least 30 million illegal immigrants in the United States today. To most Californians, 30 million seems low.

So why are Americans being insistently told that there are only 11 million illegal immigrants in the United States? When Lou Dobbs began referring to the "11 to 20 million illegal aliens" in 2006, citing the Bear Stearns report, the *Columbia Journalism Review* went apoplectic: "Lou Dobbs takes a tough look at the immigration debate—and plays loose with the numbers."[34] For simply reporting the ranges and not taking a position on the correct figure, Dobbs had shocked the conscience of the *CJR*. "Every major newspaper in the country that has reported a number over the past several days," the *Review* triumphantly reported, "has given an estimate of about 11 million or 12 million." What kind of vulgar demagogue would question "every major newspaper"?

The *CJR* dismissed the Bear Stearns report for being "light on the large-scale demographic data"—i.e., census data. In fact, however, even the Pew report touted by the *CJR* had warned that its own estimate was based on census data samples of fewer than a hundred thousand people, and added a cautionary note about the accuracy of both the underlying data and the assumptions used to make estimates.[35] *CJR* was undeterred. Amid more denunciations of Dobbs for "suggest[ing] that somehow Bear Stearns' estimate is just as valid as the better-grounded lower estimates," the screed concluded: "We are inclined to believe the much more comprehensive analysis of the Pew Hispanic Center." Merely for mentioning a report that *CJR* was less "inclined to believe," Dobbs came in for paragraph after paragraph of abuse.

Minimizing the number of illegals is evidently very important to some people. If Americans realized that there are probably three times as many illegal aliens here as we're constantly being told, upward of 30 million, it might make them angry. When it comes to immigration, the journalist's motto is: *The public can't be trusted with the truth.* People might jump to unwarranted conclusions—such as that amnesty functions as a magnet. They might notice that the country's workforce and social safety net are collapsing under the weight of 30 million poor people, while the rich and powerful are doing quite well.

IMMIGRATION: A HOMICIDE MADE TO LOOK LIKE A SUICIDE

Conservatives have been buffaloed into thinking that they're the ones who want to change the country. No, the question is: Why is it better that the ethnic population of our country be changed? There's a strange rhetorical asymmetry, where mass-immigration advocates are allowed to say, *It's fantastic that the country is becoming browner,* but no one else is allowed to say, *I don't think so.* Don't even think about asking if it's a good thing that 52 percent of *legal* immigrant households are on the dole.

Immigration of the past half century has been a national homicide made to look like suicide. It's a staged crime scene. Everyone acts as if the "browning of America" is a natural process, and immigration opponents are like King Canute trying to hold back the ocean's tide. It's more like Americans are trying to stop an Army Corps of Engineers project that will flood the valley where they live in order to build a hydroelectric plant that will help one powerful corporation. The people who live in the valley will bear all the costs, and a few rich shareholders will make all the profit.

That's not "natural." The government is artificially flooding the valley. The beneficiaries of our immigration laws try to convince us that something that is 100 percent the result of government policy cannot be changed. We are constantly being told, *The country's changing, get used to it.* This has the effect of making people crazy. They think, *I guess it is just me!* People can see the country is changing rapidly for no good purpose.

It's one thing if things are getting worse and nothing can be done about it. But there is nothing necessary about our immigration policies.

IF YOU LIKE YOUR COUNTRY, YOU CAN KEEP IT

Politicians willfully designed laws to change the nature of the country, and then act outraged when anyone says: I don't like what you've done. If it's racist to say that immigration is changing America's ethnicity, why wasn't it racist for supporters of Kennedy's 1965 bill to boast that it wouldn't? Much like the miasma of lies required to pass Obamacare, when Kennedy's immigration law was being debated, Democrats swore up and down that the country's ethnic composition would continue to be white and European. *If you like your country's ethnic composition, you can keep it!* Thus, for example, Kennedy said his immigration law "will not inundate America with immigrants from any one country or area, or the most populated and deprived nations of Africa and Asia." America, he said, would continue to have the same "ethnic mix," and "the ethnic pattern of immigration under the proposed measure is not expected to change as sharply as the critics seem to think."[36]

The *Washington Post* assured readers that "the new immigration pattern would not stray radically from the old one."[37] Senator Hiram Fong of Hawaii said that Asians "will never reach 1 percent of the population."[38] Attorney General Robert Kennedy testified that there would be only about five thousand immigrants from the Asia-Pacific Triangle "after which immigration from that source would virtually disappear."[39] Secretary of State Dean Rusk testified that "there might be, say, 8,000 immigrants from India in the next five years," but no mass migration from that part of the world.[40] Representative Emanuel Celler of New York claimed that "there will not be, comparatively, many Asians or Africans entering this country."[41] (Imagine saying something like that in public today. They'd bring back hanging.)

In the first five years after the law passed, instead of the 8,000 immigrants from India, as promised by Rusk, there were 27,859. Instead of 5,000 immigrants from Japan, as we were assured by Senator Fong, there were 20,000.[42] Through family reunification policies, immigration from those places has exploded. Contrary to Kennedy's assurance that his bill would not "inundate America with immigrants from any one country or area," more than half of all immigrants to the United States since 1970 are native Spanish-speakers.[43] That's not what the bill's proponent promised. That's not even "diversity."

Merely to point out that the bill's proponents lied, and every single one of these predictions was off by approximately 300 percent, is to invite personal calumny. The United States is being artificially transformed into Latin America solely for the benefit of Democrats and businessmen in need of cheap labor. If you object, you're a racist.

> *I promise this law will not do XYZ!*
>   Hey—your bill did XYZ!
> *You're a racist.*

As with Obamacare, had the bill's proponents told the truth, the 1965 immigration overhaul would never have passed. The difference is that, when proof of their lies about Obamacare emerged, the bill's architect, Jonathan Gruber, went into hiding; Democrats were humiliated; and Republicans triumphant. When proof of their lies about the 1965 immigration act emerged, Kennedy was made a saint, Republicans were humiliated, and Democrats triumphant. Congratulations, liberals! You won. Whoever slaps the "racism" post first, wins. (And you wonder why MSNBC calls opposition to Obamacare "racist.")

MERIT-BASED LANDSCAPERS

Supporters of the 1965 act also claimed that it would introduce a meritocracy in immigration. Attorney General Kennedy put it starkly in a letter to the *New York Times*: "The time has come for us to insist that the quota system be replaced by the merit system." Representative Celler said immigrants would "have to compete and qualify in order to get in, quantitatively and qualitatively."[44]

Fifty years later, when a Harvard PhD thesis pointed out that our immigration policies have been the opposite of a meritocracy, dragging down the national IQ by favoring immigrants from countries with IQs far below the national average, liberals called the author, Jason Richwine, a "racist." He was forced out of his job at the Heritage Foundation and made virtually unemployable. How about revisiting Bobby Kennedy's sainthood for promising a meritocracy in immigration? Apparently, that's now "racist."

They're the ones discriminating on the basis of race! Our immigration laws discriminate against the handful of countries that populated America for the first three hundred years of its existence in order to bring in poor immigrants from the Third World. Since 1970, nearly 90 percent of all *legal* immigrants have been from the Third World, and the majority of them need taxpayer assistance. The only reason liberal elites want to inundate

America with poor immigrants is because white English-speaking immigrants from developed countries won't do menial labor or bloc-vote for the Democrats.

Guess who's hurt the most by our immigration policies? Americans without a lot of job skills, especially black Americans. You know who else is hurt by the constant importation of low-skilled workers? Hispanic immigrants—the ones who were admitted last year, and the year before, and the year before that.[45] *Sorry, poor voiceless Americans—Sheldon Adelson wants to pay his maid even less!* If anyone has a right to be screaming "racism!" it's those of us opposed to the dump of a million low-wage workers on the country every year.

The reason we can't use immigration to bring in the best people is because *our* best people don't want immigrants competing with their kids. They want immigrants competing with their *landscaper's* kids. Democrats don't care that because they're continually importing more low-wage workers to the country, the immigrants already here can't get a decent-paying job. Al Sharpton's catchphrase is: Pro-lifers only care about the fetus until it's born. Well, Democrats only care about immigrants until they can vote. I promise you: If immigrants voted 8–2 for the Republicans—rather than 8–2 for the Democrats—Chuck Schumer would be down on the border with the Minutemen. How about the Democrats explain why it's so vital to constantly import more people when most Americans think we have enough already? What is it they don't like about our working class? What is it they don't like about our country?

6

IMMIGRATION AS "MYSTERY BARGAIN BIN"

A 2013 PROPUBLICA ARTICLE ABOUT A PAKISTANI ANCHOR BABY WHO BECAME a heroin dealer/terrorist described one of his drug-dealing associates this way: "Ikram Haq was a mentally impaired Pakistani immigrant. His lawyer, Sam Schmidt, convinced the jury that Headley conned his client into a heroin deal."[1] I see at least three reasons the word "immigrant" should never have been attached to the name "Ikram Haq": "mentally impaired," "Pakistani," and "heroin deal." May I talk to the immigration official who decided to admit Ikram? Please at least tell me that the mental impairment appeared after we were graced with Ikram's presence.

> U.S. immigration official: *What else can you tell me about your son?*
>
> Visa applicant: Well, he's mentally impaired and will never reach the cognitive level of a third grader.
>
> U.S. immigration official: *That's fantastic! We'll get the papers right to you.*

Since when are we required to take anyone who wants to come here, including mentally impaired Pakistanis who engage in heroin deals on a bad day and contribute absolutely nothing to society on their good days? That's not a rhetorical question—I want the exact date. Americans seem to be under the impression that we signed an agreement to participate in the Mystery Bargain Bin on immigration: It could be $10,000—or it could be a pile of dirt! Here's hoping!

America is not a public hospital in an urban neighborhood where we have to take anyone who shows up. Until 1970, American immigrants did better than the natives—as any sane immigration policy would require. They made more money, bought more houses, and were more educated. By contrast, the post-1970 immigrants are far more likely to be unemployed and live in poverty than native-born Americans. More than a third of all post–Kennedy act immigrants don't even have a high school diploma.[2] Among natives, only the sick, addled, or delinquent have failed to complete high school by the age of twenty-five—about 7 percent of all Americans.[3] Manifestly, our government has no interest in setting up a skimming-the-cream operation when it comes to immigration.

WHAT DID WE DO?

Twenty-five years of PC education has convinced Americans that we have to treat immigrants as if they're black people and we're making up for the legacy of slavery. These aren't descendants of American slaves! Why do we owe other countries anything? It is simply assumed that we must have done *something* to them.

Britain used to have an empire, meaning that it wiped out exotic diseases, ended tribal bloodshed, expanded literacy, and generally dragged primitive societies into the nineteenth century. Life was better than before, but, on the other hand, the British administrators had all the good jobs, so the natives threw the British out. *Now it works the other way, Jack.* In some bizarre notion of turn-about-is-fair-play, it is assumed that backward societies have a right to relocate to the countries of their former colonizers. I thought they hated those guys?

That's crazy enough. But America didn't have any colonies. It *was* a colony. Our racial guilt is over slavery and Jim Crow (by Democrats). Nixon didn't impose racial quotas on trade unions because he thought it would be culturally enriching for white members to work side by side with black people. He was enraged at the unions for refusing to hire blacks. The country, he said, owed African Americans a "dividend." What do we owe the Third World?

Did we all agree to turn our country into a gigantic battered women's shelter required to take in every oppressed person of the world? Why would any country do that? We're not obliged to take the world's hardest cases. In fact, I'm sure most Americans would think that's a bad idea.

What did we do to the Somalis? The only American intervention there was purely humanitarian. In the middle of a mass starvation, America leapt in to send food to this primitive warlord society. Unfortunately, the warlords intercepted our grain shipments, so the first President Bush sent troops to ensure our aid would get to the people. The Clinton administration came in and decided America was going to "embark on an unprecedented enterprise aimed at nothing less than the restoration of an entire country as a proud, functioning and viable member of the community of nations."[4] In short order, the brutalized corpses of American troops were being dragged through the streets of Mogadishu.

In other words, the Somalis owe us. But U.S. immigration officials decided: *Let's ratchet up the degree of difficulty in our immigrants. Not only will we let in the poorest, most backward people of the world, but let's not even take African Christians. Let's take the African Muslims!*

WE NEED SOME PIZZAZZ— HOW ABOUT 100,000 SOMALIS?

The reason Scandinavian Minnesota ended up with more than one hundred thousand Somalis is that liberals thought the state was too white-bread and not at all diverse. In the 1990s, the head of the Minneapolis Foundation, Emmett Carson, complained that California and New York were much more "multicultural" than Minnesota. Wouldn't Minnesota be a much cooler state with a hundred thousand Somalis? The foundation ran a public information campaign, showing a photo of three smiling Somali women in their native garb over the caption: "Maybe you're just not sure what to make of all these new Minnesotans bringing in all these strange new cultures and customs. But hey, have you ever really thought about lutefisk?" Pleased by the success of his campaign, Carson exulted: "Minnesota is changing."[5]

Yes, Minnesota used to be very boring. Now it's exciting!

Indictment: Somali Gangs Trafficked Girls for Sex

MINNEAPOLIS (AP) Twenty-nine people have been indicted in a sex trafficking ring in which Somali gangs in Minneapolis and St. Paul allegedly forced girls under age 14 into prostitution in Minnesota, Tennessee and Ohio, according to an indictment unsealed Monday.

The 24-count indictment, unsealed in U.S. District Court in the Middle District of Tennessee, said one of the gangs' goals was recruiting females under age 18, including some under age 14, and forcing them into prostitution so the defendants could get money, marijuana or liquor.

The indictment details several instances in which young Somali or African American girls were taken from place to place and forced to engage in sex acts with multiple people. One girl was under 13 when she was first prostituted.[6]

In just a few decades, Minnesota has gone from being approximately 99 percent German, Dutch, Finnish, Danish, and Polish to 20 percent African immigrant,[7] including at least one hundred thousand Somalis.[8] And that's not counting the Somalis who have recently left the country to fight with al Qaeda and ISIS. One hundred thousand is just an estimate. We don't know precisely how many Somalis the federal government has brought in as "refugees" because the government won't tell us. *The public can't be trusted with the truth.*

Since becoming more multicultural, Minnesota has turned into a hotbed of credit card skimming, human trafficking, and smash-and-grab robberies.[9] Mosques have popped up all over the state—as have child prostitutes and machete attacks.

Welfare consumption in Minnesota has more than doubled on account of the newcomers—only half of whom have jobs. Those Somalis who do have jobs earn an average of $21,000 a year, compared with $46,000 for the average Minnesotan. (Consider yourself lucky, Minnesota: In Sweden, only 20 percent of Somalis have jobs.) Eighty percent of Somalis in Minnesota live at or below the poverty line. Nearly 70 percent have not graduated from high school, compared with only 8.4 percent of non-Somali Minnesotans.[10]

But no Democrat will cross them, and no Republican will mention them: Somalis have leapfrogged past native blacks to become a major political force in Minnesota. For every white Minnesotan who becomes a Republican each year, two Somalis turn eighteen and start bloc-voting for the Democrats.

Everyone seems to agree that it is Minnesotans' responsibility to assimilate to Somali culture, not the other way around.[11] The Catholic University of St. Thomas has installed Islamic prayer rooms and footbaths in order to demonstrate, according to Dean of Students Karen Lange, that the school is "diverse." Minneapolis's mayor, Betsy Hodges, has shown up wearing a full hijab to meetings with Somalis. (In fairness, it was "Forbid Your Daughter to Work Outside the Home" Day.) A suburban Minnesota high school has "Welcome" signs written in Somali, a Somali student group, and articles in the school newspaper about how unhappy the Somalis are.

Kate Towle, the parent leader of a high school group called "Students Together as Allies for Racial Trust" explained that diversity skills "have to be developed like math, history."[12] Maybe it would be better for students to be learning math and history, rather than the important skill of: Getting Along with Somalis. It doesn't seem to be working, anyway: There are still violent ethnic brawls that send students to the hospital.

What did we do to Somalis? What did we do to Cameroonians or Senegalese? Absolutely nothing. But now these immigrants, who arrived yesterday, will get affirmative action over white Americans. Do the media really not know how the Ghanaian immigrant got accepted to ALL EIGHT Ivy League schools? According to *New York* magazine, it's because he's "better than you."[13]

"THANK YOU" WOULD BE NICE

We can't assimilate immigrants to Western ideas about pedophilia, human trafficking, and credit card fraud, but they take like fish to water to America's victim culture. People adapt amazingly quickly to a sense of entitlement. In about ten seconds, impoverished immigrants go from *Wait—I can have this?* to *Where's my money?* As a white female Sears employee told the *New York Times*, Somalis "think this is a great opportunity for them, this prejudice thing. If you look at them the wrong way or they don't have enough money, they say it's prejudice."[14] Newcomers hear American paeans to tolerance, respect, and inclusion and think: *Great! That means tolerance of ME, respect for ME, and inclusion for ME.*

In 2002, Minneapolis police shot a Somali man, Abu Kassim Jeilani, who was walking down the middle of a busy street waving a machete. While this may be common behavior in Mogadishu, it's generally frowned upon in Minneapolis. Even after being tasered a half dozen times, Jeilani continued to menace cops with his machete, charging the officers and smashing it on their squad cars. Eventually, Jeilani rushed an officer and ended up dead.[15] Luckily, every Somali in Minnesota who has a job works for an ethnic grievance outfit—for example, the Somali Justice Advocacy Center, the Somali Resources Aid Associates, the African Development Center, and the Confederation of Somali Community in Minnesota. (And those are just some of the jobs being created by immigrants!)

This allowed the Somali community to erupt in rage, claiming Jeilani's "civil rights" had been violated. Omar Jamal, of the Somali Justice Advocacy Center, denounced the shooting, claiming, unironically: "We are taxpayers. We pay these people to serve and protect us. We pay taxes and they pay taxes."[16] With half of Somalis in Minnesota unemployed and 80 percent living at or below the poverty level, one thing they are definitely not doing is "paying taxes." I think the phrase he's looking for is "accepting welfare." The Somalis' civil rights lawsuit on behalf of a man who ran at cops with a machete was unsuccessful. It was very successful, however, in wasting the resources of U.S. federal courts for five years.[17]

About a decade ago, thousands of Somalis moved to the small working-class town of Lewiston, Maine. Within the first year of their arrival, the town's welfare caseload doubled. Before the town was bankrupted, Mayor Laurier T. Raymond Jr. wrote a letter to Somali elders asking them to discourage their fellow countrymen from continuing to move to Lewiston. He respectfully explained: "We have been overwhelmed and have responded valiantly. Now we need breathing room. Our city is maxed-out financially, physically and emotionally."

In response, the Somali elders accused him of racism. Calling the mayor an "ill-informed leader who is bent towards bigotry," they said he was trying to incite "violence against our people physically, verbally and emotionally." The governor and attorney general were forced to defend the mayor from charges of racism. But the Somalis pushed on, demanding that everyone acknowledge how peachy they are. "We hope that others appreciate," they said, "the potential richness and opportunity newcomers bring to the city."[18]

At least Lewiston has shed its boring whiteness! Today, Somali boys roam the streets physically assaulting the locals. Within a few days in the summer of 2009, three separate residents were mugged, including one woman in her sixties and one man who had to be hospitalized. Another time, a gang of Somali boys attacked a woman walking her dog, beating the dog with a stick. Muggings by Somalis are so common that some Lewiston residents have been victimized more than once.

Even Somalia doesn't want Somalis. Convicted rapist Mohammed Mukhtar avoided probation by agreeing to be deported after completing his sentence.[19] Somalia, however, is unlikely to take Mukhtar back. We want him to go, he claims he wants to go, but Somalia can say, *We're leaving the rapist with you.* Our immigration laws are working fantastically well for every country in the world except our own.

THEY MOVED HERE

It's not just Somalis bringing heinous cultural behaviors here and then claiming victimhood. After an illegal alien from Mexico snatched a nine-year-old American girl off her bicycle in Ohio, dragged her to his house, and repeatedly raped her, the reaction from the Mexican community was to complain about the "negative picture of Hispanics in the minds of some," as Jason Riveiro with the League of United Latin American Citizens said.[20]

In a case the *New York Times* described as a "family drama involving clashes of cultures," a Brazilian woman and Palestinian man in St. Louis murdered their own daughter because she was a "whore" for "going out with a black boy."[21] By lucky coincidence the girl's father, Zein Isa, was a suspected terrorist, so the FBI captured the entire murder on a surveillance tape in their home—in subsidized housing, naturally. (Zein could be heard on the tape boasting about how much he loved the United States because there were so many different welfare programs to game.)

On the tape, played for the jury, the girl can be heard shrieking as her father coldly says, "Do you know that you are going to die tonight?" then stabs her to death, as Mommy Dearest holds her down.[22] One of the prosecutors described the tape as "worse than any movie, any film, anything I thought that I would ever hear in my life." Jurors, who voted for the death penalty, said they would never get it out of their minds.[23]

But the Muslim community in St. Louis complained that the verdict did not respect Islamic culture. "I feel it's not right," a Muslim neighbor told the *New York Times.* "We follow our religion." The parents, she said, would "be embarrassed in front of everybody in the country like somebody when they go without their clothes outside."[24] An anthropology professor at the State University of New York, Nicolas Gavrielides, testified for the defense, saying, "Everyone growing up in the Middle East knows being killed is a possible consequence of dishonoring the family."[25]

In another one of those madcap "clash of cultures" episodes, Salem Al-Saidy, an Iraqi immigrant living in Nebraska, forced his thirteen- and fourteen-year-old daughters into arranged marriages with Iraqi men aged thirty-four and twenty-eight, then took them to be raped by the men. When the father and "husbands" were arrested, they expressed indignation—through interpreters—that anyone thought they had done anything wrong.[26] "Nobody ever told my client," the father's lawyer said, "what the criminal laws were here in the United States, much less the state of Nebraska, much less the city of Lincoln."

A Chinese immigrant in New York, Dong Lu Chen, bludgeoned his wife to death with a claw hammer because she was having an affair. He was unashamed, greeting his teenaged son at the door in bloody clothes, telling the boy he had just killed Mom. Brooklyn Supreme Court Justice Edward Pincus let Chen off with probation—for *murder*—after an anthropologist testified that, in Chinese culture, the shame of a man being cuckolded justified murder. Judge Pincus admitted that if the exact same crime had been committed by an American, "the Court would have been constrained to find the defendant guilty of manslaughter in the first degree." But in Chen's case, the murder flowed from "traditional Chinese values about adultery and loss of manhood."[27] Why do "traditional American values" about *not* murdering your wife lose out to "traditional Chinese values" about murdering her?

The female head of the Asian-American Defense and Education Fund, Margaret Fung, applauded Chen's light sentence, saying that a harsher penalty would "promote the idea that when people come to America they have to give up their way of doing things. That is an idea we cannot support."[28] At least Chen came to the United States based on his specialized knowledge of nuclear cell extraction biology. No, I'm sorry—Chen immigrated to America with his entire family when he was fifty years old—fifteen years away from collecting Social Security—to be a dishwasher.[29]

Female immigrants from Japan periodically kill their children because they have been "shamed" by a husband's infidelity, leading to long cultural pieces in *Newsweek* calling such child murders a "tragedy" and explaining that, in Japan, "the shame of having failed at her own suicide would be regarded as punishment enough."[30] There's isn't a lot of soul-searching when an American man kills himself and his kids, though those cases also tell a tragic story about shame and failure.[31]

IMMIGRANT MASS MURDERS— LIVING TEDDY KENNEDY'S AMERICAN DREAM

Here are some of the Americans who would still be alive if the government had been a bit choosier in determining who gets to live in America. Please don't write me with your favorite story of immigrant criminality. I know each of them is special in its own way, but there just isn't the space to list them all. To keep it short, I've limited the list to recent mass murders committed by legal immigrants.

- The seven people murdered by Chechen immigrants Dzhokhar and Tamerlan Tsarnaev, who planted a bomb at the finish line of the Boston Marathon in 2013. In addition to the three people killed in the blast, including an eight-year-old boy, dozens of Americans suffered severe injuries in the marathon bombing and are still learning to live with prosthetics and other artificial devices to replace lost legs, feet, eyes, and hearing—all thanks to an immigration policy that allows other countries to dump their losers on us. Days after setting off the bomb, the duo murdered a young MIT police officer during their attempted escape, and two years earlier Tamerlan and another Muslim immigrant slit the throats of three Jewish men on the tenth anniversary of the 9/11 attack—which I believe was also the work of immigrants. CNN headline after the attack: "Boston Bombing Shouldn't Derail Immigration Reform."[32] Leaving aside the wanton slaughter, Dzhokhar and Tamerlan were tremendous assets to America. They were on welfare and getting mostly Fs in school. Good work, U.S. immigration service!

- The three people, including a fifteen-year-old girl, Ashley Chow, murdered in North Miami in 2012 by Kesler Dufrene, a Haitian immigrant and convicted felon who had already been arrested in the United States nine times. Dufrene was due to be deported, but was released when Obama halted deportations to Haiti after the 2010 earthquake.

- Sixty-seven-year-old Florence Donovan-Gunderson and three National Guardsmen—Heath Kelly, Miranda McElhiney, and Christian Riege—fatally shot in a Carson City IHOP by immigrant Eduardo Sencion in 2011. Four other IHOP patrons were left in critical condition by the Mexican-born Sencion.

- The thirteen soldiers killed at Fort Hood in 2009 by Major Nidal Malik Hasan, son of Palestinian immigrants. Hasan's parents operated a restaurant in Roanoke, Virginia—because where are we going to find Americans to open a restaurant?

- The thirteen people murdered by Vietnamese immigrant Jiverly Wong, at an American Civic Association in Binghamton, New York. Wong became a naturalized citizen two years *after* being convicted of fraud and forgery in California. Apparently, Wong decided to commit mass murder because he was upset that people disrespected him for his poor English skills, a problem that could be avoided by admitting immigrants who speak English.[33]

- The five people murdered at the Trolley Square Shopping Mall in Salt Lake City by Bosnian immigrant Sulejman Talovic in 2007. Talovic was a high school dropout with a juvenile record. INS: *No room for you, Norwegian doctor. We think this Sulejman is really going to amount to something!*

- The thirty-two people murdered at Virginia Tech in 2007 by Seung-Hui Cho, a South Korean immigrant.

- The six people killed in northern Wisconsin in 2004 by Hmong immigrant Chai Soua Vang, who shot his victims in the back after being caught trespassing on their property. Minnesota Public Radio sensitively reported that Hmong don't understand American laws about private property, endangered species—or really anything written in English.

- The six men murdered by Mexican immigrant Salvador Tapia at the Windy City Core Supply warehouse in Chicago in 2003, because he was angry about being fired. Tapia was still in this country despite having been arrested at least a dozen times on weapons and assault charges. Only foreign newspapers mentioned that Tapia was an immigrant.[34] American journalists blamed the gun.[35]

- The three people murdered at the Appalachian School of Law in 2002 by Nigerian immigrant Peter Odighizuwa, who was angry at America because he had failed out of law school. Even before his killing rampage, what was Odighizuwa's contribution to America? He was a forty-three-year-old law student. The INS thought we needed to address America's chronic shortage of forty-three-year-old lawyers?

Two of the most famous murder sprees of the 1990s were also perpetrated by legal immigrants. The 1993 Long Island Railroad massacre that left six passengers dead was committed by Jamaican immigrant Colin Ferguson. Before deciding to murder white people, the unemployed immigrant kept busy harassing women on subways, bringing endless lawsuits, applying for workman's compensation for fake injuries, and blaming all his problems on white Americans. Whites are going to be a minority in this country a lot faster if the INS keeps bringing in immigrants like Ferguson.

In 1997, Christoffer Burmeister, a twenty-seven-year-old musician, was shot in the head and killed by Palestinian immigrant Ali Hassan Abu Kamal at the top of the Empire State Building.[36] Burmeister's band mate, Matthew Gross, also took a bullet to the head, but—after eight hours of brain surgery—survived. Gross now lives in a group home in Montclair, New Jersey, with other brain-injured men, taking daily medication for his seizures.[37] The assailant, Abu Kamal, had immigrated to America with his entire family two months earlier—at age sixty-eight. It's a smart move to bring in older immigrants well past their productive years, so we can start paying out Social Security right away.

You might not have noticed the orgy of immigrant mass murder, unless you are a trained Kremlinologist, and can interpret headlines like this one from the *Los Angeles Times* about the Vietnamese immigrant who shot up the Binghamton Civic Center: "Truly an American Tragedy."[38] Between 2010 and 2012 alone, immigrants committed about a dozen mass murders in this country. The murderers were from Mexico, Afghanistan, South Korea, Vietnam, Haiti, South Africa, and Ethiopia. Curiously, none were from Britain, Australia, or Canada. English-speaking Westerners seem to fit in better and are less prone to erupt in murderous rages.

Why were any of these people here? To quote the mother of the fifteen-year-old girl murdered by a Haitian immigrant in North Miami: "Because of immigration, my daughter is not alive."[39] We have no choice about native-born criminals. We can do something about the people our government chooses to bring here and set loose on the public. Murderous immigrants aren't a naturally occurring phenomenon, like an earthquake. They are entirely a result of government policy.

BEAVER CLEAVERS WITH CLEAVERS

No one notices the immigrant crime wave because the media hide the evidence. These tribunes of the people sneer at white-picket-fence, Beaver-Cleaver Americans, but are obsessed with portraying immigrant criminals that way—especially terrorists, facilitated by the fact that the government keeps making so many of them citizens.

According to the GAO, 27 percent of terrorism convicts in the United States were lawfully admitted immigrants, on their way to becoming citizens; 57 percent were citizens, naturalized citizens, or foreigners brought into the United States for prosecution.[40] That last category—"brought into the United States for prosecution"—is especially fantastic. Attorney General Eric Holder transferred loads of Somali pirates to the United States—allegedly to stand trial. The ones convicted of piracy get life in prison, where they will have better lives than they would have had back in Somalia. But if they end up being acquitted or getting convicted of lesser offenses, they get asylum.[41]

America has even granted asylum to participants in the Rwandan genocide.[42] After having claimed refugee status to obtain U.S. citizenship, Beatrice Munyenyezi was exposed as an enthusiastic participant in the genocide that left 70 percent of Rwanda's Tutsis dead. Contrary to her claim that she had been a victim of the genocide, she was a perpetrator, identifying Tutsis to be raped and murdered by the Hutu militia.

She was convicted in federal court of procuring her naturalization unlawfully, and sentenced to ten years in prison, but Munyenyezi remains a lawful permanent resident. Only an immigration court can order her deportation, and first she must serve her criminal sentence. She may not be able to be sent home because conditions in the receiving country can change, for better or worse. (Except in Africa, which is only for the worse.) She will need a valid passport and some other country that will agree to take her, otherwise we can't put her on a plane. Why would any other country take her? Consequently, as soon as she's released from prison, the Rwandan murderess could end up living next to you, reader.

In another few years, America will be granting asylum to the ISIS and Boko Haram butchers—and you'll be reading searching articles in the *New York Times* wondering how those boys with the wide, goofy smiles went wrong.

Our official policy is to turn away astrophysicists in order to make room for illiterate Afghan peasants who will drop out of high school to man coffee carts until deciding to engage in jihad against us. That was Immigration Success Story Najibullah Zazi, who pleaded guilty in a plot to bomb the New York City subway in 2010. Zazi had been born into a tribe in eastern Afghanistan and came to America in his teens. He dropped out of high school and had an arranged marriage to his cousin in Pakistan. His ticket to entry was his father—whose ticket was, in turn, a brother living in Queens. Zazi's own uncle described him to the *New York Times* as "a dumb kid, believe me."[43] Our immigration officials said, *WELCOME, ZAZI!... Sorry, Scottish scientists—no room for you.* Instead of immigrants who could help America, we have to take entire villages of illiterates from Afghanistan, thanks to Teddy Kennedy's 1965 immigration act.

One of Zazi's coconspirators, Zarein Ahmedzay, arrived from Afghanistan willing to do a job no American would ever consider doing: drive a cab. A third accomplice, Adis Medunjanin, was born in Bosnia, prompting the *New York Times* to begin an article on his convictions: "An American citizen was convicted of a host of terrorism charges on Tuesday..."[44]

AS AMERICAN AS APPLE PIE

News accounts would have us believe that the one hundred thousand Somalis collecting welfare in Minnesota while resting up for the next jihad are just as Minnesotan as the characters in *Fargo*. A close examination of the names of "homegrown Americans" who have joined ISIS and other terrorist groups suggests otherwise. In 2008, the *New York Times* announced "the first known American suicide bomber."[45] Go USA! It was

Shirwa Ahmed, Somali immigrant to Minnesota. Who could have guessed "Shirwa Ahmed" would be America's first suicide bomber? My money had been on a guy named "Jim Peterson." In addition to the first suicide bomber, other "Americans from Minnesota" participating in terrorism included Mahamud Said Omar, Cabdulaahi Ahmed Faarax, Abdiweli Yassin Isse, Ahmed Ali Omar, Khalid Mohamud Abshir, Zakaria Maruf, Mohamed Abdullahi Hassan, and Mustafa Ali Salat.[46]

Pakistani terrorist Daood Sayed Gilani conspired with the Pakistani military to carry out four days of terrorist attacks on hotels, movie theaters, and hospitals in Mumbai in 2008. But as far as the media were concerned, he was John Wayne. The *New York Times* called him "David Coleman Headley," a "United States citizen who lived in Pakistan but recently was mainly a resident of Chicago."[47] What constitutes "mainly"?

Although born in America, Gilani was brought up in Pakistan, raised by his Pakistani Muslim father in a strict Muslim culture from infancy until age seventeen. At seventeen, Gilani moved to the United States to live with his mother in Philadelphia and adopted the name "David Coleman Headley." He failed out of a community college, became a heroin addict, and was soon busted for importing heroin from Pakistan. In 1999, Gilani was released from prison to go back to Pakistan for an arranged marriage. He moved that wife—one of two—to live in Chicago.[48]

Why, he seems to have stepped right out of a Norman Rockwell painting!

A lengthy *Times* profile of Daood laid it on thick about his American roots: "Mr. Headley felt pulled between two cultures and ultimately gravitated toward an extremist Islamic one."[49] It might help readers understand the strange attraction of Islamic extremism to an "American citizen" if they were told that Mr. Headley's real name is "Daood Sayed Gilani," that he was raised in a backward Muslim culture in Pakistan, and that his American citizenship was only that of an anchor baby. The *Times* fooled Senator Bob Casey, then the Democratic chairman of the Foreign Relations

Subcommittee on South and Central Asia, who said of Gilani: "It's really disturbing—Americans becoming radicalized."[50]

Of more than fifty articles mentioning Gilani in the *New York Times*, only five so much as mentioned his real name—dismissing it as his "birth name"[51] or "the Urdu [name] he was given at birth."[52] Similarly, the Associated Press called him: "David C. Headley, an American formerly named Daood Sayed Gilani."[53]

It is not the *Times*' consistent practice to use aliases acquired in adulthood. In the rare case when an actual American becomes a Muslim terrorist—usually after meeting one of our Muslim immigrants making America more vibrant—the media exclusively use the terrorist's birth name. Michael Finton abandoned that name when he became a Muslim and began calling himself "Talib Islam." After Finton attempted to bomb a federal building in Chicago, the *Times* used his "birth name"—the opposite of its practice with Daood. The *Times* even managed to work in a reference to Finton's "red hair" by the second paragraph.[54] It was the same with Suleyman al-Faris, whom absolutely every newspaper refers to exclusively by his birth name: John Walker Lindh.

Dropping subtlety, about a year after the explosion of articles on "American citizen" "David Coleman Headley," the *Times* ran an article titled "The Jihadist Next Door." The article noted with alarm that "[i]n the last year, at least two dozen men in the United States have been charged with terrorism-related offenses," leaving intelligence operatives "scurrying for answers."[55] The "Americans" who left government officials "scurrying for answers," were:

> Najibullah Zazi, Afghan
> Daood Sayed Gilani, Pakistani
> Umer Farooq, Pakistani
> Waqar Khan, Pakistani
> Ramy Zamzam, Egyptian

Ahmed Abdullah Minni, Eritrean
Aman Hassan Yemer, Ethiopian

It makes no sense—it's the freckle-faced boy next door!

The media's weird obsession with billing immigrant terrorists as apple-pie Americans leads to comical results, such as the panelists on MSNBC's *The Cycle* puzzling over how Aafia Siddiqui, a "U.S.-trained scientist" could have become radicalized.[56] Here's a tip for MSNBC: When you can't pronounce the terrorist's name, the rest of America isn't sitting in slack-jawed amazement. Siddiqui wasn't an American by any definition. She wasn't even an anchor baby. Rather, Siddiqui was born and raised in Pakistan and came to the United States as an adult via our seditious universities. After an arranged marriage over the phone with another Pakistani, who—luckily for America!—joined her here, she divorced and married the nephew of 9/11 mastermind Khalid Sheikh Mohammed. Who could have seen Siddiqui's radicalism coming?

Not only have our post-1965 immigration policies increased America's welfare, criminal, and terrorism caseloads, but now all Americans are being asked to give up their civil liberties to fulfill Teddy Kennedy's dream of bringing the entire Third World to live here in America. When Rand Paul carries on for thirteen hours about Obama using a drone to kill "American citizen" Anwar al-Awlaki, the term "American citizen" has lost its essential meaning. The National Security Act of 1947, creating the CIA, expressly prohibited the agency from engaging in domestic operations. But now we have to spy on "Americans" because of all the al-Awlakis, Tsarnaevs, and Zazis. We have created two huge problems where none existed before—domestic terrorism and government spying—all so the Democrats can win elections and Mark Zuckerberg can underpay his employees.

7

IMMIGRANTS AND CRIME: WHY DO YOU ASK?

YOU WILL SPEND MORE TIME TRYING TO OBTAIN BASIC CRIME STATISTICS ABOUT immigrants in America than trying to sign up for Obamacare. The facts aren't there. Those of us who want to know if a murderer is an immigrant are treated as if we're trying to keep blacks out of the country club. *What difference does it make?*

Here are some ways it might make a difference: Knowing how many criminals are immigrants might affect our opinion of our current immigration policies. It would help us evaluate Marco Rubio's proposal to legalize 20–30 million illegal immigrants, en masse. It could tell us how much money an immigration moratorium would save the taxpayers by reducing the number of police, missing persons operators, hospital emergency room doctors, surgeons, prosecutors, judges, court clerks, prison guards, and rape counselors made necessary by criminal aliens. It would be extremely relevant to the debate about whether to build a fence on our southern border.

SO TELL US!

The government doesn't collect data about immigrant crime, and the media wouldn't report it, anyway. This allows liberals to sneer at anyone else's estimate of the number of criminal immigrants: "We found no such data. This statement is both incorrect and ridiculous. Pants on Fire! The statement is not accurate and makes a ridiculous claim." That quote comes from PolitiFact's evaluation of Texas Governor Rick Perry's statement: "I think [there were] over 3,000 homicides by illegal aliens over the course of the last six years."[1]

Asked by PolitiFact to supply a source, Perry's spokesman cited the Texas Department of Public Safety's webpage, which states: "From October 2008 through July 1, 2014, Texas has identified a total of 203,685 unique criminal alien defendants booked into Texas county jails. Over their criminal careers, these defendants are responsible for at least 642,564 individual criminal charges mostly consisting of Class B misdemeanors or higher, including 3,070 homicides and 7,964 sexual assaults...."

That looks like "over 3,000 homicides" to me.[2]

But PolitiFact turned to its own expert, Northeastern University professor Ramiro Martinez Jr., who said that if Perry were correct, then illegal immigrants would have committed 46 percent of all murders in Texas—and that "boggles the mind." Strictly speaking, boggling the mind of a professor is not data. Martinez asked how so many illegal immigrants could be committing murder and "nobody noticed."[3] It might be easier to "notice" if we weren't prohibited from noticing.

Somebody's noticing the immigrant crime wave: Google *illegal alien crime* and you'll get more than 2 million hits. Google *immigrant crime* and you'll get 40 million. Only our government and media refuse to notice. Then they turn around and denounce anyone else's estimate, saying: *You don't know that.*

So tell us! We "don't know that" only because the people in a position to know have decided to keep it secret.

THE FACTS ABOUT CRIMINAL ALIENS— WITH SEVENTEEN CAVEATS

Every time you think the government has finally produced a real number of immigrants convicted of crimes in America, there's a catch. Legal immigrants will be excluded, convicted criminals whose country of birth is unknown are left out, Hispanic criminals will be classified as "white"[4]—but Hispanic valedictorians are celebrated as another illegal immigrant "success story!" In 1991, the Department of Justice produced a detailed report on the racial characteristics of inmates in both state and federal prisons from 1926 to 1986. Hallelujah! Facts! But then you notice a tiny asterisk: Mexicans are counted as "white" every year except 1926. *Thanks, government!*

I would prefer to have the actual numbers of legal and illegal aliens arrested and convicted of crimes. I would like that information much more than I wanted to know how many residents of American Samoa have no battery-powered radios in their homes. Unfortunately, the government won't tell us how many immigrants commit crimes—much less what their crimes were. It will, however, give us an *exact* count of Samoans without battery-powered radios (2,651 in 2010).[5]

The most extensive information on criminal aliens collected by the federal government is a bare-minimum estimate of the number of immigrants in American prisons and jails. This is not information the government automatically collects: It had to be expressly requested by Congress. In 2011, the Government Accountability Office reported that America was incarcerating at least—the absolute minimum estimate—351,000 criminal aliens: 55,000 immigrants in federal prison and 296,000 illegal aliens in state and local facilities.[6] In the understatement of the century, the GAO admitted that its figures included only "a portion of the total population of criminal aliens who may be incarcerated at the state and local levels...."[7]

The GAO's estimate of 351,000 incarcerated aliens *excludes*:

1. All legal immigrants in state or local prisons;
2. Convicted illegal aliens for whom the states did not submit reimbursement requests to the federal government;[8]
3. Prisoners whose country of birth could not be determined;[9]
4. Immigrants who have been naturalized;
5. Children born to illegal aliens on U.S. soil;
6. Immigrants without at least one felony or two misdemeanor convictions;
7. Immigration detainees;[10] and
8. Illegal immigrants who committed crimes after being amnestied by Reagan in 1986.

To be extra opaque, the GAO counted all immigrants in federal prisons—legal and illegal—but counted only illegal immigrants in state prisons and local jails.[11]

Why exclude legal immigrants? Isn't that worse? Only certain Republicans get excited about the difference between legal and illegal immigrants. The rest of America is trying to understand the point of the last thirty years of legal immigration. Why was this necessary? While it's nice to know a little more about the people Marco Rubio is so anxious to make our fellow citizens, why can't we be told how many rapes and murders *legal* immigrants commit? To paraphrase the line about families, you can't choose your native-born Americans—but you can choose your immigrants. Our immigration system will be working when the number of immigrants who commit crimes is zero.

Why would any country import other countries' criminals? What could possibly be on the plus side of the ledger, with "criminal" on the minus side? Since the United Nations isn't yet demanding that America allow everyone in the world to immigrate here, couldn't we at least discriminate on the basis of felon vs. non-felon? Maybe we could do a triage:

1. Helpful to country;
2. Not helpful to country, but not a felon;
3. Felon.

Here's another idea: Instead of the Census Bureau collecting detailed information about how many rental units have "broken or missing stair railings" (382,000 in 2010) or have had mold in their bathrooms in the last twelve months (1.1 million in 2010),[12] how about the government tell us how many immigrants have committed crimes? Determining the number of foreign born in the criminal justice system doesn't rely on taking surveys, trusting Americans to accurately report on their stair railings, and hiring teams of statisticians to spend years analyzing the data. We just need the government to count. Unlike mold in private homes, criminals have come into significant contact with the government—cops, prosecutors, judges, and prison guards. And we're already paying those guys' salaries. As important as the number of carports in America is, it's also important to know how many immigrants are committing crimes.

DOING THE WORK OUR MEDIA JUST WON'T DO: CLUES TO THE IMMIGRANT CRIME WAVE

With the government keeping that information locked in a steel casket at Fort Knox, one has to look at ancillary facts. The available data suggest that the crime rate among immigrants is astronomical. The Department of Homeland Security (DHS), for example, inadvertently issued a report indicating that there are twice as many foreign-born criminals as the GAO's estimate. In 2006, the DHS stated that 605,000 foreign-born criminals would be arrested by state and local law enforcement in 2007 *alone*. That's double the number of illegal aliens for whom the states requested reimbursement in 2009.[13] If the DHS's estimate is correct, then nearly a third of the 2 million prisoners in state and local facilities that year[14] were foreign born.

Piecing together state and federal reports, it appears that half the correctional population in California consists of illegal aliens. According to a state report, there were fewer than two hundred thousand inmates in the entire California prison population, including mental hospitals, in 2009.[15] That year, 102,795 illegal aliens were incarcerated in California, costing the state more than $1 billion a year.[16] Texas counts only illegal aliens who have already been fingerprinted by the Department of Homeland Security. Even with that limitation, Texas arrests more than thirty-two thousand criminal aliens *a year*.[17]

Then there is the explosion of America's prison population since we began admitting millions of Third World immigrants in the 1970s. From 1925 until 1970, a steady 0.1 percent of the population was in state or federal prison. Thus, in 1925, when the U.S. population was 100 million, there were about one hundred thousand people in prison; and in 1970, when there were 200 million Americans, there were two hundred thousand in prison.[18] Then, suddenly, just as a very different sort of immigrant began to be admitted under Teddy Kennedy's 1965 immigration act, the prison population skyrocketed. If the incarceration rate had remained the same, there would only be about 310,000 people in prison today. Instead, there are more than 2 million prisoners in America. Since 1970, the U.S. population has increased by one-third, but the prison population has nearly sextupled. A lot of factors affect incarceration rates—liberal judges, destructive social programs, illegitimacy, and social decay. But those come and go. Immigration is forever.

ONE THOUSAND DOMINICANS—ONE DANE

The New York State Department of Corrections has collected information about the top ten nationalities in its prisons for years—a practice that will presumably end as soon as this book is published. Foreign inmates were 70 percent more likely to have committed a violent crime than American criminals. They were also twice as likely to have committed a class A felony, such as aggravated murder, kidnapping, and terrorism.[19]

In 2010, the top ten countries of the foreign-born inmates were:

Dominican Republic: 1,314

Jamaica: 849

Mexico: 523

Guyana: 289

El Salvador: 245

Cuba: 242

Trinidad and Tobago: 237

Haiti: 201

Ecuador: 189

Colombia: 168[20]

Most readers are agog at the number of Dominicans in New York prisons, having spent years reading *New York Times* articles about Dominicans' "entrepreneurial zeal,"[21] and "traditional immigrant virtues."[22] Even in an article about the Dominicans' domination of the crack cocaine business, the *Times* praised their "savvy," which had allowed them to become "highly successful" drug dealers, then hailed their drug-infested neighborhoods as the "embodiment of the American Dream—a vibrant, energetic urban melting pot."[23]

Between 1996 and 2010, the only change in New York's foreign inmate population was that El Salvador and Ecuador edged out China and Panama on the "Top Ten" list, and the number of Mexicans doubled. Mexicans have been in the top ten nationalities of foreign-born inmates in New York for decades. In 2010, there were more Mexicans in New York state prisons—523—than there were inmates from the entire continent of Europe—353.[24]

In 2007—the last year the New York Department of Corrections bothered to list European inmates by country, the representation of the following countries in state prisons was:

Denmark: 1

Czechoslovakia: 2

Netherlands: 2
Switzerland: 2
Ireland: 4
Poland: 27
Germany: 46
England: 49[25]

Of course, on account of Europe's own insane immigration policies, most of the "European" criminals are probably Muslims.[26] In Denmark, actual Danes come in tenth in criminals' nationality, after Moroccans, Lebanese, Yugoslavians, Somalis, Iranians, Pakistanis, Turks, Iraqis, and Vietnamese.[27]

We do not know how many prisoners from "England" were like this one, featured in the *Orlando Sentinel* in 2014: "Brit Gets Ten Years for Seeking Child Sex for Incest Fantasy." The name of the "Brit" was: Shuhel Mahboob Ali.[28] He had flown from London to Florida in order to rape the thirteen-year-old daughter of a man he met through an online ad. Instead, the forty-year-old Ali was arrested by undercover FBI agents who had placed the ad. In his months of chatting with the fake dad, Mr. Ali provided graphic details of how he planned to create a "daughters only" incest family. He said he would "breed" with the thirteen-year-old girl, then immediately begin sexually abusing their babies, to indoctrinate them into the incest "lifestyle." "When you start with very, very, very young," he boasted, "you can mold them to believe anything and do anything you [say]."[29] Shuhel Mahboob Ali is now one of the "British" inmates in our federal prisons.

ARKRIN TAECHARATANAPRASERT OF THE BACK BAY TAECHARATANAPRASERTS

Other hints about immigrant crime come from the "Most Wanted" lists. Here is the Los Angeles Police Department's list of "Most Wanted" criminals, as of January 1, 2015:

- Jesse Enrique Monarrez (murder),
- Cesar Augusto Nistal (child molestation),
- Jose A. Padilla (murder),
- Demecio Carlos Perez (murder),
- Ramon Reyes (robbery and murder),
- Victor Vargas (murder),
- Ruben Villa (murder),[30]
- Antonio Villaraigosa (gross incompetence and mismanagement of funds).

Ninety percent of the names on the U.S. Marshals' list of most wanted criminals[31] would not have been recognizable *as* names fifty years ago—unless "Arkrin Taecharatanaprasert" or "Florin Filipescu" were little-remembered early-twentieth-century Americans. But it's nice to know that the Nguyen family has a hobby they all enjoy. (From the Marshals' list: Hieu Nguyen, Jimmy Nguyen, and Nancy Nguyen.)

Half the names on the Marshals' list are Hispanic.

The Hennepin County Sheriff's Office in Minnesota openly applies affirmative action to its "Most Wanted" lists, in order to show a "cross section" of the community, rather than telling us, as the title suggests, who actually are the "most wanted."[32] But even in a compilation of criminals front-loaded with Americans, a pattern emerges:

- Krysta Ellen MacCourt, 34: Wanted on charge of felony escape from custody and sentencing guideline violations on DWI convictions.
- Hannah Jeanette Myhre, 31: Wanted on charge of sentencing guideline violations on first-degree aggravated robbery conviction.
- Edward Francis Bates, 38: Wanted on charge of first-degree criminal sexual conduct in connection with a Brooklyn Center rape.

- Jose Guadalupe Gutierrez-Sanchez, 40: Wanted on charge of first-degree criminal sexual conduct in connection with the abuse of a girl.
- Abdihakim Mohamed Isse, 40: Wanted on charges of first- and third-degree criminal sexual conduct in connection with a sexual assault.
- Mohamud Mohamed Omar, 32: Wanted on charge of fleeing a police officer in a motor vehicle.
- Julian Alcaide Lopez, 37: Wanted on charge of criminal sexual conduct in connection with a sexual assault.
- Steven Allen Ableman Jr., 29: Wanted on charges of DWI and domestic assaults.
- Abdikani Mohamed Ahmed, 26: Wanted on charge of degree aggravated robbery in connection with an armed robbery.
- Fanuel Andies Tesfatsion, 24: Wanted on charge of prohibited person in possession of firearm.

Instead of searching law enforcement bulletins for clues, it would be terrific if our constitutionally protected guardians of liberty in the press ferreted out the truth. Judging by the interest on the internet, the public is absolutely *fascinated* with the immigration status of criminals.

IT'S RUDE TO ASK ABOUT THE IMMIGRATION STATUS OF THE SUSPECT

On the rare occasions when a reporter asks if a criminal is an immigrant, government officials summarily dismiss the question as if it would be racist to discuss the defendant's nation of birth. Ricardo DeLeon Flores killed a teenaged girl in Kansas after speeding through a stop sign and crashing into two cars. "When asked whether Flores was a U.S. citizen," the local Kansas newspaper reported, "Deborah Owens of the Leavenworth County Attorney's Office said she had no knowledge of his citizenship status."[33]

Was the Spanish translator a hint? The ICE officials showing up in court? His Oakland Raiders T-shirt? Two families' lives were forever changed by the reckless behavior of someone who should not have been in this country, but the prosecutor refused to tell a reporter that Flores was an illegal immigrant. Owens must have felt a warm rush of self-righteousness, thinking how much better she is than all those blood-and-soil types who want to know when foreigners kill Americans.

In 2012, Gerardo Beltran Rodriquez, twenty-seven, Adolfo Guzman Lopez, thirty-one, and Irving Eduardo Rodriquez-Munguia, twenty, were caught with four pounds of heroin in their car during a traffic stop. (Hispanics should become better drivers if they plan to keep transporting large amounts of heroin.) None of the men spoke English. In another act of journalistic heroism, a local reporter in Gaston, North Carolina, asked if the men were illegal aliens. The highway patrolman who arrested them, W. R. Blanton, responded that he doesn't deal with immigration.[34]

Essex County prosecutor Paula T. Dow refused to answer questions about her office's release of Jose Carranza, twenty-eight, an illegal alien indicted for child rape who then went on to murder three teenagers. Brushing off the "uproar" about Carranza's immigration status on CNN, Dow said those questions would have to "wait for another day." The assistant prosecutor, Thomas McTigue, responded to media inquiries about the decision to release an illegal alien child rapist, saying, "Our focus hasn't been his immigration status."[35] No kidding.

In this vale of ignorance, the *New York Times*' David Leonhardt announced that he was quite sure how many immigrants are in prison: Very few. Not many, at all. A tiny number. Certainly less than anything TV personality Lou Dobbs says. In another classic example of the absence of facts being used to browbeat anyone whose figures the media don't like, in 2007, Leonhardt snippily corrected Dobbs for claiming that one-third of federal prisoners "come from some other country." Announcing that he would present "the facts," Leonhardt wrote that the "percentage of non-citizens" in federal prison had fallen to 20 percent in 2005.[36]

First of all, Dobbs said "come from some other country"—not "non-citizens." Half a million people who "come from some other country" become citizens every year.[37] More than a million did in the year before Clinton's 1996 reelection.[38]

In any event, Leonhardt wasn't citing facts at all. He was citing one of several wild guesses by the government. The DOJ relies on immigrants' self-reports to determine prisoners' citizenship status. The GAO conducts its own analysis of Bureau of Prisons data. And the U.S. census simply guesses the immigration status of inmates.[39] Clearly, the government hasn't the first idea how many prisoners are noncitizens. But Leonhardt treated as gospel the Department of Justice's estimate that 20 percent of federal prisoners were illegal immigrants. That same year, the GAO said it was 27 percent[40]—which is pretty close to Dobbs's "one-third," and the GAO was only counting illegals, not all foreign born.

Leonhardt might as well have chastised Dobbs for using an incorrect estimate of the number of fish in the ocean. The difference is: The number of foreigners in American prisons is easily ascertainable, if only the government would count them. Wouldn't it be great if someone would just tell us how many immigrants have been convicted of committing crimes in America?

CRIMINAL CULTURES POURING IN TO AMERICA

America is helpless against the criminal cultures being foisted on us by immigration from the Third World. Identity theft, credit card scams, Medicare and food stamp fraud, tax rebate theft, and staged-crash insurance scams—these are not native American habits. Our criminals kill their spouses for the $30,000 life insurance policy after splashing their DNA all over the crime scene. Americans think only dumb people become criminals, but that's not true in the Third World, where criminality transcends social class.

In Nigeria, every level of society is criminal, with the smart ones running internet scams, the mid-range ones running car-theft rings, and the stupid ones engaging in piracy and kidnapping. At the University of Lagos, you can major in credit card fraud. There were almost no Nigerians in the United States until the 1970s.[41] Today, there are 380,000. We take more immigrants from Nigeria than we do from Britain.[42] There are more Nigerians in the United States than any other country in the world besides Nigeria.[43] But I'm sure our new Nigerian neighbors will have German-style rectitude about reporting ALL their income to the government.

In Mexico, every transaction between a citizen and a government official involves a cash bribe.

All of the main immigrant groups to the United States commit a wildly disproportionate amount of crime compared with native-born Americans. Russians specialize in financial fraud, arms dealing, and drug smuggling; Albanians prefer ATM thefts, home invasions, gambling, and drugs; Chinese go in for human smuggling, drug trafficking, and gambling; and Arabs specialize in drug smuggling, human trafficking, and document fraud.[44] According to the National Crime Prevention Council, Mexican gangs in Los Angeles use money from the sale of counterfeit products to fund their drug trafficking, human smuggling, and prostitution operations. Copyright theft alone costs the county nearly half a billion dollars in lost tax revenue and one hundred thousand lost jobs.[45]

We've built up no immunity to such complicated crimes, so America is like Disneyland to foreign criminals. To illustrate my point, I ran a Nexis search of the words "fraud, food stamp, Medicare and insurance." Unfortunately, my computer exploded. A compilation of the perpetrators would produce enough comical foreign names to fill this entire book. It would be a bestseller, come out in paperback, be adapted for the big screen, win a Golden Globe—and you'd still be searching Nexis for one traditional American who bilked Medicare for $20 million. For brevity, here are some of the results from *a single month*, September 2014:

Sadiq Sadruddin Lakhani, convicted in fuel fraud case;[46] Sathish Narayanappa Babu, convicted of Medicare fraud;[47] Cruz Sonia Collado, sentenced for $6.5 million Medicare fraud;[48] Andrew Jong Hack Park, Sang

Jun Park, Jose Isabel Gomez Arreoloa, Xilin Chen, Chuang Feng Chen, Aixia Chen, Hersel Neman, Morad Neman, Mehran Khalili, and Alma Villalobos, arrested for laundering drug money;[49] Taimur Khan, Javed Sunesra, Zuned Sunesra, and Bismilla Sunesra, convicted in illegal prescription-drug scam;[50] Farid Fata, convicted in $225 million Medicare theft;[51] Armen Bislamian, Khachatur Bislamyan, Sisak Saribekyan, Karlen Khatchatryan, and Hartunyun Grigoryan, charged with $2 million credit card scam;[52] Estrella Perez, Solchys Perez, and Abigail Aguila, sentenced in $20 million Miami healthcare fraud;[53] Dona Takushi, Jenny Nishida, and Nicole Cheung, convicted in credit union embezzlement;[54] Armen Bislamian, Khachatur Bislamyan, Sisak Saribekyan, Karlen Khatchatryan, and Hartunyun Grigoryan, arrested in $2 million credit card theft;[55] Akinola Afolabi, convicted in $1.5 million Medicare fraud case;[56] Amir Rasheed, Karuna Mehta, Mashhod Afzal, Mustafa Al Kabouni, Mohamad Barbour, Mohammad Amir Al Kabouni, Muhammad Eid Al Kabouni, Waqif Qadir, Asra Qadir, Glenda Lopez, and Cristina Ramirez, convicted in $3.6 million food stamp fraud;[57] Bahram Khandan, sentenced for selling $1.8 million stolen hospital supplies over the internet;[58] Felix Maduka and Stella Maduka, convicted in $4.5 million healthcare fraud scheme;[59] Moklasur Mukul, Mohamed Ali, Deshi Bazar, Ali Ahmed, Nazir Ahmed, Mustak Ahmed, Azizur Ullah, Mohammed Chadek, Mohammed Miah, Mohammed Amin, Dilshad Chowdhury, and Mohamed Ahmed arrested in food stamp fraud;[60] Fowzi Naji Tareb, charged with $6 million food stamp fraud;[61] Angel Mirabal, charged with $24 million Medicare scheme;[62] Ricardo Parga and Alien Moya, accused of faking car accident in insurance scam;[63] Dr. Vicha Janviriya, convicted in $1.3 million Medicare fraud;[64] Annilet Dominguez, sentenced in $6 million Miami home healthcare fraud;[65] Orelvis Olivera, indicted in $8 million Medicare fraud;[66] Dr. Kutub Mesiwala, Jaweed Mohammed, Mohammad Zubair Khan, and Tousif Khan, indicted in $7 million healthcare fraud;[67] Ernesto Fernandez, Dennis Hernandez, Jose Alvarez, Joel San Pedro, Alina Hernandez, and Juan Valdes, charged in $6 million Miami home healthcare fraud.[68]

By contrast, the typical American's idea of an internet scam is to photoshop the head of Hillary Clinton onto the body of Kim Kardashian.

Our government seems pretty slow at detecting the Pakistani Medicare scams. I have my doubts that we have the manpower to catch them all. How much are foreigners' elaborate frauds going to cost the taxpayer? How much are we paying to incarcerate people who have no right to be here? How much of the American economy will be devoted to the police officers, lawyers, and judges necessary to keep foreign criminals behind bars? What is the cost in murder victims, rape survivors, facial reconstruction surgeries, drug overdoses, ruined lives, stolen property, and destroyed neighborhoods? We haven't the first idea, but on the bright side, the government can tell us the precise number of Samoans without battery-powered radios.

WHY CAN'T WE HAVE ISRAEL'S POLICY ON IMMIGRATION?

WHAT DO YOU THINK ISRAELI PRIME MINISTER BENJAMIN NETANYAHU WOULD do if tens of thousands of Israelis were being murdered by Palestinians? If heroin deaths in Israel suddenly tripled and 90 percent of the heroin was coming into Israel through the Palestinian territories—some of it through a tunnel the length of six football fields?[1] If ISIS butchers were on Israel's border?

If you guessed, "Give them in-state college tuition, driver's licenses, and free medical care," you would be wrong.

In 2012, Israel had sixty thousand illegal aliens, which would be the equivalent of a mere 2 million illegals in America. Warning that the illegals would overwhelm Israel and destroy the nature of the country, Netanyahu vowed to complete a border fence. Even opposition leader Yair Lapid supported a fence, as well as "the arrest and deportation of infiltrators."[2]

Israel responded to the influx of illegal aliens by arresting them and putting them on buses out of the country. This is in contrast to our policy, which is to put them on buses *into* our country and enroll them in U.S.

schools. The *Times* quoted an Israeli bystander, observing the arrests, saying: "It must be done or tomorrow we will have no country and we will have to look for another one."[3] For refugees who could not be deported under international law, Israel built detention facilities on the border, where they were to be held until conditions in their countries improved. Netanyahu unsentimentally responded to protests over the detentions, saying, "The infiltrators who were transferred to the special detainment facility can either stay there or go back to their home countries."[4]

I admire Israel's policy and wish we could adopt it. Show me in a straight line why we can't do what they do. If Israel's ethnicity changes, the idea of Israel changes. If America's ethnicity changes, the idea of our country changes, too.

YOU KNOW WHERE HISPANICS ARE OVERREPRESENTED? U.S. PRISONS

When did Americans get together and decide we want 30 percent of all immigrants to be from a single country and that country should be Mexico? If we're going to take almost all our immigrants from a single country, why not Denmark? There appears to have been only one Danish prisoner in New York State in decades—and, again, that was a Muslim.

Sixty-six percent of the criminal aliens imprisoned in the states in 2009 were Mexican.[5] In the federal prisons, 68 percent of the criminal aliens were Mexican and nearly 90 percent were from one of eight countries: Mexico, Colombia, the Dominican Republic, Cuba, Jamaica, El Salvador, Honduras, and Guatemala.[6] Even in the beautiful mosaic of New York State, where prison inmates come from 124 different countries, the vast majority—75 percent—are from the Caribbean or Latin America.[7] Doesn't something kind of stick out like a sore thumb here? What other country on earth would be this stupid? Not Israel!

For every category the media care about, we get obsessively detailed reports on Hispanic percentages. We have studies showing Hispanics are underrepresented in Hollywood,[8] at top colleges,[9] in the federal government,[10] and in the national media.[11] We're told there are too few Hispanic veterinarians in Texas[12] and not enough Hispanic cops in Utah.[13] (An unseemly number of these reports were authored by Hispanics themselves, so one area where Latinos are definitely not deficient is self-esteem.)

You know where else Hispanics are underrepresented? In the U.S. military. You'd never know it, with the media showcasing every Hispanic troop,[14] but Hispanics are half as likely to enlist in the military as either whites or blacks. The recruit-to-population ratio for whites is 1.06. For blacks it is 1.08. For Hispanics, it's only 0.65. The media not only neglect to highlight this particular underrepresentation, they lie about it. An article published by the Population Reference Bureau—subsidized by taxpayers—is titled: "Latinos Claim Larger Share of U.S. Military Personnel." To the untrained eye, this would seem to be saying that Latinos claim a larger share of U.S. military personnel. In fact, however, by "larger share," the headline means "larger" compared with the past—not compared with other groups. The actual article admits that Hispanics constitute less than 12 percent of all enlistees, compared with 16 percent of the civilian workforce. Moreover, despite their machismo culture, a majority of Hispanic troops are women.[15]

Here's a category where Hispanics are overrepresented: Prisons. There are about four times as many whites as Hispanics in the United States, according to the census, so let's assume there are actually three times as many.[16] And yet Hispanics commit 90 percent as many assaults as whites, nearly as many violent robberies (thirty-seven thousand Hispanics to thirty-eight thousand whites), and 84 percent as many murders (thirty-eight thousand Hispanics to forty-five thousand whites).[17] Hispanics are only half as likely to be in prison for rape as whites, probably because white women in the United States are more than twice as likely to report rape as Hispanics.[18] In fact, American women will report rapes that didn't even happen. (See, e.g., University of Virginia, Columbia Mattress Girl, and Lena Dunham.) Hispanic males in the United States are more than three times as likely to spend time in prison in their lifetimes than white males are.[19] In 2010, 1,258 of every 100,000 Hispanic males were in prison, compared with 459 per 100,000 white males.[20] Evidently, the dream of many "Dreamers" is to rob, assault, and murder Americans.

LOST A FRIEND TO DRUGS? THANK A MEXICAN

The vast majority of all drugs in America—heroin, cocaine, marijuana, and, increasingly, methamphetamine—are brought in from Mexico. Most of the heroin sold in the United States is grown south of the border, and Mexican cartels transport nearly all of it.[21] Justice Brennan's invention of birthright citizenship has been a bonanza for the drug trade. Now the cartels have Mexicans on both sides of the border to complete the distribution chain. Two of the Sinaloa cartel's major American distributors, Pedro and Margarito Flores, were "Americans," born to a family of cartel members in Chicago and raised in the Mexican part of the city. We have to make Mexican drug traffickers U.S. citizens so that Arianna Huffington can have cheap gardeners.

In 2012, the U.S. government estimated that 660,000 Americans were using heroin and more than 3,000 dying of it every year because Mexico was boosting the supply.[22] About a quarter of all people who try heroin will become dependent on it, according to government estimates,[23] and the precise appeal of methamphetamine to Mexico's Sinaloa drug cartel was that it was "ragingly addictive," according to the *New York Times*.[24] *Forbes* reports that there is "little doubt" that the heroin that killed Philip Seymour Hoffman came from Mexico.[25] These aren't "big city" problems: They're Mexico-is-on-our-border problems.

Missouri had 18 heroin overdose deaths in 2001; ten years later, there were 245.[26] Heroin deaths in Minnesota shot from 3 to 98 between 1999 and 2013.[27] Michigan saw fatal heroin overdoses surge from a few dozen a year in 2002 to more than 100 a year starting in 2009.[28] In just one year, heroin-related fatalities in Connecticut nearly doubled, to 257 in 2013.[29]

Between 2007 and 2012, heroin use in the United States is estimated to have increased by almost 80 percent.[30] And that's just heroin. More than 40,000 Americans were killed from all illegal drug use in 2010, surpassing car accidents and shootings as a cause of death.[31]

The addicts who die may be the lucky ones. In 2001, a seventeen-year-old boy in New Jersey who scored 700 on the math SAT took a heroin overdose that left him unable to stand, walk, or bathe himself. His mother, a globetrotting executive with Citibank, was forced to quit her job and become his full-time caretaker. After a year of hospitalization and more than a decade of therapy, he still needs his mother to carry him to the toilet. He has no recollection of taking an overdose, but packets of heroin and marijuana were found stored in a secret compartment in his bedroom.[32]

That's what happened to one of America's brightest young men because the head of Mexico's Sinaloa drug cartel discovered tunnels. As the *New York Times* admiringly put it: "[Joaquin 'El Chapo' Guzman's] greatest contribution to the evolving tradecraft of drug trafficking was one of those innovations that seem so logical in hindsight it's a wonder nobody thought of it before: a tunnel."[33] El Chapo is married to Emma Coronel: American anchor baby.[34] In September 2011 Emma left the cartel's hideout long enough to get to California, and give birth to her own American anchor babies.[35] As soon as the twins were delivered, Emma went right back to Mexico to rejoin the man who replaced Osama bin Laden on both the FBI and Interpol's Most Wanted list.[36]

America: Do you have any respect for yourself?

HERE ARE SOME FENCES THAT WORK!

China went to war to stop Britain from addicting its people to opium. On the eve of the Opium Wars, China's drug czar said: "If we continue to allow this trade to flourish, in a few dozen years we will find ourselves not only with no soldiers to resist the enemy, but also with no money to equip the army."[37] Today, China is once again battling drug smuggling because, like America, it also has a poor, corrupt nation with a massive humanitarian crisis on its border: Not Mexico, but North Korea. Guess what China did? It built a fence! Despite stern warnings from the *New York Times*, China put a thirteen-foot barbed wire fence on its border, patrolled by armed guards. And you know what, *New York Times*? It's working![38] But America can't have a fence because a fence on the border would be a crime against diversity.

You know who else has a border fence? The only democracy in the Middle East: Israel. In 2013, the *New York Times' Latitude* blog reported the "good news" about how well Israel's fence was working: "The good news came in the form of statistics: In the last days of December, the number of illegal immigrants entering Israel dropped to zero for the first time in more than half a decade. The new fence that Israel is constructing along its border with Egypt, coupled with enhanced border-security measures, seems to be working."[39] Of the 10,365 illegal aliens who entered Israel in 2012, "9,200 were sent out."

No one tells Netanyahu, "Show me a fence, I'll show you a ladder." But that's all we hear from government officials about a fence on the U.S.-Mexican border. Give politicians a quip and they think they're Pythagoras.

- Former Homeland Security Secretary and Arizona Governor Janet Napolitano: "Show me a 50-foot wall and I'll show you a 51-foot ladder at the border."[40]
- California Democratic Representative Sheila Jackson Lee: "And I know that you've heard this quote often, and that is that you build a fence 10 feet and they will get a ladder 11 feet."[41]
- Texas Governor Rick Perry: "If you build a 30-foot wall from El Paso to Brownsville, the 35-foot ladder business gets real good."[42]

- Rick Perry, again: "The 15-foot ladder business is going to get good on that 14-foot fence."[43]
- And again—Perry: The only thing a border-wide wall "would possibly accomplish is to help the ladder business."[44]

Why doesn't Rick Perry say that to Israel?

AT LEAST MEXICO DOESN'T BEHEAD PEOPLE LIKE ISIS—WAIT, WHAT?

In 2014, the American media exploded with news of ISIS beheadings in Syria—six thousand miles away from the United States. Meanwhile, the beheading capital of the world is just to our south, a stone's throw from American homes, businesses, and ranches. When the Islamic State of Iraq and Syria first began posting videotaped beheadings online, it was as if no one had ever heard of such barbarity. In fact, decapitation porn was an innovation of the Mexican drug cartels.[45]

One "ISIS" video circulating in 2014 showed a man being beheaded with a chain saw. Then it turned out the video wasn't an ISIS beheading, at all: It was a Mexican video from 2010.[46] After American David Hartley was shot and killed by Mexican drug cartel members while jet skiing with his wife at a lake on the Mexican border, the lead investigator on the case was murdered and his head delivered in a suitcase to a nearby military installation.[47] In 2013, there was a huge outcry over Facebook's video-sharing policy when an extremely graphic video of a man beheading a woman appeared on the site. That, too, was a product of Mexico.[48]

Where is the 24-7 coverage for these champion beheaders? If it seems like you never hear about all the dismemberments in Mexico, you'd be right. In a search of all transcripts in the Nexis archive in the first eight months of ISIS's existence as a jihadist group, "beheading" was used in the same sentence as "ISIS" or "ISIL" 1,629 times. During that same time period, it was used in the same sentence as "Mexico" or "Mexican" twice.

Indeed, in the previous five years Mexican beheadings were mentioned only sixty-six times.[49] If a tree falls and beheads a woman in Mexico, does anyone hear it?

The main difference between decapitations in Syria and Mexico is that Mexicans also behead women, children, and innocent bystanders.[50] In addition to pioneering videotaped beheadings, Mexicans specialize in corpse desecration, burning people alive, rolling human heads onto packed nightclub dance floors, dissolving bodies in acid, and hanging mutilated bodies from bridges.[51]

Why are the media obsessed with ISIS's beheadings but not the more frequent head-chopping right next door? It would be as if French newspapers in 1930s obsessively covered the Chaco War between Bolivia and Paraguay, while relegating news about Germany to the back pages. While the Chaco War was important—the bloodiest South American conflict in the twentieth century—Hitler's increasing militarism was arguably of more immediate concern to France.

The American media's fixation on monsters twelve hours and several connecting flights away from the United States, while ignoring the savage butchery occurring in a country within walking distance, is so obvious that border fence advocates have taken to warning that Islamic terrorists might enter the United States through the wide-open Mexican border. It's possible, but you know what's even more possible? That Mexicans will walk across the border.

Iraqi terrorists may long to maim and rape Americans, get them hooked on heroin, burn down hundreds of acres of our national parks, and kill Americans in drunk driving accidents. But it's Mexicans who are actually doing these things.

Even *Newsweek* complained about the media's obsession with ISIS beheadings, to the detriment of beheadings in...Saudi Arabia![52] About eighty criminals suffer this punishment in Saudi Arabia every year, and while the legal proceedings might not meet Western standards of proportionality, those decapitations are administered only after a formal trial and conviction. Between 2007 and 2011, 1,300 people were beheaded by criminal gangs in Mexico—and that's in addition to the 100,000 murders by other means.[53]

One of Mexico's most notorious beheaders is now living freely in the United States because of Justice Brennan's footnote. In 2010, fourteen-year-old Edgar Jimenez Lugo beheaded four men in the wealthy resort town of Cuernavaca, Mexico, and hung their corpses from a bridge over a busy road, their heads and genitals lying nearby.[54] Although Lugo was raised entirely in Mexico, his illegal alien mother had given birth to him in San Diego. So after serving a quick three-year sentence in Mexico for four dismemberments, Lugo "returned" to America. This country was helpless to stop him—at least until someone notices that our anchor baby policy is based on the mental delusion of one Supreme Court justice. The U.S. embassy refused to say where the gruesome murderer would be living, or to discuss his case at all, due to "privacy considerations," according to Britain's *Daily Mail*.[55]

In a microscopic item on the case, the *New York Times* referred to Lugo as a "U.S. Boy."[56] So the *Times* believes a fourteen-year-old who was merely born here, but raised entirely in Mexico, is an American. But a fourteen-year-old born in Mexico and raised in the United States is also an American—a "Dreamer"! Show me the reasoning behind that, other than: *We want as many Mexicans voting here as we can get!*

HEADLESS BODY FOUND IN BORDERLESS COUNTRY

I take it that liberals would be dismayed if Mexicans began beheading people in America, based on their relentless mocking of Arizona Governor Jan Brewer's claim, in July 2010, that there had been beheadings in the Arizona desert. The *Washington Post*'s Dana Milbank sneered: "Ay, caramba! Those dark-skinned foreigners are now severing the heads of fair-haired Americans? Maybe they're also scalping them or shrinking them or putting them on a spike."[57] Salon.com cited Brewer's remark to sneer that "as you can see, Jan Brewer is crazy."[58]

Apparently, liberals considered it pretty far-fetched that Mexican cartel violence would ever, in a million years, cross into America. So if it ever did, that would be a big deal, right?

Three months after Brewer's claim, Mexicans beheaded a man in Arizona.[59] Within the next two years, a headless body turned up in the Arizona desert,[60] and the dismembered body of a nineteen-year-old American girl was found in Oklahoma.[61] All three dismemberments were believed to be the work of Mexican cartels—confirmed in the first Arizona case.[62] At that point, liberals' position was that it was no big deal, after all. In fact, Mexicans beheading people in the United States was of such utter insignificance that the media barely mentioned these beheadings and went back to the eye-rolling retort: *Show me a fence, I'll show you a ladder.*[63]

The Mexican predilection for beheadings is not limited to drug cartels. In 2004, two Mexican men decapitated three *children*, ages nine to ten, in Baltimore, Maryland, over some obscure family dispute. Everyone involved was an illegal alien, all related to one another through a series of connections that would require a Talmudic scholar to sort out, but seemed to involve a lot of baby mamas. According to the Mexican government, the executioners, Policarpio Espinoza and Adan Espinoza Canela, were the children's uncle and cousin, respectively, and the (three) parents were: Ricardo Espinoza, Mimi Quezada, and Maria Andrea Espejo. One child was completely decapitated, the other two partially decapitated. Even seasoned police officers were shaken by the grisly crime scene.[64]

If Muslim men had decapitated three Syrian children in Baltimore, do you think you would have heard about it? The *Baltimore Sun* tidied up the executions, calling them "slashing deaths."[65] How about: *The slashing death of James Foley at the hands of ISIS?*

Some Mexicans practice "Palo Mayombe," a primitive voodoo religion found throughout Latin America that holds that human sacrifice brings magical powers. The upside to their belief system is that practitioners will confess right away to committing heinous dismemberments because they believe they are invisible.[66] Americans in New Jersey and Texas have been dismembered by the cult.

Is an American citizen more likely to be murdered by a Muslim terrorist or by a Mexican? According to CNN, twenty-nine Americans have been killed in Islamic terrorist attacks in the United States since 9/11.[67] I don't know why they excluded 9/11, so by my count, it's 3,029. In fact, let's round it up to four thousand to cover the last several decades. According to the GAO's extremely conservative figures, Mexicans alone—forget other immigrants—have murdered a minimum of twenty-three thousand Americans in the last few decades.[68]

WHO'S WRONG: US OR ISRAEL?

If this were happening in Israel, forget a fence—Netanyahu would be bombing Mexico. We don't have to do that, but can't we at least build a fence? Instead of prosecuting border guards who shoot and wound illegal aliens—as President Bush did—Netanyahu would stoutly defend the agents, saying, "We didn't choose this." And if the agents killed any illegals, he'd dismiss the casualties as "telegenically dead Mexicans." Israel may have gotten its immigration policies from us, back when America was a country that defended itself. President Dwight Eisenhower put a general in charge of the INS, who proceeded to round up and deport illegals in an operation dubbed "Operation Wetback."

If this country were Israel, 80 percent of the country would be cheering a military offensive on our southern border.[69]

HBO's Bill Maher would be saying of our southern neighbors: "Americans have three hundred forty-nine Nobel Prizes; Latin Americans have sixteen. That seems like kind of a big advantage for Team America."[70] (It's worse than that. Excluding the humanities prizes, all of South and Central America combined—with a population of nearly 450 million—have won only five Nobel prizes, compared with well over three hundred Nobel Prizes in the sciences for Americans.) Maher would place the blame for violence on the border on illegal aliens themselves, saying, "If it's your father, your brother, your uncle who's smuggling drugs, guns, humans, and counterfeit goods into the United States, whose fault is it really? Do you really expect Americans not to retaliate?"

Howard Stern would denounce radio callers bleating about the alleged humanitarian crisis on our border, explaining: "The median income in the United States is $29,000 and the Mexican median income is $3,000. But the Mexicans are mad at the United States. Instead of being mad at the f***ing drug cartels running their so-called country, who are raping the country, taking all the aid that the United States actually gives to them. That they're not angry with. They're angry at the U.S." He'd point out that the United States and Canada are the only real democracies on the continent. Erupting in a volcano of expletives, he would say: "Americans get enough s*** all over the world. They get s*** on all the time. We won the Mexican-American War in 1848. We *are* the indigenous people of that area. I'm sick of the bulls***."

The above actually was said—but it was said about Israel and the Palestinians, not the United States and Mexicans.

The harm done to the United States by Mexicans is considerably greater than the harm done to Israelis by the ineffectual Palestinians. In the July 2014 conflict, Palestinians fired more than four thousand rockets into Israel.[71] In all, their bombs killed six civilians, including one Thai national. "Barrages of rockets from Gaza," the *New York Times* reported, do little damage because Palestinians are using "largely futile homemade rockets."[72]

Americans are always asked, *What would you do if rockets were being fired from Mexico into Texas?* The answer is: Absolutely nothing. My question is: What if instead of a few thousand Palestinian criminals in Israel,[73] Palestinians were committing hundreds of thousands of crimes against Israelis—murder, rape, drug trafficking, violent assaults, robbery, drunk driving homicides, and burglary? That's the equivalent of the *minimum* number of immigrants committing crimes in large parts of America.

The U.S. government admits that at least 351,000 criminal immigrants were incarcerated the United States as of 2011—the vast majority of them Mexican.[74]

According to the GAO, five jurisdictions alone—New York City; Los Angeles County; Orange County, California; Harris County, Texas; and Maricopa County, Arizona—are incarcerating more than 110,000 criminal illegal aliens.[75] The total population of those five counties is 28 million, or about three and a half times the size of Israel. The illegal alien crime wave in those parts of America, therefore, would be the same as thirty thousand Palestinians, Jordanians, and Eritreans in Israeli prisons. In fact, however, in 2012, Israel was incarcerating a total of only eighteen thousand prisoners of any type.[76]

The GAO also reports that each arrested illegal alien had committed an average of twelve offenses—or 1.32 million crimes in those five jurisdictions.[77] Illegal immigrants' most common offense was drug trafficking, except in New York, where it was murder.[78] Based on the GAO's estimate of offense types committed by criminal aliens, that would amount to approximately 2,750 drug arrests of immigrants in Israel, 5,500 motor vehicle violations, 2,750 assaults, 800 rapes, and 400 murders.[79] In fact, there were only 124 murders in Israel in the first eleven months of 2013, according to the U.S. State Department.[80] And remember: The GAO was only counting illegal aliens. We have no idea how many legal immigrants, anchor babies, refugees, asylees, and naturalized citizens were incarcerated in these five counties.

IS IT GOOD FOR THE AMERICANS?

If Israel had our open-border policies, it would be overrun with Palestinian, Jordanian, and Eritrean criminals. If we had their policies, the only criminals in America would be the guys you see on *Cops*. There would be about seven hundred thousand people in American prisons, instead of 2 million.

Jews forthrightly ask: Is it good for the Jews? Why can't Americans ask: Is it good for Americans? We're the only nation on earth that specifically seeks out immigrants whom we have to help—even those who commit heinous crimes against us. How about asking our politicians: Who's wrong—us or Israel? Chuck Schumer? Marco? Governor Christie? Hey—where'd everybody go? If any American politician thinks Israel is pursuing an inhumane immigration policy, America has the influence to stop it. I happen to think Israel's policy is perfectly sensible. But Democrats don't. Rick Perry doesn't. Jeb Bush doesn't.

Like Israel, we reached a "two-state" solution with our neighbor, but Mexico refuses to accept that settlement. Our boundary with Mexico was established in 1848; Israel's boundaries with the Palestinians were first established in 1948 and modified in 1967. Our neighbors are at least as troublesome as Israel's, but instead of lobbing impotent rockets across the border, they commit murder, child rape, vehicular homicide, narcotics crimes, assault, and arson in this country on a staggering scale. Far more Americans are murdered by Mexicans, per capita, than Israelis are murdered by Palestinians.

Could we move Israel to our southern border? They know how to defend a country.

SPOT THE IMMIGRANT!

CASE NO. 1 | FRESNO, CALIFORNIA

LET'S PLAY "SPOT THE IMMIGRANT!"

In 1998, three adolescent girls in Fresno ran away from home, then changed their minds when they had gotten about thirty miles away. They called an acquaintance to pick them up, and on the way back, he stopped to see a friend at a motel. When the girls entered the motel room with him, they were seized by two dozen men, ranging in age from fourteen to forty-five, who proceeded to gang-rape the girls over the next several hours.

Now, try to guess the ethnicity and immigration status of the perpetrators based on these representative excerpts from the single *New York Times* article on the gang rape:

> *New York Times*
> May 1, 1998
> Gang Rape of Three Girls Leaves Fresno Shaken, and Questioning
> by Don Terry[1]

FRESNO, Calif., April 27—On the edge of this working-class city, along a highway not far from the vineyards and the strawberry and cotton fields on some of the richest farmland in the nation, as many as 20 men and boys crowded into a motel room three weeks ago for what the police said was a night of rape.

The setting: Working-class farmland. Maybe the rapists were farmers?

What happened on the night of April 6 has shaken many people in this central California city of 450,000 residents. But Fresno lost its small-town innocence years ago, in what the current Mayor, Jim Patterson, called an explosion of crime.

I wonder what happened "years ago" to account for Fresno's loss of "small-town innocence" and "explosion in crime"?

"Everybody is hurt by this," said Mayor Patterson. "This is one of those God-awful things that could stigmatize a community."

The rapists must be longtime Fresno residents for the attack to "stigmatize a community."

The authorities kept the attack quiet for two weeks while they investigated and tracked down suspects. But over the last several days, as the arrests began, the assault has been front page news here.

The rapists are probably part of the "old boys network"—otherwise why would the police keep the case so hush-hush?

Last Friday, a 24-year-old man was picked up at his home and a teen-ager was taken into custody at his high school, bringing the total under arrest in the attack to five adults, the oldest 31, and seven juveniles. The police are hunting for three to five more suspects.

So we know the rapists included a "man," "adults," and some "juveniles." They must have no other relevant identifying characteristics, such as "football players" or "members of the Rotary Club."

"We've had gang rapes occur before but not of this magnitude," said Lieut. Jerry Davis, the commander of the city's crimes-against-persons unit. "The crime itself is bad enough, but this was directed at children. It's mind boggling."

The police's minds are boggled. The rapists must be boy-next-door types.

A rally is planned on Friday at California State University here to show support for the girls and to demonstrate to the community "that this could be your daughter, that this could happen to any of us," said Kathryn Forbes, a lecturer of women's studies at the university.

This could happen to "your daughter." The rapists are definitely plain vanilla Americans.

But everyone, from Fresno's Mayor to rape counselors, agree that what happened here could have happened anywhere, perhaps in a fraternity house or in a basement in a predominantly white suburb like Glen Ridge, N.J., where a group of high school football players sexually assaulted a mentally retarded teen-age girl with a bat and a stick in 1989.

Wait—why are we talking about a fraternity gang rape? And how did a decade-old sexual assault of a mentally disabled girl in Glen Ridge, New Jersey, come into this? Was the Duke lacrosse team involved?

Bernard Lefkowitz, who wrote a book about the assault in Glen Ridge, *Our Guys* (University of California Press, 1997), said: "For a lot of boys, acting abusively toward women is regarded as a rite of passage. It's woven into our culture."

For some reason, the Times *is going on an extended exegesis about a freakishly rare sexual assault on a mentally handicapped girl, in another state, from the 1980s. It was sick, but it was more an abuse-of-the-mentally-disabled case than a rape case, since the girl, who was their age, didn't object.*

Woven into Fresno's subculture are gangs, and the police report on the attack linked some suspects with one called the Mongolian Boys Society. There are a multitude of ethnic gangs here, including a white supremacist gang called the Peckerwoods.

Why is the Times *talking about a white supremacist gang? Is the "Mongolian Boys Society" a white supremacist gang?*

Martha Moreno, 13, said she had not been surprised by what happened because too many boys "think girls are their slaves."…"It really scared me when I heard about what happened," she said. "It makes you think anything can happen to you. But I still tell boys, I'm not a slave."

I have no idea what that little vignette illustrates, but neither the victims of this gang rape nor their assailants had names like "Martha Moreno."

The surprise ending—which *Times* readers WOULD NEVER BE TOLD—was that the Fresno gang rapists were Hmong immigrants, as were their victims. Over the next year, about three dozen Hmong men were indicted for a series of gang rapes and forced prostitution of young girls in the Fresno area, including the gang rape that reminded the *Times* of high school football players in New Jersey a decade earlier.[2]

Apart from a random reference to the "Mongolian Boys Society," the only hint that the Fresno gang rape was entirely an immigrant affair was this passage: "Ms. Eager, the director of the Fresno rape center, said people had called her office asking if the girls had been wearing sexy clothing or if they had done something to provoke the attack. One man called to say that because the girls had walked into the motel room, it was not fair to call it rape."

Only on Lifetime TV for Women, would an American man call the prosecutor to ask if child victims of a gang rape were wearing "sexy clothing."

Why does the public have to search for clues in a news story? News is not supposed to be a suspense novel. The *Times* knew, so why not tell us? Instead, it deliberately hid the truth by launching into a pointless reverie about a 1989 rape in Glen Ridge, nonspecific "fraternity rapes," and a "white supremacist gang" in Fresno. Never did the *Times* inform its readers that the Fresno gang rape was committed by Hmong, nor did the *Times* provide the names of the suspected rapists—not through their arrests, indictments, pleas, and convictions.[3] Everyone else was named—law enforcement officials, the mayor, rape crisis counselors. Why not the perps?

The media would sooner publish the names of rape *victims* than the names of their "diverse" rapists. Gang rape is a strength! Wait, did I get that right?

Eventually, twenty-three Hmong were indicted in the Fresno child rape, which sounds kind of newsworthy to me. But only two newspapers and one TV network informed the public that the rapists were Hmong: The *St. Paul Pioneer Press* (Minnesota), the *Washington Post*, and CNN.

Why would a newspaper in Minnesota report on a gang rape in California, you ask? Only someone in the news business could be expected to notice, but a rape epidemic has been sweeping through all the Hmong hot spots in America: Fresno, California; St. Paul, Minnesota; Green Bay, Wisconsin; Boulder, Colorado; and Detroit, Michigan.[4] And that's to say nothing of the sudden appearance of polygamy, opium use, and animal sacrifice.[5]

After another Hmong rape in Fresno, the *Times* sympathetically explained that in Hmong culture, "no" means "yes." In that case, a twenty-three-year-old Hmong man kidnapped a coed from her dorm room, took her to his parents' house, and raped her. Oozing with cultural understanding, the *Times* noted that this was how the Hmong propose marriage. How does a woman decline the offer? Hang herself? According to a lawyer quoted by the *Times*, the American witnesses to the girl's abduction had simply misunderstood her "ritual protests" and called the police. Apparently, the rape victim didn't understand either, inasmuch as she filed rape charges. The *Times*' article about the rape was titled: "Asian Tradition at War with American Laws."[6]

A few years after that, in 1988, a Hmong immigrant kidnapped a young Laotian woman from her Fresno office and forcibly raped her. The American judge sentenced the rapist to only 120 days in jail after his lawyer said that, in Hmong culture, if a woman doesn't fight her rapist with sufficient ferocity, the rapist and victim are considered married.[7] (Note to Hmong: You might want to put this on your Match.com profile.)

In 1991, Hmong immigrants in Colorado purchased a fifteen-year-old girl from her Hmong parents in Fresno for $8,300, not including shipping. The girl was taken to Colorado, where she was sexually assaulted by the family's twenty-one-year-old son. *Happy birthday, Son!* She escaped by slipping a note to a neighbor that read, "I'm not his wife. They force me here and I want to go back to Fresno." (You know someone's being held prisoner if they return voluntarily to Fresno.) When the police showed up, the Colorado Hmong were indignant, saying they had paid good money for the girl and announcing that the purchase of teenaged brides was "a custom among members of their ethnic group."[8]

In 1996, it was a multicultural fantasy camp when Dominican immigrant Judge Ramona Gonzales[9] presided over the criminal trial of Hmong immigrant Sia Ye Vang. Convicted of habitually sexually molesting his stepdaughters, aged ten and eleven, Vang faced up to eighty years in prison. Instead, Judge Gonzales sentenced him to...English lessons! Perhaps she'd found a new treatment for sex offenders.

> *You need a new hobby. How about learning English?*
> You think that will stop these cravings, Doc?
> *It's worth a try!*

The child molester's lawyer had argued that sex with girls is accepted in Vietnam, the defendant's native country.[10] Had I been there, I would have pointed out, *We're not in Vietnam.*

In 1999, nine Hmong men pleaded guilty to luring four teen and pre-teen girls from Wisconsin to Detroit, where the girls were held captive and repeatedly gang-raped.[11] In 2003, a group of Hmong men took turns raping young girls "to see whether their small bodies were large enough to accommodate adult customers."[12] In November 2011, a Hmong woman helped a Hmong man rape a sixteen-year-old girl with a beer can, brutalizing the girl so badly that her blood soaked through two blankets and a carpet. The unconscious girl had to be airlifted to the Mayo Medical Clinic.[13]

Thank you, Teddy Kennedy!

The prosecution of Hmong rapists is hindered by the fact that neither the girls nor their families are inclined to report the rapes. (*Rolling Stone* magazine might want to look into this.) The Associated Press reports, "In

Hmong culture, a girl who loses her virginity before marriage may be looked down upon by her own relatives, even if she is forcibly raped."[14] *Do tell me more about these colorful, fascinating people!*

Around the time of the Hmong rape in Fresno that made the *Times* think of fraternity rapes, Hmong armed burglars in St. Paul forced a Hmong woman to strip naked, then fondled her in front of her husband and nine children. They robbed the family and, before leaving, raped the mother and her eleven-year-old daughter. According to Hmong cultural anthropologists, the assailants believed that the sexual assaults would prevent the family from reporting the robbery.[15] In fact, the family reported the robbery right away, but waited days to mention the rapes.

In November 2011, a fifteen-year-old Hmong girl was gang-raped after a Hmong friend offered to give her a ride home from school, but, instead, took her to an abandoned house, where about two dozen Hmong men and boys were waiting. The men dragged the girl, kicking and screaming, from the car and gang-raped her. She didn't report the crime because of the shame to her family. Eventually, school officials discovered the attack and called the police.[16]

After a twelve-year-old Hmong girl in Minnesota was gang-raped by at least ten men, neither she nor her family told the police. Over the next several weeks, she continued to be abducted and gang-raped. Returning home after one brutal episode, limping in pain, a female relative said to her: "You're just a little slut."[17] A fourteen-year-old Hmong girl who was gang-raped in 1998 reports that her Hmong classmates "look at me like I'm just a tramp."[18] A sixteen-year-old Hmong girl who was gang-raped and forced into prostitution by some Hmong men never told her parents about it, explaining that her mother would only say, "You deserved it."[19] Like I haven't heard that before! This exact episode has appeared on *Law & Order* a dozen times, but the rapists were always preppie fraternity guys.

When a disturbed girl at the University of Virginia tells three different stories about being gang-raped at a fraternity house, her story is scooped up by *Rolling Stone* magazine and becomes major national news. But an actual gang-rape epidemic sweeping California, Minnesota, Michigan, and Wisconsin is deliberately hidden from the public. You can't make a governing Democratic coalition without breaking a few girls.

Even if the press were dying to report on the Hmong gang-rape spree, the police won't tell them about it. A year before the Hmong gang rape that reminded the *Times* of a rape in Glen Ridge, New Jersey, the police in St. Paul issued a warning about gang rapists using telephone chat lines to lure girls out of their homes. Although the warning was issued only in Hmong, St. Paul's police department refused to confirm to the *St. Paul Pioneer Press* that the suspects were Hmong, finally coughing up only the information that they were "Asian."[20]

And the gang rapes continue. The *Star Tribune* counted nearly one hundred Hmong males charged with rape or forced prostitution from 2000 to June 30, 2005. More than 80 percent of the victims were fifteen or younger. A quarter of their victims were not Hmong.[21] The police say many more Hmong rapists have gone unpunished—they have no idea how many—because Hmong refuse to report rape. Reporters aren't inclined to push the issue. The only rapes that interest the media are apocryphal gang rapes committed by white men.

Was America short on Hmong? These backward hill people began pouring into the United States in the seventies as a reward for their help during the ill-fated Vietnam War. That war ended forty years ago! But the United States is still taking in thousands of Hmong "refugees" every year, so taxpayers can spend millions of dollars on English-language and cultural-assimilation classes, public housing, food stamps, healthcare, prosecutors, and prisons to accommodate all the child rapists.[22] By now, there are an estimated 273,000 Hmong in the United States.[23] Canada only has about eight hundred.[24] Did America lose a bet? In the last few decades, America has taken in more Hmong than Czechs, Danes, French, Luxembourgers, New Zealanders, Norwegians, or Swiss. We have no room for them. We needed to make room for a culture where child rape is the norm.[25]

A foreign gang-rape culture that blames twelve-year-old girls for their own rapes may not be a good fit with American culture, especially now that political correctness prevents us from criticizing any "minority" group. At least when white males commit a gang rape the media never shut up about it. The Glen Ridge gang rape occurred more than a quarter century ago, and the *Times* still thinks the case hasn't been adequately covered.

THE WITCH DOCTOR IS IN

If liberals will excuse rape when committed by immigrants, it's the work of a moment for them to drop their reverence for "science" when it conflicts with primitive beliefs of tribal people transplanted to the United States.

A Fresno man—an actual Fresno man, not a "Fresno man"—was horrified when he looked out his window and saw his Hmong neighbors clubbing a German shepherd puppy to death. The police arrived and found out the Hmong were practicing a ritual slaughter to appease the gods because the woman of the house was sick—all of which was reported with great sensitivity by the *Los Angeles Times*. True, an American doctor had told the woman that she just had diabetes, but, as the *Times* reported, "she isn't so sure."[26]

An American doctor said she had diabetes. She had diabetes. Is that really an open question at the *LA Times*? Other Hmong in California weren't "so sure" when American doctors told them their kids had measles, club feet, and even cancer, deferring instead to their "ancient folk ways" over the white man's science. As a result, at least nine Hmong children died of measles in a single year, one Hmong was condemned to live with club feet, and a Hmong girl with ovarian cancer suddenly disappeared, never receiving the chemotherapy she needed.[27] It was the gods' punishment for an ancestor's evil ways!

The *LA Times* was practically lactating with cultural understanding about the Hmong's canine murder, titling the article: "Hmong's Sacrifice of Puppy Reopens Cultural Wounds." It seems that Americans were creating "cultural wounds" by complaining about the Hmong clubbing Fido to death. How about the puppy's wounds? Could we get an article on that? *Hello, PETA? Stop hassling that kid for eating a hamburger—I got a real story for you!*

When even animal-rights activists abandon their concern for helpless creatures out of political correctness toward immigrants, the brainwashing has reached a crisis point. Instead of criticizing the Hmong's house pet holocaust, the head of Fresno's Humane Society, Don Pugh, called Americans racist for objecting to it. Pugh told the *LA Times* that he got more calls about animal sacrifice than he found animal carcasses. Thus, he concluded, complaints about Hmong clubbing dogs to death was "racism, pure and simple."[28] On Pugh's logic, Jimmy Hoffa is still alive.

Notwithstanding Pugh's searing analysis, it is a fact that Hmong ritually sacrifice animals. They brag about it. They demand First Amendment protection for it. They submit court documents requesting victim restitution payments for their animal sacrifices. The Hmong "shaman" who killed the German shepherd puppy, for example, boasted to the *LA Times* that he sacrifices animals every year "to release the souls of the animals who helped him during the year, so that they can be reborn." The husband of the diabetic Hmong woman demanded to know what else they were supposed to do. "We burned the paper money," he said, casually admitting to another crime. "We did the chicken and the pig. But still my wife gets no better. What was I to do? I am a shaman and this is what we believe. So I bought this dog for $5 and did the ceremony right here."[29] No word on whether plans mandated by Obamacare cover animal sacrifice.

After a Hmong in Minnesota, Txawj Xiong, was stabbed by a Minnesota man—probably driven mad by seeing a puppy clubbed to death—he submitted a victim restitution statement to the court requesting repayment for:

Cow for sacrifice for Hu Plig ceremony–$540.00

Pig for sacrifice for Hu Plig ceremony–$90.00

Two chickens for sacrifice for Hu Plig ceremony–$10.00

Roast Pig for Hu Plig ceremony–$155.15

Shao woman to conduct Hu Plig ceremony–$200.00

Xiong's legal filings explained that animal sacrifices are necessary "to restore the soul of a victim." This is contained in an official court record in the United States of America. And the trial court approved most of it, ruling only that the two chickens were "excessive." The assailant ordered to pay for this insane hokum appealed on Establishment Clause grounds. He lost. The Minnesota Supreme Court upheld victim restitution expenses for an animal sacrifice.[30] But the Humane Society's Don Pugh says the idea that the Hmong engage in animal sacrifice is "racism, pure and simple."[31]

After Minnesota experienced a rash of Hmong gang rapes, animal sacrifices, and one child murder, as well as a particularly shocking mass slaying of Minnesota hunters, a local talk radio host suggested that the Hmong "either assimilate or hit the road." The *Baltimore Sun* somberly reported his "hateful words," adding with sadness that no one had ever "dared to blurt out [such sentiments] publicly."[32]

What is the formal, book-writing equivalent of: ARE YOU F-ING KIDDING ME? When a proposal that tribal Laotians living in Minnesota temper their enthusiasm for mass murder, child rape, and puppy killing is treated like something out of *Mein Kampf*, the country may be a few tweaks away from a serious effort at assimilation.

In 1987, a Hmong father and son beat the crap out of twenty-three-year-old Michael Speropulous in a road rage incident in Chicago. As Speropulous approached their car, Bravo Xiong, thirty-eight, leapt out and began hitting him on the head with a steel bar. Bravo's father, Ching, joined in, holding Speropulous in a bear hug so the son could continue the attack.

At trial, the Hmong men testified that it was Speropulous who had dragged Bravo from his car and beaten him. All witnesses contradicted their account—as did Speropulous's hospital records. Unfortunately, we can't expect Hmong to tell the truth, unless everybody in the courtroom drinks rooster blood first. This, the Hmong defendants requested in their court papers. It seems these vibrant people believe that a person who lies after drinking rooster blood will die within a year and the rooster will take the person's spirit, preventing the liar from being reincarnated as a human. So at least there's solid science behind it. Although the judge ruled against drinking rooster blood, he imposed no punishment on the Hmong for a vicious assault that sent an American to the hospital, instead ordering them to take English lessons and a class in cultural assimilation.[33]

People who never should have been in America in the first place get affirmative action in jobs, in college admissions, in newspaper coverage of their crimes—and in actual criminal sentencing.[34] We used to have equality before the law. We used to have Western medicine. We used to have color-blind aspirations. But now we have Third World immigrants.

PUBLIC WARNED TO BE
ON LOOKOUT FOR "MAN"

GANG RAPE, CHILD RAPE, INCEST—IT'S BEEN A LONG TIME SINCE WE'VE SEEN much of that in the United States. Of course, there are lots of things we thought had been abolished a hundred years ago that our mass-immigration policies are bringing back. Every society has monsters. But why are we importing primitive cultures that are centuries behind the West in their regard for women and children?

When it comes to multiculturalism, you can't say, *We love the empanadas—but we don't want forty-year-old men raping their nieces.* You don't get to choose. This is not a buffet. It's sheer madness for a First World country with unprecedented freedoms for women to be welcoming cultures with medieval views on the sexes.

A nation's "culture" consists of the habits of its people. In the groundbreaking book *Albion's Seed: Four British Folkways in America*, historian David Hackett Fischer illustrates how hardwired a people's culture is by tracing various behavioral patterns of twentieth-century Americans back to distinct regions of Britain. The Northeast got the urbane, morally straight, literate East Anglians, while Appalachia was dominated by the wild and woolly Scots-Irish. Centuries later, we can still see the influence of the East Anglians in Massachusetts, the state with the most college graduates, and of the Scots-Irish in TV shows like *Cops*.

It's worth asking, therefore, what cultures is America importing today at a rate of more than a million people a year?

Academics, popular culture, Democratic senators, and Melissa Harris-Perry fill our brains with apocryphal tales of predatory white males in fraternities and the military, while carefully concealing the evidence that women have the least to fear from white Anglo-Saxon men. As Olatokunbo Olukemi warned, with perfect lucidity, about powerful, privileged, straight white men, in an article in the *Columbia Journal of Gender and the Law* that is absolutely not a joke: "A group in the dominant role in terms of gender, race, and sexuality will encode/decode an occurrence in a manner consistent with its own privileged position and view of 'reality' and thus in a manner different from a marginalized group. Due to the hegemony created by the dominant group, the marginalized group may also ascribe to the manner in which the powerful group codes, resulting in false consciousness."[1]

On the other hand, all the gang rapes keep being committed by immigrants.[2]

With the media actively covering up the crimes of immigrants, it may take a while to notice, but Anglo-American men were the best women ever had it. Feminists see women as a community apart from men, but the truth is, America is a nation apart from the rest of the world. In no area is that clearer than the treatment of women and children. Latin Americans, Arabs, Asians, and Indians take a distinctly less respectful view of the gentler sex. Even Continental Europeans can't compete with American men. They don't have the gusto for gang rape, incest, and child rape of our main immigrant groups, but they fall far short of what the English-speaking world considers gallant behavior.[3]

It's as if Ted Bundy designed our immigration policies to ensure that the most misogynist cultures go to the head of the line. American employers get the cheap labor, Democrats get the votes, and American girls get the rapes.

This would be blindingly obvious, except that the media refuse to report anything but good news about immigrants.

SUSPECT DESCRIBED AS "MAN"

Here's a typical headline from a local Nashville TV station in 2011 about an illegal alien child rapist: "Man Wanted for Raping Girl, 11, Robbing Her Family." The story never used the word "immigrant," but rather described the suspects as: "Man," "a 26-year-old man," "the men," and "the pair." One of them "had recently been living at the Clairmont apartments on Patricia Drive." A Clairmont-apartments man, then! The "men" were suspected in a rash of armed home invasions, during which they also sometimes raped the occupants, including children. Careful news readers would notice that the police had to deploy "Spanish-speaking officers" on the case, and also that the names of the suspects were "Olbin Sabier Euceda" and "Benson Olman Euceda." Only after the first forty-one indictments were handed up against Sabier Euceda two years later did the *City Paper* (Nashville, Tennessee) finally cough up the information that he was a "suspected illegal immigrant." Why only "suspected"? Doesn't anyone know? Sabier Euceda had been captured at a bus station headed to Mexico. (I wonder if flight is a problem with criminal suspects who are citizens of another country?)

Another "Man" in the news was Milton Mateo Garcia—just the sort of hardworking immigrant we keep hearing so much about from Marco Rubio and the *New York Times*. Garcia had *three* jobs. Even after he was caught sneaking into the country illegally from Honduras in 2013, he wasn't discouraged. Through sheer pluck and determination, Garcia came right back, and began working as a dishwasher. (You just can't get Americans to wash dishes. They won't do it at any price.) After less than a year back in the United States, Garcia grabbed a twenty-six-year-old doctor walking to her apartment in the well-do-to Rittenhouse Square area of Philadelphia, forced her into her apartment, and repeatedly raped her. He left with her keys, so when he realized he'd forgotten his bag, Garcia simply let himself back into the woman's apartment, raped her again, collected his things, and left. Suggesting why there's no Honduran Silicon Valley, Garcia also took his victim's cell phone. The cops found him by calling the phone.[4]

Here are the newspaper headlines about this illegal alien's rape of a female doctor:

> "Man Allegedly Forced Philadelphia Doctor into Her Apartment and Raped Her"
>   —UPI, by Frances Burns
> "Man Charged with Rittenhouse Doctor's Rape"
>   —NBC10.com, by Vince Lattanzio
> "Kitchen Worker Arrested in Rittenhouse Rape"
>   —*Philadelphia Daily News*, by Dana DiFilippo

Even news stories about immigrant crimes that mention deportation proceedings get headlines like this one: "Holly Springs Man Faces Child-Sex Charge."[5] The defendant in that case, Oscar Sanchez Lopez, was no more a "Holly Springs man" than a burglar at the mayor's residence is a "Gracie Mansion man." Lopez was a Mexican man who raped a child in a country where he had no legal right to be.

SECRET DECODER RING FOR IMMIGRANT CRIMES

It's great living in America and having to interpret news stories as if we're reading *Pravda*. Usually, the only way to tell if a crime story involves an immigrant is if:

1. The crime involves a uniquely perverse sexual assault, such as gang rape, child rape, or incest;
2. The rapist is shocked that anyone thinks he did something wrong;
3. A woman is involved in the rape or the cover-up;
4. The rapist's name would not be found in a phonebook from the 1960s;
5. Newspapers informatively refer to the rapist in their headlines as: "Man."

But those telltale signs allow only an educated guess that the perpetrator is an immigrant. To confirm it, one must search for words such as "ICE" or "translator." In a way, we're lucky immigrants don't bother learning English, or the "translator" search wouldn't work.

"THEY WERE UNSURE OF HIS IMMIGRATION STATUS"

A case out of Seattle had all the main ingredients of an immigrant crime story. First, the crime consisted of the repeated rapes of five little girls between the ages of four and ten. Second, the rapist's lack of remorse led to gasps in the courtroom. Third, the rapes went on for at least four years without the intervention of the victims' mother, even though the rapist was her boyfriend. Fourth, the rapist's name was "Salvador Aleman Cruz." And finally, the *Seattle Times*—the only newspaper to cover the case—headlined the article on his conviction "Man Convicted on 7 Counts in Child-Rape Case."[6]

While not the gripping page-turner of a stripper falsely accusing Duke lacrosse players of rape, the Cruz case did have some newsworthy aspects. A twenty-one-year-old girl whom Cruz had begun raping when she was four years old went to the top of the courthouse and threatened to jump, rather than face him in court, where he was acting as his own lawyer in order to taunt and intimidate his victims. She was excused from testifying, which wasn't a problem since there were so many other victims.

There are exactly six news stories on Cruz's case in the entire Nexis archive, all from the *Seattle Times*—plus an Associated Press report that no newspaper seems to have picked up. The only clue about Cruz's immigration status was this, from the *Seattle Times*: "After the assaults...Cruz fled to Mexico, prosecutors said. They were unsure of his immigration status."[7]

They were "*unsure of his immigration status*"? Did anyone ask?

In the case of a blindingly false allegation of rape against Duke lacrosse players, reporters pursued details about the accused men like starved bloodhounds. We were told the men's grades, their classes, their professors' impressions of them, the value of their parents' homes, their private e-mails, their every encounter with the police—and on and on.[8] But a child rapist named "Salvador Aleman Cruz" needs a Spanish translator in court and flees to Mexico after raping at least five little girls—and both the government and media say, *Oh yeah, we don't know his immigration status. Why do you ask?*

People who want cheap maids will tell you: *Of course Salvador Aleman Cruz isn't the kind of immigrant we want to legalize!* But what are they doing to stop it? They're happy to take the cheap labor and never trouble themselves with figuring out how to keep the Salvador Aleman Cruzes out.

Another hardworking illegal immigrant from Mexico is Palemon Vargas Reyes. He would already be a legal resident, on his way to citizenship, if the American public hadn't stopped House Speaker John Boehner from taking up Marco Rubio's "comprehensive immigration reform." (The media learned their lesson: Henceforth, they will not inform us when Congress is considering an amnesty bill.) Reyes owned a construction business! He's a married father of five! In April 2014—about a year after the U.S. Senate passed Rubio's bill—Reyes was arrested for serially raping a fourteen-year-old girl. One of the rapes took place at a job site, so he really is a hard worker. The headline on this story was: "Columbus Resident Charged with Molestation."[9]

ONE FOR THE "NOT OUR PROBLEM" FILE

The defendant in a story the *Chattanooga Times Free Press* headlined "Smuggling Case Nets 15-Year Sentence"[10] was "man"—as he was called in another *Free Press* headline—thirty-six-year-old German Rolando Vicente-Sapon, an illegal alien from Guatemala. He had persuaded his sixteen-year-old first cousin, Yuria Vicente-Calel, to join him in the United States, where he immediately began raping her, got her pregnant, and then began sexually abusing their infant daughter.[11]

So the good news is: They have an anchor baby!

What are the odds an American woman could be held as a sex slave by her cousin in a foreign country without her parents ever mentioning anything? But Yuria continued to be raped by Vicente-Sapon for five years with no complaint from her parents. And now, with Yuria's incest anchor baby, they can come to the United States and get free healthcare, food stamps, and Social Security. *You don't want to break up families, do you?*

If you were wondering how an illegal alien was able to rape his cousin for five years before finally catching the eye of our immigration officials, the answer is: Lots of people who are subsidized by the taxpayer conspired to bring them to this country, and turn them into public charges. In order to get Yuria across the border to be his sex slave, Vicente-Sapon had hired human smugglers suggested to him by a tax-exempt Hispanic church in East Ridge, Tennessee. (He's a churchgoer!) After he began sexually abusing his anchor baby infant daughter, publicly supported lawyers helped Yuria obtain a restraining order against him. Government officials with the Hamilton County Department of Children's Services issued the order, but none of them contacted immigration authorities. They didn't notice that neither Yuria nor her pedophile cousin spoke English?

Throughout Vicente-Sapon's criminal proceedings—and appeals!—American taxpayers paid for Spanish translators, child services employees, investigators, judges' salaries, court costs, and so on. Now taxpayers will be on the hook for his room and board in a state penitentiary. All this, for a case that should have gone into a file labeled "Not Our Problem." We have our own underclass that needs help. We don't need other countries' under-classes moving in, too.

The *Chattanooga Times Free Press*'s story on Vicente-Sapon's convic-tion was headlined "Illegal Alien Arrested for Incest, Child Rape, Kidnap-ping, and Sex Slavery." Just kidding! It was: "Man Guilty in Case of Human Smuggling."[12] *Oh, it was a MAN. How fascinating.* The *Free Press* never mentioned that the human smuggler was an illegal alien. That information was available only in the federal district court opinion dismissing Vicente-Sapon's motion to exclude his statements to the police on the grounds that the Spanish translator misunderstood him. But at least the *Free Press* reported the story. According to Nexis, it was the only news outlet to do so.

ANOTHER ADVANTAGE OF NOT SPEAKING ENGLISH

Vicente-Sapon wasn't the first immigrant criminal to game the system by claiming "translation" problems. In 2010, Annie Ling, a child-abusing Malaysian immigrant, got a new trial—thanks, American Civil Liberties Union!—after the Georgia Supreme Court held that criminal defendants who allege, after trial, that they are deficient in English are entitled to new trials with taxpayer-provided certified translators.[13] In Annie's case, in Mandarin.

In 2011, the Arkansas Supreme Court overturned Jose Luis Mendez's sixty-year sentence for rape and attempted murder on the grounds that the Spanish translator misunderstood his confession. This was despite the fact that the victim personally knew Mendez and testified in court that she had awoken to see Mendez on top of her, strangling her,[14] and that the doctor who examined her immediately after the attack testified that her injuries showed that she had been strangled, beaten, and raped.[15]

Even when police present the defendant with a tape recording and written document giving Miranda warnings in Spanish, that won't prevent an appeal based on translation problems. That's how Guillermo Paniagua

Paniagua appealed his conviction for driving drunk on the wrong side of the road, running headlong into the chief of police of Needville, Texas, killing him, then fleeing the accident on foot.[16]

So it's kind of relevant when the defendant is an immigrant. Taxpayers are footing the bill for all those translators as well as the appeals denouncing the translators. With the amount of money an immigration moratorium would save U.S. taxpayers on court interpreters alone, we could build three border fences and revive NASA.

But when it comes to immigrant criminals, all the media notice is that the perp is a "man."

THERE SEEMS TO BE SOME INTEREST IN IMMIGRANT CHILD RAPISTS

With the media aggressively hiding information about immigrant crime, citizens take to the internet to document the legions of Americans murdered, maimed, and raped by immigrants. In 2012, Malaysian immigrant Dwipin Thomas Maliackal was arrested after going to a meeting with an undercover cop who had posted on an "incest chatroom" as a father offering up his ten- and thirteen-year-old daughters for sex.[17] Maliackal, posting under the name "Horny_Indian,"[18] had told the undercover "dad" that he "would love to get [the ten-year-old] pregnant, if you're OK with that." He detailed various sex practices he wanted to perform on the girls—which the *Orlando Sentinel* decorously refused to print. He also admitted to having already had sex with other children, including a five-year-old neighbor. Horny_Indian was convicted and sentenced to prison for fourteen years.

On the website Libertarian Republican, Eric Dondero posted a story about Horny_Indian, and howled about the silence from the American media:

A mystery. The distinguished and hugely popular worldwide London *Daily Mail* has a feature story on alleged child rapist

Dwipin Thomas Maliackal; yet no national media in the U.S. has deemed it newsworthy. Only local coverage in the *Orlando Sentinel* and *Tampa Bay Tribune.*

Is it because it doesn't quite fit the template? The alleged perpetrator is a South Asian from an immigrant family. He is the immediate past president of his college fraternity. He went to a college, University of South Florida, notorious for hard-left politics, multiculturalism and vicious Republican-bashing. Maliackal was an aspiring journalist. And a Bob Costa wannabee sportscaster. Minority. Went to the right school. Good chosen career path. He was a walking talking poster boy for the liberal media.

But it turns out, he is also an alleged child molester.[19]

The comments section was boiling with rage—except for one commenter, who made the important point that Dondero was a racist for noticing that the child molester was an immigrant:

Apparently every time a Muslim gets charged with a sex offense it's supposed to be national news. Because Eric is a racist coward.

That a man had admitted to having sex with a five-year-old could wait. The important point was that it was "racist" to notice that a sexual predator against American children was an immigrant. (Dondero hadn't mentioned that the pedophile was a Muslim, but that's good to know if I'm ever on *Jeopardy* and the category is "Immigrant Child Rapists.")

IF IT BLEEDS, IT LEADS— UNLESS THE PERP IS AN IMMIGRANT

Stories like this are never broken by the mainstream media. It's always some right-wing blog that publicizes immigrant crimes. Journalists love to claim they only print what the public wants to know. But for as long as there has been news, people have been interested in crime stories. That's why we have the cliché: "If it bleeds, it leads." Quite obviously, there's an enormous interest in stories about immigrant crime. But no amount of the public wanting to know will end the media blockade on negative information about immigrants.

Jorge Juarez-Lopez, an illegal immigrant from Mexico, began raping his illegal alien girlfriend's illegal alien daughters, ages eleven and thirteen—or possibly nine and eleven[20]—on a drive from Sacramento, California, to North Carolina. He continued raping the girls over the next couple of years, while living with them as their father. At first Juarez-Lopez would wait for their mother to leave for work, and sneak up on the girls saying: "I have a surprise for you!" But soon he was forcing the girls to perform oral sex on him even when Mom was home, as he watched for her to come up the stairs. When Juarez was caught, he shrugged and told the police—in Spanish, of course—"I belong to the government now," a thrill, I'm sure, for North Carolina taxpayers.

Showing little anguish for what he had done, Juarez kept writing to the girls' mother from prison, asking her "to weigh how we have lived, everything I've given you." In addition to supporting Juarez in prison for the next thirty-six to fifty-three years, taxpayers will be the ones giving things to the mother, now. She also doesn't speak English. All this so that the farming and meatpacking industries in North Carolina can refuse to mechanize their operations for a few more years, and the Democrats have a shot at turning the state blue.

Although he made quite a splash on the internet websites covering illegal alien crime, Juarez-Lopez appears in only one document on Nexis: *Indyweek*, an alternative newspaper out of Durham covering mostly music and culture. Yes, the same newspapers that had blanketed the state with daily updates about a (nonexistent) rape by the Duke lacrosse team had no interest in a real child rape case going on for years right under their noses.

Even when an illegal alien child molester is arrested in an exciting caper just a block from the *New York Times* building, they won't report it. In 2012, illegal alien Ricardo Martinez-Gomez, who had already been deported three times, reappeared in Granville, New York, and sexually molested an eight-year-old girl at a sleepover with his girlfriend's daughter. The little girl reported the abuse to Martinez-Gomez's girlfriend, but she told no one, giving her boyfriend time to escape. By the time the victim told her mother, and she contacted the police, Martinez-Gomez was on a bus from Albany to New York City. Notified by the Granville police to be on the lookout, Penn Station police were waiting for Martinez-Gomez's bus, but he somehow slipped past them. As the cops headed back to an office to review videotapes of the departing passengers, Detective Warren K. Davis happened to be walking through the station on his lunch break and spotted the accused child molester. Officer Davis asked Martinez-Gomez for identification, saw "Gerardo Cruz" on the man's Social Security card, and recognizing it as the suspect's alias, arrested him.[21]

If Martinez-Gomez had made it out of Penn Station and strolled one block south, he might have walked right into the *New York Times* building. The *Times* would have given him sanctuary, called in La Raza attorneys, and never written a word about the case—unless it was to describe Martinez-Gomez as a hardworking immigrant with a "shy smile." Only one news outlet wrote about the illegal alien child molester's arrest within shouting distance of the *New York Times* building: Manchester Newspapers. It's not even clear if the story ran in any of Manchester's actual newspapers, or just online. When Martinez-Gomez was sentenced, only the Schenectady *Daily Gazette* reported it, in a small news blotter item.[22]

Flimsy rape accusations against college athletes will be pursued to the ends of the earth. But as soon as a rape suspect is determined to be an immigrant, all news interest vanishes. On August 22, 2014, a local Milwaukee TV station posted a short item: "Illinois Fugitive Is One of Wisconsin's Most Wanted, He's Armando Romero-Gutierrez."[23] Armando was a thirty-six-year-old Mexican wanted for sexually assaulting an eleven-year-old family member. U.S. Marshals believed he was either with a brother in Wisconsin—or back in Mexico.[24] But then the media trail goes cold. It's been almost a year. Have they found Armando?

IT MIGHT BE WORTH PAYING MORE FOR YOUR YARD WORK

Then there was the child rape case illustrating the perils of cheap lawn care. In 2012, immigrant Francisco Marquez Martinez, thirty-eight, raped a twelve-year-old girl after coming to mow her family's lawn a day early when the girl and her nine-year-old sister were home alone. He asked to come inside when it began to rain, but she refused, so Marquez forced his way in, chased the girl to her parents' bedroom, then to the bathroom, where he raped her in the bathtub.

The internet was ablaze with the news that a thirty-eight-year-old landscaper had raped a client's twelve-year-old girl. But not one newspaper stated that Marquez was an immigrant, much less an illegal immigrant. The truth first emerged when Marquez's lawyer argued that his client had confessed only because he didn't speak English. Still, somehow, Marquez managed to convey through his government-provided translator, in the alternative: He didn't do it; he did it, but the girl seduced him; the sex was consensual; he thought she was seventeen; and, on final thought, he didn't have sex with her at all since he's a married man who preached at his church.

These were the headlines about the case from the only newspaper on Nexis that covered the story, at all, the *Winston-Salem Journal*:

> "Girl Says Man Hired by Family to Mow Lawn Raped Her"
> "Man Accused of Raping Girl Told Police He Thought She Was Older"
> "Man Accused of Raping Girl, 12, Tells Different Version of Incident"

"Man Gets 25 Years for Rape of Girl, 12"[25]

So again, readers would know the child rapist was a "man." The *Winston-Salem Journal* was absolutely clear on that point. It isn't a space problem: The newspaper was capable of packing all sorts of information into its headlines, such as the fact that the rapist was hired to mow the lawn, that he claimed he thought she was older, and that he was sentenced to twenty-five years. What's the matter with "Illegal Alien Gardener Convicted of Raping Girl, 12"?

The *Journal*'s articles on the case religiously noted that the paper "does not identify victims of sexual assault or their families." (Except when the accused is a Kennedy or a Clinton.) Why not add: "or information about rape suspects' immigration status"? It's perfectly obvious that rape victims aren't being identified, but readers have no way of knowing that "man" means "immigrant."

SPOT THE IMMIGRANT!

CASE NO. 2 | HOMECOMING DANCE

N 2009, A ONE-HUNDRED-POUND SIXTEEN-YEAR-OLD WHITE GIRL WAS GANG-RAPED by about a dozen men outside her homecoming dance at Richmond High School in San Francisco's Bay Area. She had gotten bored with the dance and gone outside to call her father for a ride home when a boy she'd known since the seventh grade invited her to drink brandy with his friends in the courtyard.

BRUTAL ATTACK

The men got her drunk, at one point forcing brandy down her throat. Over the next few hours, the girl, an English honors student, was savagely beaten, gang-raped, sodomized, raped with a foreign object, and dragged over the concrete by her feet to the dumpster. The men even urinated on her.[1] The attack was so brutal, one of the suspects tried to help his case by immediately admitting to the police, "I'll be straight up with you, all I did was pee on her and take her ring."[2] When the ringleader was arrested, he shouted that it wasn't rape because she was so drunk, "she didn't even know what was going on." In the alternative, he said, "She wanted it—she wanted all of us."[3]

Throughout the two-hour gang rape, other men stood and watched—some cheering—without calling the police. One witness said he thought she was dead: "I saw people, like, dehumanizing her; I saw some pretty crazy stuff.... She was pretty quiet; I thought she was like dead for a minute but then I saw her moving around, I was like, 'Oh.'"[4] The victim, called "Jane Doe," survived, but was left with bone fractures, burns, hypothermia, and head lacerations. She was in too much pain for nurses to insert a speculum for the rape exam,[5] though they did remove the foliage from her anus.[6]

Here are the first few paragraphs from a classic MSM column about the Richmond gang rape:

Los Angeles Times
November 7, 2009
Saturday Home Edition
A Deeper Lesson in Gang Rape
by Sandy Banks[7]

When a public tragedy like this occurs,

It's a "tragedy"! I don't remember the fake UVA fraternity gang rape being called a "tragedy."

...it is our instinct—our responsibility, even—to try to understand it. We look for clues to its cause, its meaning in personal stories, official actions and social forces.

Are the kids deranged? Did the school do something wrong? Is this just a reflection of a violent culture?

Is it the school's fault? America's violent culture? She couldn't possibly be referring to a foreign culture we're required to import because Democrats need votes...

In the Richmond gang rape case, I was surprised that so many readers made race the subtext. And they took me to task for not mentioning the race of the victim or her attackers.

YOU DIDN'T MENTION THE RACE OF THE VICTIM OR HER ATTACK-ERS?????????

"The discomfort you folks feel in acknowledging racial attacks on whites prevents you from writing the facts," one reader's e-mail said.

I admit to feeling "discomfort" as I tried to get a grip on the racial dimensions of the assault. The victim was white; her attackers were described to me by students as mostly Latino, with one black and one white.

Actually, the "white" one was a Mexican, too—one of our famous "white Hispanics," Cody Smith. That's according to the victim,[8] who had known him since seventh grade.[9] And the charges against Smith were later dismissed.[10]

But I didn't mention race in my column because I don't believe that explains the attack.... Gang rape—and bystander inaction—didn't migrate here from across the border; it's not the province of any one ethnic group, income level or generation.

Journalists are supposed to report facts, not decide what "explains" the crimes they're reporting on and then give us only the facts that support their side.

Just ask the woman who told me about the gang rape of her college roommate at a fraternity party in 1972 on the University of Virginia campus.

Excellent counterexample! A non-disprovable story from forty years ago.

It was gossip fodder on campus, but the girl was too ashamed to come forward. "It was never reported, no one was ever arrested and all the perpetrators are now probably lawyers [and] businessmen," she wrote.

We'll be here all week if we're allowed to start citing gossip that includes words like "probably."

Why is it that whenever immigrants commit a shocking gang rape, newspaper columnists wander off into fictitious rapes committed by white fraternity members? I'm not saying there has never been a gang rape at a college fraternity that resulted in actual convictions. I am saying that if that had happened, we would know about it. In fact, the media would never stop talking about it. A white fraternity gang rape would be world-famous. There would be Hollywood movies, television documentaries, Broadway plays, a plaque, a law named after the incident, women's studies courses—perhaps entire college majors on the case. At the very least, it would not be hard to find.

By contrast, the way we know about immigrant gang rapes—often the only way we know—is that there are case numbers, defendants, and convictions. Usually there are a few people in the community who know the facts, so the truth seeps out, in spite of media censorship.

We know the facts of the Richmond gang rape not because of bald accusations of the sort regularly printed in the *New York Times* about hoax campus rapes, but because there were trials, sworn testimony, and DNA evidence against specific named defendants. The men convicted for the gang rape attack were Manuel Ortega, twenty; Elvis Torrentes, twenty-three; Ari Morales, seventeen; Marcelles Peter, eighteen; Jose Montano, nineteen; and John Crane Jr., forty-three—five Mexicans and one African American.

The rape of a high school sophomore at her homecoming dance is not a hazy memory of something my college roommate told me about: Ortega admitted in court that he initiated the rape, beat up the victim, ripped her clothes off, forced his penis into her mouth, and dragged the unconscious girl around the courtyard. Other witnesses testified in court that Ortega also stomped on the girl's head and tried to penetrate her with a skateboard.[11]

WE DIDN'T EVEN NOTICE THEIR RACE!

As for Ms. Banks's claim that she didn't even notice that the gang rapists were Mexican and their victim white, YOU HAVE GOT TO BE KIDDING ME. The media *always* notice race. It is the first thing they look for in any crime—hoping against hope to have finally found Tom Wolfe's "great white defendant." They'll even turn a Hispanic perpetrator white, as the *New York Times* did with George Zimmerman. After the police shooting in Ferguson, did anyone need to ask: *Hey, does anyone know the race of the cop or the race of the guy he shot?*

Like Banks, the author of the *New York Times*' (sole) article on the Mexican gang rape also studiously avoided any mention of the attackers' ethnicity. It began: "Around 4 p.m. on Oct. 24 of last year, Cynthia Avalos saw a short young man with close-cropped brown hair walking near Richmond High School, drunk."[12] The man was lead rapist Ortega. How is the fact that he is short or had "close-cropped hair" relevant? Does that explain the attack? Are gang rapes the province of any one stature or hairstyle?

The reason the Richmond rapists' Mexican-ness is wildly relevant is that the rape never had to happen. A sixteen-year-old girl at her homecoming dance was gang-raped and left for dead because the Democrats need more voters. We could save a lot of soul-searching about "our" violent culture if journalists didn't hide the fact that gang rapes are generally committed by people who are not *from* our culture. Outside of a fictional television drama—and secondhand tales of college rapes that might have occurred forty years ago—you are not going to find a group of white men raping young girls. Gang rape, child rape, elder rape, and murder rape are highly correlated with specific ethnic groups—ethnic groups we are bringing to America by the busload. Sixteen-year-old honors students in Richmond, California, have no familiarity with the cultural norms being imposed on the nation, which no one asked for, which Americans didn't consent to, and about which they certainly have received no warning.

10

HERE'S A STORY, *ROLLING STONE*!

THE MEDIA BALANCE OUT THEIR CENSORSHIP OF NEWS ABOUT IMMIGRANT rapists with false accusations of rape against American white men. The whiter and more American, the better—white cops, white prosecutors, white lacrosse players, white military contractors, white fraternity members. (Tawana Brawley, Duke lacrosse, Jamie Leigh Jones, and the *Rolling Stone*'s hoax gang rape.) Instead of body cameras on cops, what we really need are body cameras on journalists and neurotic women.

The fake rape cases always produce a blizzard of articles with such titles as: "Does Privilege Breed Contempt?,"[1] "When Peer Pressure, Not a Conscience, Is Your Guide,"[2] and "Why Soldiers Rape: Culture of Misogyny, Illegal Occupation, Fuel Sexual Violence in Military."[3] It's getting to be like a decades-long performance art piece to see if the media can get people to believe that white American men are huge gang rapists.

The *New York Times* alone has ceaselessly run front-page stories, editorials, letters, and book-length articles on the subject of alleged, but unproved, date rapes on college campuses.[4] In the nine months between March 29, 2006, and the end of 2006, the *Times* ran more than fifty stories about a rape at Duke University *that never happened.*[5] It's as if the media were prospecting for ice in the Mojave Desert. Are you sure you don't want to try the Antarctic? If the *Times* dedicated 1 percent as much coverage to rapes committed by foreigners on U.S. soil, it might actually reduce the number of women who are raped by helping remove the main perpetrators from the country.

In order to get the *Times*' attention, here are a few immigrant rapes that took place on college campuses:

- In March 2013, two Penn State girls were kidnapped and sexually assaulted by a couple of illegal aliens from Mexico, after the illegals offered the girls a ride to their dormitory. The attacks were interrupted when a campus police officer saw a woman's leg dangling out of the Mexicans' pick-up truck.[6]
- In November 2013, a student at Goldey-Beacom College in Delaware was raped by Carlos E. Bastardo, an immigrant on a student visa from Brazil. Unlike "date rape" cases featured in the *Times*, the victim wasn't drunk and didn't wait to report the rape. After being assaulted, she ran from the room, went straight to a hospital, and called the police.[7]
- In February 2013, Diego Gomez-Puetate, an Ecuadoran student at the College of Idaho, raped an unconscious student at an "International House" party, stopping only when he was caught by her friend. He was convicted of the rape in August of that year.[8]
- In August 2012, a Skidmore College international student— and residence hall assistant—Ajibu Timbo from Sierra Leone was arrested for sexually assaulting a college employee.[9]

None of these sexual assaults was ever mentioned in *Times*, despite providing an opportunity for the *Times* to drone on about the "campus rape culture." If only immigrants were college athletes, newspapers might report their sex crimes, and *Law & Order* could finally have a plotline "ripped from the headlines" that's not ludicrous.

ILLEGAL IMMIGRANT BEATS GAY

After decades of the media's hiding the ethnicity of any rapist who isn't white, in 2014, *Boston Globe* columnist James Carroll asked: "Why do hard-drinking fraternity members and entitled athletes stand at ground zero of the danger zone?...Why are the brightest and most privileged people in America the owners of this grotesque problem?"—and so on.[10] Carroll's conclusion? We need to import yet more illegal immigrants from Latin America![11]

I'm fairly certain more immigration from Latin America will not reduce the incidence of rape. In fact, the evidence suggests that it would do exactly the opposite.

About the same time Carroll was bleating about the rape culture of privileged white men, Mexican immigrants went on trial in Richmond, California, for the violent gang rape of a lesbian. Humberto Salvador had smashed the woman on the head with his flashlight, forced her to strip naked on the sidewalk, and raped her. His fellow Mexican gang members then joined in, taking her to an abandoned building where they passed the naked woman back and forth among them. While raping her, Salvador kept asking her—in Spanish—"You like men now, don't you? Tell me you like men."[12]

Not one single news outlet mentioned that the lesbian's assailants were Mexican,[13] allowing half-wits like Carroll to keep penning pieces about the "brightest and most privileged people in America" having a rape problem. In the PC ranking, evidently, "Hispanic immigrant" beats "gay." News coverage about the vicious hate crime described Salvador as "Richmond Man"—or the more lavishly specific "Man":

"Richmond Man Convicted in Gang Rape of Lesbian"
—Associated Press, December 19, 2013

"Richmond Man Sentenced to 411 Years, Four Months for Gang
   Rape"
      —*Contra Costa Times* (California), May 16, 2014
"411-Year Term Given in Rape of Lesbian"
      —*San Francisco Chronicle*, May 20, 2014
"Man Sentenced in California Gang Rape of Lesbian"
      —Associated Press, May 20, 2014

Also about the same time Carroll was hoping for more poor Central
American illegal immigrants to pour in and put an end to America's infernal rape culture, Juan Carlos Sanchez was charged with raping his stepdaughters, aged nine and eleven—with the assistance of his wife and
mother-in-law, who were also charged with child abuse.[14]

That Juan Carlos Sanchez should not be confused with the Juan Carlos Sanchez who was one of Colorado's "Most Wanted Sex Offenders,"
convicted in 2005 for raping a twelve-year-old girl after slipping a muscle
relaxer into her drink.[15]

Nor was it the Juan Carlos Sanchez, twenty-two, charged with statutory
rape for having sex with a thirteen-year-old girl in North Carolina in 2007.[16]

And it was not the thirty-five-year-old Juan Carlos Sanchez *Ayala*
arrested in Sacramento in 2004 for molesting a five-year-old boy.[17]

It was a different Juan Carlos Sanchez. Sometimes, it seems like we're
not getting the crème de la crème when it comes to immigrants. Maybe it
would work better if the decision of who gets to live here were made by us,
not them. Perhaps we should consider qualifications more stringent than
"lives within walking distance."

HERE ARE SOME RAPE CULTURES FOR YOU!

Outside of the West, all countries have flourishing rape cultures.
Every year the State Department puts out a report ranking countries in

terms of human sex trafficking, and every year, countries with the least human trafficking include all of the West (America, Canada, Australia, New Zealand, nearly all of Western Europe, and Israel), plus South Korea and Taiwan. With only two exceptions—Nicaragua and Colombia (and they're cooking the books)—the rest of the world is awash in the human sex trade.[18]

In lying to its readers about another subject—the heterosexual transmission of AIDS[19]—the *New York Times* inadvertently revealed how women and children are treated in Thailand:

> Five young women in casual clothes sit opposite them on similar benches, but behind a display window of cheap glass. They chat among themselves, brushing each other's hair or playing with the brothel dog.
>
> In the unshaded light of a pink fluorescent tube, their makeup looks coarse, their lipstick purple. One young woman wears a "Snoopy and his friends" T-shirt dress. Over her breast is a blue, heart-shaped pin with a number. Some women wear yellow pins. These are price tags.
>
> In this establishment, with its chatty mama-san, shrine to the Buddha and small table of snacks for indecisive clients, a half-hour of sex with a woman with a blue pin costs 65 baht, or $2.60; with a yellow pin, $2.
>
> These young women live at the brothel, a shabby building of bamboo and thatch, roofed with tin, in the Thai city of Chiang Mai. They are always on call, and each has between 10 and 20 customers a day. In this area, in this kind of brothel, four of five women carry the AIDS virus.[20]

We take more immigrants from Thailand than from Ireland, Australia, and New Zealand *combined*.[21]

INDIA'S RAPE CULTURE

The *New York Times* reports that India is "one of the most unsafe countries in the world for women,"[22] ranking just slightly ahead of Jeffrey Epstein's Palm Beach mansion. Gang rapes are common and cause little alarm.

In December 2012, a fifteen-year-old girl was gang-raped while she was walking home from school in a northern province of India, putting her in the hospital in critical condition. The girl's rape was not reported for three days because of "family pressure," according to the police.[23] The next day, a female medical student boarded a bus with a male companion in Delhi, where at least six men attacked the two with metal rods, dragged the woman to the back of the bus, and gang-raped her. The victims were then tossed from the moving bus. The rape victim had to undergo several surgeries, requiring most of her intestines to be removed. She eventually died of her injuries. Men in Delhi blamed the woman. "In most cases, it's the girl's fault," Ram Singh told a *Times* reporter.[24]

National Public Radio attributes the high rate of gang rape in India to "unelected, all-male village councils" that "influence attitudes toward women."[25] America was bristling with "all-male village councils" from around 1620 to 1960, and yet women here were astonishingly safe.

LATIN AMERICAN RAPE CULTURE

India's rape culture is impressive, but, according to Professor Carlos Javier Echarri Cánovas of El Colegio de Mexico, who studies violence against women: "The fact is that the rate of rape in Mexico is higher than in India."[26] A report from the Inter-American Children's Institute explained that Latin America is second only to Asia in the sexual exploitation of women and children because sex abuse is "ingrained into the minds of the people." Women and children are "seen as objects instead of human beings with rights and freedoms."[27]

Try to imagine waking up to this report on American cities: "Women, especially if they are young, working class and poor, run the risk of being murdered and having their mutilated and raped bodies show up some morning in the streets of numerous Latin American cities, as evidenced by the more than 1,500 cases reported in the last decade that remain unsolved and unpunished."

That's from a report by the Inter Press Service titled "Latin America: Women Murdered, Raped—and Ignored."[28] The women's corpses are typically defaced, especially the genital areas, and their bodies are "positioned so that their sex organs are exposed." Commenting on the sexually macabre murders, Claudio Nash, the coordinator of the Centre for Human Rights at the University of Chile, said that in Latin America, "being subjected to these kinds of attacks is almost intrinsic to being a woman. They are not seen as violations of basic human rights."[29]

There are sex-segregated buses in Mexico[30] and a sex-segregated metro system in Delhi.[31] How will sex-segregated subway cars go over in New York City? Will Justice Ruth Bader Ginsburg approve that in our new country? While we're at it, why not let the Hottentots replace Supreme Court justices? They'll make the court more vibrant.

MUSLIM RAPE CULTURE

By now, Muslim rape culture is well known in Sweden, Norway, and Denmark on account of their own deranged immigration policies. A 2001 police study in Oslo, Norway, for example, found that two out of three rapes were committed by Muslims.[32] But—as in America—the local press neurotically portray the Muslim rapists as "Swedish men."[33] Muslim gang rapists taunt their victims in court.[34] The "grand mufti" of Australia, Sheikh Taj el-Din al-Hilali, gave a speech blaming the Muslim rape epidemic on Australian women, for not being veiled. ("If you take uncovered meat, put it on the street...and the cats eat it, is it the fault of the cat or the uncovered meat?")[35] In the middle of the internationally covered "Arab Spring" protests in Egypt, a mob of Muslim men sexually assaulted a female CBS reporter, Lara Logan.

What do Muslims have to do to get the media to shift their focus from apocryphal fraternity rapes by preppie white guys to real rapes by these barbaric, alien cultures being foisted on the West?

The CBS broadcast in which Lara Logan described her "brutal sustained sexual assault" by Egyptian men celebrating in Tahir Square topped the Nielsen ratings.[36] But the *New York Times* devoted less newspaper ink to Logan's actual rape than it did to a nonexistent rape by Duke lacrosse players. In fact, the *Times* published less about the sexual assault on Logan than it did on the Augusta National Golf Club's all-male membership policy.

ALL CULTURES ARE EQUAL— EXCEPT AMERICA'S, WHICH IS THE WORST

This is how PC kills. Political correctness requires that American women not be warned that, when they leave the West, they will be encountering cultures that do not share our Protestant virtues of self-restraint and legal equality.

Here are some news accounts of sexual assaults on Western tourists from a just few months in 2013 and 2014:

In February 2013, an American photographer from Staten Island was murdered on a "safe" street of Istanbul by a Turkish man, who hit her with a rock because she wouldn't kiss him. A local storeowner downplayed the murder, saying, "If the woman does not flirt, a man would not attempt to do anything," and adding, "Everything starts with a woman." A thirty-year-old tour operator also blamed the murdered victim, saying, "She was asking for trouble."[37] You know, by being a woman.

That same month, a female tourist from Italy was gang-raped by police in Mexico when she refused to pay a bribe[38]—the same police force accused by a Canadian tourist of gang rape just a year earlier.[39] Around the same time, masked men broke into an Acapulco beach villa and gang-raped six tourists from Spain. A seventh woman was told she was not raped because she was a Mexican.[40] I'm trying to imagine what would happen if a group of white men gang-raped a half dozen Latinas, but skipped one woman because she was white.

The following month, in March 2013, a twenty-four-year-old Dutch woman working in Dubai was raped by a Sudanese colleague. When she reported the rape to the police, they asked her, "Are you sure you just didn't like it?"[41] For reporting the rape, she was charged with the crime of having unlawful sex and sentenced to sixteen months in prison. A few months later, the polygamist ruler of Dubai pardoned her for the crime of being raped—and simultaneously pardoned her rapist.[42]

In March 2013, a Swiss woman was gang-raped by seven or eight men while on a bicycle trip with her husband in India. The rapists tied her husband to a tree for him to watch.[43] That same month, a British tourist leapt from her third-floor hotel room in India to avoid being raped by *the hotel owner.*[44] In April, a twenty-one-year-old American student was gang-raped for six hours inside a moving public transit minivan on the Copacabana Beach in Brazil. Her boyfriend was tied up and forced to watch. Among the accused rapists was the bus's fourteen-year-old fare-taker.[45]

In one month, January 2014, a Danish woman was robbed and gang-raped at knifepoint for three hours by men she had stopped in a popular Indian shopping district to ask for directions;[46] a Polish tourist traveling with her two-year-old daughter in India was raped by a cabdriver, then thrown along with her child to the side of the road;[47] and an eighteen-year-old charity worker from Germany was sexually assaulted on a train in India.[48]

In March that year, a British woman was raped by a security guard who was walking her back to her room in a five-star hotel in Egypt. By the Egyptian government's own account, staff at that one upscale hotel had been responsible for three other rapes as well as numerous sexual assaults in the previous two years.[49]

BUT AMERICAN MEN ARE NO PICNIC, EITHER!

Lauren Wolfe, director of Women Under Siege at the Women's Media Center, recounted many of these adventures in Third World travel in the *New York Times*, but smothered the facts with PC palaver about how it could happen anywhere. "Reports of rape *in all countries* [emphasis added]," she dutifully wrote, are undermined by "corruption and a cultural willingness to ignore violence considered 'normal,' even close to home."[50]

In all countries? Even when reporting on innocent American women being raped and molested throughout the Third World, the media won't question their dogma that all cultures are equal—except American culture, which is the worst!

Wolfe admitted that when she searched for articles about tourists being raped in the United States, she didn't find any. Instead, she kept getting more articles about American tourists being raped abroad. But Wolfe checked with Julia Drost, the policy and advocacy associate in women's human rights at Amnesty International, and Drost confirmed that sexual violence "knows no national or cultural barriers."[51] Most women travelers, Wolfe said, would agree that "bad things can happen when you get in a taxi in New York."[52] Well, yeah: 99 percent of New York taxi drivers are immigrants.[53]

IMMIGRANTS FLED THESE CULTURES!

Today, thanks to Teddy Kennedy, even Americans who haven't technically left home are being forced to encounter these foreign rape cultures in their own country. Immigrants who thought they were fleeing backward, misogynistic societies are being attacked by the same rapists they knew back home. In 2009, illegal immigrant Juan Carlos Conseco-Figueroa raped a Hispanic immigrant in her Annapolis, Maryland, home, forcing the woman to perform oral sex on him at knifepoint, in front of children. He then grabbed the six-year-old, ripped off her clothes, and dragged her into a bedroom. As he was raping the child, police broke down the door.[54]

Among the things that Conseco-Figueroa's rape victim must have thought she was escaping by coming to America was the Hispanic rape culture. But without an immigration moratorium, soon the only difference between America and Mexico will be that in the United States, you'll be able to push "one" for English. Immigrants may wonder why they bothered coming. Another few years of our current immigration policies, and we'll all have to move to Canada to escape the rapes.

SPOT THE IMMIGRANT!

CASE NO. 3 | DEATH SENTENCE CHAMPIONS

INTERNATIONAL LAW WAS CREATED DURING THE BUSH ADMINISTRATION BECAUSE a group of Mexicans—and one African American—gang-raped and murdered two teenaged girls in Houston, Texas.[1] The crime made history in another way: It led to the most death sentences handed out for a single crime in Texas since 1949.[2] Do you even know about this case?

The only reason the media eventually admitted that the lead rapist, Jose Ernesto Medellin, was an illegal alien from Mexico was to try to overturn his conviction on the grounds that he had not been informed of his right, as a Mexican citizen, to confer with the Mexican consulate.

Journalists have an irritating tendency to skimp on detail when reporting crimes by immigrants, a practice that will not be followed here.

One summer night in June 1993, fourteen-year-old Jennifer Ertman and Elizabeth Peña, who had just turned sixteen, were returning from a pool party, and decided to take a shortcut through a park to make their 11:30 p.m. curfew. They encountered a group of Hispanic men, who were in the process of discussing "gang etiquette," such as not complaining if other members talked about having sex with your mother.[3] The girls ran away, but Medellin grabbed Jennifer and began ripping her clothes off. Hearing her screams, Elizabeth came back to help her friend.

For more than an hour, the five Hispanics and one black man raped the teens, vaginally, anally, and orally—"every way you can assault a human being," as the prosecutor put it.[4] The girls were beaten, kicked, and stomped, their teeth knocked out and their ribs broken. One of the Hispanic men told Medellin's fourteen-year-old brother to "get some," so he raped one of the girls, too. But when it was time to kill the girls, Medellin said his brother was "too small to watch" and dragged the girls into the woods.[5]

There, the girls were forced to kneel on the ground and a belt or shoelace was looped around their necks. Then a man on each side pulled on the cord as hard as he could. The men strangling Jennifer pulled so hard they broke the belt. Medellin later complained that "the bitch wouldn't die." When it was done, he repeatedly stomped on the girls' necks, to make sure they were dead.[6] At trial, Medellin's sister-in-law testified that shortly after the gruesome murders, Medellin was laughing about it, saying they'd "had some fun with some girls" and boasting that he had "virgin blood" on his underpants.[7] It's difficult to understand a culture where such an orgy of cruelty is bragged about at all, but especially in front of women.

By the time the girls' corpses were found four days later, their bodies were so badly decomposed that dental records were required for identification. The decomposition was especially pronounced in the head, neck, and genital areas.[8] Jennifer's father, tipped off that bodies had been found, rushed to the scene, but the police held him back, as he shouted, "Does she have blond hair? Does she have blond hair?"

Activist Ralph Reed tells the *New York Times* that Republicans should take a more "charitable" view of immigration.[9] When he's a fourteen-year-old

American girl being raped and murdered by Mexicans, we'll be more interested in his ideas on charity.

GANG RAPIST SEES HIMSELF AS "THE GOOD GUY"

Arrested a few days later, the Mexican gang rapists were "utterly without remorse"—as the *New York Times* said in its one, lonely article on the case. Entering the court, the defendants cursed at reporters and kicked a news camera to the ground.[10] To the surprise of the police, Medellin not only confessed, but bragged about the grisly rape-murder.

He was convicted and sentenced to death—a sentence that was repeatedly appealed and repeatedly upheld. Unable to grasp that he had done anything wrong, Medellin wrote on his prison webpage: "My life is in black and white like old western movies, but unlike the movies, the good guys don't always finish first."[11] A strictly impartial observer might not concur with Medellin's assessment of himself as "the good guy." The first of the men executed for the crime was the only black assailant, Sean O'Brien. He had tearfully confessed upon his arrest[12] and his last words were: "I am sorry. I have always been sorry."[13] At his execution, Medellin said, "Don't ever hate them for what they do."[14]

Hate *them?* No worries there—it's you we hate. Jennifer's father, Randy Ertman, summarized our feelings toward Medellin in his statement to the court when the last three defendants were sentenced to death: "I hope you rot in hell. I honest to God mean that. I hope they rot in hell, sir. I hope to be there when you die, you sick pieces of (censored). Thank you, Your Honor, for allowing me to speak. I appreciate it, sir."[15] That doesn't move the story along; I just admired his eloquence. Before Mr. Ertman spoke, one of the sheriff's deputies said they'd give him a few minutes to talk and "if he comes over the rail, we'll give him a few more."[16]

Medellin's aunt, Reyna Armendariz, denounced the death sentence for her nephew, saying: "We acknowledged that he committed a crime!"[17]

Unironically, his cousin Reyna Armendariz agreed, saying, "Only God has the right to take a life."[18]

WHAT IS IT ABOUT OUR CULTURE?

Of course, it's hard to see the cultural divide with the media hiding the fact that five of the six rapist-murderers were Hispanic, at least one an illegal alien, and his brother either illegal or an anchor baby. One of the victim's parents later said, "The problem with the youth of America starts in the home. So parents, please be there for your children, always."[19] However true that may be, the problem with these particular youths mostly started in Mexico.

For more than a decade after this widely publicized crime, the only clue that it was not a problem of "America's youth" was the perpetrators' names. For my readers who enjoy puzzles, try to spot any similarities: Jose Ernesto Medellin (Hispanic), Vernancio Medellin (Hispanic), Peter Anthony Cantu (Hispanic), Derrick Sean O'Brien (Black), Efrain Perez (Hispanic), Raul Omar Villareal (Hispanic).

It was not until the media saw a chance to spring the leader of this murderous gang rape that the word "Mexican" appeared within a mile of the defendants' names. There are nearly one thousand articles in the Nexis archives about the case—even the *New York Times* wrote about it, despite the absence of an illegal alien valedictorian anywhere in the story. But apart from one *Houston Chronicle* article that described Medellin as "Mexico-born,"[20] American news consumers only found out Medellin was an illegal alien when that fact was used to try to overturn his death sentence. The girls were murdered on June 24, 1993; the first time Medellin was identified as a Mexican citizen[21] was in a November 28, 2004, *Chicago Tribune* column by a Northwestern University law professor, calling on President Bush to show respect for the World Court in "a Texas case involving Mexican citizen Jose Medellin."[22] That, incidentally, was the professor's full description of Medellin's crime: "a Texas case." Seeing a chance to nullify Medellin's death sentence, the media suddenly exploded with references to his Mexican-ness.

EUROS SIDE WITH MEXICAN GANG RAPIST

Mexico, President Bush's dearest international ally, brought a lawsuit against the United States in the International Court of Justice on behalf of its native son, Jose Ernesto Medellin, arguing that Texas failed to inform him of his right to confer with the Mexican consulate. It probably didn't occur to the police to ask Medellin if he was Mexican, with the media referring to the suspects exclusively as: "five Houston teens," "five youths," "the youths," "young men," "members of 'a social club,'" "a bunch of guys," "six young men," "six teen-agers," and "these guys"[23] (and, oddly, "America's hottest boy band").

The World Court agreed with Mexico, confirming my suspicion that any organization with "world" in its title—International World Court, the World Bank, World Cup Soccer, the World Trade Organization—is inherently evil. The court ordered that Mexican illegal aliens in American prisons must be retried unless they had been promptly advised of their consular rights—a ruling that would have emptied Texas's prisons.

It wasn't as if America had shanghaied Medellin and dragged him into our country. He sneaked in illegally, demanded the full panoply of rights accorded American citizens, and when things didn't go his way, suddenly announced he was an illegal alien entitled to rights as a Mexican citizen. Or as the *New York Times* hyperventilated: A failure to enforce the World Court's ruling "could imperil American tourists or business travelers if they are ever arrested and need the help of a consular official."[24] If an American tourist or business traveler ever gang-rapes and murders two teenaged girls in a foreign country, I don't care what they do to him.

WOULDN'T ANOTHER BUSH BE GREAT IN THE WHITE HOUSE?

Texas Governor Rick Perry, Solicitor General Ted Cruz, and the Texas state court said, Thanks for your thoughts, World Court, but rulings from the Hague are not American law, so we're ignoring it. Medellin appealed Texas's decision to the Supreme Court, but before the Court could hear the case, President Bush sent a letter to the Department of Justice, announcing that he had decided that the United States would obey the ICJ ruling.

With this odd development, the Supreme Court sent Medellin's case back to Texas. State officials were incredulous. *We have to obey some guys in the Hague? And our president says we have to do that? Why does he claim to be* our *president, then?* They couldn't believe the ICJ order was being taken seriously by anyone, regarding it as equivalent to a resolution from the Seventh International Congress of Star Trek Fans—impressive to fellow enthusiasts, but not something anyone could expect actual lawyers to treat as law.

Texas courts proceeded to rule that a presidential memorandum isn't federal law, either. So the case went back to the Supreme Court and, this time, the Court seconded Texas's plan to disregard Bush's idiotic memorandum. It was a 6–3 decision with you-know-who dissenting.[25] (Justices Breyer, Souter, and Ginsburg). Historical note: That same day, the Supreme Court upheld another death sentence out of Texas, against Ruben Cardenas, a forty-year-old illegal immigrant from Mexico, convicted of raping and murdering his sixteen-year-old cousin.[26]

Medellin was finally executed on August 5, 2008.

11

WHY DO HISPANIC VALEDICTORIANS MAKE THE NEWS, BUT CHILD RAPISTS DON'T?

ALL PEASANT CULTURES EXHIBIT NON-PROGRESSIVE VIEWS ON WOMEN AND children; Latin America just happens to be the peasant culture closest to the United States.

Mexicans alone constitute more than one-third of all legal immigrants and about 80 percent of illegal immigrants. They now surpass every other immigrant group in America, having long since overtaken the once-dominant Germans.

If America had taken in 40 million Norwegians[1] over the past few decades, wouldn't we get a few articles about these strange Nordic people's brusque manners?[2] Of course, we couldn't actually take 40 million Norwegians because there are only about 5 million of them in Norway. To approximate the number of Mexicans who have come to the United States since 1970, we'd have to import the entire populations of Austria, Switzerland, Denmark, Finland, Norway, and Ireland.

What will America be like when it's majority Hispanic in order to give the Democrats votes and businesses cheap labor? The media could have made this easy to see by reporting the truth about immigrant sex crimes. But they won't do that. We'll never know the story of FLORENTINO LOPEZ-PALOMINOS, listed on the Yakima County docket as charged with "SEX MISCONDUCT 1 DV; INCEST 1 DV"—though you might notice a pattern in the incest cases if you ever peruse your local criminal dockets. To bypass media censorship, we'll look at a few famous sex crimes, ICE raids and international reports, and the prevalence of prepubescent birth mothers.

NOT BEN FRANKLIN'S AMERICA

The three young girls kidnapped and held as sex slaves for more than a decade in a boarded-up house in Cleveland had been held by Ariel Castro. Even the *New York Times* couldn't avoid reporting that story. But then it turned out Castro wasn't the only Hispanic raping young girls—*on his block*. While investigating the Castro case, detectives happened upon Elias Acevedo, forty-nine, who had lived down the street from Castro. Acevedo, they discovered, had routinely raped his own daughters when they were children. He had also raped his brother's common-law wife when she was eighteen years old and pregnant. And he had raped and killed two of his neighbors in the 1990s. All in all, it wasn't a great street to go trick-or-treating on. Acevedo pleaded guilty to 173 counts of rape, 115 counts of kidnapping, and one count of gross sexual imposition. The only mention in the *Times* of this case of incest, child rape, and murder—on the same block as the sensational Ariel Castro case—was a tiny Associated Press item on page A-18, headlined: "Ohio: Life Sentence in Murders and Rapes."[3] Possible *New York Times* obituary for Hitler: "Austrian Painter Kills Self."

Chandra Levy's killer turned out *not* to be Democratic Congressman Gary Condit, but Ingmar Guandique—an illegal alien from El Salvador, given temporary amnesty by President Bush.[4] (Does that guy have any brothers? I'd love to see another one like him in the White House!) The one Central Park rapist that even liberals admit was guilty was Hispanic: Matias Reyes.[5] After the other attackers had finished with the victim, Reyes came across the jogger's beaten and bloody body, and raped her himself.[6] Among Reyes's many, many other rapes, he had also raped and killed a pregnant woman in the presence of her children, and he had even raped his own mother.[7]

PENIS-CHOPPING IMMIGRANTS

The incessant rape in Hispanic societies seems to have driven the women mad. American doctors pioneered penis reattachment surgery after Ecuadoran immigrant Lorena Gallo chopped off the one belonging to her husband, John Bobbitt. After her arrest, Lorena told the police that she had chopped it off because: "He always have orgasm, and he doesn't wait for me to have orgasm. He's selfish."[8] (Whatever happened to the silent treatment?)

For scholars: The only other instance of this particular crime being committed against an American man occurred in 2011—by another immigrant. The man's Vietnamese bride, Catherine Kieu, cut off her husband's penis, then ground it up in the garbage disposal. Apparently, she was angry that he was divorcing her. Luckily for Kieu, she was from Vietnam, allowing her lawyer to blame her behavior on the trauma of growing up in a war-torn, impoverished nation.[9]

BABY HOPE

The 1991 discovery of a child's decaying body in a cooler led to a twenty-two-year search for her rapist-murderer.[10] Finally, in 2013, police got a tip that led them to Baby Hope's rapist and murderer: It was her cousin, fifty-two-year-old Conrado Juarez, an illegal alien from Mexico, who admitted to smothering the four-year-old while raping her. The girl's name was

Anjelica Castillo and her parents were also illegal immigrants from Mexico. In all, about six family members knew something about the crime but never said anything.[11] Juarez said that it was his sister, Balvina Juarez-Ramirez, who helped him dispose of the girl's body.[12] At the time of Juarez's arrest, Baby Hope's mother was still living illegally in New York with some of her ten children. After several weeks of interrogation, the mother finally admitted that she always suspected Baby Hope was her daughter, but never told the police.[13]

This case of incest, child rape, and murder was entirely an illegal immigrant affair. Baby Hope's parents were illegal immigrants, the cousin who raped and murdered her was an illegal immigrant, and the cousin who helped dispose of the body was an illegal immigrant. Wouldn't that be an important fact to put right up there in the headline? To even mention, at all? New York taxpayers had spent a kazillion dollars trying to solve the Baby Hope case. Weren't they entitled to know?

PROSECUTORS AND THE PRESS AS FORTHCOMING AS USUAL

The Manhattan District Attorney's office sent out a press release on Juarez's indictment that said nothing about Juarez being an immigrant of any sort, certainly not illegal.[14] The NYPD spent twenty-two years and a small fortune trying to solve a case that never should have happened in this country in the first place. How many other crimes went unsolved because, for two decades, the police were pouring resources into a manhunt for a Mexican illegally in this country, who committed child rape and murder in New York City?

Nor did the *New York Times* mention that Baby Hope's killer and his accomplices were all illegal aliens from Mexico. The *Times'* extensive reporting managed to cover that the child, Anjelica Castillo, had been born in Elmhurst Hospital Center in Queens in 1987, that her murderer worked as a dishwasher at Trattoria Pesce Pasta on Bleecker Street, and that Juarez and his sister had hidden the cooler containing the girl's dead body "in a wooded area near the Dyckman Street exit off the Henry Hudson Parkway." The *Times* described how the cops had eventually tracked down the child rapist. (A tip from a woman whose friend had mentioned that her sister had been murdered led the police to DNA on an envelope licked by Baby Hope's mother, and finally to Juarez.) The *Times* also recounted how Juarez's daughter had lied to the police, telling them her father "had been in Mexico for the last 12 years," just before Juarez's wife admitted that he had left for work downtown at 7:00 a.m. that morning.

I guess the fact that the whole lying, murdering, child-molesting, body-disposing family were illegal immigrants from Mexico would have taken the *Times* over its word limit. Instead the paper lied about the family's immigration status, calling Baby Hope's father "an immigrant from Mexico."[15] Reporting the "immigrant" part but not the "illegal" part implies that he had immigrated legally.

It would be like a bulletin on President Lincoln's assassination:

Shots Fired at President
  WAS HE HIT???
Oh yeah, he died. What? Did we say anything that was untrue?

The rest of our constitutionally protected guardians of liberty were similarly tight-lipped on the "illegal alien" aspect of this monstrous crime:

- Neither CBS[16] nor ABC News[17] disclosed that Juarez was not just your regular boy-next-door American child rapist.
- *Newsday* of Long Island also gave no indication that Juarez was an immigrant.[18]
- CNN's story on Juarez's capture did not mention that he was an immigrant, although keen observers might have noticed

that Juarez needed a translator.[19] (Yes, after being in the United States for twenty-five years, the child rapist still couldn't speak English.)

- The *New York Daily News* didn't mention that Juarez was an immigrant, but did provide a crucial clue, saying: Juarez "only speaks Spanish."[20]

- Even *People* magazine, famous for mentioning the unmentionable, said nothing about Juarez's illegal status.[21]

The bewilderment expressed in the comments sections on news stories about Juarez's capture shows that readers hadn't the first idea that the participants were all illegal immigrants from Mexico.[22]

SOMETIMES WE'RE NOT RESCUING VICTIMS, WE'RE BRINGING IN ACCOMPLICES

This is where cultural differences can create problems. Americans aren't used to female relatives of raped and murdered children actively helping the perpetrator get away with it. They can't grasp that the girl's parents either didn't know or didn't care that she had been raped and murdered.

Far from "I am woman, hear me roar," these are cultures where women aren't accustomed to standing up to men, even men who rape kids. In 2013, illegal immigrant Bertha Leticia Rayo was arrested for allowing her former husband, an illegal immigrant from Guatemala, to rape her four-year-old daughter, then assisting his unsuccessful escape from the police. The rapist, Aroldo Guerra-Garcia, was aided in his escape attempt not only by his ex-wife, but by another woman, Krystal Galindo. (Kind of a ladies' man, was Aroldo.) Guerra-Garcia entered a plea to aggravated criminal sodomy and aggravated indecent liberties with a child and was sentenced to eleven months in prison. In a separate case, the mother of the child rape victim was indicted for cruelly beating the child.[23]

That same year, the government busted up a child pornography operation in Illinois being run out of the home of three illegal aliens from Mexico, including one woman. At least one of them, Jorge Muhedano-Hernandez, had already been deported once. *Peoria Journal Star* headline: "Bloomington Men Plead Guilty to False Documents."[24]

In 2014, Isidro Garcia was arrested in Bell Gardens, California, accused of drugging and kidnapping the fifteen-year-old daughter of his girlfriend, then forcing the girl to marry him and bear his child. The mother suspected Garcia, then thirty-one years old, had been raping her teenaged daughter, but did nothing. All three were illegal aliens from Mexico.[25]

In New Mexico, there was a father-son child rape duo. When being sentenced for repeatedly raping a three-year-old and an eight-year-old, Mexican illegal immigrant Luis Casarez's argument to the judge that he did not deserve jail time sounded like Marco Rubio's talking points about hardworking illegal immigrants with roots in America: "I have been here for many years"—Casarez said, incongruously, through a translator. "That's why," he added, "I've been working instead of getting involved with problems." Other than that one thing.

Two weeks after Luis Casarez was indicted for child rape, his son, Luis Casarez Jr., was indicted in a separate case of child rape.[26]

HISPANIC CHILD RAPISTS POP UP IN NEBRASKA, INDIANA—EVEN HAWAII

Immigration raids show a pattern completely undetectable by our media. In June 2014, immigration officials in California decided to round up what sounds like an extremely narrow category of immigration violators: previously deported illegal aliens who had been convicted in the United States of sex crimes and were living in the Los Angeles area. Within three days, they had arrested thirty-one people who fit that description.[27]

That same month, Immigration and Customs Enforcement conducted raids in six states not known for having large illegal alien populations—

Kansas, Illinois, Indiana, Wisconsin, Kentucky, and Missouri. They netted 297 illegal immigrants, nearly 80 percent of whom had been convicted of crimes in the United States, including aggravated battery of a child, sexual assault of a minor, solicitation of a child, aggravated criminal sexual assault, battery, and domestic abuse. Of the twenty-four illegal aliens arrested in the Wichita, Kansas, area, all but one were from Latin America; nineteen were from Mexico.[28]

Hispanic sexual predators show up in all sorts of legal cases. In 2013, the Nebraska Supreme Court was asked to decide whether Hector Medina-Liborio, a twenty-eight-year-old illegal alien from Mexico, could withdraw his no-contest plea to abducting and raping a four-year-old girl, on the grounds that the judge had not *expressly* advised him that his conviction for child abduction and rape could lead to deportation, even though there was evidence that he knew it. (As the kids say: Duh.) The court ruled that if judges neglect to inform illegal aliens that no-contest pleas to child abduction and rape can have immigration consequences, the defendant will be entitled to withdraw his plea.[29]

After thirty-year-old Manuel Antonio Fajardo-Santos, an illegal immigrant from Honduras, was arrested in New Jersey for molesting the nine-year-old sister of his girlfriend, he posted bail, but then went straight into the custody of U.S. Immigration and Customs Enforcement (ICE). Worried that the Honduran would be deported before he could be criminally punished, the state tried to regain custody of him by increasing his bail. The New Jersey Supreme Court ruled—in a case of first impression—that deportation proceedings constituted changed circumstances under the law, allowing the bail amount to be raised.[30]

It's great that we have so many Latin Americans in the United States, raping young girls, so the courts can work out these thorny legal issues.

Even in Hawaii, where the population is only 2.7 percent Mexican,[31] a Mexican child molester pops up. In 2012, forty-seven-year-old Jose Luis Hernandez-Dominguez was sentenced to ten years in prison for sexually molesting a five-year-old girl over an extended period, while his wife babysat the girl. Both the child rapist and the victim were illegal immigrants.[32] Hernandez-Dominguez's molestation conviction made the local news, along with the information that he was an illegal alien. Apparently, there's not a lot of white guilt among native Hawaiians.

There are so many Hispanic child rape cases that in a state like California the same judge can hear several of them. Thus, a few years after presiding over the case of immigrant rapist Guatemalan Willy Alejandro Jimenez, who had grabbed a four-year-old girl in a Palo Alto parking lot, raped her, beaten her unconscious, then thrown her naked body from a moving car,[33] the same judge also presided over the case of fifty-year-old immigrant child rapist Paul Narvios,[34] who repeatedly raped his girlfriend's nine-year-old daughter, getting her pregnant and making her one of only four girls under the age of ten to give birth in the United States.[35]

INTERNATIONAL STUDIES AND CHILD PREGNANCIES

International studies about child sex crimes in Latin America never seem to get the prominent media coverage of studies purporting to show that Fox News viewers are idiots,[36] but they exist. According to the Latin American and Caribbean Youth Network for Sexual and Reproductive Rights (REDLAC), 77 percent of reported sexual assaults in Lima, Peru, are against child victims.[37] In the late 1990s, girls between the ages of ten and fifteen accounted for more than 15 percent of all births in Argentina and 17 percent of all births in Uruguay.[38] By contrast, less than 2 percent of births in the United States are to girls in that age group—and most of those are Hispanics.[39] In the United States, Hispanics are seven times more likely to give birth between the ages of ten and fourteen (1.4 per thousand) than whites (0.2 per thousand), according to a Centers for Disease Control study.[40]

The prevalence of freakishly young birth mothers in Latin America confirms the reports. According to CNN, 318 *ten-year-old girls* gave birth in Mexico in 2011 and in the Mexican state of Jalisco alone 465 girls between the ages of ten and fourteen gave birth.[41] In the last quarter century, there's been one reported case of an American impregnating a girl that young.

You might have noticed from headlines like these—or you would if you lived in Britain, the only place where such headlines might ever appear:

- "Girl Aged Nine Who Gave Birth to Baby in Mexico Didn't Realize She Was Pregnant until Seven Months—and Her Mother Didn't Think It Was a Crime"[42]
- "Argentine Schoolgirl, 12, Gives Birth to Twin Sons (on Same Day Mexican Nine-Year-Old Became a Mother)"[43]
- "Tribal Law Protects Boy, 15, Who Impregnated 10-Year-Old Colombian Girl from Under-Age Sex Charges"[44]

Although records from the 1930s are suspect, the youngest mother in history is said to be five-year-old Lina Medina, who gave birth in Peru in 1939.[45] Counting only specific cases with provable facts reported in the news since 1900, five eight-year-old girls are known to have given birth— two in Colombia, and one each in Mexico, Peru, India (a Muslim),[46] and Chechnya (another Muslim).[47] As a result of the United States' meticulous recordkeeping, the apparent rate of medical oddities in America is inflated in every category compared with official records from most other countries. Nonetheless, no eight-year-old girls have yet given birth in the United States—unless we're counting an apocryphal story of Bill Clinton's surgeon general, Joycelyn Elders, who, while pushing sex ed for kindergartners, claimed to have heard about an eight-year-old in rural Arkansas who gave birth to twins, which no Arkansas doctors had heard of or believed.[48]

Since 1990, the media have reported on fifty-three specific girls aged ten or younger who have given birth in Latin America.[49] In the United States, with a population about 70 percent the size of the nine countries where those births occurred,[50] there were four reported births to girls that young—and three were to immigrants. Two were fathered by Hispanic immigrants, one by a Haitian illegal immigrant, and one by an American. But for William Edward Ronca,[51] there would not be a single confirmed case of a white man in the Western Hemisphere impregnating a girl ten years old or younger. Go USA.

In fact, William Ronca appears to be the only white man in the entire world who has impregnated a girl that young. In all of Western Europe, the United States, Canada, Australia, and New Zealand combined, there have been eight reported births to girls aged ten or younger. Seven of the eight involved immigrants.[52]

THEY'RE CHANGING US

In 1840 the famous chronicler of America, Alexis de Tocqueville, noted that although many criminal offenses in England had been abolished in the new country, Americans "still make rape a capital offence, and no crime is visited with more inexorable severity by public opinion."[53] He contrasted America with France, where rape was punished with far lesser penalties and "it is frequently difficult to get a verdict from a jury against the prisoner." Our Supreme Court improvidently abolished America's centuries-old tradition of permitting capital punishment for rape in 1977—over the objections of the Court's two conservative justices, William Rehnquist and Chief Justice Warren Burger. But rape is still considered a pretty serious crime.

While international organizations are constantly having to ask other nations to please take rape seriously,[54] Americans have been taking rape seriously since the first settlers arrived, four centuries ago. But our post-1965 immigration policy is creating an America more like the rest of the world. We aren't helping the women of the Third World by bringing millions of them here. As Tocqueville also said, "Nothing is more wonderful than the art of being free, but nothing is harder to learn how to use than freedom."

This is where numbers make a difference. We're not changing the immigrants, they're changing us. The rape of little girls isn't even considered a crime in Latino culture—and that culture is becoming our culture. Gloria Trevi, the international pop star known as "the Mexican Madonna," nonchalantly told a reporter for the *New York Times* that sex with a child is acceptable in Mexico. "In the United States, a minor is a minor, and that's a crime," but in Mexico, she said, if the girl is over twelve, "it's not a violation, and you can't say anything."[55] In fact, in thirty-one of thirty-two states in Mexico, the age of consent for sex is twelve. Only in Mexico State is it fourteen.[56] Credible accusations that Trevi had pimped twelve-year-old girls to her manager, Sergio Andrade, a man three times their age, only increased her popularity in Mexico.[57]

A book about police rape investigations reports that American policemen are learning to "be understanding of cultural differences" and keep an "open mind" about child rape because "the Hispanic culture is more accepting of statutory rape."[58] Describing his experiences working in one Hispanic community, an American detective said, "I have a large group of Hispanic men in their thirties and forties who are having intercourse with young girls. I'm being told it's a cultural thing." Hospitals would alert him to babies born to thirteen-year-olds impregnated by much older men, and he'd show up at the girl's home, expecting to find parents ready to string up the guy. Instead, he said, "the family will say it's a blessing and we're so happy. I'll explain it's illegal, they cut me right off. I get a lot of those too."[59]

In 2005, Mecklenburg County, North Carolina, was less than 10 percent Hispanic; more than half of all statutory rape victims were Hispanic.[60] The county gave up on prosecuting child rape cases because, as the chairman of the health committee, Norman Mitchell, said, "I don't want to waste the community's time on one item when we have a lot of items before us."[61] Has the *New York Times* published anything about this? CNN? The *Wall Street Journal*? A 2010 U.S. government study of two thousand adult Latino women in America found that 8 percent of respondents said they had been victims of childhood sexual abuse—compared with a national rate of childhood sexual abuse of about 0.1 percent, according to the U.S. Department of Health and Human Services.[62]

Transplanting millions of people, en masse, from the Third World to the United States won't change their cultures any more than moving New Yorkers to Vermont made them flinty Republicans. Instead, Vermont became socialist. The idea that backward peasants will instantly acquire the characteristics of Americans is the kind of homeopathic magic New Guinea primitives would believe.

> *I know how we'll get Third World people to give up child rape,
>   slavery, animal sacrifice, and human dismemberment!*
> Bring them Christianity? Teach them to read? Give them eco-
>   nomics textbooks?
> *No—I've noticed that successful middle-class people live in nice
>   houses in American suburbs, so we'll move illiterate peasants
>   to American suburbs.*

This is what Democrats and Marco Rubio are trying to do to our country: Bring in the depraved cultures of the Third World and pretend we're changing them, rather than them changing us. Other countries are always welcome to adopt American ideas about equality before the law and Anglo-Saxon morality. They don't need to leave home to do that. Instead, America is just bringing in a lot of rapists.

12

KEEP AMERICA ~~BEAUTIFUL~~ MULTICULTURAL

NO ONE SERIOUSLY BELIEVES THAT BRINGING IN HORDES OF THIRD WORLD people has no effect on the environment. Preserving natural resources is an idiosyncrasy of prosperous cultures: Mexico is still in the slash-and-burn stage of capitalism, about a hundred years away from caring about the environment. Our illegal alien population alone is the size of Peru. The Pew Research Center estimates that in thirty-five years the United States' population will be 438 million, of whom 100 million will be immigrants and their children. Numbers like that cannot help but to degrade America's national parks and wilderness areas.

Will that wake up the bought-off environmentalists? They used to care about gridlock, overcrowding, loss of parkland, and exhaustion of natural resources. Not anymore. Today's environmentalists turn a blind eye as 25 million people tramp through delicate ecosystems, set fire to national parks, kill livestock, dump tons of soiled diapers and Pepsi bottles in the desert, and deface ancient Native American sites. Political correctness demands that no one notice immigrants' toll on the environment.

ACCUSATIONS OF BIGOTRY GO UP IN SMOKE—ALONG WITH OUR NATIONAL PARKS

In 2011, after a series of devastating wildfires raged through Arizona, burning half a million acres of land, Senator John McCain said something uncharacteristically sensible: "There is substantial evidence that some of these fires have been caused by people who have crossed our border illegally. The answer to that part of the problem is to get a secure border."[1]

Instantly, McCain was attacked as a nativist xenophobe. *We have no idea who set the fires. It was probably a camper.* Illegal alien activist Randy Parraz sneered of McCain: "It's easier to fan the flames of intolerance, especially in Arizona,"[2] and the pro–illegal alien *Washington Post* ran this bracingly original headline: "John McCain Fans the Fires of Immigration Intolerance in Arizona."[3] La Raza's Daniel Ortega accused McCain of spreading "fear and hate." Representative Raul Grijalva, also from Arizona, put out a press release the day after McCain's remarks accusing him of provoking "an extreme anti-immigrant and anti-Latino atmosphere in Arizona."[4]

Five months later, the Government Accountability Office released its investigative report on Arizona wildfires: They're mostly caused by illegal aliens.[5]

When McCain first made his remarks about illegal aliens being behind most of the Arizona wildfires, Forest Service spokesman Tom Berglund stridently denied that illegals had caused one specific fire,[6] neglecting to mention that illegals were the single largest cause of all of Arizona's wildfires. The Environmental Protection Agency issues regulations demanding that pesticides be purer than dirt in the ground, but then the government deliberately lies to us about illegal immigrants burning down our national parks.

Of the seventy-seven human-caused fires on federal or tribal land in Arizona between 2006 and 2010 investigated by the GAO, a cause could be determined in sixty cases. Fully half of those were caused by illegal aliens. Only five were caused by campers neglecting to fully extinguish a campfire, and the rest were freak accidents.[7] One of the reasons the GAO was able to review only seventy-seven fires was that the Bureau of Land Management and the Forest Service couldn't spare any agents for investigations. They were too busy protecting "firefighters and their equipment from illegal aliens."

Apparently, when illegals see border patrol agents, they try to distract them by throwing lighted matches in the brush to start fires. Not only do illegal immigrants intentionally set wildfires, but they violently attack firefighters trying to extinguish the blazes. Fires are allowed to rage, because fire crews are forced to wait for law enforcement protection. Arizona's first major fire of 2009 occurred in Hog Canyon in the Peloncillo Mountains. With no law enforcement available to provide nighttime support, firefighters had to abandon their efforts at dusk. Overnight, the fire spread from three hundred acres to three thousand acres, eventually consuming seventeen thousand acres of parkland.

Illegal aliens also prevent firefighters from using their radios. As the Forest Service blandly states: "[F]irefighters are instructed not to use radios when they encounter illegal border crossers because illegal border crossers may believe that firefighters are reporting their location to law enforcement and react violently."[8] I wonder if it would help if firefighters didn't have to worry about being attacked by illegal aliens. And wouldn't it be a big help if there were half as many wildfires? Calculating only the cost of fires on national parks, a fence on the border is a bargain.

AMERICANS BEGIN A LIFETIME OF SERVICE TO FOREIGN LAWBREAKERS

The Forest Service had once gamely suggested trying to identify "the group most likely to start fires," but once the evidence was in, they buried it. To blame illegal aliens would be playing the old "blame the perpetrator" game.

Despite the evidence adduced by the GAO showing that illegal immigrants are both the single largest cause of wildfires and also the biggest impediment to extinguishing them, the government report dared not suggest building a fence. We can't do that because *fences don't work! Diversity is a strength!* Instead, our government decided that 100 percent of the price of illegal aliens' fire setting should be paid by Americans. Let's teach *Americans* about fire prevention.

After noticing that a lot of the wildland fires in California's Cleveland National Forest were being set by illegal aliens, for example, the Border Agency Fire Council in Southern California decided the solution was to hire Americans to go into the areas trafficked by illegals and put their fires out for them. Maybe we could cook their food and give them space heaters, too! Not incidentally, the Fire Council is made up of forty-three U.S. *and Mexican* government agencies. Weirdly, it didn't occur to them to stop the illegal activity leading to the fires. Instead of being made a laughingstock, the Fire Council's approach was touted as an innovative approach by the GAO in its report to Congress.[9]

DRUG CARTELS IN OUR NATIONAL PARKS

Starting enormous conflagrations in our national parks may be the least of illegal immigrants' attacks on this country's natural beauty. Because of new border restrictions after 9/11—I guess it *was* possible to tighten the borders!—our dear friends in Mexico moved their drug cartel operations directly into America's parks. After the 9/11 terrorist attacks—committed by immigrants—a lot of Americans decided to take their vacations here in the United States. If they went to one of our national parks, they might have been threatened with guns by other immigrants.[10]

One hunter in the Angeles National Forest was seized by illegal aliens and held at gunpoint for getting too close to their pot farm on American parkland. When law enforcement officers later approached the area, the cartel members shot an agent.[11] "These guys shoot people," a Forest Service agent told the *New York Times*, and "they do not distinguish between police, hunters or campers."[12] The Mexicans also protect their pot gardens with bear traps, trip wires rigged to shotguns, and razor blade–equipped booby traps.[13]

In 2003, a national parks spokesman confirmed that in this "new onslaught on the parks," seizures of marijuana crops in some areas had shot up by 800 percent—"far greater than anything we've ever seen before."[14] At least we get absolute honesty from the government. One month after U.S. Park Rangers had arrested eight illegal aliens from Mexico tending a marijuana farm in the middle of Sequoia National Park, President Bush hailed Mexican immigrants for their contributions to the American economy.[15]

With little media attention and complete disregard by President Bush, Mexican organized crime continued its seizure of America's national parks, undeterred. In 2010, there were three shootings in the Sonoran Desert National Monument. Two illegal alien drug smugglers were killed by other illegal alien drug smugglers and an Arizona County deputy sheriff was shot.[16] In the Tucson sector, which includes the Coronado National Forest and the Sonoran Desert National Monument, federal land officials spend 75 to 97 percent of their time responding to threats from illegal aliens.

Armed illegal aliens were in control of our national parks, so government officials leapt to action by shutting down the parks. A majority of the Organ Pipe Cactus National Monument was closed to U.S. citizens for more than a decade because it was too dangerous.[17]

Another bright idea of the government was to warn Americans not to enter federal lands where they might encounter armed illegal aliens:

DANGER—PUBLIC WARNING
TRAVEL NOT RECOMMENDED

- Active Drug and Human Smuggling Area
- Visitors May Encounter Armed Criminals and Smuggling Vehicles Traveling at High Rates of Speed
- Stay Away From Trash, Clothing, Backpacks, and Abandoned Vehicles

- If You See Suspicious Activity, Do Not Confront! Move Away and Call 911
- BLM Encourages Visitors To Use Public Lands North of Interstate[18]

Americans are not allowed in certain parts of their own national parks because of possible clashes with illegal immigrants. How long was I unconscious?

NYT: IT'S BETTER TO BE BROWN THAN GREEN

The environmental damage done to federal parkland by the Mexican pot growers is breathtaking. According to *USA Today*, the illegals "scar the landscape by crudely terracing hillsides that erode under winter rain. They spill pesticides, fertilizer and diesel fuel used to power generators that run extensive drip-irrigation systems. They dam creeks for water sources, plant salsa gardens, disfigure trees and leave behind tons of garbage, human waste and litter."[19] Park officers find deer carcasses hanging from trees, owls impaled on posts, and claws from grisly bears displayed as trophies.[20]

Except for one fully brainwashed government official, who said, "I don't want to single out one group,"[21] there was no mistaking who was dumping pesticides, chopping down trees, and threatening hikers in our parks. In 2005, James Parker, a senior narcotics agent with the Campaign Against Marijuana Planting, told *USA Today*: "In the last two or three years almost 100% of the gardens we've eradicated are Mexican drug cartel gardens."[22] Even the *New York Times* had to admit it was Mexican illegal aliens. "Ninety-nine percent of the people we arrest or investigate are from Mexico," a SWAT team leader in Tulare County told the *Times*. Forest Service Special Agent Laura Mark said, "Ninety to 95 percent of the marijuana in California is now grown by Mexican nationals who work for the drug cartels."[23]

Following this explosion of honesty in the *Times*, the paper mostly dropped the subject. The *Times* will instruct readers to put a two-liter soda bottle in their toilet tanks and to unplug DVRs for a "greener home."[24] But it hides information about illegal aliens destroying millions of acres of precious national parkland. That of course pales in comparison to the environmental damage wreaked by working toilets. Between 2001 and 2014, the *Times* ran only one other article mentioning the illegal immigrant marijuana farms in our national parks.[25] Someone should tell the *Times* the Mexican pot growers are American loggers.

Although the pot farms are entirely Mexican operated, the *Los Angeles Times* reports that the cartels are working with Middle Eastern terrorist groups, including Hezbollah. That seems like a pretty big story to me. The *New York Times* never mentioned it. *Times* readers will be so busy rigging their toilet tanks to save water, they'll never know that our national parks are being decimated in order to fund foreign terrorists.

DUMPING POLLUTANTS BY THE WORLD'S TALLEST TREE

In 2008, the National Park Service arrested five illegal aliens who had commandeered several acres of land in the Redwood National Park for a pot farm *within six miles of the world's tallest tree.* The Mexicans had dumped pesticides, fertilizer, and trash in the middle of this international landmark, doing untold damage to the forest.[26] Three of the five illegal aliens arrested at the site had already been deported once.

Like something out of *Pravda*, the *New York Times* not only neglected to report on the illegal aliens' desecration of a redwood forest, but ten days after the pot farm was discovered, prattled about "dreadlocked hippies" in houses near Redwood National Park, "where marijuana is covertly grown."[27] In the Soviet era, the only way Russians knew there had been a plane crash was that the Soviet press would suddenly be bristling with stories about American air disasters. Today, the only way for *Times* readers to know that Mexican illegal aliens are dumping pollutants next to irreplaceable sequoia trees is by reading about hippies with indoor grow-lights near a redwood forest.

The Mexican assault on America's national parks goes well beyond what is absolutely necessary to cultivate marijuana crops. Reporters who have visited the sites gape in horror at the trash illegal aliens have left behind. Amid the plethora of two (2) *New York Times* stories on the pot farms, one said that law enforcement officers have found "elaborate tree-houses, makeshift showers and, invariably, trash and pesticides, much of which ends up in streams and creeks."[28] The *Fresno Bee* reported that the illegal immigrants leave behind "tons of trash" in addition to poaching deer and other park animals.[29] The *Los Angeles Times* said of one camp: "Trash was strewn everywhere—empty cans, torn packets of noodles, a crusty leather rifle scabbard. A soggy sleeping bag was stuffed behind a tree." The chief law enforcement officer at Sequoia National Park swept his hand toward the piles of trash, saying, "Nice, eh? Welcome to your national park."[30]

LOOK AT MEXICO'S NATIONAL PARKS TO SEE OUR FUTURE

For a glimpse into America's future, consider how Mexicans treat their own environment. In Mexico's most famous national park, a ten-thousand-year-old evergreen forest designated by presidential decree as a biosphere reserve, illegal loggers chop down about seventy mature trees a day, or "a small forest a week," according to the *New York Times*.[31] While environmentalists from around the world send millions of dollars to Mexico to preserve the forest, local peasants indignantly announce that the land belongs to them and slaughter the trees.

Marijuana growers set fire to old-growth pine forests in Sierra Tara-humara, destroying two-hundred-year-old trees, simply to clear areas for growing pot. Sometimes, the locals burn huge swaths of the forest out of pique with the government. Mexican authorities are helpless against these crusading peasants, who attack officers, set fire to police cars, and storm prisons to free illegal loggers.[32]

Sending their poorest, most backward people to the United States is obviously a big help to Mexico, but it's pretty rough on America's landscape. The sheer numbers of immigrants tromping into the United States can't help but to harm our wilderness areas. That's why the largest anti-immigration group is called "*Numbers* USA," not "Hispanics Litter and Scorch the Earth." But it is also a fact that the vast majority of the Teddy Kennedy immigrants come from peasant cultures that have no concept "litter."

In 2005, the Sumidero Canyon in Chiapas, Mexico, was so jammed with garbage that it became a cause célèbre for environmentalists. In the first few days of cleanup, thirty tons of garbage were removed from the eight-mile canyon.[33] Then ten years later, the river was completely clogged again, full of plastic bottles, bags, Styrofoam cups, and plates.[34] As one Mexican environmentalist said, "[I]t's a war without end."[35] Lucy Gallagher of Mexiconservacion explained in an online video that "people actually just dump the garbage on the beach." Pointing to beer bottles, syringes, shoes, and soap carpeting the beach around her, she said, "[P]retty much anything that you can find in your house waste will be on this beach."[36]

After ritualistically noting that "[n]ot every Mexican litters," the *Houston Chronicle* said that Mexico is "choking on its refuse." Mexico City is flooded after every major rainfall because bottles and trash clog the storm drains: "Soft drink bottles, snack wrappers, used diapers and cigarette butts clog city streets, rural highways and scenic beaches. Mountains of garbage stand sentry-like in empty lots and at the edges of bucolic rural villages. Discarded plastic bags hang in trees and dangle from cactus like bitter industrial fruit."[37] Mexicans "tuck pop bottles into hedges, trees and lampposts. Schoolchildren drop snack packages wherever they please. Drivers of intercity buses instruct passengers to toss refuse out the windows rather than leave it aboard."[38] There are periodic outbreaks of dengue fever on account of the mosquitoes clustering around trash dumped on the roads.[39]

The *Chronicle* was quick to point out that it wasn't Mexicans' fault that they littered: It was the fault of a "deeply entrenched political system."[40] (My money had been on systemic racism.) The logic is murky, but it has something to do with the system discouraging "citizen input," forcing Mexicans to throw their trash on the ground.[41]

For decades, Mexican refuse ended up on San Diego's world-famous beaches by way of the Tijuana River. The "pungent flow, with its brown froth and floating bits of plastic," carried excrement from Tijuana through eight miles of rural California before landing on Southern California beaches. Border agents avoided the river, not only because of the smell, but because it "melts the wax off your boots if you step in it," as one agent told the *New York Times*. This blight on California's beaches reached a crisis point in the 1990s. One solution would have been for Mexicans to stop throwing their garbage in the river. But as San Diego County Supervisor Brian P. Bilbray said, it wasn't like dealing with Canada. "This is where the first world and the third world meet."[42] Instead, U.S. taxpayers funded a sewage treatment plant on the border at a cost of $239.4 million. Mexico chipped in $17 million.[43]

THE MEXICAN LITTERING HABIT

The Mexican cultural trait of littering is well known to everyone, except American journalists. With the rigid circling of wagons by the elites as impenetrable as ever, the truth about the rampant littering problem of Mexican immigrants mostly slips out in the nontraditional media. The comments sections of hiking blogs are a hotbed of unfiltered reporting. After Labor Day weekend in 2011, one hikers' blog wailed: "KCAL reports that in one canyon alone (they never mention which one, but it certainly looks like the East Fork of the San Gabriel River in the accompanying video) had upwards of 30,000 pounds of trash left in it over the long weekend. THIRTY. THOUSAND. POUNDS."

The comments thread was more specific:

PISSED OFF HIKER says:

September 12, 2011 at 6:42 pm

Maybe they should lower the price of water in LA county
so the Mexicans could take a shower at home and wouldn't have
to have bath day in the river.

JANETTE P. says:

September 13, 2011 at 3:58 pm

I noticed the comment about the Mexicans, sadly, this is
more than likely true. My extended family is Mexican so I know
how most of them are and the outskirts of Angeles is full of
Hispanic people. I went last week just to sit next to the river that
runs through the canyons and I wanted to shoot the people who
left their crap there—red cups, abandoned sandals, plastic
bags—immediately I gathered what I could and brought it up
to a huge green trash bin they had there. They ACTUALLY
HAD a huge trash bin. I don't understand the laziness of people.
Earth is so beautiful and I hate that people don't take the
responsibility to keep it that way as much as possible.[44]

It's not just America's national parks that are being destroyed, but its
neighborhoods. After suburban Wheaton, Maryland, flipped from majority white to majority Hispanic, the *Washington Post* reports, "[t]he grassy
medians often got treated as dumps, collecting beer bottles, dirty diapers
and fast-food trash that longtime residents still spend their weekends picking up."[45] Established residents, the *Post* reported—while absolutely not
prejudiced and, in fact, delighted by their colorful neighbors—were, however, "bothered by litter, cars parked on lawns, graffiti and a rash of auto
break-ins." Thus, local Ed Williford complimented the "beautiful things"
Hispanics do to their houses and rushed to assure the *Post* that "we don't
mind the Hispanics. We're not prejudiced." His complaint was with the
ones "who leave the trash—they have no respect." His wife elaborated,

saying, "Some leave loads and loads of beer bottles and trash. I think people get frustrated when they see that. That's not the way we like to live."[46] It's not the way Washington lobbyists like to live either, but they don't live in Wheaton. Their maids do.

In tony Palm Springs, a letter to the editor of the *Desert Sun* complained about vandalism in a local park after Mexican Independence Day. "Exercise equipment, landscape boulders, memorial plaques, utility buildings and tennis court signs," the resident wrote, "are all covered with green spray paint proudly displaying the 'tag' of some individual who must now feel very proud of this accomplishment."[47]

Similarly, in a *Los Angeles Times* Neighborhood Report on once majority-black Vermont Square in South LA, the comments section consisted mostly of black residents complaining about the littering of their new Hispanic neighbors. Endorsing another commenter's remark that the neighborhood looked like Tijuana, "Stoney" said, "I work around many different ethnicities" and "Mexicans just do not clean up after themselves. It is as if they have never thrown a piece of trash away in their lives. They just leave it all on the ground."[48] One longtime black resident, Audrey, said: "Trash in the street is an ugly sight.... Adults with children mimicking [them] seem to see no problem with their childish actions."[49] A book about Mexican immigration published by the Russell Sage Foundation disputed the notion that blacks resent Mexican immigrants for taking their jobs, saying that actually what they resented was the "litter, public hygiene, drinking outdoors and noisiness."[50]

Do you see a pattern developing?

Even a post on the Democratic Underground website reported (spelling and capitalization as in the original):

> There is at least one new beer can or bottle a day thrown out on the area I try to keep clean. Fast food debris are a close second and the final straw was having to pick up a "loaded" diaper last week.

Other property owners have given up trying to keep ahead of the stuff, the roadside looks like some third world country.

I believe a large percentage of the litter is coming from newly arrived people from south of the border. If anyone has been to Mexico (outside of the tourist areas), you know why I suspect that they may be part of the problem. We have a large Central American population that are drawn here to work on the farms and a large tyson chicken plant that employes many immigrants. I have no problem with people coming here to improve their lives. I do have a problem with people that reduce the quality of MY life.

In reply, one Democratic Underground commenter said: "When I lived in Mexico, we referred to the white plastic bag as the 'Mexican National Flower,' and that was probably being kind. Last year when I spent some time in Ireland, I never saw any litter at all...anywhere."[51] (You know what else you didn't see in Ireland? Mexicans.)

Unless we're witnessing a mass psychosis—*let's all get together and smear an innocent ethnic group*—Hispanics are prodigious litterers. Even other Hispanics notice! In 2005, a Latino group in Boston put together a program to teach fellow Hispanics to stop littering, using street mimes to communicate beyond the language barrier. When a draft of their proposal leaked, there was shock, hurt, and, of course, outrage—and not just the usual outrage associated with anything having to do with mimes. Colombian immigrant Diego Luis Peña demanded an apology for the Hispanic-run anti-littering campaign, saying, "People are very hurt." Local resident Jose Ortiz said that the anti-littering campaign "caused a lot of pain."[52]

Inasmuch as the rules of political correctness require that no one notice anything negative about Hispanic culture, maybe we should consider admitting only those immigrants we're allowed to criticize, like Germans. How can any immigrant assimilate if Americans refuse to mention their little cultural annoyances, such as littering, drunk driving, and child rape? The Irish would still be filling up the paddy wagons if America had treated them with such kid gloves. (Remember the good old days when the *Irish* were our biggest problem?) The *Houston Chronicle* explained that Mexicans throw trash on the ground because, in Mexico, no one tells them not to.[53] Unfortunately, no one tells them not to in the United States, either—provided the person doing the littering is slightly darker than Joe Pesci.

Ordinary people have noticed. But without these eyewitness accounts in blog posts and online comments, it would be impossible to make sense of news stories about park closures and mass littering.

IT'S PROBABLY "TEABAGGERS" VANDALIZING IRREPLACEABLE ARCHAEOLOGICAL TREASURES

In 2013, Joshua Tree National Park was beset by inner-city graffiti on rocks and boulders—as well as on ancient petroglyphs etched by Serrano and Chemehuevi Indians thousands of years ago. The century-old Barker Dam had graffiti carved into it. Rather than suggest that any particular group was responsible for the vandalism and garbage, federal officials closed large sections of the park.

Joshua Tree Park is located in two California counties, San Bernardino and Riverside, that had recently become majority Hispanic. Twenty years ago, both these counties were more than 80 percent white.[54] By 2010, according to the U.S. census, San Bernardino County was 51.1 percent Hispanic and 31.4 percent white,[55] while Riverside County was 46.9 percent Hispanic and 38 percent white[56]—and this from a census bureau that undercounts illegal aliens.

Luckily, Huffington Post readers drew no connection between the recent influx of Latin American immigrants and the sudden appearance of gang graffiti in our national parks, allowing them to blame "teabaggers," "kids today," and "this generation of parents."

IF_Toci

Think of short-sighted TEABAGGERS running a town of twenty-one thousand people for a dozen years. Thousands of people, only in the desert for Cheap Housing, badly wanting a MALL and looking for something to do. Looks like some of them have found something to do.

12 APR 2013 3:42 PM

SilverStacker

I'm surprised the kids today can get off Facebook long enough to do this.

12 APR 2013 7:18 PM

cjaco

Yet another sign that this generation of parents is the worst in history.

12 APR 2013 8:27 PM[57]

Later that year, all of Cucamonga Canyon in Rancho Cucamonga also had to be closed because the trails were piled high with garbage and the canyon walls covered with graffiti. In 1980, Rancho Cucamonga was 88 percent white and 16 percent Hispanic.[58] By 2010, the town was officially 42.7 percent white and 34.9 percent Hispanic.[59] *USA Today* has a nice photo gallery of "scenic Sapphire Falls," including one shot of four Hispanic men in the act of spray-painting rock cliffs.[60]

But the U.S. Fire Service stressed that it was closing the canyon not because of the trash and spray-painted gang symbols, but as a simple fire precaution.[61] Most of the canyon remains closed to this day.[62] Overwhelming popular opinion on hiking blogs was that the closure of Sapphire Falls was due to the epic amounts of trash and graffiti in the canyon, put there by Mexicans:

August 2013

Yes this is above Rancho Cucamonga, the Beverly Hills of the IE, but the problem is it's surrounded by places like Fontucky, Rialto, Ontario, and the like. Who do you think writes all that graffiti in the canyon? It's not the high-end soccer moms from Rancho. These guys find these pristine places and ruin them for the rest of us. Same thing happened to Rosarito, Mexico in the 90s (off-topic I know, but illustrates my point). I wouldn't bring my wife or teenage daughters here.[63]

March 2014

I grew up down the street from here. And as a kid (1990s), we used to gather all the neighborhood kids and walk up to the falls on hot summer days.... I have noticed the past few years, it was pretty much always crowded and the trail was littered with trash and graffiti.... The same thing happened to Joshua Tree National Park last year.... most of the Indian land is now forever closed off to the public because of the disrespect people showed for their ancient monuments....[64]

BUYING OFF THE ENVIRONMENTALISTS

Where are the environmentalists? For fifty years, they've been carrying on about overpopulation; promoting family planning, birth control, abortion; and saying old people have a "duty to die and get out of the way"—in Colorado's Democratic Governor Richard Lamm's words. In 1971, Oregon governor and environmentalist Tom McCall told a CBS interviewer, "Come visit us again.... But for heaven's sake, don't come here to live." How about another 30 million people coming here to live?

The Sierra Club began sounding the alarm over the country's expanding population in 1965—the very year Teddy Kennedy's immigration act passed[65]—and in 1978, adopted a resolution expressly asking Congress to "conduct a thorough examination of U.S. immigration laws." For a while, the Club talked about almost nothing else. "It is obvious," the Club said two years later, "that the numbers of immigrants the United States accepts affects our population size and growth rate," even more than "the number of children per family."[66] Over the next three decades, America took in tens of millions of legal immigrants and illegal aliens alike.

But, suddenly, about ten years ago, the Sierra Club realized to its embarrassment that importing multiple millions of polluting, fire-setting, littering immigrants is actually fantastic for the environment! The advantages of overpopulation dawned on the Sierra Club right after it received a $100 million donation from hedge fund billionaire David Gelbaum with the express stipulation that—as he told the *Los Angeles Times*—"if they ever came out anti-immigration, they would never get a dollar from me."[67]

It would be as if someone offered the Catholic Church $100 million to be pro-abortion. But the Sierra Club said: *Sure! Did you bring the check?* Obviously, there's no longer any reason to listen to them on anything. They want us to get all excited about some widening of a road that's going to disturb a sandfly, but the Sierra Club is totally copasetic with our national parks being turned into garbage dumps.

Not only did the Sierra Club never again say another word against immigration, but, in 2004, it went the extra mile, denouncing three actual environmentalists running for the Club's board, by claiming they were racists who opposed mass immigration. The three "white supremacists" were Dick Lamm, the three-time Democratic governor of Colorado; Frank Morris, former head of the Black Congressional Caucus Foundation; and Cornell professor David Pimentel, who created the first ecology course at the university in 1957 and had no particular interest in immigration.[68] But they couldn't be bought off, so they were called racists.

America's premiere hate group, the Southern Poverty Law Center, jumped into the fray, with multimillionaire con man and SPLC head Morris Dees running for the Sierra Club board simply to smear the three real environmentalist candidates as "white supremacists"—yes, even the former head of the Black Congressional Caucus Foundation. Dees had never before shown the slightest interest in environmentalism. But, evidently, what poor Southerners need most is a massive influx of foreign poor people competing for their jobs. And what the environment needs most is millions of poor immigrants trashing our national parks. Now the alliance makes sense, no?

In 2012, Sierra Club executive director Michael Brune announced that the Club officially supported mass immigration—amnesty, no borders, more legal immigration, the whole nine yards. "The Sierra Club," he gushed, "has thrived because of the ability for our members to engage with the full tools of democracy."[69] Businessmen seeking cheap labor take note: The Sierra Club's "tools of democracy" are new voters, who will give the Left hegemonic control of our politics. At that point, the EPA will start shutting down power plants, coal mines, oil exploration, and so on.

Environmentalists can't keep ignoring immigration forever. They have eyes. If mass-immigration enthusiasts want to make the argument that preserving America's natural wilderness is not as important as transforming our culture to a poorer and more Latin one, then they should make that argument. Instead we get bald-faced lies from the government, silence from the press, and bought-off "environmentalists" denouncing anyone who threatens their money supply.

13

CARLOS SLIM:
THE *NEW YORK TIMES'*
SUGAR DADDY

CAN WE TRUST ANYTHING THE *NEW YORK TIMES* SAYS ABOUT IMMIGRATION?
In 2008, the world's richest man, Carlos Slim Helu, saved the *Times* from bankruptcy. When that guy saves your company, you dance to his tune. So it's worth mentioning that Slim's fortune depends on tens of millions of Mexicans living in the United States, preferably illegally.

That is, unless the *Times* is some bizarre exception to the normal pattern of corruption—which you can read about at this very minute in the *Times*. If a tobacco company owned Fox News, would we believe their reports on the dangers of smoking? (Guess what else Slim owns? A tobacco company!) The *Times* impugns David and Charles Koch for funneling "secret cash" into a "right-wing political zeppelin."[1] The Kochs' funding of Americans for Prosperity is hardly "secret." What most people think of as "secret cash" is more like Carlos Slim's purchase of favorable editorial opinion in the Newspaper of Record.

It would be fun to have a "Sugar Daddy–Off" with the *New York Times*: Whose Sugar Daddy Is More Loathsome? The Koch Brothers? The Olin

Foundation? Monsanto? Halliburton? Every time, Carlos Slim would win by a landslide. Normally, Slim is the kind of businessman the *Times*—along with every other sentient human being—would find repugnant.

Frequently listed as the richest man in the world, Slim acquired his fortune through a corrupt inside deal giving him a monopoly on telecommunications services in Mexico. But in order to make money from his monopoly, Slim needs lots of Mexicans living in the United States, sending money to their relatives back in Oaxaca. Otherwise, Mexicans couldn't pay him—and they wouldn't have much need for phone service, either—other than to call in ransom demands.

Back in 2004—before the *Times* became Slim's pimp—a *Times* article stated: "Clearly...the nation's southern border is under siege."[2] But that was before Carlos Slim saved the *Times* from bankruptcy. Ten years later, with a border crisis even worse than in 2004, and Latin Americans pouring across the border, the *Times* indignantly demanded that Obama "go big" on immigration and give "millions of immigrants permission to stay."[3]

What a difference one thieving Mexican billionaire makes!

True, it's not unusual for the *Times* to root for the destruction of the United States. Maybe, in this particular instance, the *Times* agrees with every single thing Slim says. Perhaps there was a secret meeting with Slim: *You may have saved us, Carlos Slim, but this newspaper will be in no way cognizant of your financial interest in continued illegal immigration. You're just very lucky that we happen to agree with you. However, if you get into offshore drilling, we will take a VERY strong position against you.*

On the other hand, there's no question but that the *Times* has become exceptionally shrill on immigration since Slim saved the company from bankruptcy.

CARLOS SLIM: FAT, PUDGY WHITE KNIGHT

In 2008, the *Times* was hemorrhaging money. Evidently people were finding more economical means to line their birdcages. In less than a decade, the stock had collapsed from $45 a share to $15 a share. Ratings agencies were threatening to lower the *Times'* debt rating to junk bond status.[4] By the fall of 2008, advertising sales were cratering, and the company had a $400 million line of financing coming due in May 2009—with no hope of borrowing any more money. Poor minorities don't get in as much trouble with zero-down mortgages as the Newspaper of Record had with its loans.

The *Times* began offering buyouts to the news staff and then, not getting enough of them, warned of firings. Company-wide spending cuts of $230 million were announced.[5] (The announcements were published in the *Times*, so few people noticed.) As the clock ticked on the *Times'* $400 million credit line, insiders were predicting catastrophe for the Old Gray Lady. "For the first time," one *Times* employee said, "people really are thinking this place could go bankrupt."[6] According to *New York* magazine: "Fantasies about a white-knight businessman who might 'save' the *Times* with a cash infusion abound in the newsroom and in media circles across the city."[7]

The white-knight fantasies ran more toward Michael Bloomberg or Google executives than a Mexican robber baron, but beggars can't be choosers. And that's how the *New York Times* got in bed with a monopolist looter whose wealth depends on millions of Mexicans moving to the United States.

The newspaper's own Mexican correspondent questioned the deal, calling Slim "the consummate monopolist" and asking: "Does being embroiled in a business culture of back-scratching and unseen forces make him a great partner for the *Times*? I don't think so."[8] The source of Slim's wealth is his telecommunications monopoly, handed to him by Mexican President Carlos Salinas in 1990.[9] As *New York Times* financial reporter Eduardo Porter put it—one year before Slim became the *Times'* benefactor—Slim got his enormous wealth by "theft."[10]

HE'S A GENIUS! HE HAS A MONOPOLY!

In 2012, the Organisation for Economic Co-operation and Development (OECD) issued a scathing report on Slim, accusing him of impoverishing

Mexico while feathering his own nest with a telephone monopoly. Slim's control of 70 percent of the mobile market in Mexico—far higher than in any other country in the OECD—allows him to pocket a profit of nearly twice the world average for major telecommunications companies.[11]

As Porter put it in the once-trusted pages of the *Times* Business Section: "Mr. Slim is richer even than the robber barons of the gilded age.... It takes about nine of the captains of industry and finance of the 19th and early 20th centuries—Rockefeller, Cornelius Vanderbilt, John J. Astor, Andrew Carnegie, Alexander Stewart, Frederick Weyerhaeuser, Jay Gould and Marshall Field—to replicate the footprint that Mr. Slim has left on Mexico."[12]

At least those magnates created something. Slim was handed a monopoly for a fully developed product, which he has done nothing to improve upon—unless threatening to imprison your competitors is considered a major innovation. When government officials pressured Slim to stop gouging Mexicans for their Telmex phone service in 2006, Slim demanded that the officials be thrown in jail. A spokesman for Slim's Telmex later admitted the threat, clarifying to the *Columbia Journalism Review* that imprisonment was not the "goal."[13] Well, yeah—obviously. The "goal" was to block government interference in his monopoly so he could keep fleecing Mexicans.

Carlos Slim has shown more gusto for arresting Mexicans than our own border patrol has. "When competitors were eventually allowed in," the *Times*' Porter wrote in 2007, "Telmex kept them at bay with some rather creative gambits, like getting a judge to issue an arrest warrant for the top lawyer of a competitor."[14] One of Slim's business rivals, speaking anonymously, told the *New Yorker* about two guys showing up at his office and informing him "that if we didn't take down our microwave link, Telmex was going to cut all our telecommunications."[15]

That was done by the man the *New York Times* is in hock to.

Because of Slim's government-granted monopoly, Mexico is, according to the OECD:

- Dead last among OECD countries in the number of fixed telephone lines per capita—seventeen per one hundred people;
- Second to last in the number of cell phones per person; and
- Third from last in broadband penetration, with Mexico doing better than only Turkey and Chile.[16]

Mexico is far from the poorest Latin American nation—it's about mid-range—but it has the fewest cell phones per capita of any Central or South American country.[17] Ninety-eight percent of Venezuelans have cell phones. Only 78 percent of Mexicans do. The internet has changed the world—except in Mexico, where Slim's monopoly ensures that broadband is twice as expensive as in any other OECD country.[18] When Mexican professor and journalist Denise Dresser returned to Mexico after several years abroad, she was shocked to discover that the exact same telephone/internet setup she had in Los Angeles would cost three times as much. "I started studying why the Mexican economy doesn't grow," Dresser said. "So much led me back to Carlos Slim."[19] Her body has never been found. (Joke.) (I think.) In the *Economist*'s ranking of crony countries, the magazine reported that Mexico was one of the worst, "mainly because of Carlos Slim."[20]

Slim steals from the people—and the people love him! "To many Mexicans," the *New Yorker* said, "Slim's wealth is a matter of pride." A 2009 poll found Mexicans ranking Slim "the great leader Mexico needs."[21] They might want to reconsider that. Slim isn't Mexican. He's of Lebanese descent. Usually someone in Slim's position is known as an "imperialist oppressor."

This is the man to whom the *New York Times* owes its lifeblood.

Without a monopoly, Slim doesn't look like such a genius. He bought CompUSA in 2000; by 2008, the company had closed its doors.[22] He bought a gold mine in Mexico just before the floor dropped out on gold. His purchase of a portion of the UK *Independent* in 2008 was, as he admitted, a mistake—"a bad one."[23] The single good investment Slim has made may well be his decision to bail the *New York Times* out of imminent collapse.

True, the stock crashed from fifteen dollars to six as soon as Slim began acquiring shares. Even *Times* insiders thought Slim's investment was "crazy."[24] But what they don't understand is that Slim relies on immense, continuing Mexican immigration to the United States, both legal and illegal, for his fortune. Buying pro–illegal immigration coverage in America's most influential newspaper was a wise business investment.

HOW "THE RICHEST MAN IN THE WORLD" MAKES MONEY ON ILLEGAL IMMIGRATION

One of the ways Slim makes money off of illegal immigration in the United States is by overcharging Mexicans to call home, especially during World Cup soccer season. Slim takes a percentage of all cell phone calls into Mexico—and Telmex's "interconnection rates" are astronomical.[25] International roaming rates are 37 percent higher in Mexico than the average of all OECD countries.[26]

But the main way illegal immigrants benefit Slim is through their remissions. Monopolistic pricing is of little value in a poor country. A monopoly on air in Burundi would not produce the world's richest man. Luckily for Slim, Mexico is located right next to one of the wealthiest nations in the world. The OECD estimates that Slim's suffocating telecommunications monopoly costs Mexican consumers $26 billion a year, with more than half of that coming from Slim gouging his customers.[27] They would have $20 billion less to spend without 40 million Mexicans living in the United States.[28]

According to the World Bank and the International Monetary Fund, Mexican immigrants or those of Mexican descent send at least $20 billion out of America back to their relatives in Mexico each year.[29] No wonder immigrants are so reliant on welfare—they're sending so much of it out of the country! Twenty billion dollars is significantly more—about a quarter more—than the amount of money the United States sends to Mexico in direct foreign aid.[30] The $20 billion being sent to immigrants' grandmothers in Chiapas is forever eliminated from the American economy—unavailable for investment in American companies, the purchase of American products, or hiring American workers. That's a cost of immigration that Americans are never told about.

These billions of dollars being drained out of the U.S. economy every year would be bad enough if the money were coming exclusively from cheap-labor employers like Sheldon Adelson. But it's worse than that. It comes from American taxpayers. Not only do taxpayers have to support Americans who lose their jobs to low-wage immigrant laborers, taxpayers support the immigrants, too. Seventy-five percent of immigrant families from Mexico are on government assistance.[31]

Then they turn around and give the money to Carlos Slim. Seventy-three percent of legal Mexican immigrants send money back to their native land and 83 percent of *illegal* immigrants do.[32] Only because $20 billion is being sent by immigrants out of the United States, back to Mexico, can Slim continue to gouge customers for his crappy products. The majority of the money sent by immigrants to Mexico is used for "consumption"—i.e., to buy Carlos Slim's telephone service, shop at Carlos Slim's department stores, and eat in Carlos Slim's restaurants.[33] Slim's businesses account for 40 percent of all publicly traded companies on Mexico's main stock market index. He owns more than two hundred businesses—banks, retail outlets, restaurant chains, hotels, an airline, a mining company, Sears Mexico, a bottling company, a cigarette manufacturer, and construction, insurance, and real estate companies.

What would all those businesses be worth in Burundi?

That's why, in 2014, Slim was exhorting Mexican youth to cross illegally into the United States for jobs. The stated purpose of Obama's open defiance of American immigration laws was to avoid punishing "children" who were brought to the United States by their parents. Slim didn't care about that. (Then again, neither did Obama.) He just wanted more Mexicans working in America and sending dollars back to him. As the CEO of the "Carlos Slim Foundation" explained, "[O]ur goal is to reduce the access barriers for them to reach this potential...to build not just them but their families, so they're able to contribute to the economy"—i.e., the Mexican economy owned by Carlos Slim.[34]

Slim's income stream takes a circuitous route, going from American taxpayers, to government assistance programs, to the immigrant, to his relatives in Mexico, to services, food, and clothes sold by...Carlos Slim! It would be simpler if Americans cut Slim a check for $20 billion every year, but taxpayers might object to being bilked to support a Mexican plutocrat.

THE *NYT* PROTECTS SLIM'S INCOME STREAM

So the media hide the truth about this massive theft from the taxpayers to fund a foreign racketeer. One begins to understand why Slim wanted control of the "Newspaper of Record." Since Slim saved the paper in 2008, the *Times* has been fervent in support of illegal immigration. Oddly, for a newspaper based in America, the *Times* celebrates the vast amounts of money being sucked out of the U.S. economy. The *Times* thinks it's great that "the poor themselves" decide how much money to transfer from our economy to their home countries' economies.[35] But that's because such remittances are a crucial part of Slim's business plan.

In 2014, when banks raised their fees for transfers of money out of the United States to avoid abetting money laundering, the *Times* rebuked the financial institutions, saying, "[I]t is not credible for banks to suggest that it's too hard to tell suspicious transfers to, say, Sudan, from legitimate remittances to, say..." Guess which country? Guess! That's right: "Mexico." Rushing to protect Slim's money stream, the *Times* editorial demanded that "other secure, low-cost options" be found, even suggesting that the World Bank get into the remittance business.[36]

The *Times* chose to publish this editorial on transfers of money to Mexico at a time when there was other news in the world—the U.S. primary elections, a Supreme Court decision on religious freedom and Obamacare, new Obamacare website "glitches," illegal aliens pouring across the border, more shootings in Chicago, an Ebola virus outbreak in Africa, Russia violating a missile treaty, Israeli airstrikes on Palestinians, new Snowden revelations about the CIA spying on Germany, global warming still incinerating the planet, and the Republicans' infernal War on Women.

True, people have different ideas about what constitutes a major stop-the-presses story and what is D-Section stuff, but making it easier for foreigners to transfer money out of the U.S. economy was an odd choice for an editorial. Instead of another hard-hitting piece on "the glass ceiling," the *Times* chose to devote valuable editorial space to fretting over a potential slowdown in Carlos Slim's collection of $20 billion from Mexicans living in the United States. It would be as if the *Times* had been rescued by Google—and then began indignantly defending corporate tax havens.

The *New York Times* is far more compromised by having Carlos Slim as its sugar daddy than any conservative is by the Koch Brothers. The *Times* is not just beholden to Slim; he holds the very life of the paper in his pinky-ringed, perfumed, fat Mexican hand. Normally, it's easy to predict the *New York Times'* position on any issue, because: a) it never changes; and b) it is referenced on a weekly basis in the pages of the *Times*. But that's not true of immigration. Since Slim waddled in, the *Times* has altered its stance from mild concern about illegal immigration to bubble-headed cheerleading for illegal immigration.

Cheerleaders: *OUR TEAM IS AWESOME.*
But seriously, you have to admit that Duke has a better basket-
    ball team than Yeshiva.
Cheerleaders: *NO! YESHIVA ROCKS! WE RULE!*

How else can one explain the *Times* responding to a surge of hundreds of thousands of illegal immigrants into the country by calling for Congress to grant them amnesty? And with passion! According to the *Times*, Obama's "most urgent priority" in response to an invasion along our southern border "should be giving these children lawyers and caregivers."[37] This wasn't run-of-the-mill liberal insanity. A few days earlier, *Washington Post* editor Charles Lane wrote: "Only by showing people there is nothing to be gained by paying traffickers for the traumatic voyage through Mexico will the chaos cease."[38] Of course, Lane hadn't been bailed out of bankruptcy by Carlos Slim.

THE *TIMES* CHANGES ITS TUNE

If the lunacy of the *Times*' editorials doesn't grab you, how about the fact that the newspaper has become noticeably hysterical about illegal immigration since Carlos Slim came on board? In 1997—the pre-Slim days—the *Times* had editorialized: "Fighting illegal immigration is a difficult and important job. But Congress should do it in a way that will deter illegal entry at the border."[39] Another editorial that year complained that the Immigration and Naturalization Service had "done a poor job of keeping out illegal aliens, deporting criminals [and] processing requests for asylum."[40] This wasn't even Bush-bashing—Clinton was president!

Post-Slim, the *Times* tends more toward deranged hectoring in favor of illegal immigration. In the *Times*' 2014 "Go Big" editorial—the one insisting that Obama grant permanent residence to illegal immigrants streaming across the border—the *Times* sniped: "Republicans will howl over Mr. Obama's solo actions. Let them."

The *Times* should never stop hearing about Carlos Slim. By all the rules of the Left, you're not supposed to trust someone beholden to a rich man, especially one with a specific interest in public policy. If Slim had saved any company in the world other than the *New York Times*, his sleazy insider deals and business model based on mass illegal immigration to the United States would absolutely be a problem. *But you forgot something—we're the* New York Times! *We're the good guys. You're not factoring that in.*

SOLVING "THE SERVANT PROBLEM"

From Carlos Slim to urban professionals, ethnic activists, greedy "churches," and Republican lobbyists, no one who supports mass immigration does not benefit financially from it. *New York Times* sugar daddy Carlos Slim is just a particularly repellant example of the bald self-interest behind the demand for a never-ending tide of poor immigrants to the United States. *Don't you understand? People on Wall Street are about to have to pay minimum wage for a nanny!* It's not about loving Hispanics—it's about cheap servants.

Republicans are terrified of saying anything about immigration for fear of being called "racist." It's kind of lucky for American billionaires—and one Mexican billionaire—that the vast majority of our immigrants are Latin America's poor, not Poland's poor. The fact that most immigrants are Hispanic provides excellent cover for the elite's monumental self-interest.

Here's a tip for the GOP: Don't talk about the illegal aliens. Talk about Carlos Slim. Talk about rich Americans finding a solution to "the servant problem." Talk about one-hit-wonder Mark Zuckerberg underpaying his computer programmers while 32 percent of American graduates in STEM fields (science, technology, engineering, and math) can't get jobs and the rest haven't seen their salaries rise for more than a decade.[41]

Talk about how Bill Clinton couldn't find someone to be his attorney general because of the prevalence of illegal alien employees in households of the "1 percent." Determined to appoint a woman attorney general, Clinton kept producing women with illegal alien nannies. In the end, he had to get around the rich's dependence on cheap domestics by nominating Janet Reno to fill the spot.

Clinton first nominated Zoë Baird, an in-house lawyer for Aetna Life and Casualty. Then it turned out Baird had employed illegal aliens, Lillian and Victor Corderos, as her household's nanny and chauffeur. The media ferociously defended Baird, explaining how "commonplace" illegal alien workers were in professional households. "It's just a reality of life," one head of an employment agency told the *Times*, "that without the illegal girls, there wouldn't be any nannies, and the mommies would have to stay home and mind their own kids."[42] Are you grasping the full horror of the situation?

Another employment agency admitted it was just about saving the rich money: "No matter how you slice it, the reason that people hire immigrants without papers is that they're looking to save. If they want legal, they can get it, but it costs."[43] Baird, for example, who was making half a million dollars a year, got two illegal alien servants for forty-two dollars a day each, plus room and board.[44] The *Times* cheerfully described illegal alien help for the rich as a "pragmatic" arrangement "linking illegal immigrants and middle-class homes." The newspaper said that as "more American women with young children moved into the workplace, the demand for housekeepers increased exponentially."[45]

Notwithstanding the *Times*' heartfelt defense of the rich and their maids, Americans responded by deluging the Capitol switchboard with enraged calls assailing Baird's employment of illegals. The phone calls were running 50–1 against her, according to Democratic Senator Howard Metzenbaum of Ohio.[46] It was left to Senator Joe Biden, Delaware Democrat, to explain to the Clinton White House that most Americans do not have a retinue of illegal alien servants.

Baird was forced to withdraw her name from consideration and returned to her half-a-million-dollar-a-year job. The Corderos were not so fortunate. Solely on account of the ruckus over Baird's nomination, they were forced to return to Peru, under threat of deportation. And thus ended the humanitarian crisis in Peru as far as Zoë Baird was concerned.

Even after seeing what had happened with Baird, Clinton's next nominee, Kimba Wood, also had an illegal alien nanny! In three interviews for the job—twice by White House counsel Bernie Nussbaum, and once by the president himself—Wood flatly denied that she had a "Zoë Baird problem," apparently on the grounds that when she first hired her illegal alien

Trinidadian nanny it was not technically against the law. In her withdrawal letter, Wood kept obtusely insisting that she had not broken the letter of the law.[47]

The elites just can't grasp that most Americans raise their own kids, make their own beds, cook their own food, and drive their own cars. A decade later, another pro–illegal immigration activist saw her nomination go up in flames over an illegal alien employee. President-Elect Bush chose Linda Chavez as his labor secretary, but she was forced to withdraw when it was revealed that she, too, had hired an illegal alien domestic. Defending the rich's need for cheap labor, Chavez said, "I do believe that Zoë Baird was treated unfairly."[48]

BUT IT'S GREAT FOR THE RICH!

The push for mass immigration from "developing" countries has nothing to do with solving world poverty. It would be an odd way to do it: *I know—let's move all the poor people to American suburbs!* According to the World Bank, 2.4 billion people—about a third of the earth's population—live on less than two dollars a day.[49] Until the world economy reaches perfect equilibrium and there is no reason for anyone to move from one country to another, billions of desperate people will want to come to America. We can't take them all, so which billion of the starving masses are liberals going to exclude? Will it involve death panels? Are liberals going to trample on the rights of Bangladeshis? They're dying of cholera! Is it their brown skin liberals don't like? Sorry, liberals, but your white picket fence sense of America and fear of "Furriners" can't hold back the 2.4 billion in this worldwide humanitarian crisis.

Our current immigration law's preference for destitute people from backward cultures is merely a convenience for the 1 percent. The elites will be gung-ho for a fence just as soon as every college graduate—at least from one of the better schools—can afford a maid, a nanny, a chef, and a gardener. At that point, the elite will stop pretending to care about the world's poor. America will be Brazil, with a well-pampered, itty-bitty upper class, amid an ocean of poor people.

Half a century of Kennedy's immigration law already has us well on our way to becoming a nation of Have-Everythings and Have-Nothings. Fabulously wealthy towns like Malibu, California; Atherton, California; Woodside, California; Greenwich, Connecticut; New York's Upper East Side; and Palm Beach, Florida, are lily-white—and getting whiter! But in the rest of the country, once-white towns are going majority Hispanic like dominoes: Van Nuys, California; San Bernardino, California; Oxnard, California; Shelbyville, Kentucky; Danbury, Connecticut; Monroe, North Carolina; and Siler City, North Carolina—home of *The Andy Griffith Show*'s "Aunt Bee." It's a sweet deal the elites have: They get to have cheap nannies and lawn boys in the whitest towns in America—*and* feel morally superior at the same time! What's not to like about that?

Immigration isn't about rescuing the 2.4 billion people of the world living on less than two dollars a day. It's about enriching the already rich, who like to laugh at blue-collar people being ground down by cheap labor. It's about Carlos Slim, Zoë Baird, Kimba Wood, Mark Zuckerberg, and Sheldon Adelson getting richer. It's about the gilded class being able to afford a battery of servants. It's about ethnic activists increasing their power and media desirability. It's about Democrats winning a permanent political majority. And it's about Republican officeholders pleasing their well-heeled donors and clinging to power, at least for a few more years. What use does New Jersey Governor Chris Christie have for an out-of-work roofer when Mark Zuckerberg wants to be his friend? The only people not benefiting from immigration are ordinary Americans. But who cares about them?

Certainly not the *New York Times*. They just want to keep Carlos Slim happy.

SPOT THE IMMIGRANT!
CASE NO. 4 | INDIAN SEX SLAVES IN BERKELEY

ONE MAY IMAGINE MARCIA POOLE'S SURPRISE WHEN SHE WAS DRIVING through Berkeley one day in 1999 and saw a group of Indian men carrying an oddly shaped, rolled carpet to the back of a van. As Poole continued to watch, she saw a woman's leg fall out of the carpet. Nearby, other men were trying to drag a crying Indian girl into the same van with the rolled-up human body.

Poole tried to intervene, but the head Indian yelled at her to butt out of a "family affair." Then, at the sound of police sirens, all the Indians scattered, leaving her alone with the van, the rolled-up body, and the crying girl.

As Poole was telling the police what she'd seen, the Indians returned one by one, as if they happened to be strolling through the neighborhood. *Oh look—a van with an unconscious thirteen-year-old girl rolled up in a carpet!*

On closer inspection, the police found not only the girl in the van, but another young female body in the building's stairwell.

The head Indian turned out to be multimillionaire real estate magnate Lakireddy Bali Reddy. He told the police that the girls were his nieces. Their roommate—the crying girl—had come back to their shared apartment, which he owned, to find them unconscious. All three worked in his restaurant, so the girl called him and the big happy family was in the process of transporting the girls to a hospital. In a rolled-up carpet.[1] The girl in the stairwell was dead. Both victims had suffered from carbon monoxide poisoning, though the one in the carpet later recovered.

Would any of this seem at all suspicious if white men were caught doing it?

It was not suspicious to the Berkeley police. In a flash of investigative genius Inspector Clouseau would admire, the policewoman on the scene allowed Bali Reddy to translate for the crying girl, who did not speak English. Amazingly, she confirmed his story! Lieutenant Cynthia Harris, chief of detectives for the Berkeley Police Department, later acknowledged that "in hindsight, we should not have done that."[2] "How does "Chief of Police Harris" sound, Cynthia?

Reddy was assessed a fine for the carbon monoxide leaking from a broken heater in his building. And that was the end of that, as far as the police and the media were concerned. Lakireddy Bali Reddy—another immigrant success story!

LAKIREDDY BALI REDDY'S "HIGH-TECH WORKERS"

Except then a local high school journalism class decided to investigate the story. Not having attended Columbia Journalism School, the young scribes were unaware of the prohibition on committing journalism that reflects poorly on Third World immigrants. Thanks to the teenagers' reporting, it was discovered that Reddy had become a multimillionaire by using H-1B visas to bring in slave labor from his native India. Dozens of Indian slaves were working in his buildings and at his restaurant. Apparently, some of those "brainy" high-tech workers America so desperately needs include busboys and janitors.

And concubines. The pubescent girls Reddy brought in on H-1B visas were not his nieces: They were his concubines, purchased from their parents in India when they were twelve years old. The sixty-four-year-old Reddy flew the girls to America so he could have sex with them—often several of them at once. (We can only hope this is not why Mark Zuckerberg is so keen on H-1B visas.)

The third roommate—the crying girl—had escaped the carbon monoxide poisoning only because she had been at Reddy's house having sex with him, which, judging by the looks of him, might be worse than death. As soon as a translator other than Reddy was found, she admitted that "the primary purpose for her to enter the U.S. was to continue to have sex with Reddy." The day her roommates arrived from India, she was forced to watch as the old, balding immigrant had sex with both underage girls at once.[3] She also said her dead roommate had been pregnant with Reddy's child. That could not be confirmed by the court because Reddy had already cremated the girl, in the Hindu tradition—even though her parents were Christian. In all, Reddy had brought seven underage girls to the United States for sex—smuggled in by his brother and sister-in-law, who lied to immigration authorities by posing as the girls' parents.[4]

Reddy's "high-tech" workers were just doing the slavery Americans won't do. *No really—we've tried getting American slaves! We've advertised for slaves at all the local high schools and didn't get a single taker. We even posted flyers at the grade schools, asking for prepubescent girls to have sex with Reddy. Nothing. Not even on Craigslist.*

Reddy's slaves and concubines were considered "untouchables" in India, treated as "subhuman"—"so low that they are not even considered part of Hinduism's caste system," as the *Los Angeles Times* explained. To put it in layman's terms, in India they're considered lower than a Kardashian. According to the Indian American magazine *India Currents*: "Modern slavery is on display every day in India: children forced to beg, young girls recruited into brothels, and men in debt bondage toiling away in agricultural fields." More than half of the estimated 20.9 million slaves worldwide live in Asia.[5]

Thanks to American immigration policies, slavery is making a comeback in the United States! A San Francisco couple "active in the Indian community" bought a slave from a New Delhi recruiter to clean house for them, took away her passport when she arrived, and refused to let her call her family or leave their home.[6] In New York, Indian immigrants Varsha and Mahender Sabhnani were convicted in 2006 of bringing in two Indonesian illegal aliens as slaves to be domestics in their Long Island, New York, home.[7]

In addition to helping reintroduce slavery to America, Reddy sends millions of dollars out of the country in order to build monuments to himself in India. "The more money Reddy made in the States," the *Los Angeles Times* chirped, "the more good he seemed to do in his hometown." That's great for India, but what is America getting out of this model immigrant? Slavery: Check. Sickening caste system: Check. Purchasing twelve-year-old girls for sex: Check. Draining millions of dollars from the American economy: Check. Smuggling half-dead sex slaves out of his slums in rolled-up carpets right under the nose of the Berkeley police: Priceless.

HIGH SCHOOL REPORTERS BREAK THE CASE

He would have gotten off scot-free, with no one the wiser, except for a high school journalism class. Remember: The truth about Reddy's human smuggling racket was broken not by the *San Francisco Chronicle*, but by a high school newspaper, the *Berkeley High Jacket*.[8] Even after high school kids did the work American reporters just won't do, the media ignored the story. The *New York Times* never wrote about Reddy's slaves, unless we're counting a brief reference to Reddy's use of H-1B visas thousands of words into an article on the difficulties employers face in bringing high-tech workers to America.[9]

You've heard about Officer Darren Wilson shooting Mike Brown in Ferguson, Missouri. You've heard about the nonexistent rapes at UVA, the Duke lacrosse team rape case, and that ridiculous woman carrying a mattress around on her back at Columbia University. You've heard that Senator Kirsten Gillibrand claims male senators spoke in sexist language to her. Now ask yourself: Why have you never heard of Lakireddy Bali Reddy?

REPUBLICANS STILL FIGHTING DEMOCRATS OVER SLAVERY

Not just the media, but government officials refused to acknowledge that Reddy had done anything wrong. He's diverse! America is too "white-bread." Slavery is colorful! The appropriately named federal prosecutor, John Kennedy, allowed Reddy to plead to a few counts of tax and immigration fraud and to the importation of two underage girls for sex. For this, Kennedy recommended a sentence of six years. Six years! Before having his sham conviction overturned by the Texas Court of Appeals, former Representative Tom Delay was facing three years in prison for putting campaign funds in the wrong account.

The Republican-appointed black female judge, Saundra Brown Armstrong, apparently thought six years a bit lenient for slavery and ordered the lawyers to come up with a longer sentence. Pressed to the wall, Kennedy recommended *eight* years, which is all that Reddy got. It's one thing for people in Reddy's native village to consider him a king, but did the American prosecutor have to? The American Civil Liberties Union took Reddy's side in the child rape/slavery case. ACLU attorney Jayashri Srikantiah strenuously argued that any sentence longer than six years was too harsh for a model citizen like Reddy.[10] Nothing says "American Civil Liberties" like a sixty-four-year-old Indian importing little girls for sex!

Reddy still lives in California, as do his pimp brother and sister-in-law. So do all of Reddy's victims—and not just his victims in America, but his victims back in India *who had never been to America*. In order to bring a case that ended in a lousy eight-year prison sentence, government officials traveled to India to locate more of Reddy's child rape victims. They were all brought to America and given asylum, despite the fact that none of them would testify against Reddy.[11] Indeed, a few years into Reddy's sentence, five of his concubines came to court to praise Reddy and urge his early release from prison.[12]

So that was a great deal for America. We got the Indian pedophile. We got his H-1B scams. We got a caste system that defines some humans as "untouchable." We got a bunch of girls who think it's normal for their parents to sell them to a sixty-year-old man for sex and who even defend the pedophile. As the *Los Angeles Times* put it, these girls don't understand "just how abhorrent sexual abuse of minors is in U.S. culture."[13] I'm so happy to have them as my fellow Americans. It bodes well for the future of our country.

14

EVERY SINGLE IMMIGRATION CATEGORY IS A FRAUD

THE VAST MAJORITY OF ALL LEGAL IMMIGRANTS—TWO-THIRDS—GET IN ON "family reunification" policies each year. In other words, America has no say about the single largest category of immigrants and we end up with gems like Octomom, the Boston Marathon bombers, and one hundred thousand Somalis in Minnesota. Entire villages from Pakistan are dumped on the country, based not on their expertise in nuclear engineering, but because everyone in the village is related to the first guy who got in. If they're not, in the strict sense, related, they'll lie. In 2008, the State Department suspended the family reunification part of the African refugee program because DNA testing showed that only 20 percent of "family members" were actually related.[1] We'll still take as many refugees from Africa, but they won't have to lie about being related anymore.

The government can't even police marriage fraud. It's a felony to engage in a sham marriage with an immigrant, but no one ever gets caught. In 1997 a thirty-year-old, down on her luck, two-time divorcée married an eighteen-year-old Ethiopian man—and was suddenly $5,000 richer! That seemed totally believable to our immigration officials. The immigration "marriage" was exposed as a scam only when the woman turned up in Oregon fifteen years later as the Democratic governor's "first lady."[2] By then it was too late to prosecute, forget revoking the Ethiopian's citizenship.

MUSLIM TERRORIST FARMWORKERS

The special agricultural amnesty of 1986 is a good example of how even the most reasonable-sounding immigration law will inevitably be turned into a pipeline for criminals, welfare cases, and terrorists. As Congress debated the amnesty bill, newspapers were full of stories about "beleaguered" farmers with crops rotting in the fields who were "sick with worry" that the law would "rob" them of "the migrant workers who are the backbone of the field labor force," as the *Los Angeles Times* put it.[3]

Coming to the rescue was then-Representative Chuck Schumer! (Words that should chill you to the bone.) Illegal alien farmworkers who could prove they had done seasonal farmwork for a total of ninety days between May 1, 1985, and May 1, 1986, would be granted temporary legal status. What could go wrong?

In the first three years of the program, 888,637 agricultural amnesty applications were identified as fraudulent—but only 60,020 of those were denied.[4] Overwhelmed with amnesty applications under just this one provision, the INS found it to be a big time-saver to simply ignore fraud.[5] As one longtime INS employee explained, "Since documentation wasn't required, the burden was on the government to prove the aliens were not farmers. Fraud was widespread and enforcement virtually impossible."[6] Consequently, more than eight hundred thousand deceitful applications for amnesty were granted.

Among the fraudulent farmworker amnesties approved by the INS was one from Egyptian Mahmud Abouhalima,[7] or—as he was known in the terrorist community—"Mahmud the Red." Mahmud had come to the United

States as a "tourist" from Germany—where he had been denied political asylum, but got around that by marrying an emotionally disturbed alcoholic, and then married another German woman after divorcing the first when she objected to his taking a second wife.[8] At the end of 1985, Mahmud and his second wife took a "three-week" trip to the United States on tourist visas and promptly settled into an apartment in Brooklyn.[9] Luckily for Mahmud, just as his tourist visa was expiring six months later, Schumer's farmworker amnesty became law. So Mahmud submitted an application, claiming to have worked on a farm in South Carolina, despite having never left New York, except one short visit to the Michigan Islamic community.[10]

Mahmud was approved. Otherwise, crops would rot in the fields! And what a wonderful agricultural worker Mahmud was. He became a limo driver in New York, where he repeatedly had his license suspended for ripping off customers and speeding through red lights because he was busy reading the Koran. But exhibiting that can-do spirit we so admire in immigrants, Mahmud simply drove without a license, delighting his customers with the Arabic sermons blaring from the car's tape player.[11]

Two years after receiving his "farmworker" amnesty, Mahmud was granted temporary legal residence in the United States. For the next few years, he repeatedly flew to Pakistan for combat training. In 1990, Mahmud became a U.S. permanent resident. That was a big year for Mahmud. In 1990, Mahmud busied himself:

- driving Sheikh Omar Abdel-Rahman, the terrorist known as "the Blind Sheikh" (who managed to stay in the United States by repeatedly applying for asylum);
- murdering Omar's chief rival, Mustafa Shalabi (suspected, crime unsolved);
- providing the getaway car for El Sayyid Nosair, after he assassinated Rabbi Kahane in Brooklyn, although Nosair ended up jumping in the wrong Arab's taxi.[12]

Three years later, Mahmud was one of the main conspirators in the 1993 World Trade Center bombing, which blew a hole in the skyscraper five stories deep, cratered the ceiling of a PATH train, killed six people, injured thousands, and caused half a billion dollars in property damage. Mahmud then fled the country—leaving crops to rot in the field! He was captured by the Egyptians, tried in the United States, and convicted. Without her husband's terrorist income to support her, his German wife now lives on welfare in the United States.[13]

Mohammed Salameh, another terrorist convicted in the 1993 World Trade Center bombing, was also in the United States because of Schumer's special agricultural worker amnesty. The unskilled nineteen-year-old first came to the United States on a tourist visa because, as the U.S. consulate later explained, someone in the office "took a chance" on Mohammed.[14] Mohammed not only had never worked on a farm, but he was not even in the country until 1988, two years *after* the special amnesty became law, though it was explicitly limited to those who had worked on farms in the United States *in the year before May 1, 1986.*

By the most basic definition of the law, Mohammed was not eligible, but he was allowed to stay in the United States and obtain a work visa— while the INS processed his petition. Moving with the lightning speed of a government agency, the INS rejected his petition for amnesty as a farmworker three years later. Then, Mohammed applied for a general amnesty, claiming he had been living continuously in the United States from 1982 to 1986. Actually, he was a teenager in Jordan then, but again, Mohammed was allowed to stay while the INS considered his request. As it was considering, Mohammed bombed the World Trade Center.[15]

Even if someone at the INS had promptly rejected his application, noticing that Mohammed only arrived in the United States in 1988—he still couldn't have been deported. Schumer had included a provision prohibiting the INS from taking any action against any immigrant who merely *applied* for agricultural amnesty. That might discourage fraudulent applications! No matter how laughably fictional, Mohammed's request for a farmworker amnesty immunized him from deportation. He would still be setting off bombs as a frustrated farmworker had he not returned the van used in the bombing to the Ryder rental agency to get his deposit back.[16] Gosh, we really are getting the smartest immigrants.

The ringleader of the 1993 World Trade Center bombing was Ramzi Yousef. He came to the United States without a visa but claimed asylum and was released into the country. He got a free immigration lawyer from the white-shoe law firm Willkie Farr & Gallagher.[17] With pinpoint timing, one year before the World Trade Center bombing—committed by a couple of "farmworkers," an asylum seeker, and several "tourists"—the *New Republic* published an indignant screed about the heartless storm troopers at the INS, who see their jobs as "enforcement" rather than "providing public services and immigration benefits"—in the words of Ignatius Bau of San Francisco's Coalition for Immigration Reform.[18]

NOT-SO-HIGH-TECH WORKERS

What about all those brainy, high-tech H-1B immigrants that Senator Orrin Hatch keeps telling us about?

The media gush about the legions of star-performer immigrants, but, suspiciously, they always list the exact same ones—all white, all male, and of British, Dutch, German, and Russian stock: Peter Thiel of PayPal, Palantir Technologies, etc. (born in Germany); Elon Musk of X.com, Tesla, etc. (born in South Africa—to a Canadian mother and a South African–born British father); Sergey Brin of Google (born in Russia). None of them came to the United States on H-1B visas.

For an objective view of high-tech immigrants, the *New York Times* turned to Vivek Wadhwa, who boasted that "over half of Silicon Valley tech start-ups and a quarter of those nationwide were founded by immigrants from 1995–2005." It's probably not a coincidence that Wadhwa did not say what fraction of these "start-ups" were either successful or original. There are lots of me-too startups ripping off investors and adding nothing to the economy. Wadhwa excitedly added that a "majority" of Indian and Chinese immigrants who go home "want to start a company."[19] Yes, and a majority of girls who go to Hollywood "want to be movie stars."

Wadhwa said it was "troubling" that "47 percent of all U.S. science and engineering workers with doctorates are immigrants." If doctorates in science or engineering are so important, why don't any of the stars in Silicon Valley have one? A lot of the biggest names—Gates, Jobs, and Zuckerberg—don't even have undergraduate degrees.

As long as the media hide the details, it's easy for Indian American Wadhwa to claim that "[t]he next Google could well be cooked up in a garage in Guangzhou or Ahmedabad."[20] Where are all the Indian Googles and Paypals now? This importation of cheap tech workers has been going on for decades.[21] Already, 65 percent of all high-tech visas go to Indians. Sixty-five percent! The next-largest H-1B visa holders are the Chinese, filling 12 percent of the slots. We better be getting a few Asian geniuses.

But judging by the articles they write, Indians' main talent is self-promotion. Ron Banerjee—another objective source—gloats in the *Financial Post* that "the wealth and success of Indian immigrants is undeniable."[22] In the *International Business Times*, Harichandan Arakali asks: "India's Startup Scene: Will VC Dollars Create the Next Amazon?"[23] The *Washington Post*'s Vinod Dham says, "Indian engineers on H-1B visas have…contributed significantly to advancing innovation in high technology."[24] Yet another article about how awesome Indians are—written by Neesha Bapat—is titled: "How Indians Defied Gravity and Achieved Success in Silicon Valley."[25]

Apparently, Indians think they're just peachy! If white Americans expressed this much regard for themselves, it would be "racist." Here's how such an article might read:

How White American Men Defied Gravity and Achieved Success in Silicon Valley

Did you know Twitter was created by four American white men? Yes, Jack Dorsey, Evan Williams, Biz Stone, and Noah Glass defied gravity and achieved success in Silicon Valley. All white Americans!

How about these companies also created by white American men? Netscape (Jim Clark and Marc Andreessen), Mozilla Firefox (Dave Hyatt and Blake Ross), Netflix (Marc Randolph and Reed Hastings), Oracle (Larry Ellison, Bob Miner, and Ed Oates), Apple Computer (Steve Jobs and Steve Wozniak [the adopted Jobs's biological father was a Syrian immigrant, admitted under the pre-1965 immigration act], Pandora (Will Glaser, Jon Kraft, and Tim Westergren), Zillow (Richard Barton), Wikipedia (Jimmy Wales), Craigslist (Craig Newmark), Uber (Garrett Camp and Travis Kalanick—technically a Canadian white man), Zynga (Mark Pincus), and Yelp (Jeremy Stoppelman and Russel Simmons).

This list goes on! Why, the next Google might well be cooked up in a garage in Ft. Benton, Montana, or Camden, Maine.

If you think about it, white men have actually accomplished quite a lot.

The cheap-labor advocacy group Partnership for a New American Economy excitedly tweeted that two—yes TWO (2)—of the five LinkedIn founders were, I quote: "born in Europe"![26] They were born in Germany and France. Here's my counter-tweet: "98.7% of the founders of important Silicon Valley companies were born in America! 99 percent are white men!"

H-1B VISAS: INDENTURED SERVITUDE

One person to analyze H-1B visas who's not in it for either cheap labor or ethnic chauvinism is Professor Norman Matloff, who has been writing about so-called high-tech visas for years. He says: "The vast majority of H-1Bs, including those hired from U.S. universities, are ordinary people doing ordinary work, not the best and the brightest. On the contrary, the average quality of the H-1Bs is LOWER than that of the Americans." We're not going to get the guys who designed the Indian nuclear bomb. They're doing fine in India. Why leave?

The main advantage of foreign labor over native workers, Matloff explains, is that H-1B workers are indentured servants: They can't quit without risking deportation, so American employers get to pay less for standard computer programming work. You can imagine what a huge cost-saver that is! Foreign workers go off in cubbyholes, type away at their code for twelve hours, then collapse. Tons of Americans could do the same work, but, the problem is, they want to be paid.

"Employers know they have these workers over a barrel," business professor Sankar Mukhopadhyay explains. "They aren't going to demand a raise during those six years [of green card sponsorship], even if they deserve it, and they aren't going to move on to another company, because they know doing those things will jeopardize their chances of getting their green cards in time." As Benjamin Franklin said in 1751, the main advantage of slaves and indentured servants isn't that their work is better—it's worse. It's that "Slaves may be kept as long as a Man pleases," whereas "hired Men are continually leaving their Master."[27]

CALLING JASON RICHWINE

Microsoft's Bill Gates pleaded with Congress to give him more cheap foreign workers, claiming computer giants like Microsoft were just trying to bring in "smart people," and that H-1B visa holders were so immensely qualified that their salaries started at $100,000 a year.[28] Then it turned out that only 12.4 percent of Microsoft's H-1B holders were paid as much as $100,000—mostly lawyers and other executives.[29] Even worse, since the introduction of the H-1B visa, Microsoft has been laying off American workers by the bushel.[30]

Intel's chairman Craig Barrett must have needed a thesaurus to write his op-ed on the brilliance of H-1B workers. He called them "the world's top talent...highly educated workers...working in high-need jobs...in highly skilled professions...valuable foreign-born professionals—including badly needed researchers, scientists, teachers and engineers...scientists and engineers...highly educated graduates...the top minds...driv[ing] innovation and economic growth...professional talent."[31]

Then Barrett used the H-1B program to fire American workers and replace them with underpaid foreign workers.[32]

If Gates, Barrett, and the rest of them really want "the world's top talent," where were they when Jason Richwine was being crucified for proposing that we do just that? Quite obviously, high-tech employers neither seek, nor desire, "smart people." They want cheap people. Mass-immigration advocates push ethnic stereotypes about high-IQ immigrants, but then go crazy whenever anyone suggests we actually bring in high-IQ immigrants.

As long as we must be incessantly hectored about Indians as high-IQ computer whiz kids, let's take a look at their IQs. You can't play the high-IQ game when it suits your cheap-labor interests, then cry "racism" when those claims are examined. The average Indian IQ is staggeringly low: 82. That's about the same as the average IQ in Afghanistan—84; Panama—84; Dominican Republic—82; Paraguay—84; Yemen—85; Pakistan—84; and Tonga—86.

Yet we take more immigrants from India than from Canada—in fact, we take more from India than from Canada and Great Britain combined. We take more immigrants from India than from Austria, Belgium, Denmark, Finland, Greece, Iceland, Ireland, the Netherlands, New Zealand, Sweden, Switzerland, Spain, and the Czech Republic put together. Why are we discriminating against Canadians, British, Danes, Swiss, and Swedes? The answer is: Because those immigrants would tend to fill the kinds of jobs rich people have. Immigrants are always great—unless they might take your job. Facebook's Mark Zuckerberg isn't looking to bring in people who will take *his* job; he wants immigrants to take his employees' jobs.

It's so obvious what employers like Gates, Barrett, and Zuckerberg are doing that even Public Radio International has noticed. In a story about H-1B visa workers abused by their American employers, PRI quoted one who said, "I'm being paid less, which sucks for me, and it also sucks for American developers because I am a threat to them. I am cheaper."[33]

Indentured servitude was abolished in America in 1867, two years after the Thirteenth Amendment was ratified. Henceforth, *all* employees would have the right to quit. It didn't matter if the employment contract was entered into voluntarily. If a worker couldn't quit, it was serfdom, prohibited by the Peonage Act of 1867.[34]

The great abolitionist senator—Republican, of course—and future vice president Henry Wilson cited the example of New Mexico after it eradicated the "wretched system" of indentured servitude. "[P]eons who once worked for two or three dollars a month," he said, "are now able to command respectable wages, to support their families, elevate themselves, and improve their condition."[35] Democratic Senator Charles Buckalew said the inability to quit resulted in conditions that were "always exceedingly unfavorable to" the employee, adding that the system "degrades all—both the owner of the labor and the laborer himself."[36]

So more than a century ago, everyone agreed: No more indentured servitude. But today's employers have conspired to bring it back with H-1B visas, then they strut around like they're Martin Luther King by invoking the magical word "immigration." Immigration covers a multitude of sins because we have all agreed to pretend mass immigration from the Third World is the same thing as black civil rights.

In the 1960s, leftists were at least self-destructive: They wanted to damage the country in ways that would hurt *them*, *their* parents, and *their* kids. The New Left has found a way to be self-righteous only after checking to make sure they've completely exempted themselves from the destruction they're wreaking. Liberals will pull every string imaginable to prevent their own kids from having to compete with immigrants—and then demand cheap employees for themselves. The middle class and lower class take it in the shorts—and the elites get to feel noble.

15

SHUT IT DOWN

THE ONLY THING THAT STANDS BETWEEN AMERICA AND OBLIVION IS A TOTAL immigration moratorium. There's no possibility of quick fixes. The entire immigration bureaucracy has to be shut down. It's evident that the government can't be trusted to use three brain cells in admitting immigrants, so its discretion has to be completely revoked. No matter how clearly laws are written, government bureaucrats connive to confer citizenship on people that a majority of Americans would not want to let in as tourists, much less as our fellow citizens. Instead of trying to do the "Sorcerer's Apprentice" thing, mopping the floor while the water is still pouring in, we need to stop the inflow, then take time to assimilate the immigrants already here.

No other fix will work. Congress could just insist that immigrants pay taxes, learn English, not collect welfare, and have good moral character, except the problem is: It already has. All those laws were swept away by INS officials, judges, and Democratic administrations. Doing it again won't produce a different result.

We trusted the government, and it screwed up.

We can't even expect our immigration officials not to make citizens of convicted felons.[1] Tens of thousands of immigrants have been granted citizenship *after* being convicted of crimes in the United States. And, no, you can't see their names or read about their crimes.

A year before the 1996 presidential election, the Clinton White House worked feverishly to naturalize 1 million immigrants in time for Clinton's reelection. Criminal background checks were jettisoned for 200,000 applicants, so that citizenship was granted to at least 70,000 people with FBI criminal records and 10,000 with felony records.[2] Murderers, robbers, and rapists were all made our fellow Americans so the Democrats would have a million new voters by the 1996 election. In 2013 alone, the Obama administration released 36,007 convicted criminal aliens with about 88,000 convictions among them—including 426 for rape and 193 for murder.[3] They'll soon be your fellow citizens, too.

Usually, we only find out about all the convicted felons our government is making citizens when there's a political scandal. But it's a daily practice. Consider this small news item from 2011: Twice in one day, the border police arrested Mexicans who had previously been convicted of sex offenses against children in the United States. Neither of the men's original child sex convictions made the news. The truth came out only when the border patrol accidentally mentioned the convictions in press releases about their rearrests.[4] One was illegal alien Eduardo Rodriguez-Lopez, who had been convicted in the United States for sex with a child and deported. The other, Antonio Batista, was a U.S. citizen. He had previously been arrested for human smuggling, sex assault on a minor, and sex abuse.[5]

What does it take to be turned down for citizenship in the United States?

SEND THE LEFTISTS BACK TO PERU

Even if we could trust the government on immigration—and again, we can't—there are the legions of immigration lawyers, lobbyists, nonprofits, and general miscreants whose single-minded mission is to turn America into the Third World hellhole of liberal fantasies.

Everyone in the entire immigration apparatus is working frantically to bring the hardest cases to our shores. Left-wing traitors, who used to honeymoon in Cuba and fight with peasant revolutionaries in Peru, bring endless lawsuits to ensure every genocidal Rwandan can get on the American gravy train. Immigration lawsuits are decided by judges who come from the same nonprofits, and Democratic-appointed federal judges issue lunatic rulings to ensure that there will never be a pause in the transformation of America.

The country won't be safe until the following outfits are out of business:

The ACLU's Immigrants' Rights Freedom Network; the National Immigration Forum; the National Immigration Law Center; the National Immigration Project of the National Lawyers Guild; the National Network for Immigrant and Refugee Rights; the Office of Migration and Refugee Services; the American Immigration Law Foundation; the American Immigration Lawyers Association; the Border Information and Outreach Service; Atlas: DIY; the Catholic Legal Immigration Network; the Clearinghouse for Immigrant Education; the Farmworker Justice Fund; Grantmakers Concerned with Immigrants and Refugees; the Immigrant Legal Resource Center; the Immigrants Support Network; the International Center for Migration, Ethnicity, and Citizenship; the Lesbian and Gay Immigration Rights Taskforce; the Lutheran Immigration and Refugee Service; the National Association for Bilingual Education; the National Clearinghouse on Agricultural Guest Worker Issues; the National Coalition for Dignity and Amnesty for Undocumented Immigrants; the National Coalition for Haitian Rights; the National Council of La Raza; and the National Farm Worker Ministry.

Look at that list and ask yourself if it is possible that anything short of a total immigration moratorium can save this country. And that's just a fraction of the anti-American immigration groups.

The billion-dollar immigration industry has turned every single aspect of immigration law into an engine of fraud. The family reunifications are frauds, the "farmworkers" are frauds, the high-tech visas are frauds—and the asylum and refugee cases are monumental frauds.

WHY DO WE ALWAYS GET LAST PICK IN THE GLOBAL REFUGEE DRAFT?

The biggest scams in immigration law are the humanitarian cases. One hundred percent of refugee and asylum claims are either obvious frauds or frauds that haven't been proved yet. The only result of our asylum policies is that we get good liars. Taxpayers subsidize sleazy immigration activists who coach immigrants to lie to immigration officials. Document mills produce phony passports, school records, and medical reports. Often, asylum applicants know nothing about the country they claim as home.

As the *New York Times* described the asylum con: "West Africans claim genital mutilation or harm from the latest political violence. Albanians and immigrants from other Balkan countries claim they fear ethnic cleansing. Chinese invoke the one-child policy or persecution of Christians, Venezuelans cite their opposition to the ruling party, and Russians describe attacks against gay people. Iraqis and Afghans can cite fear of retaliation by Islamic extremists."[6] (Don't worry: Carlos Slim's money stream is not affected by the asylum cases!)

One Russian woman claimed asylum on the grounds that she had been persecuted because she was gay. When her lawyer asked her to elaborate, she huffily told him, "I'm not gay at all. I don't even like gay people."[7]

To weed out the frauds we'd need a Pulitzer prize–winning journalist to investigate each individual asylum claim. Someone like, say, the *Times*' Nicholas Kristof. A few years ago Kristof wouldn't shut up about Somaly Mam, a Cambodian victim of sex trafficking. Mam claimed that as a child she had been beaten and prostituted by her abusive grandfather and sold to a brothel, where she was tortured with electrodes hooked up to a car battery. But in a testament to the human spirit, Mam escaped from the brothel and went on to found a multimillion-dollar organization to combat child sex-trafficking—all of which is recounted in Mam's international bestseller *The Road of Lost Innocence.*

After a decade of tributes, honors, awards, and gobs of donations, Mam turned out to be full of crap. Her childhood friends, contacted by *Newsweek,* described her as "a happy, pretty girl with pigtails," who was "well-known and popular in their small village." She lived with her parents and attended village schools all the way through high school.[8]

At least Long Pross, one of Mam's rescued Cambodian child prostitutes, was real. As Kristof described her in a column titled "If This Isn't Slavery, Then What Is?": "Glance at Pross from her left, and she looks like a normal, fun-loving girl, with a pretty face and a joyous smile. Then move around, and you see where her brothel owner gouged out her right eye." Then it turned out she had lost her eye during eye surgery on a nonmalignant tumor. *Newsweek* even had the medical records.

It took a decade of Mam touring the world as an internationally recognized celebrity for her deceptions to be exposed. She had been one of *Time*'s one hundred most influential people, interviewed by Oprah, feted at Manhattan and Beverly Hills soirees, and embraced by Secretary of State Hillary Clinton, actress Meg Ryan, and Facebook's Sheryl Sandberg.

How is a U.S. immigration judge supposed to do better? How, specifically, are U.S. officials going to investigate claims of gang rape in Nigeria? They don't: They just grant asylum. Knowing full well that asylum is the most fraud-ridden of all immigration programs—which is saying something—immigration judges approve 92 percent of all "credible fear" asylum applications.[9]

NAFISSATOU DIALLO

The only cases that ever get disproved are the ones where the asylees somehow become famous. Hotel maid Nafissatou Diallo became an international sensation when she accused the head of the International Monetary Fund, Dominique Strauss-Kahn, of raping her at the Sofitel hotel in New York. That turned out to be just another immigrant get-rich-quick scheme,[10] but her rape claims brought unwanted attention to her asylum application.

It turned out Diallo had cooked up the yarn about being gang-raped in her native Guinea in order to win asylum in the United States. The whole thing was a fairy tale she had memorized by listening to a tape given to her by an American immigration activist.[11] If Diallo hadn't made a spectacle of herself by trying to shake down the IMF chief, no one would have ever been the wiser. Diallo, of course, is still in the United States, collecting welfare.

AMADOU DIALLO

Another Diallo whose asylum application was exposed as a pack of lies only after he became famous was Amadou Diallo, shot by four New York City police officers. While looking for a violent Bronx rapist one night in 1999, the cops shouted at Diallo to put his hands up, but he didn't obey because he didn't speak English and he wasn't sufficiently familiar with American customs to know that when police officers are shouting and pointing guns at you, the best practice is to show them your hands.

Only because Diallo got himself killed for not speaking the language[12] did we find out about all the immigration frauds he had committed to be here. He first got to America by falsely stating he was a "student," though he never attended any school in the United States. After arriving on a student visa, Diallo was granted asylum based on his claim that he was from Mauritania and his parents had been murdered by the government.

In fact, he was raised in a well-to-do Guinean family and had lived in Bangkok and Singapore as a child, traveling with his father's job. After Diallo's death-by-lack-of-English-skills, his allegedly murdered parents suddenly materialized and demanded $61 million from New York City taxpayers. The city gave them $3 million—at that point the largest wrongful-death settlement in New York history for a person earning less than $10,000 a year.[13]

Why were hardworking New Yorkers forced to bear the cost of a problem that was caused entirely by incompetent federal immigration officials? Four cops' lives were nearly ruined because an immigrant who didn't speak English scammed the system to stay in the United States. Even before the shooting, Diallo wasn't a major boon to the country. He eked out a living selling baseball caps, tube socks, and bootleg videotapes on East 14th Street in Manhattan,[14] clogging up the sidewalk and engaging in intellectual property theft.

No American media outlet would ever admit it, but any legal immigrant making less than $10,000 is collecting food stamps as well as other government benefits. With the money they received from New York taxpayers, Diallo's parents built a computer lab—in rural Guinea.[15] Despite the pain it must cause them to be reminded of their son's death in America, both his parents now live here, too,[16] the better to denounce American police officers.[17] Federal officials, whose salary you pay, give away American citizenship like a consolation prize.

Diallo's cost to America: Millions of dollars in immigration and criminal court costs, judges' salaries, welfare payments, a $3 million settlement, in addition to the cost of government attorneys to work out the deal, and the loss of four good officers to the New York police force.

Benefits to America: $0.00.

EDWIN BULUS

Another asylum applicant became famous only because the *New York Times* decided to champion his cause. In 1997, the *New York Times* ran a Pulitzer-bait story about Nigerian political refugee Edwin Bulus, who said the Nigerian government "is bent on genocide against my entire family. I'm afraid that, like others, I will be killed."[18] He said he became a target of

Nigerian political authorities after his brother, Happy Bulus, attempted a military coup. Edwin himself was part of the pro-democracy movement at the University of Lagos, having become "very inquisitive about political ideologies like those of Jean Jacques Rousseau and Thomas Jefferson."[19]

Somehow Edwin managed to escape and flee to America, using documents he admitted were fake. When he arrived, he said, he found out both his parents had died. Dr. L. Hankoff, a government psychiatrist, diagnosed Edwin with depression. "He sits with his hands in his lap and his head bent," Dr. Hankoff observed, "making some eye contact, but often apathetic and appearing dejected." Edwin blamed himself for his parents' deaths, saying, "I just pray they rest in peace."[20]

But instead of finding sanctuary in the United States, the *Times* said, Edwin had ended up in a "Kafkaesque" web of INS bureaucracy. Guards at the detention facility had thrown out his papers—the very papers he needed to make his case! Not only that, but they had "stomped on him, forced him to kneel naked for hours, pushed his head in a toilet, left him to sleep naked on a bare mattress and subjected him to racist invective."[21]

Still, Edwin's many supporters had high hopes! Edwin was going to receive another hearing as soon as his cousin could send a photo ID card and affidavits attesting to the fact that Edwin was Happy Bulus's brother. His asylum application was supported by everyone—Amnesty International USA, the Florida Immigrant Advocacy Center, a government psychiatrist, and a law firm in Nigeria. An immigration official who had interviewed Edwin for two hours found him credible. And, of course, it had to help that the Newspaper of Record was broadcasting his story.

Alas, instead of shaking up the INS, the *Times* inadvertently shook out the truth. The Nigerian acting consul in New York read the *Times* article. So did a businessman visiting from Nigeria. And so did Nigerians living as far away as Australia and Oregon. It turned out that Happy Bulus did not have a brother named Edwin. Edwin had never attended the University of Lagos. Edwin's parents were alive and well. Happy's parents were alive and well—and none too happy about this imposter using their family's name. Edwin's name wasn't even "Edwin," it was "Muhtaru."[22]

The only reason Edwin's lies were exposed was because the *Times* believed every word he said. Of course, anyone could have been fooled by a wily deceiver like Edwin. When confronted with the discrepancies in his story, Edwin claimed that there must be *two* lieutenant colonels named "Happy Bulus" who were arrested for plotting military coups against the Nigerian government. "The issue before me," he said, "is a double identity clash."[23] His immigration lawyer believed him.

In the end, Edwin probably got asylum. As his lawyer explained, Edwin had actually bolstered his case for asylum by lying because, while he might not have been wanted by Nigerian officials before, since defaming them in his application, "he's in danger. He's been targeted."[24] Most likely, Edwin is currently engaging in credit card schemes from a housing project in Staten Island.

OSCAR FOR PLAYING A GANG-RAPE VICTIM

In 2001, the *New Yorker* described the dramatic performance of one immigrant during her asylum interview. The applicant, Caroline, wept, closed her eyes, and whispered as she told her story of being repeatedly arrested, beaten, sodomized, and raped by soldiers in her country. They "took me by the head and they put my head against their penis," she said. "They spat on us. They wanted us to do things.... They beat us up and did horrible things to us.... They forced us to do fellatio and they put objects in our genitals. They stamped on us, they trampled us for three days. I suffered many infections because of the rape. My kidneys got infected."

Although Caroline claimed she had been repeatedly hospitalized on account of these barbarities, she could produce no evidence "because of all the riots and the pillages." She had no proof of her abortion because "I don't want any documentary evidence of this abortion because it happened as a result of a rape." If she were sent back, she said, "I might be killed on the road, because I am a member of the opposition."

The immigration officer interviewing Caroline was notoriously tough-minded, but after hearing a tearjerker like that, he granted her asylum.

The truth, Caroline admitted to the *New Yorker*, was that she had come to the United States with her family for a wedding the previous summer and decided to stay. The "immigrant community" in the United States provided her with fake identity cards and Social Security numbers and those heinous rape stories. They had initially suggested she claim genital mutilation, but female circumcision is not practiced in her country, so she went the rape/torture route. "I have never been raped," she laughingly told the *New Yorker*.[25]

Asked about the lenient approach of our immigration system toward asylum claims, Dana Marks, president of the National Association of Immigration Judges, said she always errs on the side of granting asylum because the "mistake of granting a fraudulent asylum case is far less disastrous than denying a genuine one."[26] Disastrous for whom?

AUTOMATIC ENTRY FOR THE WORST CULTURES IN THE WORLD

The entire world outside of America, Canada, Australia, New Zealand, and parts of Western Europe is a humanitarian crisis. We're not even rescuing the real victims, who are either dead or can't catch an international flight to the United States. In any event, that's not our job.

When by some freak accident an English-speaking, non–welfare receiving, Christian Western European family applies for asylum, the government will spend six years trying to hound them out of the country. That's what happened to the young German family that sought asylum on the (actually true) grounds that the German government was going to take their children away unless they ceased homeschooling them. As a huffy Ralph De La Cruz complained in the *Dallas Morning News*: "If not having the right to home school" in Germany constitutes persecution, "wouldn't something like beheadings of the local population by drug cartels, also qualify?"

That's how asylum is used to turn America into a dumping ground for the most backward people on earth. No advanced country could ever produce the sort of persecution our immigration laws reward, so the asylum welcome mat gets rolled out only for criminals, scam artists, and terrorists. They're less persecuted than the German family was, but they come from horribly backward cultures, so it's easy to cook up a good story. After six years of litigation, the Department of Homeland Security finally stopped trying to deport the German family, granting them "indefinite deferred-action status." You can see them on display in my Immigration Museum as the only asylum applicants in fifty years who didn't immediately go on welfare.

SHUT IT DOWN

The only way to stop the nonsense is to have an immigration moratorium. It would be nice to get some British and Dutch immigrants again, but it's not worth the risk of keeping our immigration bureaucracy in business.

Just shut it down. No more family reunification, no more scam marriages, no more refugees, no more phony asylum cases (which is all of them), and no more "high-tech workers" providing slave labor to Microsoft and concubines to Indian pedophiles. No legal fixes can make a dent in our behemoth immigration apparatus. Until every last special pleader for mass immigration from the Third World is out of the business, the country cannot be safe.

A moratorium should be music to the ears of aspiring immigrants! They won't want to "cry" because "they don't feel wanted" and are "abused in many ways"—as immigrants to America do, according to Dr. Manuel Carballo, executive director of the International Center for Migration,

Health, and Development at Columbia University.[27] They will no longer be subjected to "hate crimes and discrimination" in America—as put by Pramila Jayapal, who was born in India, but now represents Seattle in the Washington State House.[28] They won't experience "harassment, hardship and discrimination" in Alabama—as the Southern Poverty Law Center says they do.[29] Have immigrants heard about America's gun fetish? The college rape epidemic? The lack of safe and easy access to abortion? We're doing them a favor.

If America could get a timeout on endless immigration from the Third World, we'd have a chance to reform ourselves and drain these deep sewers of depravity, racism, and xenophobia that liberals keep finding around every corner. They'll be happier. We'll be happier. After a half century of taking in the hardest cases in the world, America needs a little "me time."

16

I WROTE THIS CHAPTER AFTER NOTICING HOW STUPID RICH PEOPLE ARE

HISTORICALLY, WHEN REPUBLICANS IGNORE WHITE VOTERS, THEY LOSE. WHEN they ignore minorities and drive up the white vote, they win. Reagan took out a sitting president in 1980 by sweeping the New Deal coalition, "except for blacks and Hispanics," according to a *Washington Post* analysis.[1] Four years later, Reagan's share of the black vote declined further. He won 9 percent of the black vote[2]—the smallest percentage captured by any Republican presidential candidate between Lyndon Johnson's 1964 landslide and Barack Obama's candidacy in 2008.[3]

He also won the largest electoral landslide in U.S. history.

Explaining the Democrats' drubbing in the 1984 presidential election, the *Washington Post*'s Richard Harwood said Democrats had made a historic "miscalculation" by obsessing over the black vote. Although Southern blacks came through and voted 90 percent for Walter Mondale, Reagan swept the South with 75 percent of the white vote.[4]

Rule of thumb, Republicans: If you aren't being called "racist" by the *New York Times*, you're losing.

With Democrats always gassing on about how Hispanics are going to turn Texas blue, as happened to California, no one seems to have noticed that Texas already has more Hispanics than California.[5] Hispanics in Texas are no different from the ones in California: Both bloc-vote for Democrats by about 60 to 75 percent. The difference is: White Texans vote overwhelmingly Republican, whereas white Californians split their vote. In 2012, whites were 55 percent of the California electorate, but they voted only 53 percent for Romney.[6] That same year, whites were 56 percent of the Texas electorate—but they voted 80 percent for Romney.[7] *Eighty percent!* The *New York Times*' famed statistician, Nate Cohn, estimates that in 2012 Obama got the smallest percentage of the white vote in Texas of any Democrat in history, at 18.9 percent.[8]

So how have the media, Democrats, and cheap-labor enthusiasts managed to convince Republicans to focus like a laser beam on winning slightly more of the Hispanic vote? We must consider the possibility that they do not have Republicans' best interests at heart. Blacks and Hispanics are not swing voters—whites are. It would be as if Republicans tricked the Democrats into devoting all their efforts to getting a tiny sliver more of the fundamentalist Christian vote. The GOP's addiction to lobbyists' money is killing the party.

THE OFF-THE-CHARTS POPULARITY OF OPPOSING ILLEGAL IMMIGRATION

In 1994, Governor Pete Wilson of California pulled off an amazing come-from-behind victory by tethering himself with titanium cords to Proposition 187, which prohibited illegal aliens from collecting public services. Wilson went from a catastrophic 15 percent job-approval rating[9] to a landslide victory. Suddenly he was being touted as presidential material.[10]

This wasn't the California of Richard Nixon and Ronald Reagan, a storybook era when Republicans could easily win that state. Just two years earlier, Republicans had been walloped in three statewide elections—two senate elections and a presidential election.[11] But Wilson won his 1994 reelection with 55 percent of the vote, which was the largest percentage of any Republican running statewide in California in the last thirty years, other than Hollywood movie star and virtual Democrat Governor Arnold Schwarzenegger, who won his 2006 reelection by precisely one point more than Wilson got in 1994.

Before the election, the *New York Times* had the exact same advice for Wilson that it does for the Republican National Committee today. The *Times* urgently warned Wilson that he was headed for a humiliating defeat by supporting Proposition 187, which was, in the words of the *Times*, a "nativist abomination,"[12] "xenophobic,"[13] and a "platform of bigotry, racism and scapegoating."[14] Republicans faced an epic loss unless they repudiated Prop. 187 and leapt on the Hispandering bandwagon—and pronto. There wasn't a moment to spare!

Luckily, Wilson wasn't RNC Chairman Reince Priebus, so he didn't take the *Times*' advice.

As it turned out, Proposition 187 got even more votes than Wilson, winning 59 percent to 41 percent. It was supported by two-thirds of white voters, 56 percent of black voters, 57 percent of Asian voters—and even a third of Hispanic voters.[15] It won in every county of California except San Francisco, a city where intoxicated gay men dressed as nuns performing sex acts on city streets is not considered unusual. In heavily Latino Los Angeles County, Proposition 187 passed by a twelve-point margin. The "nativist abomination" lifted Republicans across the state and ended the Democrats' quarter-century control of the California State Assembly.[16] Even Michael Huffington nearly beat popular incumbent Senator Dianne Feinstein in an election that wasn't called until days later.

Contrary to the media's predictions, Proposition 187 "did not motivate more Latinos to come out to vote," according to Susan Pinkus, director of the *Los Angeles Times*' exit poll.[17] Refugio Trujillo, for example, a lifelong Democrat with a sign for Wilson's opponent in his lawn, was among the one-third of Hispanics who supported the initiative, telling the *San Jose Mercury News*: "We have too many aliens out here."[18] Not only did one-third of Hispanics support Proposition 187, but black voters came out in droves— for Wilson. In House races nationwide that year, Republicans won only 8 percent of the black vote. Wilson won 21 percent of black voters.[19] Interestingly, that's nearly the identical percentage Romney won from young black males in 2012 by refusing to budge in his opposition to illegal immigration.

To give you a sense of what a monumental Republican triumph Prop. 187 was, after the election, the media lashed out at California voters, calling them "bitter" and "angry."[20]

Unfortunately for her, Wilson's Democratic opponent Kathleen Brown didn't realize that the *Times'* hectoring on Prop. 187 was a gag. It was only supposed to fake out *Republicans*. Convinced that opposition to Proposition 187 was surging, days before the election, Brown asked voters to "send a message that says we understand that in diversity is our strength"![21] Landslide for Wilson. Only ten percent of Brown's voters cited her opposition to the proposition as a reason to support her.[22] But nearly a third of Wilson's voters cited his support of it as their number one reason for supporting him.

Is Kathleen Brown advising the RNC on its Hispanic outreach?

NICE TRY, GRINGOS!

The response from Mexico was swift. Mexican President Carlos Salinas de Gortari wailed, "Will they return to Mexico, wash windshields in California, sell newspapers on the streets or beg?" Evidently, he wasn't worried about losing Mexico's top talent to America through illegal immigration. His government began setting up homeless shelters on the Mexican side of the border. Masked men stormed McDonald's franchises, smashed plate-glass windows, turned over cash registers, threw hamburgers on the floor, and spray-painted anti-American slogans on the walls.[23] (Our new country is going to be great!)

The response from American liberals was swifter. The ACLU and other anti-American groups brought suit and got the initiative overturned by the courts, courtesy of Carter-appointed District Court Judge Mariana Pfaelzer. Apparently, shots were fired by brave patriots in 1775 on the North Bridge in Concord so that their descendants might one day be forced to support any Mexican who manages to sneak across the border.

Today, Los Angeles is the second-biggest Mexican city in the world. Its taxpayers are required to spend billions of dollars for education, health-care, food, housing, and jail cells for illegal immigrants. According to the California Department of Education, two-thirds of the public school students in the Los Angeles Unified School District are Hispanic.[24] Sun-drenched California suddenly has all the problems of a Third World country because the Third World has moved there.

DON'T WORRY, REPUBLICANS, THEY'LL RESPECT YOU IN THE MORNING

After getting a court to nullify the popularly enacted Prop. 187, the Left's most urgent priority was to make sure Republicans never tried anything like that again. At the time, of course, no one could deny the truth. On the eve of the election, ABC reported that Proposition 187 had brought Wilson "from behind into a narrow lead in a year when incumbents everywhere are threatened with extinction."[25] The *Economist* magazine said that even in heavily Democratic Oregon, the Republican gubernatorial candidate Denny Smith "made late gains in his campaign by saying he thought Proposition 187 a fine thing."[26]

But as soon as memories faded, the media began relentlessly rewriting the story of Proposition 187 as a catastrophe for the GOP. If I didn't know better, I'd say the media don't want the GOP to win landslide victories.

Republicans fall for it every time.

Nearly twenty years later, after the 2012 presidential election, the RNC paid $10 million for a report that concluded: "To broaden its appeal, the party must...embrace and champion comprehensive immigration reform. If we do not, our party's appeal will continue to shrink." (I could have told them how to lose for, say, $8 million.) It all sounds vaguely familiar...wait—I remember! That's the exact advice given to Wilson in 1994 by the *New York Times*, the Republicans' dearest, most trusted friend in the whole wide world.

In fact, however, if Romney had won 71 percent of the Hispanic vote in 2012, instead of 27 percent, he still would have lost. On the other hand, had he won just 4 percent more of the white vote, he would have won.[27] So what did Reince Priebus, Jeb Bush, Marco Rubio, Rand Paul, John Boehner, and all rich Republicans decide their sole mission should be after the 2012 election? Win a few points more of the Hispanic vote! The *Washington Post*'s Chris Cillizza was totally impressed. He cited the report's conclusion, saying: "That's 100 percent right."[28] And when Chris Cillizza tells Republicans they're on the right track, the party had better sit up and listen!

Pete Wilson's victory on the back of Proposition 187 ought to be studied by today's GOP like General Eisenhower's Operation Overlord. Not only was it a stunning success in defiance of the *Times*' predictions, but contemporary America has nearly the exact same demographic makeup as California did in 1994—a.k.a. "the California Republicans Swept with an Anti–Illegal Alien Initiative." In 1994, California was 75 percent white, 12 percent Hispanic, 6 percent Asian, and 7 percent African American.[29] Today, the American electorate is 72 percent white, 10 percent Hispanic, 3 percent Asian, and 13 percent African American.[30]

Will any rich Republican donor ever notice?

BUSH EMPTIES THE REPUBLICAN PARTY

President Bush's record-breaking 40 percent of the Hispanic vote in his 2004 reelection is cited as a model for Republican office-seekers. Let's review: Reagan ticked off the only minority group that mattered in 1984, and won a historic landslide; Bush sucked up to Hispanics and barely won his reelection as a wartime president running against a complete nincompoop.[31]

And look at what Bush had to do to get 40 percent of the Hispanic vote! He carried his half-Mexican nephew, George P. Bush, around on the campaign trail as if he were an extra appendage, giving him a primetime slot at the Republican National Convention for a speech delivered partially in Spanish. He was the first president to give weekly radio addresses in Spanish and also added a Spanish-language page to the White House website. He campaigned—in America—with Mexico's president. He held a huge Cinco de Mayo fiesta at the White House. He gave speeches to the racist National Council of La Raza, promising $100 million in federal funds to speed immigration applications.[32]

Bush's Hispandering didn't even win him a majority of Hispanics! But it did tick off his base, leading to a blowout loss for his party two years later.

The conservative Christian base that had carried Bush to victory in 2004 turned against him with a vengeance over amnesty, wiping out Bush's party in the House, Senate, and state governorships. In the 2006 election, only 77 percent of conservatives voted Republican, compared with 91 percent of liberals who voted Democrat.[33] Thirty-six percent of voters said they cast their votes specifically to oppose Bush—and he wasn't on the ballot. That's even more than the 27 percent who voted to oppose Bill Clinton in the 1994 Republican sweep of Congress.[34]

It's hard to argue that Bush's betrayal of conservatives on immigration was not the central factor in Republicans' catastrophic 2006 losses. Other than Bush's obsessive fixation on passing amnesty, there wasn't much new that year.[35]

Liberals like to tell the story of how their courageous opposition to the Iraq War finally won the public's hearts and minds, ushering in a Democratic Congress in 2006, but that's not what public opinion surveys show. Dozens of Gallup polls on the Iraq War from the moment we invaded in March 2003 to June 2014 show public support for the war declining from 75 percent to 50 percent two years into the war, then mostly remaining in the 40s thereafter.[36]

It was Bush's neurotic demand that the Senate take up "comprehensive immigration reform" in March 2006 that enraged Americans. A *Washington Post*–ABC News Poll in April 2006 showed more Americans approved of Bush's handling of the Iraq War than approved of his handling of immigration.[37]

In nearly every poll on Bush's handling of immigration that year, about 60 percent of the public disapproved, with only 25 percent approving—the latter figure giving us a rough estimate of how many Americans acquire their opinions exclusively from the *New York Times* or the *Wall Street Journal*.

- *Newsweek*, May 11, 2006: 61 percent "disapprove[d] of the way Bush is handling immigration policy"; only 25 percent approved.
- *New York Times*/CBS News poll, May 4–8, 2006: 58 percent "disapprove[d] of the way George W. Bush is handling the issue of immigration"; 26 percent approved.
- Pew Center for the People and the Press, April 7–16, 2006: 62 percent "disapprove[d] of the way George W. Bush is handling the nation's immigration policy"; 25 percent approved.
- *Time* magazine poll, March 29, 2006: 56 percent "disapprove[d] of the job President Bush is doing in handling the immigration problem"; 25 percent approved.[38]

Gallup has been asking Americans to name "the most important problem facing this country" for years. Going back decades, immigration had ranked as the "most important problem" for only about 4 to 5 percent of respondents. Then, suddenly, in April 2006—just after Bush had launched his plan for "comprehensive immigration reform"— immigration shot to the number one problem for 30 percent of Republicans, 16 percent of independents, and 11 percent of Democrats.[39]

Lest there be any misunderstanding, poll respondents didn't think immigration was a "problem" the way Bush thought it was a "problem." Sixty-one percent of Americans wanted to criminalize illegal aliens.[40] Fifty-three percent of Pew respondents said illegal immigrants should be required "to go home."[41] Twenty percent of respondents in a *Washington Post*–ABC News Poll agreed with: "Declare all illegal immigrants to be felons."[42] Compiling results from a series of polls in February and March 2006, Pew Research found that about 90 percent of Americans called illegal immigration a "serious problem," while a clear majority called it a "very" or "extremely" serious problem.[43]

Seventy-nine percent of those with "less tolerant" views on immigration, as ABC News put it, said immigration would be a "top issue" in their vote.[44]

As long as Bush had brought it up, Americans said they wanted to stop *legal* immigration, too. In the Quinnipiac poll, 72 percent of respondents wanted immigration to decrease or stay at the same levels (39 percent for "decrease," and 33 percent for "stay the same"). In the Pew Hispanic Center poll, 77 percent of Americans wanted immigration to decrease or stay the same (40 percent to 37 percent). Even in the *New York Times*/CBS poll, 73 percent opposed an increase in legal immigration (34 percent for "decreased" and 39 percent "kept at present level").[45]

More Americans support Obamacare than support an increase in legal immigration.

Gallup found that nearly 60 percent of Americans considered the country's future "population growth" a "major problem"—and those with "less formal education" were "most likely to correctly attribute population growth to immigration, while Americans with post-graduate education are least likely to do so."[46] Apart from the maid, immigration is barely noticeable in the better neighborhoods.

Midterm elections, the *New York Times* has said, "tend to be won by whichever side can motivate more true believers to vote." There's no question but that Bush's push for amnesty in 2006 infuriated his base. In June 2006, influential conservative leaders including Brent Bozell, Phyllis Schlafly, and Howard Phillips issued a statement lambasting the amnesty plan being pushed by Bush, as well as a "compromise" measure proposed by Republican Congressman Mike Pence. The leaders pledged to oppose any member of Congress who voted for either bill.[47]

YOU'VE GOT ONE MOVE, GOP

It's a sucker's game to think that Republicans can ever get to the Democrats' left on immigration. A terrible year for Democrats is winning only 60 percent of the Hispanic vote. The vast majority of the Democrats' ethnic base is voting for them no matter what. There could have been a 1929 stock market crash in 2012, and Obama would still have won more than 90 percent of the black vote and upward of 70 percent of the Hispanic and Asian vote. When they're being honest, Democrats admit that Republicans "are delusional if they think they're making any inroads with Latinos," as Texas Democratic Party spokesman Rebecca Acuna said in 2012. Acuna noted that out of 728 elected Hispanic officials in Texas, 668 of them were Democrats. Only 60 were Republicans.[48]

The GOP's only move is to run the table on white voters, as Reagan did.

By unapologetically opposing the transformation of America into a Third World country, the GOP would sweep the white vote—once white people recovered from the shock of any candidate asking for their vote. Why should Republicans be ashamed of getting white votes? How about the party work on getting more of them? By fighting for black jobs, Republicans will also win a lot more black voters—as Romney did in 2012, winning a jaw-dropping 20 percent of the young black male vote.[49]

Unfortunately, the public's opinion is of little interest to Republican consultants who have hefty college tuition bills to pay. Their solitary interest is in pleasing big donors by constantly apologizing to Hispanics for not moving fast enough on amnesty. They would rather engineer a forty-nine-state defeat than abandon the cheap-labor advocates on immigration.

What might these genius GOP operatives think about a presidential candidate running ads bashing immigrant welfare scams? Something like: "She is collecting Social Security on her cards. She's got Medicaid, getting food stamps, and she is collecting welfare under each of her names. Her tax-free cash income is over $150,000." What if a Republican presidential candidate accused self-appointed Hispanic leaders of running "organizations based on keeping alive the feeling that they're victims of prejudice"? I'm guessing that wouldn't impress the big thinkers in the GOP who are squeamish about "self-deportation."

But Reagan said all that—and was called a racist.[50] And he won the largest electoral landslide in history.

17

MOST OF OUR CHAMPIONS ARE SELLOUTS—HALF OF THE REST ARE INCOMPETENT

THE PRACTICED LIARS IN THE REPUBLICAN PARTY KNOW DAMN WELL Americans do not want more immigration, but the leadership won't give it up. To please well-heeled donors, elected Republicans compulsively push for amnesty, in-state tuition, driver's licenses, and welfare payments to illegals. And the media cover for them: *Don't worry, we won't write about what you're doing with immigration! And if we do, it will only be to talk about your moral courage, Marco.* Only when they need actual voters do Republicans suddenly start saying: "Complete the dang fence!" (2008 McCain campaign).

It's always interesting to see what politicians lie about. At least they know what's actually popular with voters. Back when he was running for office, Senator Marco Rubio criticized "comprehensive immigration reform," saying, an "'earned path to citizenship' is basically code for 'amnesty.'"[1] He pledged, "I will never support—never have, and never will support—any effort to grant blanket legalization amnesty to folks who have entered this country illegally."[2] Then Rubio got to Washington and spent the next three years pushing for amnesty. Representative Renee Ellmers of North Carolina came out for a path to legalization and, as a result, was headed for defeat, until Mark Zuckerberg came to her rescue with election ads that claimed her position was "No amnesty. Period." Within a month of returning to Congress, Ellmers voted in favor of Obama's executive amnesty. I guess it depends on what the meaning of the word "period" is.

So we know they know where Americans stand on immigration. (*Please stop!*) In February 2015, more Americans said they had a favorable opinion of North Korea (11 percent)[3] than wanted to increase immigration (7 percent).[4]

The baffling question is why Americans are so utterly incapable of influencing public policy on immigration. True, all the money and power are on the other side of the issue. Zuckerberg, Rupert Murdoch, Michael Bloomberg, Sheldon Adelson, Rudy Giuliani—all of them support amnesty and mass immigration. But the rich and powerful also support gun control and abortion—again, Zuckerberg, Murdoch, Bloomberg, Adelson, and Giuliani. Money and power don't seem to help them on those issues.

It is impossible to imagine a Republican candidate for president who is not pro-life and pro-gun. But it's becoming increasingly impossible to imagine a Republican candidate for president who *doesn't* support amnesty—Marco Rubio, Rand Paul, Rick Perry, Mike Huckabee, George, Jeb, Zeppo, and Shemp Bush. Why is that? At least as many Americans would like to see a total immigration moratorium as support gun rights and oppose abortion. So why does National Right to Life have decisive influence over the Republican Party, while Numbers USA has none? Why do Gun Owners of America always win, while immigration opponents always lose? More Americans oppose amnesty than oppose restrictions on guns. But even after the mass shooting at a grade school in Newtown, Connecticut, Congress was able to enact no new gun laws. By contrast, even after immigrants bombed the Boston Marathon, Congress went ahead and funded Obama's unconstitutional amnesty.

The reason the National Rifle Association wins is because it knows how politics works. Gun activists do not try to discern what a politician believes in his heart or try to take the measure of the man. They look at voting records—specifically, a politician's record on guns. Rather famously, the NRA will not oppose any politician who votes right on guns, no matter how awful he is on every other issue (Harry Reid); and they will not support a politician who opposes gun rights no matter how wonderful he is on other issues (Rudy Giuliani). The NRA doesn't demand some impossible political purity. If a politician votes to protect gun rights, the NRA won't insist that he also celebrate "Gun Appreciation Day." Vote for gun rights and you will be rewarded on Election Day; oppose gun rights and you will be punished. Left to their consultants, most elected officials would be terrified to oppose gun control. Instead, they're terrified to oppose the NRA.

By contrast, most immigration opponents seem to have no concept of how to influence politicians. They announce that Senator Jeff Sessions or Representative Steve King are the only acceptable presidential candidates, and think their job is done. Consequently, Americans who would like to vote on immigration have no idea which governors granted illegals in-state tuition and which governors vetoed those bills. Conservative leaders won't tell them. Their long-term plan is to keep demanding that Jeff Sessions run for president and stay home and pout if Tom Tancredo isn't anywhere on the ballot. There are plenty of enticements for selling out on immigration, but none for doing the right thing.

If the NRA behaved this way, the country would be living under the policies of Moms Demand Action for Gun Sense in America. How about we look at politicians' actual records on this one issue? America's suicidal immigration policies are the single biggest threat facing the nation. What happens with immigration will determine whether America continues to exist or becomes a Third World republic that will never elect another Republican—in other words, "California." It's more important than gun rights, right to life, taxes, or Iran's nuclear program—or whatever other issue you care to cite, because immigration will decide all issues, once and for all, in favor of the Democrats.

VOTER GUIDE

Now ask yourself if you had any idea where the following presidential candidates stood on immigration and tell me if immigration activists are doing their job.

JEB BUSH

Jeb Bush is what's known as "a wolf in wolf's clothing" on immigration. As governor of Florida he aggressively pushed a bill that would allow illegal aliens to obtain driver's licenses, *less than three years after thirteen of nineteen terrorists in the September 11 attack had used Florida driver's licenses to board the planes.*[5] (And Jeb is supposed to be "the smart one.") In 2012, Jeb openly refused to endorse Romney before the Florida primary because of Romney's opposition to amnesty. He made it well known to the press that he was offended by Romney's statement that illegal aliens would "self-deport" when the jobs dried up. The day before the primary, Laura Bush showed up in Sarasota, Florida, and announced that both she and George wished Jeb were in the race.[6]

Demonstrating the Bush family's uncanny feel for the concerns of ordinary Americans, the next day Romney swept the Florida primary, winning 46 percent of the vote in an eight-person field. He did better among Florida's Hispanic voters than with Republican voters at large. Throughout the rest of the year, Jeb kept running to the press saying Romney should "tone down his harsh rhetoric on issues like illegal immigration," as the *New York Times* admiringly put it. This was fantastically helpful in a close presidential election. About once a month since then, one or another Bush has issued a statement lecturing Republicans about Romney's "harsh tone" on immigration.[7] This always makes the *New York Times* swoon. Needless to say, the *Times* could barely contain its esteem for Jeb when, in April 2014, he called illegal immigration "an act of love."[8]

RICK PERRY

Texas Governor Rick Perry pushed for Texas's in-state tuition for illegals and then lectured Republicans about it, saying, "If you say that we should not educate children who've come into our state for no other reason than they've been brought there by no fault of their own, I don't think you have a heart." (Romney's response: "I think if you're opposed to illegal immigration, it doesn't mean that you don't have a heart, it means that you have a heart and a brain.")[9] Perry opposes E-Verify.[10] He also opposes a fence, either on the grounds that he has that witty quip about ladders[11] or because "the idea that you're going to build a wall from Brownsville to El Paso, it's just—it's ridiculous on its face."[12] (Wait until Perry hears about the Great Wall of China!) He opposed the Arizona law allowing state officers to check the immigration status of those they detained, as did Jeb Bush and Marco Rubio.[13]

CHRIS CHRISTIE

Governor Chris Christie was famously duped by Senator Chuck Schumer into supporting comprehensive immigration reform. Schumer considered Christie such a patsy that he immediately leaked the news that he had buffaloed Christie on amnesty in a single thirty-minute phone call. Christie's Senate appointee then voted for the bill. A few months later, Christie doubled down on amnesty by giving in-state tuition to illegal aliens.

RAND PAUL

Senator Rand Paul calls illegal aliens "undocumented citizens" and has fully banished the word "amnesty" from his vocabulary, using the word "normalize" instead. He even refers to Reagan's amnesty—which everyone calls "amnesty"—as a time "when we normalized people back in 1986." Paul frequently cites the imaginary tax boon we'll get by dumping 30 million poor people on the country.[14] He coos to illegal immigrants—or "undocumented citizens"—"We will find a place for you" and "We're saying you don't have to go home," demanding that we acknowledge that "we aren't going to deport 12 million illegal immigrants." Instead of a fence, the libertarian wants the government to tell us when the border is secure.

Under pressure from his base, Paul voted against the Schumer-Rubio amnesty, but promptly backtracked. In under a year, Paul was warning conservatives that "the Hispanic community is not going to hear us until we get beyond this [immigration] issue,"[15] and cutting ads for the amnesty-supporting Chamber of Commerce.[16] He got fantastic press from the *New York Times*, which was expected, but he also continued to be cited as a true-blue conservative warrior by alleged conservatives. Even after Paul's about-face on amnesty, Chris Chocola, then-president of the Club for Growth, hailed him as one of the important tea party conservatives who "influenced the rest of them."[17]

RICK SANTORUM

In his twelve years in the Senate, Santorum showed no interest in immigration—a point made by his 2006 Democratic opponent Bob Casey when Santorum tried to use illegal immigration as an election issue. (Republicans are fiercely opposed to immigration whenever they need our votes!) Santorum did vote against the 2006 Kennedy-McCain amnesty,[18] but he also voted against sanctions on employers who hire illegals—another point made by Casey, who ended up winning the election.[19] In his 2012 presidential campaign, Santorum continued to oppose punishing employers who use illegal alien labor.[20]

TED CRUZ

In September 2012, Senator Ted Cruz told the *New York Times*, "I have said many times that I want to see common-sense immigration reform pass." He expressly rejected the idea of self-deportation, saying that "he had never tried to undo the goal of allowing them to stay." His main interest in immigration, he told the *Times*, was the "real need for labor" by farmers and ranchers.[21] He said he also wanted to change the law so that even more Mexicans and Chinese could immigrate here legally.

Cruz voted against the Rubio amnesty bill, but proposed amendments to it that would *double* legal immigration from 675,000 to 1.3 million a year and quintuple the number of "high tech" H-1B visas, from 65,000 to 325,000 per year.[22] Even Rubio's bill only increased "high tech" visas—a.k.a. tickets into the country for Lakireddy Bali Reddy's concubines—to 180,000 a year.[23] Cruz also offered an amendment that would theoretically prevent amnestied illegal aliens from ever obtaining citizenship. Most amnesty opponents breathed a sigh of relief when it failed: It would have been overturned by a court in five minutes, but would have made the amnesty bill deceptively attractive.[24]

After the Schumer-Rubio bill passed, Cruz blasted it as "amnesty"—a word that few other elected Republicans are willing to use under any circumstances. So perhaps, like Governor Scott Walker, Cruz has flip-flopped to America's side on immigration. Given the likely field of GOP presidential candidates, purer-than-thou conservatives better get ready to do some flip-flopping of their own on flip-flopping candidates.

MITT ROMNEY

As governor of Massachusetts, Mitt Romney repeatedly vetoed bills giving illegal aliens in-state tuition, and the legislature was never able to override him. He made clear he would also veto any bill allowing driver's licenses for illegal aliens, so those never made it to his desk. He vetoed a bill to give health coverage to illegal aliens—but the legislature overruled him. About the time Jeb Bush was pressuring the Florida legislature to give illegals driver's licenses, Romney sought and received a special agreement with federal immigration officials allowing Massachusetts state troopers to arrest illegal aliens.[25] Romney was Jan Brewer before Jan Brewer was Jan Brewer.

For this, Romney was unremittingly attacked by Third World–immigration boosters such as Senator Teddy Kennedy and activist Ali Noorani.[26] The Democratic attorney general of Massachusetts, Thomas Reilly, called a press conference to denounce Governor Romney as "mean-spirited" for vetoing the bill to give illegals in-state tuition. In response, Romney invited the press to his office and showed them that the proposed reduction in tuition for illegals would cost the state millions of dollars a year.[27]

Romney is the only serious presidential candidate ever to support E-Verify and a fence on the border—unequivocally. The media, GOP consultants, the big donors, and the Bush family all attacked him for his suggestion that illegal aliens would "self-deport." Media darling John McCain blustered to the *New Yorker* that "everybody agrees" that Romney's "biggest mistake" was to say "quote, self-deport." Chuckling at the madness of it, McCain said, "I didn't know whether to laugh or cry when I heard that, because you can't have eleven million people self-deport." How does McCain think they got here?

Despite ferocious blowback and zero support from people allegedly opposed to amnesty, Romney never backed away from his immigration positions, not even after Rupert Murdoch insisted that he change his position in a private meeting a few months before the election.

The point of this exercise is to ask: Why didn't you know that, reader? Why—to this day—do so many conservatives tout Rand Paul, Marco Rubio, and Ted Cruz as "bold colors, no pastels" Republicans—especially compared with that miserable establishment RINO, Mitt Romney? Would the NRA hide truthful information about candidates' positions on guns from their members? Immigration groups do! Numbers USA gave Romney a "C+" on immigration. C+! Anti-immigration websites carped about Romney throughout the campaign. What does he have to do? Build the fence himself?

Fake conservatives and tea partiers followed the crowd and slammed Romney as an "establishment" Republican. Alleged conservative spokesmen put Romney in the same camp as Chris Christie and Jeb Bush. It would be as if gun-rights supporters couldn't tell the difference between

Senator Joni Ernst and Representative Carolyn McCarthy, or pro-lifers described Rick Santorum and Susan Collins in the same breath.

On the eve of the Republican sweep in the 2014 midterm elections, Romney predicted on *Fox News Sunday* that a Republican Congress would "deal with those who come here illegally"[28]—heaven help him if he had said "self-deport" again! Conservatives went ballistic, accusing him of supporting amnesty, betraying them, losing his marbles. Within hours, Breitbart.com was headlining Sarah Palin's denunciation of Romney: "Gov. Romney Is in Never-Never Land on This One."[29]

Maybe "amnesty" is what Romney meant when he said "deal with the illegal immigrants already here," although he had never supported it before, despite enormous pressure to do so. But do these hairy-chested amnesty opponents know that every other possible GOP presidential candidate has said *explicitly* what they're accusing Romney of saying implicitly? There's some weird psychological block when conservatives are fiery with indignation at Romney for a vague statement about immigration—because it could be interpreted to mean what every other Republican says in no uncertain terms.

The NRA never loses and the anti-immigration groups never win because immigration opponents don't lift a finger to help politicians who are on their side. Voters are *dying* to send a message on immigration, but all they get is lies from alleged conservatives about how to do that. Romney must wonder why he bothered holding a position so unpopular with his donors on immigration. Perhaps he genuinely believes that turning America into Mexico is a bad idea.

CHAMBER OF COMMERCE: YOU CAN'T HAVE EVERYTHING

Democrats have no choice but to keep pushing to admit ever more poor immigrants: They can't win without the votes of the Third World. The intentional transformation of America into some other country ought to be killing them at the polls, but it's not, because Democrats have hoodwinked Republicans into pushing for the exact same thing. How did Republicans end up on the wrong side of the question: *Should the Democrats be able to establish their political hegemony for all time?*

Any party incapable of winning the vote of white men ought to hang its head in shame. Instead, Democrats denounce and abuse white people, and Republicans act embarrassed about having whites vote for them. Why are white votes bad? (To be sure, black Americans don't like mass immigration, either, but Democrats don't care what blacks think.)

Senate Majority Leader Mitch McConnell needs to get business lobbyists in a car and drive them around with a gun to their heads for an hour, explaining: *We can give you regulatory reform, OSHA reform, tax relief, tort reform. But if we give you immigration, we won't be in a position to give you anything else, ever again, and you'll have to take your chances with Nancy Pelosi.* The Chamber of Commerce has got to learn: You can't have it all.

Then, Republicans should ask Democrats: Why is it so vitally important to keep bringing in new workers to compete with low-skilled Americans and drive down their wages?

Americans love to mock the French for rolling over for Hitler, but at least they had Panzers rolling through Paris. America has chosen to do nothing as our country is taken away from us without a shot fired. The endless flow of needy immigrants is soaking up every last dollar of government aid, every low-wage job, every hour of assistance, every quantum of charitable giving. After all the country has been through only since 9/11— two wars, repeated terrorist attacks, the housing crash, widespread unemployment, and underemployment—America needs to worry about Americans. How much is the price of guilt for having a successful society before we're entitled say to the poor of the world, *Enough! We gave at the office.*

ACKNOWLEDGMENTS

LEGIONS OF PEOPLE WHO HAVE READ THIS BOOK SHALL REMAIN NAMELESS, ON account of the maniacal blacklisting in store for anyone with second thoughts about turning America into Mexico. But some in my crowd are either crazy enough, or love their country enough, to allow me to thank them publicly without even using aliases.

Ned Rice is, as ever, a joke-writing machine. I'd rush to finish chapters just to see what jokes he'd come up with—many for my own amusement, but a lot also made it into the book.

Same with Jim Hughes, who does not write professionally, but rather saves his best work for when he signs on to the computer late at night after a few cocktails. His lengthy late-night rants were so hilarious that I've made him publish some of them. (See, e.g., "Maybe the Obamacare Enrollment Figures Are on That Malaysian Airliner!," Daily Caller, April 24, 2014.)

Trish Baker and Robert Caplain have been on this subject for years, sending me news items, in addition to religiously reading and editing every chapter. Melanie Graham, one of my Circle of Deciders, always e-mailed back immediately and gave me a line that still makes me laugh. Merrill Kinstler, one of my regular talking partners for about fifteen years, let a few of my books slip by without comment. Not this one.

Noticeably, Ned, Jim, Trish, Robert, Melanie, and Merrill are all Californians, so they have a close-up view of what our new country is going to be like. In fact, nearly all my friends who were willing to be named are Californians. It's remarkable how quickly people in a state that has been overwhelmed with illegal aliens are able to grasp the fine points of my thesis. If it's not a hit in 2015, this book will be HUGE as soon as the other forty-nine states become California (without the great weather and gorgeous beaches). I'm sorry to be the one to inform you of this, but that will make all of you the Kardashians.

Others who have helped with this book, mostly by reading chapters and voting on titles, but in other ways, as well, are: Bill Armistead, Jon Caldara, Rodney Conover, Mallory and Thomas Danaher, David Friedman, James Fulford, Ron Gordon, Kevin Harrington, David Limbaugh, Jay Mann, Jim Moody, Dan Travers, Jon Tukel, Marshall Sella, Peter Thiel, Kelly Victory, and Younis Zubchevich. Also, thanks to Regnery for publishing this book and to my editors, Elizabeth Kantor and Marji Ross, for helping me cut 150 pages when it was approaching the length of *The Story of Civilization* by Will and Ariel Durant. Challenge any sentence in this book, and I've got fifty more examples waiting in the outtakes.

Finally, everyone mentioned here agrees with every single word in this book. Don't let them tell you otherwise.

NOTES

CHAPTER ONE: THE END OF AMERICA WON'T BE TELEVISED

1. Heather MacDonald, "Myth Debunked: A Latin Conservative Tidal Wave Is Not Coming," *National Review*, July 24, 2006, http://www.nationalreview.com/article/218274/myth-debunked/heather-mac-donald; and "Young Latinas and a Cry for Help," editorial, *New York Times*, July 21, 2006 ("The experience of International Planned Parenthood across Latin America shows…the high prevalence of unplanned pregnancies, sexually transmitted infections and H.I.V., and sexual violence among this demographic group.").
2. See, e.g., "Young Latinas and a Cry for Help," editorial, http://www.nytimes.com/2006/07/21/opinion/21fri3.html. ("About one-quarter of Latina teens drop out [of high school], a figure surpassed only by Hispanic young men, one-third of whom do not complete high school.")
3. See, e.g., "Young Latinas and a Cry for Help." ("Latinas, especially those in recently arrived families, often live in poverty and without health insurance.")
4. MacDonald, "Hispanic Family Values? Runaway Illegitimacy Is Creating a New U.S. Underclass," *City Journal*, Autumn 2006, http://www.city-journal.org/html/16_4_hispanic_family_values.html.

5.   See, e.g., Mark Hugo Lopez, "Three-Fourths of Hispanics Say Their Community Needs a Leader," Pew Research Center Hispanic Trends Project, October 22, 2013, http://www.pewhispanic.org/2013/10/22/three-fourths-of-hispanics-say-their-community-needs-a-leader/.

6.   See, e.g., Alexis G. Garcia, "Puerto Ricans vs. Dominicans: A Never-Ending Controversy," Latinitas, February 22, 2012, http://mylatinitas.com/profiles/blogs/puerto-ricans-vs-dominicans-a-never-ending-controversy; and Cristina Saralegui, "Bashing Hispanics Who Are 'Too' White," *Chicago Tribune*, September 29, 1994 ("After having spent my entire life in Miami and never having been subjected to prejudice of any kind from English-speaking Americans, I learned for the first time that there was such a thing as Hispanics versus Hispanics bashing.").

7.   Drew Griffin and Kathleen Johnston, "Obama Played Hardball in First Chicago Campaign," CNN.com, May 30, 2008, http://www.cnn.com/2008/POLITICS/05/29/obamas.first.campaign/.

8.   See, e.g., Joseph Katz, "Legal Background to the 'Palestinian Right of Return,'" EretzYisroel, http://www.eretzyisroel.org/~jkatz/legal.html. ("Clearly, the 'rights' and 'general welfare' of the great majority of Israel's citizens would not long survive the admission of some 4 to 5 million Palestinian refugees [for this is the number of refugees that the Palestinians now claim] who neither owe the country allegiance nor identify themselves as Israelis.")

9.   Richard Rubin, "Kenneth Lay, Deceased Enron CEO, Triumphs over IRS in Tax Court," Bloomberg News, August 30, 2011, http://www.bloomberg.com/news/articles/2011-08-29/enron-ceo-kenneth-lay-bests-irs-in-tax-court. ("The U.S. government continues to pursue a $12.6 million civil forfeiture case against Linda Lay, which was initiated three months after her husband's death. The Justice Department sued to recover $10.1 million from a family investment partnership, as well as $22,680 in cash and at least $2.5 million from the couple's penthouse condominium in Houston.")

10.   Quoted on *NBC Nightly News* with Brian Williams, June 20, 2013.

11.   Border Security, Economic Opportunity, and Immigration Modernization Act, S. 744, 113th Congress (2013), Section 2537; and Jon Feere, "Immigration Bill Contains Slush Funds for Pro-Amnesty Groups," Center for Immigration Studies, May 1, 2013, http://cis.org/feere/immigration-bill-contains-slush-funds-pro-amnesty-groups.

12. "California Latino Voters," Moore Information Opinion Research, March 2011, question 17, http://www.moore-info.com/wp-content/uploads/2011/03/NewPoll-LatinoVoterViewsonGOPinCA.pdf.

13. Univision, "Winning with Hispanics in Midterms: The Why, the How, and the What," 18, available on Docstoc: http://www.docstoc.com/docs/172113794/Univision%20Survey%20CA%20Latino%20Voters.pdf.

14. Michael Dear, "Mr. President, Tear Down This Wall," *New York Times*, March 11, 2013, http://www.nytimes.com/2013/03/11/opinion/mr-president-tear-down-this-wall.html.

15. Andrew Rice, "Life on the Line," *New York Times*, July 28, 2011, http://www.nytimes.com/2011/07/31/magazine/life-on-the-line-between-el-paso-and-juarez.html?pagewanted=all&_r=0.

16. *Border Patrol Strategy: Progress and Challenges in Implementation and Assessment Efforts: Testimony before the Subcommittee on Border and Maritime Security, Committee on Homeland Security House of Representatives; Statement of Rebecca Gambler, Acting Director: Homeland Security and Justice Issues* (Washington, DC: Government Accountability Office, May 8, 2012), 5, http://www.gao.gov/assets/600/590686.pdf.

17. See, e.g., "Immigrants, History and the House," *New York Times*, August 19, 1982, http://www.nytimes.com/1982/08/19/opinion/immigrants-history-and-the-house.html (calling the Simpson-Mazzoli bill a "one-time amnesty").

18. "The Seven Amnesties Passed by Congress," Numbers USA, June 7, 2011, https://www.numbersusa.com/content/learn/illegal-immigration/seven-amnesties-passed-congress.html.

CHAPTER TWO: TEDDY: WHY NOT THE THIRD WORLD?

1. "Reproductive Health: Preterm Birth," Centers for Disease Control and Prevention, October 30, 2014, http://www.cdc.gov/reproductivehealth/MaternalInfantHealth/PretermBirth.htm; and American Congress of Obstetricians and Gynecologists, "Prenatal Care Is Important to Healthy Pregnancies," open letter, February 21, 2012, http://acog.org/-/media/Departments/Government-Relations-and-Outreach/20120221FactsareImportant.pdf?la=en ("[T]he economic burden associated with preterm birth in the United States was at least $26.2 billion annually, or $51,600 per infant born preterm.... Preterm birth accounts for approximately 35% of all U.S. health care spending on infants...").

2. Mila Koumpilova, "New Somali Refugee Arrivals in Minnesota Are Increasing," *Minneapolis (MN) Star Tribune*, November 1, 2014, http://www.startribune.com/local/minneapolis/281197521.html.

3. Ibid.

4. See, e.g., "Federal Government Grants to Support USCCB MRS [Migration and Refugee Services] Programs and Services," United States Conference of Catholic Bishops, no date, http://www.usccb.org/about/migration-and-refugee-services/federal-government-grants-to-support-usccb-mrs-programs-and-services.cfm.

5. Fifty-seven percent of households with children headed by any immigrant, legal or illegal, use at least one welfare program, compared with 39 percent of native households with children. Steven A. Camarota, "Welfare Use by Immigrant Households with Children: A Look at Cash, Medicaid, Housing, and Food Programs," Center for Immigration Studies, April 2011, http://cis.org/immigrant-welfare-use-2011.

6. Fifty-seven percent of household with children headed by all immigrants, legal and illegal, collect at least one form of welfare. Camarota, "Welfare Use by Immigrant Households with Children."

7. Camarota, "Immigrants in the United States, 2010: A Profile of America's Foreign-Born Population," Table 10, Center for Immigration Studies, August 2012, http://www.cis.org/sites/cis.org/files/articles/2012/immigrants-in-the-united-states-2012.pdf.

8. Ibid.

9. Ibid.

10. Philip Martin and Elizabeth Midgley, *Immigration: Shaping and Reshaping America*, Population Bulletin, Population Reference Bureau, December 2006; Robert Pear, "Bush Plan Seeks to Restore Food Stamps for Noncitizens," *New York Times*, January 10, 2002, http://www.nytimes.com/2002/01/10/us/bush-plan-seeks-to-restore-food-stamps-for-noncitizens.html; and Shawn Fremstad, "Immigrants and Welfare Reauthorization," Center of Budget and Policy Priorities, February 4, 2002, http://www.cbpp.org/cms/index.cfm?fa=view&id=1477.

11. According to the pro–Third World immigration Migration Policy Institute, in 1960, 75 percent of all immigrants living in the United States were European; by 2010 only 12 percent were and most of those were Eastern European. Joseph Russell and Jeanne Batalova, "European Immigrants in the United States," Migration Policy Institute, July 26, 2012, http://www.migrationpolicy.org/article/european-immigrants-united-states. See also

Judith Waldrop and Kimberly Crews, "Now and Then: The U.S. Reaches 300 Million," *Social Education*, September 1, 2006. ("In 2004, the foreign-born residents who entered the United States in 2000 or later were 10 percent European, 23 percent Asian, and 59 percent Latin American. Among the foreign born who settled in the United States before 1970, 39 percent were European, 14 percent were Asian, and 37 percent were Latin American.")

12.   See e.g., Barbara Pinto, "Muslim Cab Drivers Refuse to Transport Alcohol, and Dogs," ABC News, January 26, 2007, http://abcnews.go.com/International/story?id=2827800.

13.   See, e.g., Gregory Hywood, "Democrats Seek Market Formula," *Australian Financial Review*, March 2, 1988 ("In the 10 elections since Mr Franklin D. Roosevelt's 1932 victory, no Democratic candidate has received more than 50 per cent of the white vote. In the past five elections, only one candidate—Mr Jimmy Carter in 1976—received more than 40 per cent."); and Stephan Thernstrom and Abigail Thernstrom, *America in Black and White: One Nation, Indivisible* (New York: Simon & Schuster, 2009), 291 ("Few Americans realize it, but the Democratic party would have lost every presidential election from 1968 and to the present if only whites had been allowed to vote. Jimmy Carter carried only 47 percent of the white vote in 1976, but was elected because his 83 percent support from blacks more than made up the deficit. Bill Clinton did even worse among white voters, getting only 39 percent of their vote in 1992 and 43 percent in 1995. But Clinton, too, got five out of six black votes and that was enough to give him wins over George Bush in 1992 and Bob Dole in 1996.").

Between FDR and Johnson's rout in 1964, only two Democratic presidents were elected: John F. Kennedy and Harry Truman. Kennedy won 49 percent of the white vote to Nixon's 51 percent. "Election Polls—Vote by Groups, 1960–1964," Gallup, http://www.gallup.com/poll/9454/election-polls-vote-groups-19601964.aspx.

Truman won a bare majority of the white vote at about 47 percent to Dewey's 44 percent, but Truman captured two-thirds of the black vote, carrying him to electoral victory. See Manning Marable, *Race, Reform, and Rebellion: The Second Reconstruction and Beyond in Black America, 1945–2006* (Jackson: University Press of Mississippi, 2007), 23, available online at http://books.google.com/books?id=qifpm1zjCLkC&pg=PA23&lpg=PA23&dq=could+truman+have+won+without+the+black+vote?&source=bl&ots=iZR2AWYoP4&sig=LvtqfUNu9HPNepA_fiYYFzwf5OE&hl=en&sa=X&ei=RLdKVLODIoLCsASAuYDQDQ&ved=0CE4Q6AEwBg#v=o

nepage&q=could%20truman%20have%20won%20without%20the%20
black%20vote%3F&f=false; and Tom Curry, "How Truman Defied the Odds
in 1948," NBC News, September 12, 2008, http://www.nbcnews.com/
id/26661213/ns/politics-decision_08/t/how-truman-defied-odds/.

14.　Patrick Reddy, "Immigration: The *Real* Kennedy Legacy," *Public Perspective*,
Roper Center, October/November 1998, http://www.ropercenter.uconn.
edu/public-perspective/ppscan/96/96018.pdf.

15.　See, e.g., William Branigin, "INS Accused of Giving In to Politics; White
House Pressure Tied to Citizen Push," *Washington Post*, March 4, 1997.

16.　See ibid.

17.　Ibid.

18.　See, e.g., Esther Cepeda, "Latino Republicans Get No Respect," *Seattle
Times*, December 18, 2010, http://www.seattletimes.com/opinion/latino-
republicans-get-no-respect/?syndication=rss. ("Traitor. Sellout. Lino
[Latino in name only]. These are some of the epithets Latino Republicans
are called by fellow Hispanics who can't imagine why any self-respecting
descendant of Latin American immigrants would ever carry water for the
Republican Party.")

19.　Ruy Teixeira, "The Emerging Democratic Majority Turns 10," *Atlantic*,
November 10, 2012, http://www.theatlantic.com/politics/archive/2012/11/
the-emerging-democratic-majority-turns-10/265005/.

20.　Jesse Mills, "Somali Social Justice Struggle in the U.S.: A Historical
Context," *Race, Gender, and Class* 19, no. 3 (2012), 52–74.

21.　Pew categorized conservatives into two groups, "Business Conservatives"
and "Steadfast Conservatives," who were, respectively 81 percent and 72
percent "proud to be American." *Beyond Red vs. Blue: The Political Typology*,
Section 9: Patriotism, Personal Traits, Lifestyles, and Demographics, Pew
Center for the People and the Press, June 26, 2014, http://www.people-press.
org/2014/06/26/section-9-patriotism-personal-traits-lifestyles-and-
demographics/.

22.　William Booth, "One Nation, Indivisible: Is It History?," *Washington Post*,
February 22, 1998, http://www.washingtonpost.com/wp-srv/national/
longterm/meltingpot/melt0222.htm.

23.　Cheryl K. Chumley, "Rep. Gutierrez: Obama Assured Me He'll 'Stop the
Deportation of Our People,'" *Washington Times*, July 21, 2014, http://www.
washingtontimes.com/news/2014/jul/21/luis-gutierrez-obama-assured-
me-hell-stop-deportat/.

24. Arian Campo-Flores, "Pushing Obama on Immigration Reform," *Newsweek,* November 29, 2010, http://www.newsweek.com/pushing-obama-immigration-reform-70093.

25. Among many other immigration facts that "no one knows" is this one: Exactly how many of the approximately 125,000 Mariel boatlift "refugees" have been convicted of crimes in America? The U.S. Coast Guard, which oversaw the transfer, estimated about ten thousand of them had been convicted of crimes by 2005. See Dan Horn, "Refugee Repaid Kindness with Crime," *Cincinnati (OH) Enquirer,* May 16, 2005.

26. See, e.g., "Letter to IRS Commissioner Mark W. Everson Re: Potential IRS Actions on the Individual Taxpayer Identification Number (ITIN)," October 22, 2003, http://www.aila.org/content/default.aspx?docid=9536. This special pleading on behalf of illegal alien welfare recipients was signed by the following:

David Marzahl
Salvador Gonzalez
Center for Economic Progress
Janell Duncan
Consumers Union
Michele Waslin
Brenda Muniz
National Council of La Raza
Jean Ann Fox
Consumer Federation of America
Chi Chi Wu
National Consumer Law Center
Rebecca Smith
National Employment Law Project
Josh Bernstein
Joan Friedland
Marielena Hincapie
National Immigration Law Center

27. "An Image Problem," *Washington Times*, April 3, 2006, http://www.washingtontimes.com/news/2006/apr/3/20060403-091645-7346r/.

28. Rove was quoted on *Lou Dobbs Tonight*, CNN, February 9, 2007.

29. "Young Voters Supported Obama Less, but May Have Mattered More," Pew Research Center, November 26, 2012, http://www.people-press.

org/2012/11/26/young-voters-supported-obama-less-but-may-have-mattered-more/.

30. What Lenin actually said was: "[C]apitalists…will toil to prepare their own suicide." William Safire, "On Language: Useful Idiots of the West," *New York Times*, April 12, 1987, http://www.nytimes.com/1987/04/12/magazine/on-language.html.

31. In 2012, Lutheran Family Services Rocky Mountains' gross revenue was $12,915,054; $10,812,318 came from government contracts. Ann Corcoran, "Lutheran Family Services Rocky Mountains Largely Funded by Government Contracts," Refugee Resettlement Watch, October 29, 2014, https://refugeeresettlementwatch.wordpress.com/2014/10/29/lutheran-family-services-rocky-mountains-largely-funded-by-government-contracts/.

32. Louis D. Brandeis, "True Americanism," speech, 1915, text available at http://www.zionism-israel.com/hdoc/Brandeis_True_Americanism.htm.

33. Ibid.

34. Patrick Tierney, *The Highest Altar: The Story of Human Sacrifice* (New York: Viking Adult, 1989), 183–85.

35. Associated Press, "Court: School Ban of US Flag Shirts Allowed," *Daily Mail* (UK), February 28, 2014, http://www.dailymail.co.uk/wires/ap/article-2569975/Court-School-ban-US-flag-shirts-allowed.html.

36. Martha Farnsworth Riche, "We're All Minorities Now," *American Demographics*, October 1991.

37. Al Bravo, "Official English Groups Opposing Spanish Citizenship Ceremony," Associated Press, June 22, 1993, http://www.apnewsarchive.com/1993/Official-English-Groups-Opposing-Spanish-Citizenship-Ceremony/id-7cd6506c6cd5095d966c72c1076f0c86.

38. Hyon B. Shin with Rosalind Bruno, "Language Use and English-Speaking Ability: 2000," U.S. Census Brief, U.S. Census Bureau, October 2003, http://www.census.gov/prod/2003pubs/c2kbr-29.pdf.

39. Camille Ryan, "Language Use in the United States: 2011," U.S. Census Bureau, Table 2, August 2013, http://www.census.gov/prod/2013pubs/acs-22.pdf.

40. Margaret Talbot, "Baghdad on the Plains," *New Republic*, August 11, 1997.

CHAPTER THREE: AMERICA TO THE MEDIA: WHATEVER YOU WANT, JUST DON'T CALL US RACISTS

1. Rand Paul, "From Illegals to Taxpayers," *Washington Times*, February 11, 2013, http://www.washingtontimes.com/news/2013/feb/11/from-illegals-to-taxpayers/.

2. Paul Colford, "'Illegal Immigrant' No More," *Definitive Source* (Associated Press blog), April 2, 2013, http://blog.ap.org/2013/04/02/illegal-immigrant-no-more/.

3. Julie Turkewitz, "In Colorado, Calls to Change a Restaurant's Name from 'Illegal Pete's,'" *New York Times*, November 16, 2014, http://www.nytimes.com/2014/11/17/us/in-colorado-calls-to-change-a-restaurants-name-from-illegal-petes.html?action=click&contentCollection=U.S.&region=Footer&module=MoreInSection&pgtype=article.

4. "California Newspaper Office Vandalized over Use of 'Illegal' Immigrant Label," FoxNews.com, January 9, 2015, http://www.foxnews.com/us/2015/01/09/california-newspaper-office-vandalized-over-use-illegal-immigrant-label/.

5. Jennifer Medina, "McCarthy's Role Is Debated in His Land of Immigrants," *New York Times*, June 23, 2014, http://www.nytimes.com/2014/06/23/us/mccarthys-role-is-debated-in-his-land-of-immigrants.html.

6. Ibid.

7. "Hypocrisy: Harry Reid Said in 1993 What Republicans Say Now about Illegal Immigrants," PopModal Videos, http://www.popmodal.com/video/20143/HYPOCRISY—Harry-Reid-said-in-1993-what-Republicans-say-now-about-Illegal-Immigrants.

8. "Press Release: Reid Introduces Bill to Overhaul Immigration Laws; Slashes Immigrant Influx by More Than 50 Percent," PR Newswire, August 5, 1993.

9. Oforji v. Ashcroft, 354 F.3d 609 (7th Cir. 2003) (Posner concurring).

10. Justice Hugo Black wrote:

    [T]he chief interest of the people in giving permanence and security to citizenship in the Fourteenth Amendment was the desire to protect Negroes. The *Dred Scott* decision had shortly before greatly disturbed many people about the status of Negro citizenship. [Senators] expressed fears that the citizenship so recently conferred on Negroes by the Civil Rights Act could be just as easily taken away from them by subsequent Congresses, and it was to provide an insuperable obstacle against every governmental effort to strip Negroes of their newly acquired citizenship that the first clause was added to the Fourteenth Amendment. (Afroyim v. Rusk, 387 U.S. 253 [1967] [citations omitted])

Although he dissented from the court's opinion in that case, Justice John Marshall Harlan agreed on the purpose of the Fourteenth Amendment:

Its sponsors evidently shared the fears of Senators Stewart and Wade that, unless citizenship were defined, freedmen might, under the reasoning of the Dred Scott decision, be excluded by the courts from the scope of the Amendment. It was agreed that, since the "courts have stumbled on the subject," it would be prudent to remove the "doubt thrown over" it. The clause would essentially overrule *Dred Scott* and place beyond question the freedmen's right of citizenship because of birth. It was suggested, moreover, that it would, by creating a basis for federal citizenship which was indisputably independent of state citizenship, preclude any effort by state legislatures to circumvent the Amendment by denying freedmen state citizenship. (Afroyim v. Rusk, 387 U.S. 253 [1967] [Harlan dissenting] [citations omitted])

11. The "better view," according to the *Yale Law Journal*, was that of Chief Justice Melville Fuller, who explained the idiocy of relying on feudal laws to determine *American* citizenship in a dissent: "Manifestly, when the sovereignty of the Crown was thrown off and an independent government established, every rule of the common law and every statute of England obtaining in the Colonies in derogation of the principles on which the new government was founded was abrogated." "Jetsam and Flotsam: Citizenship of Chinaman Born in the United States," *Yale Law Journal*, June 16, 1898.

12. Madeleine Pelner Cosman, "Illegal Aliens and American Medicine," *Journal of American Physicians and Surgeons* 10, no. 1 (Spring 2005), 6, http://www.jpands.org/vol10no1/cosman.pdf.

13. Ibid., 7; and Eduardo Porter, "Tighter Border Yields Odd Result: More Illegals Stay," *Wall Street Journal*, October 10, 2003, http://www.wsj.com/articles/SB106574684985644800 (also discussing the Silverio extended family's reliance on government support and anchor baby scams).

14. Cosman, "Illegal Aliens and American Medicine"; see also Porter, "Tighter Border."
15. U.S. v. Wong Kim Ark, 169 U.S. 649 (1898) (Fuller dissenting).
16. *Dual Citizenship, Birthright Citizenship, and the Meaning of Sovereignty: Hearing before the Subcommittee on Immigration, Border Security, and Claims*, 109th Cong. (2005) (testimony of Stanley A. Renshon).
17. Nasser al-Awlaki, "The Drone That Killed My Grandson," *New York Times*, July 17, 2013, http://www.nytimes.com/2013/07/18/opinion/the-drone-that-killed-my-grandson.html.
18. Nexis search in English language news, previous two years, for "immigration and (majority or Americans) w/s (support! or agree or want) w/s pathway to citizenship" on November 21, 2014: 475 documents.
19. *Fox News Sunday*, Chris Wallace, host, April 14, 2013.
20. NBC News/*Wall Street Journal* survey November 2014, question 24, http://online.wsj.com/public/resources/documents/WSJNBCpoll11192014.pdf. (The last of three polls dropped only the "who have jobs" part of the question.)
21. Jon Feere, "Five Myths about Amnesty for Illegal Immigrants in Senate Bill," Center for Immigration Studies, May 15, 2013, http://cis.org/feere/5-myths-about-amnesty-illegal-immigrants-senate-bill.
22. Ibid.
23. David North, "Lessons Learned from the Legalization Programs of the 1980s," ILW.com, http://www.ilw.com/articles/2005,0302-north.shtm; and David S. North and Anna Mary Portz, *The U.S. Alien Legalization Program* (Washington, DC: TransCentury Development Associates, June 1989), 82–90.
24. North, "Lessons Learned."
25. In case that's not clear enough, in April 2013 Senate negotiators debated whether to require employers of illegal aliens to calculate the Social Security taxes that would have been collected from an American worker. "They chose the milder approach," Politico reported, requiring illegal aliens to pay only those taxes already "assessed" by the IRS. Which, again, is: Zero. Kelsey Snell, "Gang of Eight Rolls Dice on Immigration," Politico, April 18, 2013, http://www.politico.com/story/2013/04/gang-of-eight-rolls-dice-on-immigration-90313.html.
26. See, e.g., Snell, "Gang of Eight Rolls Dice on Immigration."

27. Robert Rector and Jason Richwine, "The Fiscal Cost of Unlawful Immigrants and Amnesty to the U.S. Taxpayer," Heritage Foundation, May 6, 2013, http://www.heritage.org/research/reports/2013/05/the-fiscal-cost-of-unlawful-immigrants-and-amnesty-to-the-us-taxpayer.

28. Jan C. Ting, "IRS: Illegal Aliens Can Qualify for Earned Income Tax Credit," *Brandywine to Broad* (blog), NewsWorks, May 6, 2011, http://www.newsworks.org/index.php/blogs/brandywine-to-broad/item/19005-irs-illegal-aliens-can-qualify-for-earned-income-tax-credit. ("On June 9, 2000, a 'Chief Counsel Advice' was published in the name of 'Mary Oppenheimer, Acting Assistant Chief Counsel [Employee Benefits],' though it was signed by 'Mark Schwimmer, Senior Technician Reviewer.' This document advises IRS employees that illegal aliens who are disqualified from receiving the EITC can retroactively receive EITC benefits for years worked without a valid Social Security number if, after receiving a valid Social Security number, they file an amended return for the previous years worked.")

29. Steven A. Camarota, "Welfare Use by Immigrant Households with Children: A Look at Cash, Medicaid, Housing, and Food Programs," Center for Immigration Studies, April 2011, http://cis.org/immigrant-welfare-use-2011.

30. *Fox News Sunday*, April 14, 2013, transcript available online at FoxNews.com, http://www.foxnews.com/on-air/fox-news-sunday-chris-wallace/2013/04/14/sen-rubio-defends-gang-8-immigration-overhaul-sens-durbin-cornyn-chances-bipartisan#p//v/2300904976001.

31. The Field Poll, "Near-Universal Support for Allowing Long-Time Undocumented Residents to Stay and Become Citizens under Certain Conditions," press release, February 22, 2013, http://www.field.com/fieldpollonline/subscribers/Rls2439.pdf.

CHAPTER FOUR: THE LIE: THERE'S NO SUCH THING AS AMERICA

1. As Edmund Burke put it, "This fierce spirit of liberty is stronger in the English colonies probably than in any other people of the earth." Edmund Burke, "Speech on Conciliation with the Colonies," March 22, 1775, available in Philip B. Kurland and Ralph Lerner, eds., "Fundamental Documents," chapter 1 of *The Founders' Constitution* (Chicago: University of Chicago Press and the Liberty Fund, 1987), available online at http://press-pubs.uchicago.edu/founders/documents/v1ch1s2.html.

2. Samuel Huntington, *Who Are We? The Challenges to America's National Identity* (New York: Simon & Schuster, 2005), 93.

3. Snopes.com, "Fact Check: Michelle Obama Said Declaration Signers Not 'Born American,'" *Traverse City (MI) Record-Eagle*, July 25, 2014, http://www.record-eagle.com/opinion/fact-check-michelle-obama-said-declaration-signers-not-born-american/article_7fd51a6c-3b90-56ff-8eb3-17393f5e23ae.html.

4. Japan is about 145,000 square miles; the British Isles (Ireland and the United Kingdom), 120,000 square miles; and the Netherlands, 16,000 square miles.

5. Huntington, *Who Are We?*

6. Ibid.

7. "The Nation: Children of the Founders," *Time*, July 5, 1976, available online at http://content.time.com/time/subscriber/article/0,33009,917015-1,00.html.

8. Leonard W. Boasberg, "Phila. and Japan: Quite a Connection There Are Lots of Them, as a New Book Shows, Going Back Even to Franklin," *Philadelphia (PA) Inquirer*, April 25, 1999, http://articles.philly.com/1999-04-25/living/25520225_1_japanese-woman-felice-fischer-american-japanese.

9. Huntington, *Who Are We?*

10. Campbell Gibson and Kay Jung, "Historical Census Statistics on Population Totals by Race, 1790 to 1990," U.S. Census Bureau, September 2002, http://www.census.gov/population/www/documentation/twps0056/twps0056.html (Table 1, "United States–Race and Hispanic Origin: 1790 to 1990," http://www.census.gov/population/www/documentation/twps0056/tab01.pdf).

11. See George Athan Billias, *General John Glover and His Marblehead Mariners* (New York: Henry Holt and Company, 1960).

12. Huntington, *Who Are We?*, 44.

13. Ibid.

14. See Félix V. Matos Rodríguez, "Puerto Ricans in the United States: Past, Present, and Future," presentation given at the Council of State Governments, Eastern Regional Conference, December 9, 2013, slides available online at http://www.csgeast.org/2013annualmeeting/documents/matos.pdf; and "Puerto Ricans in the United States: Research Roundup," Journalist's Resource, July 2, 2013, http://journalistsresource.org/studies/government/immigration/puerto-ricans-in-the-united-states-research-roundup#sthash.BjXLBhNz.dpuf.

15. "Ellis Island," National Parks Service, http://www.nps.gov/elis/historyculture/index.htm.

16. See, e.g., Josiah Henry Benton, *Warning Out in New England, 1656–1817* (Boston: W. B. Clarke Co., 1911), available online at https://ia700404.us.archive.org/8/items/warningoutinnewe00josi/warningoutinnewe00josi.pdf; and Steven R. Hoffbeck, "'Remember the Poor' (Galatians 2:10): Poor Farms in Vermont," *Vermont History: The Proceedings of the Vermont Historical Society*, Fall 1989, https://vermonthistory.org/journal/misc/Remember_v57.pdf.

17. Huntington, *Who Are We?*, 186–87.

18. Alejandro Portes and Ruben Rumbauthow, *Legacies: The Story of the Immigrant Second Generation* (Berkeley: University of California Press, 2001), 39.

19. See, e.g., Steven A. Camarota, "Immigrants in the United States, 2010: A Profile of America's Foreign-Born Population," Center for Immigration Studies, Table 5, August 2012, http://cis.org/2012-profile-of-americas-foreign-born-population#5.

20. UPI, "The Almanac—Weekly," April 3, 2012.

21. [Argentina-born] Andres Oppenheimer, "Racists Will Love New 'Hispanic Threat' Book," *Miami Herald*, March 3, 2004, http://web.archive.org/web/20040413045004/http://www.miami.com/mld/miamiherald/news/columnists/andres_oppenheimer/8043803.htm.

22. Burke, "Speech on Conciliation with the Colonies."

23. Samantha Critchell, "Ralph Lauren Throws 40th Anniversary Party during Fashion Week in New York," Associated Press, September 9, 2007, available online at *Sydney (AU) Morning Herald*, http://www.thestar.com.my/story/?file=%2f2007%2f9%2f9%2fapworld%2f20070909125001&sec=apworld; and Johanna Neuman, "Modern Jewish History: From Ghetto to Glamour—How Jews Redesigned the Fashion Business," Jewish Virtual Library, http://www.jewishvirtuallibrary.org/jsource/History/NeumanFashion.html.

24. Margaret Talbot, "Baghdad on the Plains," *New Republic*, August 11, 1997.

25. David Gregory, *Meet The Press*, NBC, November 8, 2009.

26. Al Sharpton, *Politics Nation*, MSNBC, April 24, 2013.

27. For example, every segregationist governor and every segregationist senator was a Democrat. For the details, see Ann Coulter, *Mugged: Racial Demagoguery from the Seventies to Obama* (New York: Penguin, 2012).

28. Robert D. Putnam, "*E Pluribus Unum*: Diversity and Community in the Twenty-First Century," *Scandinavian Political Studies* 30, no. 2 (2007),

available online at http://www.aimlessgromar.com/wp-content/
uploads/2013/12/j-1467-9477-2007-00176-x.pdf.

29. Ibid.
30. As Putnam described it: "[I]nhabitants of diverse communities tend to withdraw from collective life, to distrust their neighbours, regardless of the colour of their skin, to withdraw even from close friends, to expect the worst from their community and its leaders, to volunteer less, give less to charity and work on community projects less often, to register to vote less, to agitate for social reform *more,* but have less faith that they can actually make a difference, and to huddle unhappily in front of the television." Ibid.
31. Michael Jonas, "The Downside of Diversity," *New York Times*, August 5, 2007, http://www.nytimes.com/2007/08/05/world/americas/05iht-diversity.1.6986248.html.
32. Putnam, "*E Pluribus Unum.*"
33. Ibid., Figure 4.
34. All demographic data on cities come from "State & County QuickFacts," U.S. Census Bureau, http://quickfacts.census.gov/qfd/index.html. Putnam was using 2000 Census data.
35. Putnam, "*E Pluribus Unum*," Figures 3 and 5.
36. Jeffrey S. Passel and D'Vera Cohn, "U.S. Population Projections: 2005–2050," Pew Research Center Hispanic Trends Project, February 11, 2008, http://www.pewhispanic.org/2008/02/11/us-population-projections-2005-2050/. ("The Hispanic population, 42 million in 2005, will rise to 128 million in 2050.")

CHAPTER FIVE: THIRTY MILLION MEXICANS

1. Diego Ribadeneira, "A Tenure Born in Tumult of Busing Comes to End at S. Boston High," *Boston Globe*, November 16, 1989.
2. Malaika Brown, "Tustin: Flags Unfurl as Tribute to Diversity," *Los Angeles Times*, April 8, 1992, http://articles.latimes.com/1992-04-08/local/me-557_1_cultural-diversity.
3. "A. G. Currie Middle School, 2009" [the most recent year for which the scores were available], Homefacts, http://www.homefacts.com/schools/California/Orange-County/Tustin/A-G-Currie-Middle.html.
4. Ibid.

5. Sara Gates, "Hollywood High School: Latino Population Dominates Student Body," Huffington Post, February 22, 2012, http://www.huffingtonpost. com/2012/02/22/hollywood-high-latinos_n_1294569.html.

6. City News Service, April 30, 2010 ("Three Hollywood High School students...Josue Bran, Jessy Guerrero and Hugo Ascencio—each 19 and from Hollywood—were booked on suspicion of grand theft...."); "City Attorney Delgadillo, Council President Garcetti Announce Launch of New School Safety Project to Hollywood High School," US States News, April 18, 2008; Susannah Rosenblatt, "Teen Shot, Hurt in Attack Near School," *Los Angeles Times*, December 4, 2007, http://articles.latimes.com/2007/ dec/04/local/me-briefs4.s1; and Global Broadcast Database, ABC, April 14, 2006 ("Oceanside investigators arrested a 19-year-old Hollywood High School student for allegedly molesting a 13-year-old Oceanside girl.").

7. *CNN Newsroom*, February 21, 2012.

8. Andrew Rice, "Life on the Line," *New York Times*, July 28, 2011, http://www. nytimes.com/2011/07/31/magazine/life-on-the-line-between-el-paso-and- juarez.html?pagewanted=all.

9. Anna Brown and Eileen Patten, "Hispanics of Mexican Origin in the United States," Pew Research Center Hispanic Trends Project, 2011, http://www. pewhispanic.org/2013/06/19/hispanics-of-mexican-origin-in-the-united- states-2011/. ("An estimated 33.5 million Hispanics of Mexican origin resided in the United States in 2011, according to the Census Bureau's American Community Survey.")

10. "Facts for Features: Hispanic Heritage Month 2014: Sept. 15–Oct. 15," U.S. Census Bureau, September 8, 2014, http://www.census.gov/newsroom/ facts-for-features/2014/cb14-ff22.html.

11. See generally "Hispanic Americans by the Numbers, 2012," U.S. Census Bureau, 2012, http://www.infoplease.com/spot/hhmcensus1.html#ixzz3AlIoS52Z; John P. Tuman, David F. Damore, and Maria José Flor Ágreda, "Immigration and the Contours of Nevada's Latino Population," Brookings Mountain West, June 2013, http://www.unlv.edu/sites/default/files/24/BrookingsReport- ImmigrationAndContours.pdf.

12. "State and County QuickFacts," U.S. Census Bureau, accessed 2014, http:// quickfacts.census.gov/qfd/states/35000.html; and Mark Hugo Lopez, "In 2014, Latinos Will Surpass Whites as Largest Racial/Ethnic Group in California," Pew Research Center, January 24, 2014, http://www. pewresearch.org/fact-tank/2014/01/24/in-2014-latinos-will-surpass-whites- as-largest-racialethnic-group-in-california/.

13. U.S. Census Bureau, "Facts for Features."
14. "Table 19: California—Race and Hispanic Origin: 1850 to 1990," U.S. Census Bureau, http://www.census.gov/population/www/documentation/twps0056/tab19.pdf.
15. Lopez, "In 2014, Latinos Will Surpass Whites."
16. In the last a decade, the white population of California has plummeted from 47 percent to 39 percent, while the Hispanic population has grown from 32 percent to 39 percent. Today, Hispanics make up 53.25 percent of the students in all California schools. All "minorities"—i.e., nonwhites—constitute 75 percent of the school population. "Fingertip Facts on Education in California—*CalEdFacts*," California Department of Education, 2013, http://www.cde.ca.gov/ds/sd/cb/ceffingertipfacts.asp.
17. "Rise in Public Benefits to Children of Illegal Immigrants in L.A. County Has Supervisor 'Very Concerned,'" *Los Angeles Times*, September 3, 2010, http://latimesblogs.latimes.com/lanow/2010/09/rise-in-public-benefits-to-children-of-illegal-immigrants-in-los-angeles-county-concerns-supervisor-michael-antonovich.html.
18. Don E. Albrecht, "State of Nevada," Western Rural Development Center, 2008, http://wrdc.usu.edu/files/uploads/Regional%20Data/NV/Nevada_WEB.pdf.
19. Tuman, Damore, and Flor Ágreda, "Immigration and the Contours of Nevada's Latino Population."
20. Elizabeth M. Grieco, Edward Trevelyan, et al., "The Size, Place of Birth, and Geographic Distribution of the Foreign-Born Population in the United States: 1960 to 2010," U.S. Census Bureau, October 2012, Table 1 and p. 8, http://www.census.gov/population/foreign/files/WorkingPaper96.pdf.
21. Ibid., Table 1 and p. 8.
22. Joseph Russell and Jeanne Batalov, "European Immigrants in the United States," Migration Policy Institute, July 26, 2012, http://www.migrationpolicy.org/article/european-immigrants-united-states; Grieco, Trevelyan, et al., "The Size, Place of Birth, and Geographic Distribution," Table 1 and p. 8.
23. Ana Gonzalez-Barrera and Mark Hugo Lopez, "A Demographic Portrait of Mexican-Origin Hispanics in the United States," Pew Research Center Hispanic Trends Project, May 1, 2013, http://www.pewhispanic.org/2013/05/01/a-demographic-portrait-of-mexican-origin-hispanics-in-the-united-states/.

24. Based on a 5 percent sample, the Census Bureau estimated that there were about 1.9 million Spanish-speaking white people in the United States in 1940. "United States—Race and Hispanic Origin: 1790 to 1990," U.S. Census Bureau, Table 1, http://www.census.gov/population/www/documentation/twps0056/tab01.pf.

25. Grieco, Trevelyan, et al., "The Size, Place of Birth, and Geographic Distribution," 8.

26. Jeffrey Passel and D'Vera Cohn, "Unauthorized Immigrant Population: National and State Trends, 2010," Pew Research Center Hispanic Trends Project, February 1, 2011, http://www.pewhispanic.org/files/reports/133.pdf.

27. Michael Hoefer, Nancy Rytina, and Bryan C. Baker, "Estimates of the Unauthorized Immigrant Population Residing in the United States: January 2008," Department of Homeland Security, February 2009, http://www.dhs.gov/xlibrary/assets/statistics/publications/ois_ill_pe_2008.pdf.

28. See, e.g., Roger Lowenstein, "The Immigration Equation," *New York Times Magazine*, July 9, 2006, http://www.nytimes.com/2006/07/09/magazine/09IMM.html. ("The latest estimate is that the United States has 11.5 million undocumented foreigners, and it's those immigrants—the illegal ones—who have galvanized Congress.")

29. Robert Justich and Betty Ng, "The Underground Labor Force Is Rising to the Surface," Bear Stearns Asset Management, January 3, 2005, http://www.steinreport.com/BearStearnsStudy.pdf.

30. Carl Bialik, "In Counting Illegal Immigrants, Certain Assumptions Apply," *Wall Street Journal*, May 7, 2010, http://www.wsj.com/articles/SB10001424052748704370704575228432695989918.

31. Ibid.

32. Margolis found a similarly massive undercount of Brazilians living in Boston, by comparing census figures with the number counted by the Boston Archdiocese and the Brazilian consulate. Justich and Ng, "The Underground Labor Force."

33. Donald L. Barlett and James B. Steele, "Illegal Aliens: Who Left the Door Open?," *Time*, March 30, 2006, http://content.time.com/time/subscriber/article/0,33009,995145,00.html.

34. Edward Colby, "Dobbs Pins Down Illegal Immigrants, Give or Take 9 Million," *Columbia Journalism Review*, March 31, 2006, http://www.cjr.org/politics/dobbs_pins_down_illegal_immigr.php?page=all#sthash.IkG9Z6cD.dpuf.

35. See Passel and Cohn, "Unauthorized Immigrant Population"; and Hoefer, Rytina, and Baker, "Estimates of the Unauthorized Immigrant Population Residing in the United States," 2.

36. "Three Decades of Mass Immigration: The Legacy of the 1965 Immigration Act," Center for Immigration Studies, September 1995, http://cis.org/1965ImmigrationAct-MassImmigration, citing *Hearings before the U.S. Senate Subcommittee on Immigration and Naturalization of the Committee on the Judiciary*, 89th Cong. 1–3 (1965).

37. Ibid., citing *Washington Post*, October 4, 1965, p. 16.

38. Ibid., citing *Hearings before the U.S. Senate Subcommittee on Immigration and Naturalization of the Committee on the Judiciary*, 89th Cong. 71, 119 (1965).

39. Ibid., citing U.S. Congress, House, 1964 hearings, 418.

40. Ibid., citing *Hearings before the U.S. Senate Subcommittee on Immigration and Naturalization of the Committee on the Judiciary*, 89th Cong. 65 (1965).

41. Ibid., citing *Congressional Record*, August 25, 1965, p. 21812.

42. "Three Decades of Mass Immigration."

43. William Branigin, "Immigrants Shunning Idea of Assimilation," *Washington Post*, May 25, 1998, http://www.washingtonpost.com/wp-srv/national/longterm/meltingpot/melt0525a.htm.

44. "Three Decades of Mass Immigration."

45. Nancy Foner, *From Ellis Island to JFK: New York's Two Great Waves of Immigration* (New York: Russell Sage Foundation, 2000), finding that employers were more likely to hire immigrants over American blacks and Hispanics, expecting them to be more docile and hardworking, cited in Kimberly A. Huisman, "Why Maine? Secondary Migration Decisions Of Somali Refugees," *Ìrìnkèrindò: A Journal of African Migration*, no. 5 (December 2011), 81, 98, http://www.africamigration.com/Issue%205/Articles/PDF/Kimberly-Huisman_Why-Maine.pdf.

CHAPTER SIX: IMMIGRATION AS "MYSTERY BARGAIN BIN"

1. See, e.g., Sebastian Rotella, "The American behind India's 9/11—and How U.S. Botched Chances to Stop Him," ProPublica, January 24, 2013, http://www.propublica.org/article/david-headley-homegrown-terrorist#chapter-3.

2.   William Booth, "One Nation, Indivisible: Is It History?," *Washington Post*, February 22, 1998, http://www.washingtonpost.com/wp-srv/national/ longterm/meltingpot/melt0222.htm.

3.   Steven A. Camarota, "Immigrants in the United States: A Profile of America's Foreign-Born Population," Center for Immigration Studies, Table 7, August 2012, http://www.cis.org/sites/cis.org/files/articles/2012/ immigrants-in-the-united-states-2012.pdf.

4.   Then–UN Representative Madeleine K. Albright quoted in John Bolton, "Wrong Turn in Somalia," *Foreign Affairs* 73, no. 1, February 1994, http:// www.foreignaffairs.com/articles/49438/john-r-bolton/wrong-turn-in- somalia.

5.   Leslie Brooks Suzukamo, "Campaign Aims to Raise Awareness about Immigrants," *St. Paul (MN) Pioneer Press*, 1999.

6.   Minnesota News in Brief at 8:58 p.m. CST, the Associated Press State and Local Wire, November 9, 2010.

7.   "African-Born Population in U.S. Roughly Doubled Every Decade since 1970," Census Bureau Reports, U.S. Census Bureau, October 1, 2014, http:// www.census.gov/newsroom/press-releases/2014/cb14-184.html.

8.   *Hearing: Beyond the Streets: America's Evolving Gang Threat, House Committee on the Judiciary Subcommittee on Crime, Terrorism, and Homeland Security*, 112th Cong. (July 25, 2012) (testimony of Richard W. Stanek, sheriff of Hennepin County, Minnesota), available at http:// judiciary.house.gov/_files/hearings/Hearings%202012/Stanek%20 07252012.pdf. See also Dan Van Lehman and Omar Eno, "The Somali Bantu: Their History and Culture," Center for Applied Linguistics, February 2003, available at http://www.hartfordinfo.org/issues/wsd/ immigrants/somali_bantu.pdf, estimating that forty thousand Somalis lived in Minnesota in 2003. Well over ten thousand have immigrated to Minnesota since then. See, e.g., Martha H. Bigelow, *Mogadishu on the Mississippi: Language, Racialized Identity, and Education* (Malden, MA: Wiley-Blackwell, 2010). See also Karla Hult, "Somali Minnesotans, through the Eyes of Three Generations," KARE-11, May 3, 2013, http://archive. kare11.com/rss/article/1024223/14/somali-minnesotans-through-the-eyes- of-three-generations; and "Total Ancestry Reported: Minnesota," 2008– 2012 American Community Survey 5-Year Estimates, U.S. Census Bureau, http://factfinder2.census.gov/faces/tableservices/jsf/pages/productview. xhtml?src=bkmk. (Within the category of "Subsaharan African," thirty- three thousand Minnesotans identify as "Somalian" and thirty-one

thousand identify as "African." It is believed that these figures undercount Somalians for a variety of reasons, such as overcrowding in rental units.)

9. See, e.g., "Feds: Twin Cities Human Traffickers Enslaved Girls Younger Than 13 for a Decade," *St. Paul (MN) Pioneer Press*, November 7, 2010, http://www.twincities.com/ci_16555475 ("Charges in the 24-count indictment include sex trafficking of juveniles and conspiring to sex-traffic juveniles, obstruction of justice, perjury, auto theft and credit card fraud."); Laura Yuen, "3 Guilty in Somali Gang Sex Trafficking Case," Minnesota Public Radio News, May 4, 2012, http://www.mprnews.org/story/2012/05/04/sex-trafficking; and *Hearing: Beyond the Streets.*

10. See Tino Sanandaji, "Don't Believe the Hype: Somali Immigration to Minnesota Is a Complete Failure," *Super-Economy* (blog), September 4, 2010, http://super-economy.blogspot.com/2010/09/dont-believe-hype-somali-immigration-to.html, citing the 2008 U.S. Census Bureau's American Community Survey; and Elizabeth Dunbar, "Comparing the Somali Experience in Minnesota to Other Immigrant Groups," Minnesota Public Radio News, January 22, 2010, http://www.mprnews.org/story/2010/01/25/comparing-the-somali-experience-in-minnesota-to-other-immigrant-groups-of-immigrants-.

11. See, e.g., "Mayors Seek Closure of Troubling Gaps," *Minneapolis (MN) Star Tribune*, January 7, 2014. ("Changing people's thinking about the value of every part of the city is essential to closing the income gap, achievement gap, health gap and all the other income- and race-based disparities that afflict the Twin Cities.... The arc of history has truly bent toward diversity and inclusivity.")

12. Kelly Smith and Paul Walsh, "Food Fight Erupts into Melee at South H.S.," *Minneapolis (MN) Star Tribune*, February 15, 2013.

13. See, e.g., Joe Coscarelli, "Long Island Teen Just Happened to Get into All 8 Ivy League Schools," *New York*, April 1, 2014, http://nymag.com/daily/intelligencer/2014/04/kwasi-enin-accepted-eight-ivy-league-schools.html. ("Kwasi Enin is 17 years old and better than you.")

14. See, e.g., Pam Belluck, "Mixed Welcome as Somalis Settle in a Maine City," *New York Times*, October 15, 2002, http://www.nytimes.com/2002/10/15/us/mixed-welcome-as-somalis-settle-in-a-maine-city.html.

15. Hassan v. City of Minneapolis, 489 F.3d 914 (8th Cir. 2007), available online at http://caselaw.findlaw.com/us-8th-circuit/1378661.html.

16. Art Hughes, "Somalis Outraged by Police Shooting," Minnesota Public Radio News, March 11, 2002, http://news.minnesota.publicradio.org/features/200203/11_hughesa_mplsshooting/.

17. *Hassan v. City of Minneapolis.*

18. See, e.g., Belluck, "Mixed Welcome."

19. Scott Dolan, "Portland Teen Admits Break-In, Rape," *Portland (OR) Press Herald*, April 18, 2013, http://www.pressherald.com/2013/04/18/portland-teen-pleads-guilty-to-break-in-rape/.

20. Lisa Cornwell, "Man Caught in Mexico Sentenced in Ohio Child Rape," Associated Press, March 16, 2012, available online at the *Alliance (OH) Review*, http://www.the-review.com/latest%20headlines/2012/03/15/man-caught-in-mexico-sentenced-in-ohio-child-rape.

21. State v. Isa, 850 S.W.2d 876 (1993) (S. Ct. MO), March 23, 1993, available online at http://www.leagle.com/decision/19931726850SW2d876_11671.xml/STATE%20v.%20IS.

22. *State v. Isa*; Judith VandeWater and Tim Bryant, "From 1991: FBI Tapes Implicate Father in Daughter's Death," *St. Louis (MO) Dispatch*, October 23, 1991, http://www.stltoday.com/news/local/crime-and-courts/from-fbi-tapes-implicate-father-in-daughter-s-death/article_efafe11f-f568-5f92-95da-1bf8beebfab5.html; Joe Treen, "'Die, My Daughter, Die!,'" *People*, January 20, 1992, http://www.people.com/people/archive/article/0,,20111801,00.html; and "Terror and Death at Home Are Caught in F.B.I. Tape," *New York Times*, October 28, 1991, http://www.nytimes.com/1991/10/28/us/terror-and-death-at-home-are-caught-in-fbi-tape.html.

23. "Terror and Death at Home."

24. Ibid.

25. Ibid.

26. Margaret Talbot, "Baghdad on the Plains," *New Republic*, August 11, 1997.

27. Doriane Lambelet Coleman, "Culture, Cloaked in *Mens Rea*," *South Atlantic Quarterly* 100, no. 4 (Fall 2001), http://scholarship.law.duke.edu/cgi/viewcontent.cgi?article=1924&context=faculty_scholarship.

28. Talbot, "Baghdad on the Plains."

29. Coleman, "Culture, Cloaked in *Mens Rea*."

30. Michael Reese, "A Tragedy in Santa Monica," *Newsweek*, May 6, 1985.

31. Ibid.

32. Ruben Navarrette, "Boston Bombing Shouldn't Derail Immigration Reform," CNN Wire, April 20, 2013, http://www.cnn.com/2013/04/20/opinion/navarrette-immigration-boston/.

33. Associated Press, "Friends Say N.Y. Shooter Angry at America," *Anderson (SC) Independent-Mail*, April 5, 2009. ("Jiverly Wong was upset over losing his job at a vacuum plant, didn't like people picking on him for his limited English and once angrily told a co-worker, 'America sucks.'")

34. "Ople: No Filipino Killed in Chicago Shootout," INQ7.net (Manila), August 29, 2003, http://web.archive.org/web/20031219113344/http://www.inq7.net/brk/2003/aug/29/brkofw_2-1.htm. ("Ople said, however, he ordered the consulate to verify and ensure that no Filipinos were harmed when the gunman, identified as Mexican-born Salvador Tapia shot and killed six people in an auto parts warehouse before being shot and killed by the police on Wednesday.")

35. See, e.g., Frank Main and Carlos Sadovi, "Gun First Bought in Suburb in 1967," *Chicago Sun-Times*, August 29, 2003, http://web.archive.org/web/20030830025858/http://www.suntimes.com/output/news/cst-nws-lucky29.html.

36. Frank Bruni, "Rock Band's Promise Was Bright Until Gunman Shattered Their Hope," *New York Times*, February 25, 1997, http://www.nytimes.com/1997/02/25/nyregion/rock-band-s-promise-was-bright-until-gunman-shattered-their-hope.html.

37. Melissa Healy, "Matthew Gross' Life Changed at the Empire State Building," *Los Angeles Times*, January 24, 2011, http://articles.latimes.com/2011/jan/24/health/la-he-matthew-gross-20110124.

38. Geraldine Baum and Anna Gorman, "Binghamton, N.Y., Mass Shooting Leaves Some Dead," *Los Angeles Times*, April 4, 2009, http://articles.latimes.com/2009/apr/04/nation/na-binghamton-shooting-hostage4. ("This is truly an American tragedy....")

39. David Ovalle, "Immigration Authorities Released Man Who Went On to Kill 3 in North Miami," *Miami Herald*, January 22, 2012.

40. *Report to Congressional Requesters: Criminal Alien Statistics* (Washington, DC: United States Government Accountability Office, March 2011), 24, http://www.gao.gov/new.items/d11187.pdf. (Forty-three percent of those convicted of terrorism-related offenses were "aliens with or without legal immigration status," and 65 percent of those were lawful permanent residents.)

41. Josh Gerstein, "Failed Somali Pirate Prosecution Fuels Terror Trial Fears," Politico, February 10, 2014, http://www.politico.com/story/2014/02/somali-pirate-prosecution-103328.html; and Daniel Greenfield, "Somali Pirate May Receive Asylum in US," FrontPage Magazine, February 17, 2014, http://

www.frontpagemag.com/2014/dgreenfield/somali-pirate-may-receive-asylum-in-us/.

42. Transcript of sentencing hearing of *U.S. v. Beatrice Munyenyezi*, USDC (NH), July 15, 2013.

43. Michael Wilson, "From Smiling Coffee Vendor to Terror Suspect," *New York Times*, September 26, 2009, http://www.nytimes.com/2009/09/26/nyregion/26profile.html?pagewanted=all&_r=0.

44. Mosi Secret, "Terror Defendant Convicted in New York Subway Plot," *New York Times*, May 1, 2012, http://www.nytimes.com/2012/05/02/nyregion/terror-defendant-convicted-in-plot-to-bomb-new-york-subways.html?_r=0.

45. Andrea Elliot, "A Call to Jihad, Answered in America," *New York Times*, July 11, 2009, http://www.nytimes.com/2009/07/12/us/12somalis.html?pagewanted=all.

46. Spencer S. Hsu, "U.S. Says Men Ran Terror Network," *Washington Post*, November 24, 2009, http://www.washingtonpost.com/wp-dyn/content/article/2009/11/23/AR2009112303999.html. See also Brandt Williams, "Kamal Said Hassan, Mahamud Said Omar Sentenced in al-Shabab Terrorism Trial," Minnesota Public Radio News, May 14, 2013, http://www.mprnews.org/story/2013/05/14/news/sentence-alshabab-terrorism-trial.

47. David Johnston and Eric Schmitt, "Ex-Military Officer in Pakistan Is Linked to 2 Chicago Terrorism Suspects," *New York Times*, November 19, 2009, http://www.nytimes.com/2009/11/19/world/asia/19mumbai.html?pagewanted=all.

48. See Rotella, "The American behind India's 9/11."

49. Ginger Thompson, "A Terror Suspect with Feet in East and West," *New York Times*, November 22, 2009, http://www.nytimes.com/2009/11/22/us/22terror.html?pagewanted=all.

50. Joseph Tanfani et al., "American Suspect in Mumbai Attack Was DEA Informant," *Philadelphia (PA) Inquirer*, December 14, 2009, available online at http://www.mcclatchydc.com/2009/12/14/80622_american-suspect-in-mumbai-attack.html?rh=1#storylink=cpy.

51. Ginger Thompson and David Johnston, "U.S. Man Accused of Helping Plot Mumbai Attack," *New York Times*, December 8, 2009, http://www.nytimes.com/2009/12/08/world/asia/08terror.html.

52. Thompson, "A Terror Suspect with Feet in East and West."

53. Associated Press, "Plea in Terrorism Case," *New York Times*, January 28, 2010, http://www.nytimes.com/2010/01/28/us/28brfs-PLEAINTERROR_ BRF.html.
54. Dirk Johnson, "Suspect in Illinois Bomb Plot 'Didn't Like America Very Much,'" *New York Times*, September 28, 2009, http://www.nytimes. com/2009/09/28/us/28springfield.html.
55. Andrea Elliott, "The Jihadist Next Door," *New York Times*, January 31, 2010, http://www.nytimes.com/2010/01/31/magazine/31Jihadist-t.html.
56. *The Cycle*, MSNBC, August 29, 2014.

CHAPTER SEVEN: IMMIGRANTS AND CRIME: WHY DO YOU ASK?

1. W. Gardner Selby, "Rick Perry Claim about 3,000 Homicides by Illegal Immigrants Not Supported by State Figures," PolitiFact, July 17, 2014, http: www.politifact.com/texas/statements/2014/jul/23/rick-perry/rick-perry-claim-about-3000-homicides-illegal-immi/.
2. These may or may not include convicted criminals who are *legal* immigrants. As in all immigrant crime statistics, that is unclear. But Texas's figures do only include immigrant criminals who have been fingerprinted by the Department of Homeland Security.
3. Gardner Selby, "Rick Perry Claim about 3,000 Homicides."
4. *National Crime Victimization Survey: Interviewing Manual for Field Representatives* (Washington, DC: Bureau of Justice Statistics, 2003). See "Helping You Make Informed Decisions," Item 71 (Offender's Race): "If the respondent's answer is 'Spanish, Hispanic or Latino' or any other ethnic origin, such as French or German, mark Box 1 'White' and do NOT mark Box 3 'Other' and do NOT enter the ethnic origin on the 'Specify' line."
5. "Fact Finder: 2010," U.S. Census Bureau, http://factfinder2.census.gov/ faces/tableservices/jsf/pages/productview.xhtml?pid=DEC_10_DPAS_ ASDP4&prodType=table.
6. *Report to Congressional Requesters: Criminal Alien Statistics* (Washington, DC: United States Government Accountability Office, March 2011), 7 (criminal aliens in federal prison: 55,000) and pp. 6 and 10 (illegal aliens as defined by the GAO in state and local facilities: 296,000), http://www.gao. gov/new.items/d11187.pdf.
7. Ibid., 49–50.
8. The GAO's estimate of three hundred thousand illegal immigrants in non-federal lock-ups is based on the number of incarcerated illegal aliens for

whom the states requested reimbursement from the federal government. But states don't always request reimbursement. A half dozen states have failed to file the forms for some years, including Illinois and Virginia. In 2009, Illinois was imprisoning more than ten thousand criminal aliens, and Virginia had nearly five thousand. *Report to Congressional Requesters*, 62. "For each individual name submitted, ICE reports to DOJ that it (1) verified the individual was illegally in the United States at the time of incarceration (called SCAAP illegal aliens), (2) lacked documentation to confirm an individual's immigration status (called SCAAP unknown aliens), or (3) verified that the individual was an alien legally in the United States or a United States citizen and therefore not eligible for reimbursement under SCAAP." Of the illegal immigrants for whom reimbursement was requested, the GAO counts only those whom both the state and the federal government agree are here illegally or whom the state believes are illegal and the federal government can't prove otherwise.

9. *Report to Congressional Requesters*, 14, note 19.

10. "Briefing for Congressional Requesters: Information on Criminal Aliens Incarcerated in Federal and State Prisons and Local Jails," slides from briefing prepared by the Government Accountability Office, March 29, 2005, p. 9, http://www.gao.gov/assets/100/93090.pdf.

11. Thus, the GAO stated: "The number of *criminal aliens* in federal prisons in fiscal year 2010 was about 55,000, and the number of *SCAAP criminal alien incarcerations* in state prison systems and local jails was about 296,000 in fiscal year 2009 (the most recent data available), and the majority were from Mexico [emphasis added]." *Report to Congressional Requesters*, summary page and also p. 7 ("the number of criminal aliens incarcerated in federal prisons increased...to about 55,000 in fiscal year 2010") and p. 10 ("the number of SCAAP criminal alien incarcerations in state prison systems and local jails increased...to about 296,000 in fiscal year 2009"). The report (see p. 9) goes on to define "criminal aliens"—the ones counted in federal prison—as both legal and illegal immigrants and to define "SCAAP criminal aliens"—the ones counted in state and local facilities—as only those aliens "whom ICE verified were illegally in the United States at the time of incarceration" and "[i]ndividuals whom states and local jurisdictions believe to be illegally in the United States, [but] ICE lacks documentation to confirm their immigration status."

12. "American Housing Survey for the United States: 2011," U.S. Census Bureau, September 2013, http://www.census.gov/content/dam/Census/programs-surveys/ahs/data/2011/h150-11.pdf.

13. Office of Inspector General Department of Homeland Security, *Detention and Removal of Illegal Aliens* (Washington, DC: Department of Homeland Security, April 2006), http://www.oig.dhs.gov/assets/Mgmt/OIG_06-33_Apr06.pdf.

14. See Heather C. West and William J. Sabol, "Prisoners in 2007," bulletin, Bureau of Justice Statistics, December 2008, http://www.bjs.gov/content/pub/pdf/p07.pdf (1,398,698 in state prisons); and William J. Sabol and Todd D. Minton, "Jail Inmates at Midyear 2007," bulletin, Bureau of Justice Statistics, June 2008, http://www.bjs.gov/content/pub/pdf/jim07.pdf (780,581 in local jails).

15. A California Department of Corrections and Rehabilitation report listed 160,866 people in "institutions and camps," "community correctional centers," and state mental health hospitals. It's not clear if "institutions" includes county jails. The county jails had about 30,000 sentenced offenders, for whom the state might have requested reimbursement under SCAAP, which would make it 190,866 inmates in all correctional facilities. Magnus Lofstrom and Brandon Martin, "California's County Jails," Public Policy Institute of California, chart, June 2013, http://www.ppic.org/main/publication_show.asp?i=1061.

16. *Report to Congressional Requesters*, 40.

17. "Texas Criminal Alien Arrest Data," Texas Department of Public Safety, http://www.txdps.state.tx.us/administration/crime_records/pages/secureCommStatsTx.htm.

18. Kathleen Maguire, ed., *Sourcebook of Criminal Justice Statistics, 1995* (Washington, DC: Bureau of Justice Statistics, 1996), 554, available online at http://books.google.com/books?id=xU8HPBfoGfQC&pg=PA554&lpg=PA554&dq=U.S.+Department+of+Justice,+Bureau+of+Justice+Statistics,+Prisoners+1925-+81,+Bulletin+NCJ-85861&source=bl&ots=ZHWkQw-flm&sig=K1Z7LL9T18mpymlt4n3xvl0IfkE&hl=en&sa=X&ei=idRqVKWAIoHrggSAgoOIDg&ved=0CDoQ6AEwBA#v=onepage&q=U.S.%20Department%20of%20Justice%2C%20Bureau%20of%20Justice%20Statistics%2C%20Prisoners%201925-%2081%2C%20Bulletin%20NCJ-85861&f=false; see also Table 6.28.2008 in the "Sourcebook of Criminal Justice Statistics Online," University at Albany, http://www.albany.edu/sourcebook/pdf/t6282008.pdf.

19. State of New York Department of Correctional Services, *The Impact of Foreign-Born Inmates on the New York State Department of Correctional Services* (Albany: State of New York Department of Correctional Services, July 2008), 1, http://www.doccs.ny.gov/Research/Reports/2008/Impact_of_Foreign-Born_Inmates_2008.pdf.

20. David D. Clark, "The Foreign-Born under Custody Population," New York State Department of Corrections and Community Supervision, 2010, http://www.doccs.ny.gov/Research/Reports/2011/ForeignBorn_IRP_Report_2010.pdf.

21. Sara Rimer, "Between 2 Worlds: Dominicans in New York—a Special Report," *New York Times*, September 16, 1991, http://www.nytimes.com/1991/09/16/nyregion/between-2-worlds-dominicans-new-york-special-report-between-2-worlds-dominicans.html.

22. Allen R. Myerson, "Thriving Where Others Won't Go," *New York Times*, January 7, 1992, http://www.nytimes.com/1992/01/07/business/thriving-where-others-won-t-go.html; and Daisann McLane, "Dominican Restaurants: A New Beat in Nueva York," *New York Times*, May 27, 1992, http://www.nytimes.com/1992/05/27/garden/dominican-restaurants-a-new-beat-in-nueva-york.html.

23. Michael Massing, "Crack's Destructive Sprint across America," *New York Times Magazine*, October 1, 1989, http://www.nytimes.com/1989/10/01/magazine/crack-s-destructive-sprint-across-america.html.

24. Clark, "The Foreign-Born under Custody Population."

25. State of New York Department of Correctional Services, *The Impact Of Foreign-Born Inmates*, 1.

26. See, e.g., Richard A. Greene, "Mohammed Retakes Top Spot in English Baby Names," *Belief* (blog), CNN, August 14, 2012, http://religion.blogs.cnn.com/2012/08/14/mohammed-retakes-top-spot-in-english-baby-names/.

27. "Kriminalitet Blandt Indvandrere," Danish State's Bureau of Statistics, 2007, http://hodja.files.wordpress.com/2008/12/crime_stat_3.png, cited in Robert Spencer and Nicolai Sennels, "Report from the Therapy Room: Why Are Muslims More Violent and Criminal?," Jihad Watch, April 27, 2012, http://www.jihadwatch.org/2012/04/nicolai-sennels-report-from-the-therapy-room-why-are-muslims-more-violent-and-criminal.

28. Although thousands of online sites carried stories about Mr. Ali and his incest family, the local *Orlando Sentinel* was the only U.S. newspaper to report Ali's case, in just a single article, according to Nexis. Amy Pavuk, "Shuhel Mahboob Ali: Brit Gets 10 Years for Seeking Child Sex for Incest

Fantasy," *Orlando (FL) Sentinel*, March 4, 2014, http://articles.orlandosentinel. com/keyword/online/recent/4.

29. Ibid.

30. "Top Ten Most Wanted," Los Angeles Police Department, http://www. lapdonline.org/top_ten_most_wanted/most_wanted_view/24353.

31. "Profiled Fugitives," U.S. Marshals Service, updated August 15, 2014, http:// www.usmarshals.gov/profiled.htm. ("The following is a consolidated listing of the fugitives which are profiled on the U.S. Marshals Service website. The list includes 15 Most Wanted fugitives, Major Case fugitives and local fugitives wanted by U.S. Marshal District offices. It does not represent all fugitives wanted by the U.S. Marshals Service.")

32. As the *Star Tribune* explained it, the listed criminals "aren't necessarily the most dangerous offenders on the lam"; the list is "designed to raise awareness about a cross-section" of the county's criminal offenders. Kevin Duchschere, "Most-Wanted List Features Cross-Section," *Minneapolis (MN) Star Tribune*, September 12, 2012.

33. Shawn Linenberger, "Driver in Accident That Killed Amanda Bixby Pleads Not Guilty," *Tonganoxie Mirror*, June 27, 2007.

34. "Suspected Illegal Immigrants Part of Huge Heroin Bust," ncfire, July 2012, http://www.ncfire.info/july2012.pdf (citing a *Gaston [NC] Gazette* story).

35. Staff and Wire Reports, "Morristown Man Arrested in Newark Shootings," *Daily Record* (Morristown, NJ), August 10, 2007.

36. David Leonardt, "Immigrants and Prison," *New York Times*, May 30, 2007, http://www.nytimes.com/2007/05/30/business/30leonside.html?_r=0.

37. "Naturalization Fact Sheet," U.S. Citizenship and Immigration Services, October 24, 2012, http://www.uscis.gov.

38. William Branigin, "Audit Faults INS Practices; Criminals May Still Be Getting Citizenship," *Washington Post*, April 19, 1997.

39. Steven A. Camarota and Jessica Vaughan, "Immigration and Crime: Assessing a Conflicted Issue," Center for Immigration Studies, November 2009, http://cis.org/ImmigrantCrime.

40. *Report to Congressional Requesters*, 6–7.

41. John Powers, *Encyclopedia of North American Immigration* (New York: Infobase Publishing, 2009), 213.

42. Randall Monger and James Yankay, "Annual Flow Report: U.S. Legal Permanent Residents, 2006," Table 3, Department of Homeland Security, May 2014, http://www.dhs.gov/sites/default/files/publications/ois_lpr_ fr_2013.pdf.

43. "The Nigerian Diaspora in the United States," Migration Policy Institute, July 2014.

44. See, e.g., Stefanie Cohen, "Gangs of New York—the Ethnic Mobs That Are Giving the Italian Mafia a Run for Their Money," *New York Post*, May 10, 2009.

45. National Crime Prevention Council, "Intellectual Property Theft: Get Real," NCPC.org, http://www.ncpc.org/topics/intellectual-property-theft/gangs-and-organized-crime-1.

46. Associated Press, "Arkansas Man Sentenced in Fuel Fraud Case," September 4, 2014.

47. Dawn Rhodes, "Doctor Pleads Guilty to Illegal Prescriptions, Medicare Fraud," *Chicago Tribune*, September 5, 2014, http://www.chicagotribune.com/suburbs/bolingbrook-plainfield/ct-doctor-guilty-drugs-met-0905-20140904-story.html.

48. "Owner of Home Health Care Company Sentenced to 75 Months in Prison for $6.5 Million Medicare Fraud Scheme," press release, U.S. Department of Justice, September 8, 2014, http://www.justice.gov/usao/fls/Press Releases/2014/140908-01.html.

49. Melissa Pamer et al., "Millions in Cash Found in L.A. Fashion District Takedown of Alleged Drug-Money Laundering Operations," KTLA, September 10, 2014, http://ktla.com/2014/09/10/feds-raid-l-a-s-fashion-district-in-drug-money-laundering-probe-2/.

50. "Canadian National Pleads Guilty to Illegally Importing Prescription Drugs into the United States," States News Service, September 12, 2014.

51. "Detroit Doctor Pleads Guilty to Administering Unnecessary Chemotherapy to Defraud Medicare," WFIN—1330 AM, September 16, 2014.

52. "Four Charged with Making Credit Cards with 'Skimmed' Info [stealing $2 million]," City News Service, September 18, 2014.

53. "Three Patient Recruiters Sentenced in $20 Million Miami Health Care Fraud Scheme," press release, U.S. Department of Justice, September 18, 2014, http://www.justice.gov/opa/pr/three-patient-recruiters-sentenced-20-million-miami-health-care-fraud-scheme.

54. "Final in Trio of Women Who Embezzled a Half a Million Dollars from Credit Union Is Sentenced," *Hawaii Reporter*, September 19, 2014, http://www.hawaiireporter.com/final-woman-of-trio-who-embezzled-a-half-a-million-dollars-from-credit-union-is-sentenced.

55. "Four Defendants in Custody for Allegedly Making Credit Cards with 'Skimmed' Information in Schemes That Cost Banks at Least $2 Million," States News Service, September 18, 2014.

56. Greg Yee, "Long Beach Man Sentenced to Federal Prison in Medicare Fraud Case [and ordered to pay nearly $1.5 million in restitution]," *Press-Telegram* (Long Beach, CA), September 22, 2014. http://www.presstelegram.com/general-news/20140922/long-beach-man-sentenced-to-federal-prison-in-medicare-fraud-case.

57. W. Zachary Malinowski, "Sentences Given for [$3.6-million] Food Stamp Fraud," *Providence (RI) Journal*, September 22, 2014.

58. "O.C. Resident Sentenced to Federal Prison for Selling Stolen Hospital Supplies over Internet in Scheme That Brought Him $1.8 Million," States News Service, September 22, 2014.

59. "Owner of Home Health Agency Sentenced to Five Years in Prison for Structuring $1.8 Million in Cash Withdrawals to Conceal a $4.5 Million Healthcare Fraud Scheme," press release, U.S. Justice Department, September 25, 2014, http://www.justice.gov/opa/pr/owner-home-health-agency-sentenced-five-years-prison-structuring-18-million-cash-withdrawals.

60. Gus Burns, "Feds Say They've Uncovered Rampant Food-Stamp Fraud in Hamtramck," M Live—Michigan, September 23, 2014, http://www.mlive.com/news/detroit/index.ssf/2014/09/feds_say_theyve_uncovered_ramp.html.

61. "Brooklyn Man Charged with Facilitating $6 Million Food Stamp Fraud in New York," States News Service, September 25, 2014.

62. Emon Reiser, "Miami Man Arrested, Charged in $24M Medicare Scheme," *South Florida Business Journal*, September 26, 2014, http://www.bizjournals.com/southflorida/news/2014/09/26/miami-man-arrested-charged-in-24m-medicare-scheme.html.

63. Adam Sacasa, "Couple Accused of Faking Crash; Husband, Wife Were Paid $2,000 Each, Report Says," *Sun-Sentinel* (Fort Lauderdale, FL) September 26, 2014.

64. "Michigan Physician Pleads Guilty for Role in Medicare Fraud Scheme," press release, U.S. Department of Justice, September 26, 2014, http://www.justice.gov/opa/pr/michigan-physician-pleads-guilty-role-medicare-fraud-scheme-0.

65. "Administrator Sentenced to 68 Months in Prison for Role in $6 Million Miami Home Health Care Fraud Scheme," press release, U.S. Department

of Justice, September 29, 2014, http://www.justice.gov/opa/pr/administrator-sentenced-68-months-prison-role-6-million-miami-home-health-care-fraud-scheme.

66.   "Miami Home Health Care Agency Owner Indicted in $8 Million Medicare Fraud Scheme," press release, U.S. Department of Justice, September 30, 2014, http://www.justice.gov/opa/pr/miami-home-health-care-agency-owner-indicted-8-million-medicare-fraud-scheme.

67.   "Detroit-Area Doctor and Three Others Indicted for Their Alleged Roles in $7 Million Health Care Fraud," press release, U.S. Justice Department, September 30, 2014, http://www.justice.gov/opa/pr/detroit-area-doctor-and-three-others-indicted-their-alleged-roles-7-million-health-care-fraud.

68.   "Six Defendants Charged in $6 Million Miami Home Health Care Fraud Scheme," press release, U.S. Department of Justice, September 30, 2014, available online at the FBI website, http://www.fbi.gov/miami/press-releases/2014/six-defendants-charged-in-6-million-miami-home-health-care-fraud-scheme.

CHAPTER EIGHT: WHY CAN'T WE HAVE ISRAEL'S POLICY ON IMMIGRATION?

1.   See, e.g., David Sim, "Photos of Drug Smuggling Tunnels between Mexico and the US," *International Business Times*, May 23, 2014, http://www.ibtimes.co.uk/photos-drug-smuggling-tunnels-between-mexico-us-1449770.

2.   Robert Mackey, "African Migrants Attacked in Tel Aviv," *The Lede* (blog), *New York Times* blogs, May 24, 2012, http://thelede.blogs.nytimes.com/2012/05/24/african-migrants-attacked-in-tel-aviv/.

3.   Isabel Kershner, "Crackdown on Migrants Tugs at Soul of Israelis," *New York Times*, June 18, 2012, http://www.nytimes.com/2012/06/18/world/middleeast/crackdown-on-african-immigrants-tugs-at-israels-soul.

4.   Kershner, "Israel: Migrants Protest New Law," *New York Times*, December 18, 2013, available online under the headline "African Refugees Protest Detainment in Israel," at http://www.nytimes.com/2013/12/18/world/middleeast/african-refugees-protest-detainment-in-israel.html.

5.   *Report to Congressional Requesters: Criminal Alien Statistics* (Washington, DC: United States Government Accountability Office, March 2011), 15, http://www.gao.gov/new.items/d11187.pdf.

6.   Ibid., 9.

7. David D. Clark, "The Foreign-Born under Custody Population," New York State Department of Corrections and Community Supervision, 2010, http://www.doccs.ny.gov/Research/Reports/2011/ForeignBorn_IRP_Report_2010.pdf.

8. Reuters, "Study Shows Minorities, Hispanics Most Underrepresented in Hollywood," *Las Vegas (NV) Review Journal*, August 4, 2014, http://www.reviewjournal.com/entertainment/movies/study-shows-minorities-hispanics-most-underrepresented-hollywood; Anna Bahr, "Latinos Onscreen, Conspicuously Few," *New York Times*, June 18, 2014, http://www.nytimes.com/2014/06/19/upshot/latinos-onscreen-conspicuously-absent.html; and Mireya Navarro, "Trying to Get beyond the Role of the Maid; Hispanic Actors Are Seen as Underrepresented, with the Exception of One Part," *New York Times*, May 16, 2002, http://www.nytimes.com/2002/05/16/movies/trying-get-beyond-role-maid-hispanic-actors-are-seen-underrepresented-with.html.

9. Josh Keller, "At Top Colleges, an Admissions Gap for Minorities," *New York Times*, May 7, 2013, http://www.nytimes.com/interactive/2013/05/07/education/college-admissions-gap.html?_r=0; John Benson, "Latino and Low-Income Students Underrepresented at Top Colleges," Huffington Post, August 7, 2013, http://www.huffingtonpost.com/2013/08/07/latino-college-students_n_3720705.html; "Minority Enrollment: Black and Hispanic Students Underrepresented at Highly Selective Colleges, Stanford Study Finds," Huffington Post, July 17, 2012, http://www.huffingtonpost.com/2012/07/17/stanford-study-finds-blac_n_1681136.html; and Jens Manuel Krogstad and Richard Fry, "More Hispanics, Blacks Enrolling in College, but Lag in Bachelor's degrees," Pew Research Center, April 24, 2014, http://www.pewresearch.org/fact-tank/2014/04/24/more-hispanics-blacks-enrolling-in-college-but-lag-in-bachelors-degrees/.

10. Rosa Ramirez, "Hispanics Still Underrepresented in Federal Workforce, OPM Study Finds," *National Journal*, July 31, 2012, http://www.nationaljournal.com/thenextamerica/workforce/hispanics-still-underrepresented-in-federal-workforce-opm-study-finds-20120731; Sean Daly, "New Study Finds 'Brownout' on Sunday Talk Shows: Hispanics Underrepresented, Black People and Women Too," *Tampa Bay (FL) Times*, February 10, 2012, http://www.tampabay.com/blogs/media/content/new-study-finds-brownout-sunday-talk-shows-hispanics-underrepresented-black-people-and-women; and Darryl Fears, "Hispanics Underrepresented in the Federal Workforce," *Washington Post*, January 3, 2006, http://www.washingtonpost.com/wp-dyn/content/article/2006/01/02/AR2006010201716.html.

11.   S. J. Main, "Latinos in Mainstream Media Are a Disappearing Act: The Latino Media Gap Crisis," Huffington Post, July 21, 2014, http://www.huffingtonpost.com/sj-main/the-latino-media-gap-crisis_b_5604714.html; Mark Garrison, "Report Finds Latinos Are Underrepresented in the Media," Market.org, June 26, 2014, http://www.marketplace.org/topics/economy/report-finds-latinos-are-underrepresented-media; and Ruben Navarrette Jr., "Latinos Underrepresented in National Media," *My San Antonio*, September 14, 2012, http://www.mysanantonio.com/opinion/commentary/article/Latinos-underrepresented-in-national-media-3866388.php.

12.   Corrie MacLaggan, "Lack of Hispanics in Veterinary Programs," *New York Times*, August 14, 2014, http://www.nytimes.com/2014/08/15/us/lack-of-hispanics-in-veterinary-programs.html.

13.   Jessica Miller, "Utah's Police Forces Lack Latino Officers," *Salt Lake (UT) Tribune*, September 22, 2014, http://www.sltrib.com/sltrib/news/58398191-78/police-community-officers-department.html.csp.

14.   David Plouffe and Steve Schmidt, "Pass the Immigration Bill," Politico, July 15, 2013, http://www.politico.com/story/2013/07/plouffe-immigration-op-ed-94162.html.

15.   Mady Wechsler Segal and David R. Segal, "Latinos Claim Larger Share of U.S. Military Personnel," Population Reference Bureau, October 2007, http://www.prb.org/Publications/Articles/2007/HispanicsUSMilitary.aspx.

16.   According to the U.S. census, there were 3.7 times as many whites as Hispanics in 2014, but the census undercounts illegal aliens, a majority of whom are Hispanic, so we'll make it about three times as many. See "U.S. Census State and County QuickFacts: USA, 2014," http://quickfacts.census.gov/qfd/states/00000.html.

17.   E. Ann Carson and Daniela Golinelli, "Prisoners in 2012—Advance Counts," bulletin, Bureau of Justice Statistics, Table 10, July 2013, http://www.bjs.gov/content/pub/pdf/p12ac.pdf.

18.   Callie Marie Rennison, "Reporting to the Police by Hispanic Victims of Violence," *Violence and Victims* 22, no. 6 (2007). Hispanics are especially less likely than whites to report child rape, and the least likely to report childhood sex abuse of any ethnic group, according to a study by the National Institute of Justice. Carlos A. Cuevas and Chiara Sabina, *Final Report: Sexual Assault among Latinas (SALAS) Study* (Washington, DC: National Institute of Justice, April 2010), https://www.ncjrs.gov/pdffiles1/nij/grants/230445.pdf. The same study found that Hispanics are more likely

to report a simple assault than whites and that the rate of sex crime reporting was unrelated to immigration status.

19. Michael E. Roettger and Demetrius S. Semien, "Employing Du Bois and Myrdal to Analyze the U.S. Criminal Justice System," *Race, Gender, and Class* 20, no. 1 (2013). ("Cumulatively, it is estimated that 33% of all black men, 17% of all Hispanic men, and 5% of all white men will spend time in state or federal prison [Bonczar, 2003].") See also Joy M. Thomas, "Mass Incarceration of Minority Males: A Critical Look at Its Historical Roots and How Educational Policies Encourage Its Existence," *Race, Gender, and Class* 20, no. 1 (2013).

20. Paul Guerino, Paige M. Harrison, and William J. Sabol, "Prisoners in 2010," bulletin, Table 14, Bureau of Justice Statistics, December 2011, revised February 9, 2012, http://www.bjs.gov/content/pub/pdf/p10.pdf.

21. Nick Miroff, "Tracing the U.S. Heroin Surge Back South of the Border as Mexican Cannabis Output Falls," *Washington Post*, April 6, 2014, http://www.washingtonpost.com/world/tracing-the-us-heroin-surge-back-south-of-the-border-as-mexican-cannabis-output-falls/2014/04/06/58dfc590-2123-4cc6-b664-1e5948960576_story.html.

22. See, e.g., Arian Campo-Flores and Zusha Elinson, "Heroin Use, and Deaths, Rise," *Wall Street Journal*, February 3, 2014, http://online.wsj.com/news/articles/SB10001424052702304851104579361250012275942; and Katharine Q. Seelye, "A Mother Lifts Her Son, Slowly, from Heroin's Abyss," *New York Times*, August 10, 2014, http://www.nytimes.com/2014/08/11/us/a-mother-lifts-her-son-slowly-from-heroins-abyss.html.

23. "DrugFacts: Heroin," National Institute on Drug Abuse, April 2013, http://www.drugabuse.gov/publications/drugfacts/heroin.

24. Patrick Radden Keefe, "Cocaine Incorporated," *New York Times Magazine*, June 15, 2012, http://www.nytimes.com/2012/06/17/magazine/how-a-mexican-drug-cartel-makes-its-billions.html.

25. Dolia Estevez, "Philip Seymour Hoffman's Death Casts Light on Mexico's Leading Role in U.S. Heroin Epidemic," *Forbes*, February 6, 2014, http://www.forbes.com/sites/doliaestevez/2014/02/06/did-phillip-seymour-hoffman-overdose-on-mexican-drug-lord-el-chapo-guzmans-heroin/.

26. Associated Press, "Snapshot of Heroin Use, Deaths in 26 States," April 5, 2014, available online under the headline "Snapshot of Heroin Use, Deaths in 26 States, including Louisiana," at http://www.nola.com/crime/index.ssf/2014/04/snapshot_of_heroin_use_deaths.html.

27. Ibid.

28.   Michigan Bureau of Disease Control, Prevention, & Epidemiology, Unintentional Drug Poisoning Deaths in Michigan, 2012, available at http://www.michigan.gov/documents/mdch/1_3-13-13_MortalityData 9910_431271_7.pdf.

29.   Associated Press, "Snapshot of Heroin Use."

30.   Miroff, "Tracing the U.S. Heroin Surge Back South."

31.   "Number of Deaths from Drug-Induced Causes, by Sex and Race, 1979–2010," Table 38 of the *National Drug Control Strategy Data Supplement, 2013* (Washington, DC: Executive Office of the President of the United States, 2013), http://www.whitehouse.gov/sites/default/files/ondcp/policy-and-research/2013_data_supplement_final2.pdf (putting the number of drug deaths in 2010 at 40,393). See generally Harold Pollack, "100 Americans Die of Drug Overdoses Each Day. How Do We Stop That?," *Washington Post*, February 7, 2012, http://www.washingtonpost.com/blogs/wonkblog/wp/2014/02/07/100-americans-die-of-drug-overdoses-each-day-how-do-we-stop-that/.

32.   Seelye, "A Mother Lifts Her Son, Slowly."

33.   Keefe, "Cocaine Incorporated."

34.   Some websites, most of them in Spanish, claim that her mother, Blanca Estela Aispuro Aispuro, was an "American." If so, she was an anchor baby herself. Both mother and daughter have lived their entire lives in Mexico—except for quick trips to America to have anchor babies; see Michael Daly, "Drug Cartel Beauty Queens Face an Ugly End," Daily Beast, February 26, 2014, http://www.thedailybeast.com/articles/2014/02/26/drug-cartel-beauty-queens.html; and Orlando Oliveros, "Emma Coronel, la última Mujer del Chapo Guzmán," February 25, 2014, http://www.unioncancun.mx/articulo/2014/02/25/nacion/emma-coronel-la-ultima-mujer-del-chapo-guzman.

35.   Emma's uncle is Ignacio (Nacho) Coronel—the "Steve Jobs" of Mexico, according to Anabel Hernández. "He saw the future," she exuded. It was methamphetamine. Emma's other family members working for the Sinaloa cartel included Ernesto Coronel Peña, Juan Jaime Coronel, Juan Ernesto Coronel Herrera, and Gael Carbel Aldana—all arrested in 2010, according to Daily Entertainment News, which has some of the most penetrating English-language coverage of Mexican drug cartels. "Emma Coronel Guzman—Joaquin El Chapo Guzman's Wife," Daily Entertainment News, February 24, 2014, http://dailyentertainmentnews.com/breaking-news/emma-coronel-guzman-joaquin-el-chapo-guzmans-wife/.

36. "Beauty Queen Wife of Mexico's Most Wanted Drug Lord Crosses Border to Give Birth to Twins in California," *Daily Mail* (UK), September 28, 2011, http://www.dailymail.co.uk/news/article-2042397/Sinaloa-drug-lord-Joaquin-Guzmans-wife-Emma-Coronel-gives-birth-twins-California.html.

37. Philip V. Allingham, "England and China: The Opium Wars, 1839–60," Victorian Web, http://www.victorianweb.org/history/empire/opiumwars/opiumwars1.html.

38. Peter Foster, "China Builds Higher Fences over Fears of Instability in North Korea," *Telegraph* (London), March 30, 2011, http://www.telegraph.co.uk/news/worldnews/asia/northkorea/8415490/China-builds-higher-fences-over-fears-of-instability-in-North-Korea.html.

39. Shmuel Rosner, "Rape, Lies and Videotapes," *Latitude* (blog), *New York Times* blogs, January 2, 2013, http://latitude.blogs.nytimes.com/2013/01/02/a-rape-in-israel-becomes-tinder-for-ugly-anti-immigration-politics/.

40. Reece Jones, "Something There Is That Doesn't Love a Wall," *New York Times*, August 28, 2012, http://www.nytimes.com/2012/08/28/opinion/Border-Fences-in-United-States-Israel-and-India.html.

41. "Rep. Peter T. King Holds a Markup on Homeland Security Authorization," Political Transcript Wire, October 13, 2011.

42. Peggy Fikac, "Perry's Border Fence Quip Rings a Bell," *Houston (TX) Chronicle*, October 3, 2011.

43. Ibid.

44. Ibid.

45. Ed Vulliamy, "How Arrest of the Last Don Heralds Ruthless New Era for Mexico," *Guardian* (UK), October 5, 2014, http://www.theguardian.com/society/2014/oct/05/mexico-war-on-drugs-hidden-story-joaquin-guzman-war-us.

46. Patrick Radden Keefe, "The Blogger Who Tracks Syrian Rockets from His Sofa," *Telegraph* (London), March 2014, http://www.telegraph.co.uk/news/worldnews/middleeast/syria/10730163/The-blogger-who-tracks-Syrian-rockets-from-his-sofa.html; and Vulliamy, "How Arrest of the Last Don Heralds Ruthless New Era."

47. Emily Friedman, "Mexican Investigator Searching for Killers of American David Hartley Is Decapitated," ABC News, October 12, 2010, http://abcnews.go.com/US/mexican-drug-gang-decapitates-investigator-homicide-american-david/story?id=11863267.

48. "Beheading Videos on Facebook: Cruelty and the Crowd," *Guardian* (UK), October 23, 2013, http://www.theguardian.com/commentisfree/2013/oct/22/beheading-videos-facebook. See also Karis Hustad, "Facebook Updates Explicit Content Policy," *Christian Science Monitor*, October 23, 2013, http://www.csmonitor.com/Technology/2013/1023/Facebook-updates-explicit-content-policy.

49. Nexis search of "All Transcripts" for: "beheading" within the same sentence as "ISIS" or "ISIL" between July 1, 2014, and March 1, 2015: 1,231 documents. Same search, but for "beheading" within the same sentence as "Mexic!": 66 documents, then the same search for the previous five years.

50. See, e.g., Moises Castillo for the Associated Press, "Mexican Cartel Beheaded 29—Including Women and Children—in Saturday Night Massacre," CNS News, May 16, 2011, http://www.cnsnews.com/news/article/mexican-cartel-beheaded-29-including-women-and-children-saturday-night-massacre; Ashley Fantz, "The Mexico Drug War: Bodies for Billions," CNN, January 20, 2012, http://www.cnn.com/2012/01/15/world/mexico-drug-war-essay/.

51. See Vulliamy, "How Arrest of the Last Don Heralds Ruthless New Era."

52. Janine DiGiovanni, "When It Comes to Beheadings, ISIS Has Nothing over Saudi Arabia," *Newsweek*, October 14, 2014, http://www.newsweek.com/2014/10/24/when-it-comes-beheadings-isis-has-nothing-over-saudi-arabia-277385.html.

53. Nick Miroff and William Booth, "Mexico's Drug War Is at a Stalemate as Calderon's Presidency Ends," *Washington Post*, November 27, 2012, http://www.washingtonpost.com/world/the_americas/calderon-finishes-his-six-year-drug-war-at-stalemate/2012/11/26/82c90a94-31eb-11e2-92f0-496af208bf23_story_1.html.

54. "Hitman, 15, on Trial for Beheading Victims," *New Zealand Herald*, July 21, 2011, http://www.nzherald.co.nz/world/news/article.cfm?c_id=2&objectid=10739809; "Teenage Drug Cartel Hit Man, Who Beheaded Four Victims, on His Way Home to US After Serving 3 Years in Jail," *Daily Mail* (UK), November 26, 2013, http://www.dailymail.co.uk/news/article-2514101/Edgar-Jimenez-Lugo-BEHEADED-4-victims-freed-heading-US.html. Lugo is also featured in a YouTube video—seen beating a man with a two-by-four as the man hangs from a rope.

55. "Teenage Drug Cartel Hit Man."

56.   Associated Press, "Mexico: U.S. Boy Charged as Killer," *New York Times*, February 11, 2011, A-8, available online at http://www.nytimes.com/2011/02/11/world/americas/11briefs-Assassin.html.

57.   Dana Milbank, "Headless Bodies and Other Immigration Tall Tales in Arizona," *Washington Post*, July 11, 2010, http://www.washingtonpost.com/wp-dyn/content/article/2010/07/09/AR2010070902342.html.

58.   Alex Pareene, "This Week in Crazy: Jan Brewer; The Arizona Governor Spins Wild Tales of Lawless Arizona, Runs Away When Asked to Explain References to Beheadings," Salon, September 4, 2010, http://www.salon.com/2010/09/04/this_week_crazy_jan_brewer/.

59.   "Around Arizona Briefs," *Arizona Republic* (Phoenix), March 8, 2013 ("Crisantos Moroyoqui-Yocupicio made the plea Monday to second-degree murder in the death of Martin Alejandro Cota-Monroy, 38, at an apartment in Chandler on Oct. 10, 2010"); and Laurie Merrill, "Police Call Beheading Revenge for Drug Theft," *Arizona Republic* (Phoenix), March 3, 2011 ("The man whose decapitated body was found in a Chandler apartment apparently was killed in retaliation for stealing 400 pounds of marijuana from a Mexican drug-trafficking organization, a police report reveals.... Those three suspects, Juan Campos Morales Aguilar, Jose David Castro Reyes and a third man whose full name is not known, were among a group drinking with Cota Monroy the day he was killed, the report says.").

60.   Veronica M. Cruz, "Headless Man's Identity Still Unknown," *Arizona Daily Star* (Tucson), January 12, 2012. ("The autopsy of the decapitated man found west of Tucson last week revealed few details about his identity. The man, whose hands and feet had also been removed, was found on the side of a dirt road Jan. 6.... Investigators believe the man was killed in another location and his body was later dumped in the desert....")

61.   The main suspect was Luis Ruiz, a drug dealer. As one often finds in Mexico, the prosecutor in the Oklahoma dismemberment refused to bring charges on grounds that the three witnesses were unreliable. Tim Willert, "'Flawed' Police Work Cited in Charge Dismissal," *Daily Oklahoman* (Oklahoma City, OK), March 3, 2013. For the evidence, see "Information, Oklahoma County v. Jimmy Lee Massey and Luis Enrique Ruiz," http://localtvkfor.files.wordpress.com/2012/07/saunders-murder.pdf.

62.   "Expert Says Beheadings in U.S. Look like Work of Cartels," KRGV Channel 5, January 18, 2012, http://www.borderlandbeat.com/2012/01/expert-says-beheadings-in-us-look-like.html. See also Patrick Radden Keefe, "The Snow Kings of Mexico," *New York Times*, June 17, 2012, available online under

the headline "How a Mexican Drug Cartel Makes Its Billions," at http:// www.nytimes.com/2012/06/17/magazine/how-a-mexican-drug-cartel-makes-its-billions.html. ("One convicted Sinaloa trafficker [in the United States] told me that it often took him more time to count the money he collected from his customers than it did to actually move the product. It may also help that the penalty for defaulting could involve dismemberment.")

63. See, e.g., "The GOP's Nonsense on Immigration," *Washington Post*, September 12, 2011. ("[F]ences are costly and easily defeated [think ladders and tunnels.]")

64. "Two Arrested After 1 Child Beheaded; 2 Partially Decapitated," WBALTV. com (Baltimore, MD), December 30, 2004, http://www.wbaltv.com/news/ maryland/baltimore-city/Two-Arrested-After-1-Child-Beheaded-2-Partially-Decapitated/8900586.

65. "Guide to the Case," *Baltimore (MD) Sun*, June 30, 2006, http://www. baltimoresun.com/news/maryland/bal-fallstaffsummary0630-story.html.

66. Matt Fernandez, "20th Anniversary of Mark Kilroy Death and Cult Killings," March 12, 2009, KVEO.com (TX), http://www.kveo.com/ news/20th-anniversary-of-mark-kilroy-death-cult-killings.

67. Peter Bergen and David Sterman, "U.S. Right Wing Extremists More Deadly Than Jihadists," CNN, April 15, 2014, http://www.cnn.com/2014/04/14/ opinion/bergen-sterman-kansas-shooting/.

68. A minimum of 351,000 criminal immigrants are in prison in America (296,000 in state and local facilities, plus 55,000 in federal prisons). *Report to Congressional Requesters*, 7 and 10. Between 66 and 68 percent of them are Mexican. Ibid., 9 and 15. One percent of all criminal aliens have committed murder in the U.S. Ibid., 19–21, Figure 9 (showing percentage of criminal aliens arrested at least once by offense category). That adds up to a minimum of 23,000 murders in America committed by Mexicans—and legal immigrants weren't even counted in state prisons, which is where most murderers reside.

69. See generally Janine Zacharia, "Israel's Media Blackout: Why Aren't Israeli Journalists Questioning Their Military's Devastation in Gaza?," Slate, July 24, 2014, http://www.slate.com/articles/news_and_politics/foreigners/2014/07/ israel_s_gaza_reporting_why_so_few_questions_about_the_war_and_ palestinian.html.

70. "Andrew Kirell, Bill Maher, and Conservative Guest Surprisingly Agree on Who's to Blame for Gaza Civilian Deaths," Mediaite, July 18, 2014, http://

www.mediaite.com/tv/bill-maher-and-conservative-guest-surprisingly-agree-on-whos-to-blame-for-gaza-civilian-deaths/.

71. See, e.g., Isabel Kershner, "Israel Says Hamas Is Hurt Significantly," *New York Times,* September 3, 2014, http://www.nytimes.com/2014/09/03/world/middleeast/israel-says-hamas-is-hurt-significantly.html; "Gaza-Israel Conflict: Is the Fighting Over?," BBC, August 26, 2014, http://www.bbc.com/news/world-middle-east-28252155.

72. Jodi Rudoren, "Israel Kills 3 Top Hamas Leaders as Latest Fighting Turns Its Way," *New York Times*, August 22, 2014, http://www.nytimes.com/2014/08/22/world/middleeast/israel-gaza-strip.html.

73. According to the *Times of Israel*, there are about 4,700 Palestinians incarcerated in Israel, some pending formal charges. Gavriel Fiske, "3,000 Palestinian Inmates Refuse Meals," *Times of Israel*, April 17, 2013, http://www.timesofisrael.com/palestinians-mark-prisoners-day/.

74. There were 296,000 in state and local facilities, plus 55,000 in federal prisons. *Report to Congressional Requesters*, 7 and 10.

75. Sixty-five percent of the approximately 170,000 SCAAP criminal aliens are held in these five local jurisdictions, which comes to 110,500. *Report to Congressional Requesters*, 15.

76. Matt Lebovic, "Israel a 'Prisoners' Paradise,' Says American Cable Series," *Times of Israel*, September 15, 2012, http://www.timesofisrael.com/israel-a-prisoners-paradise-says-american-cable-series/.

77. See note 76 above.

78. *Report to Congressional Requesters*, 28–34.

79. Criminal alien offense types: drug arrests: 17 percent; motor vehicle violations: 14 percent; assault: 7 percent; rape: 2 percent; and murder: 1 percent. *Report to Congressional Requesters*, 19–21, Figure 9 (showing percentage of criminal aliens arrested at least once by offense category).

80. "Israel 2014 Crime and Safety Report: Tel Aviv," United States Department of State, February 27, 2014, https://www.osac.gov/pages/Content ReportDetails.aspx?cid=15230.

SPOT THE IMMIGRANT! CASE NO. 1: FRESNO, CALIFORNIA

1. Don Terry, "Gang Rape of Three Girls Leaves Fresno Shaken, and Questioning," *New York Times*, May 1, 1998, http://www.nytimes.com/1998/05/01/us/gang-rape-of-three-girls-leaves-fresno-shaken-and-questioning.html.

2. See, e.g., Associated Press, "New Indictment Charges 23 Hmongs with Series of Rapes," October 20, 1999, available online at the *Los Angeles Times*, http://articles.latimes.com/1999/oct/21/news/mn-24690. ("A separate 500-count indictment last year charged 14 defendants, who are scheduled for trial Nov. 15.")

3. Nexis search of *New York Times* archives after May 1, 1998, for: "Hmong w/s (rape or sex! or assault!) and (motel or fresno)": No results.

4. Mei-Ling Hopgood and Jeff Gerritt, "Crime Wave Sends Ripples through Close-Knit Group of Laotian Immigrants," *Detroit (MI) Free Press*, October 27, 1999. See also Michael Reese, "A Tragedy in Santa Monica," *Newsweek*, May 6, 1985. ("In California's San Joaquin Valley, for example, four Hmong refugees from the remote mountains of Laos have been prosecuted on kidnap and rape charges for engaging in what to them is the customary way of claiming a young bride.")

5. Katherine Bishop, "Asian Tradition at War with American Laws," *New York Times*, February 10, 1988, http://www.nytimes.com/1988/02/10/us/asian-tradition-at-war-with-american-laws.html.

6. Ibid.

7. Myrna Oliver, "Immigrant Crimes, Cultural Defense—a Legal Tactic," *Los Angeles Times*, July 15, 1988, http://articles.latimes.com/1988-07-15/news/mn-7189_1_cultural-defense.

8. Associated Press, "Three Arrested in Alleged Purchase of Girl," July 17, 1991.

9. "La Crosse County Court Officials: Judge Ramona Gonzales," La Crosse County Clerk of Courts, http://www.co.la-crosse.wi.us/departments/court/docs/Judges.htm. ("Birth Place: Dominican Republic.")

10. "Wisconsin: Molester Sentenced to English Lessons," *Los Angeles Times*, August 29, 1996, http://articles.latimes.com/1996-08-29/news/mn-38707_1_english-lessons.

11. See, e.g., Pam Louwagie and Dan Browning, "Shamed into Silence," *Minneapolis (MN) Star Tribune*, March 23, 2012, http://www.startribune.com/local/11594631.html; and Hopgood and Gerritt, "Crime Wave Sends Ripples."

12. Louwagie and Browning, "Shamed into Silence."

13. Ibid.

14. Associated Press, "Indictment Charges 23 Hmong."

15. Ruben Rosario, "St. Paul Immigrant Family Enduring Ultimate Tragedy after Crime," *St. Paul (MN) Pioneer Press*, May 11, 1998.

16. Amy Doeun, "2011 Gang Rape Case Brought to Court in St. Paul," *Hmong Times* (St. Paul, MN), December 26, 2012, http://hmongtimes.com/main. asp?SectionID=31&SubSectionID=190&ArticleID=4630&TM=44237.

17. Louwagie and Browning, "Shamed into Silence."

18. Ibid.

19. Ibid.

20. Robert F. Moore, "Police Warn Hmong after Rapes," *St. Paul (MN) Pioneer Press*, December 19, 1997.

21. Louwagie and Browning, "Shamed into Silence."

22. See, e.g., ibid.

23. "American FactFinder: Hmong," U.S. Census Bureau, 2013, http://factfinder2.census.gov/faces/tableservices/jsf/pages/productview.xhtml?pid=ACS_13_1YR_B02015&prodType=table.

24. "Statistics Canada: Hmong," 2006 Census topic-based tabulations, http://www12.statcan.gc.ca/census-recensement/2006/dp-pd/tbt/Rp-eng.cfm?LANG=E&APATH=3&DETAIL=0&DIM=0&FL=A&FREE=0&GC=0&GID=0&GK=0&GRP=1&PID=92333&PRID=0&PTYPE=88971,97154&S=0&SHOWALL=0&SUB=0&Temporal=2006&THEME=80&VID=0&VNAMEE=&VNAMEF=.

25. *2010 Yearbook of Immigration Statistics* (Washington, DC: Department of Homeland Security, August 2011), https://www.dhs.gov/xlibrary/assets/statistics/yearbook/2010/ois_yb_2010.pdf.

26. Mark Arax, "Hmong's Sacrifice of Puppy Reopens Cultural Wounds," *Los Angeles Times*, December 16, 1995, http://articles.latimes.com/1995-12-16/news/mn-14591_1_hmong-community.

27. Ibid.

28. Ibid.

29. Ibid.

30. Minnesota v. Tenerelli, 598 N.W.2d 668, 672 (Minn. 1999), available online at http://mn.gov/web/prod/static/lawlib/live//archive/supct/9908/c398318.htm.

31. Arax, "Hmong's Sacrifice of Puppy Reopens Cultural Wounds."

32. Kirsten Scharnberg, "Surviving Culture Shock," *Baltimore (MD) Sun*, March 8, 1999, http://articles.baltimoresun.com/1999-03-08/news/9903080127_1_hmong-culture-shock-immigrants.

33. See, e.g., Joseph Tybor, "Eye of Newt, Wool of Bat: Is This What the Future Holds for American Courts?," *Chicago Tribune*, August 21, 1988, http://archives.chicagotribune.com/1988/08/21/page/84/article/eye-of-newt-wool-

of-bat-is-this-what-the-future-holds-for-american-courts; and Terry Wilson, "2 Hmong Convicted of Beating Motorist," *Chicago Tribune*, May 5, 1988, http://articles.chicagotribune.com/1988-05-05/news/8803140564_1_hmong-rooster-battery.

34.   Doriane Lambelet Coleman, "Culture, Cloaked in *Mens Rea*," *South Atlantic Quarterly* 100, no. 4 (Fall 2001), http://scholarship.law.duke.edu/cgi/viewcontent.cgi?article=1924&context=faculty_scholarship.

CHAPTER NINE: PUBLIC WARNED TO BE ON LOOKOUT FOR "MAN"

1.   Olatokunbo Olukemi "Street Smut: Gender, Media, and the Legal Power Dynamics of Street Harassment, or 'Hey Sexy' and Other Verbal Ejaculations," *Columbia Journal of Gender and the Law* 14, no. 1 (2005).

2.   Here are recent Department of Justice statistics for white-on-black rape:
DOJ Criminal Victimization in the United States, 2008:
White Offender/Black Victim—Rape/Sexual Assaults: 0.0

DOJ Criminal Victimization in the United States, 2007:
White Offender/Black Victim—Rape/Sexual Assaults: 0.0

DOJ Criminal Victimization in the United States, 2006:
White Offender/Black Victim—Rape/Sexual Assaults: 0.0

DOJ Criminal Victimization in the United States, 2005:
White Offender/Black Victim—Rape/Sexual Assaults: 0.0

DOJ Criminal Victimization in the United States, 2004:
White Offender/Black Victim—Rape/Sexual Assaults: 0.0

DOJ Criminal Victimization in the United States, 2003:
White Offender/Black Victim—Rape/Sexual Assaults: 0.0

DOJ Criminal Victimization in the United States, 2002:
White Offender/Black Victim—Rape/Sexual Assaults: [Sample based on 10 or fewer]

DOJ Criminal Victimization in the United States, 2001:
White Offender/Black Victim—Rape/Sexual Assaults: [Sample based on 10 or fewer]

DOJ Criminal Victimization in the United States, 2000:

White Offender/Black Victim—Rape/Sexual Assaults: [Sample based on 10 or fewer]

DOJ Criminal Victimization in the United States, 1999:
White Offender/Black Victim—Rape/Sexual Assaults: 0.0

DOJ Criminal Victimization in the United States, 1998:
White Offender/Black Victim—Rape/Sexual Assaults: [Sample based on 10 or fewer]

DOJ Criminal Victimization in the United States, 1997:
White Offender/Black Victim—Rape/Sexual Assaults: 0.0

 During the same time period, blacks were raping whites at a clip of several thousand per year—and raping black women at a rate of many multiple thousand per year, according to Department of Justice victimization surveys. (Victimization surveys are obviously the most accurate measure of who is committing crimes because someone who has just been the victim of a crime is not going to lie about the race of his assailant for the good of the race.)

3. According to the *New York Times* the two nations that send the most tourists on Thai sex tours are Japan—and Germany. We've seen evidence of what Alexis de Tocqueville called the French's "contempt of women," not only with the Gallic hilarity over Americans' minding that a U.S. president was using female underlings for oral sex, but more recently, when Dominique Strauss-Kahn, head of the International Monetary Fund, was accused of raping a hotel maid in New York City. That rape charge turned out to be another immigrant scam—at least in the sense that the sex was consensual. Still, when the story first broke, Natalie Nougayrede, diplomatic correspondent for France's *Le Monde* newspaper, pointed out that it took a day and a half for the media in France to say, "Well, maybe we should be expressing some concern and, you know, empathy for this woman and not just be scandalized about how he was dealt with by the American police."

4. Frances Burns, "Man Allegedly Forced Philadelphia Doctor into Her Apartment and Raped Her," United Press International, June 24, 2014, available online under the headline "Man Charged with Raping Young Doctor in Philadelphia's Upscale Rittenhouse Square Neighborhood," at http://www.upi.com/Top_News/US/2014/06/24/Man-charged-with-raping-young-doctor-in-Philadelphias-upscale-Rittenhouse-Square-

neighborhood/8991403632733/; Vince Lattanzio, "Man Charged with Rittenhouse Doctor's Rape," NBC10.com (Philadelphia), June 25, 2014, http://www.nbcphiladelphia.com/news/local/Charges-in-Rittenhouse-Doctors-Rape-264370101.html#ixzz3F108wEhC; and Dave Boyer, "Illegal Immigrant Charged with Rape While in Sanctuary City," *Washington Times*, July 7, 2014, available online under the headline "Two-Time Illegal Immigrant Charged with Rape in Philly's Sanctuary City," at http://www.washingtontimes.com/news/2014/jul/6/illegal-immigrant-charged-with-rape-while-in-sanct/?page=all.

5. "Holly Springs Man Faces Child-Sex Charge," *News & Observer* (Raleigh, NC), July 18, 2013.

6. None of the *Seattle Times'* headlines identified the rapist as an immigrant: Jennifer Sullivan, "Judge in Rape Case Denies Defendant's Mistrial Motion," *Seattle Times*, November 9, 2010; Sullivan, "Man Convicted on 7 Counts in Child-Rape Case; Attacks on Four Victims in 1990s—Charges Involving Alleged 5th Victim Dropped," *Seattle Times*, December 9, 2010; Sullivan, "Child Rapist Sentenced to 53 Years; His Nonchalance Shocks Families—Man Represented Himself in Court," *Seattle Times*, January 22, 2011.

7. Ibid.

8. See, e.g., Susannah Meadows and Evan Thomas, "What Happened at Duke?," *Newsweek*, May 1, 2006.

9. Sarah Fowler, "Columbus Resident Charged with Molestation," *Commercial Dispatch* (Columbus, MI), April 24, 2014, http://www.cdispatch.com/printerfriendly.asp?aid=32863. ("He also has a hold for immigration according to officials with the Lowndes County Adult Detention Center.")

10. Todd South, "Smuggling Case Nets 15-Year Sentence," *Chattanooga (TN) Times Free Press*, May 25, 2013.

11. See U.S. v. German Rolando Vicente-Sapon, USDC (Eastern Dist. Tenn.), November 14, 2012; and "German Rolando Vicente-Sapon Sentenced to Serve 15 Years in Prison for Transporting a Minor across the Mexican Border for Unlawful Sexual Activity," press release, U.S. Attorney's Office, Eastern District of Tennessee, May 24, 2013, http://www.fbi.gov/knoxville/press-releases/2013/german-rolando-vicente-sapon-sentenced-to-serve-15-years-in-prison-for-transporting-a-minor-across-the-mexican-border-for-unlawful-sexual-activity.

12. South, "Man Guilty in Case of Human Smuggling," *Chattanooga (TN) Times Free Press*, November 16, 2012, http://www.timesfreepress.com/news/local/story/2012/nov/16/man-guilty-in-case-of-human-smuggling/93022/.

13. Ling v. Georgia (S. Ct. GA), November 22, 2010, available online at http://caselaw.findlaw.com/ga-supreme-court/1545439.html#sthash.AUwRwIqS.dpuf.

14. Mendez v. State, Supreme Court of Arkansas, December 15, 2011, available online at http://law.uark.edu/documents/2012/08/Bailey-Mendez-v.-State1.pdf.

15. Ron Wood, "Mendez Gets 60 Years in Prison," May 28, 2010, *Northwest Arkansas Times*, http://webmedia.newseum.org/newseum-multimedia/tfp_archive/2010-05-28/pdf/AR_NAT.pdf.

16. Barry Halvorson, "Court Rejects Paniagua's Second Application for Appeal," *East Bernard (TX) Express*, March 4, 2010, available online at http://smalltownnews.com/article.php?catname=Regional%20Government&pub=East%20Bernard%20Express&pid=7pub=East%20Bernard%20Express&aid=62998.

17. "Man, 24, 'Traveled for Sex with Sisters, 10 and 13, and Said He Wanted to Make One His Girlfriend and Get Her Pregnant,'" *Daily Mail* (UK), December 28, 2012, http://www.dailymail.co.uk/news/article-2254158/Man-traveled-sex-sisters-10-13-told-father-wanted-pregnant.html.

18. Ibid.

19. Eric Dondero, "Why Is the U.S. Media Ignoring the Story Out of S. Florida of the Would-Be Child Rapist 'BIG Horny Indian,'" LibertarianRepublican.net, December 29, 2012, http://www.libertarianrepublican.net/2012/12/why-is-us-media-ignoring-story-out-of-s.html.

20. The girls may have been nine and eleven years old when he began raping them. The one news story about the case never alters their ages over a two-year period—they're eleven and thirteen standing outside the courtroom in 2014 and they were eleven and thirteen in 2012, when he first raped them. John H. Tucker, "Jorge Juarez-Lopez Sentenced to a Minimum of 36 Years for Sex Offenses," *Indy Week* (Durham, NC), February 26, 2014, http://www.indyweek.com/indyweek/jorge-juarez-lopez-sentenced-to-a-minimum-of-72-years-for-sex-offenses/Content?oid=3875729.

21. Matthew Rice, "Accused Sex Offender Flees Area, Found, Jailed," Manchester Newspapers, January 24, 2012, http://manchesternewspapers.com/2012/01/24/accused-sex-offender-flees-area-found-jailed/.

22. Nexis search, *Daily Gazette* (Schenectady/Albany), August 4, 2012.

23. Jenna Sachs, "Illinois Fugitive Is One of Wisconsin's Most Wanted, He's Armando Romero-Gutierrez," FOX-6 WITI (Milwaukee, WI), August 22,

2014, http://fox6now.com/2014/08/22/u-s-marshals-looking-for-illinois
-fugitive-armando-romero-gutierrez/.

24. Ibid.

25. Michael Hewlett, "Man Accused of Raping Girl Told Police He Thought
She Was Older," *Winston-Salem (NC) Journal*, July 24, 2014, http://www.
journalnow.com/eedition/mapping/man-accused-of-raping-girl-told-
police-he-thought-she/article_a9241cb4-73ee-5520-92a8-bfeadbf4865d.
html; Hewlett, "Man Accused of Raping Girl, 12, Tells Different Version of
Incident," *Winston-Salem (NC) Journal*, July 25, 2014, http://www.
journalnow.com/eedition/mapping/man-accused-of-raping-girl-tells-
different-version-of-incident/article_d472708f-196a-58dc-8ff0-
03811019ee82.html; and Hewlett, "Man Gets 25 Years for Rape of Girl, 12,"
Winston-Salem (NC) Journal, July 26, 2014, http://www.journalnow.com/
eedition/mapping/man-gets-years-for-rape-of-girl/article_d5c63ec5-f81f-
5d2b-9526-35deb6de55bf.html.

SPOT THE IMMIGRANT! CASE NO. 2: HOMECOMING DANCE

1. Shoshana Walter, "A Brutal Attack outside a School Continues to Horrify
One Year Later," *New York Times*, December 24, 2010, http://www.nytimes.
com/2010/12/24/us/24bcrape.html?; and Fareed Abdulrahman, "Haunting
Chronology of Events Detailed in Homecoming Gang-Rape Case,"
Richmond Confidential, June 24, 2013, http://richmondconfidential.
org/2013/06/24/haunting-chronology-of-events-detailed-in-homecoming-
gang-rape-case/.

2. Mark Oltmanns, "The Witness List," Richmond Confidential, December
15, 2010, http://richmondconfidential.org/2010/12/15/the-witness-list/.

3. Walter, "A Brutal Attack outside a School."

4. Oltmanns, "Tracking the Testimony in the Richmond Rape Case,"
Richmond Confidential, December 15, 2010, https://www.baycitizen.org/
news/crime/tracking-testimony-richmond-rape-case/.

5. Ibid.

6. Oltmanns, "Nurse Recounts Exam of Richmond Rape Victim," Bay Citizen,
November 19, 2010, https://www.baycitizen.org/news/crime/nurse-
recounts-interview-richmond-rape/.

7. Sandy Banks, "A Deeper Lesson in Gang Rape," *Los Angeles Times*,
November 7, 2009, available online under the headline "Finding a Deeper

Lesson in High School Gang Rape," at http://articles.latimes.com/2009/nov/07/local/me-banks7.

8.   "Anamaree Rea, a licensed nurse and sexual assault response team coordinator at the hospital," who interviewed the victim the day after the assault, "testified that of the five men, the student knew two by name: Cody Smith, whom she described as a white-Mexican school friend; and Elvis—someone she had just met. The other three men were unknown by the girl, but she identified one as a 21-year-old Mexican." Oltmanns, "Nurse Recounts Victim's Memories and Injuries," Richmond Confidential, November 19, 2010, http://richmondconfidential.org/2010/11/19/nurse-recounts-victims-memories-and-injuries/.

9.   Anne Brice, "Richmond Rape Victim: 'Do My Parents Know?,'" Bay Citizen, November 23, 2010, https://www.baycitizen.org/news/crime/richmond-rape-victim-do-my-parents-know/.

10.   Caroline Black, "Richmond High Gang-Rape: Six Male Defendants Ordered to Stand Trial for Calif. Homecoming Sex Assault," CBS News, December 22, 2010, http://www.cbsnews.com/news/richmond-high-gang-rape-six-male-defendants-ordered-to-stand-trial-for-calif-homecoming-sex-assault/.

11.   See, e.g., Malaika Fraley, "Man Convicted in Richmond High Gang Rape Testifies about Former Co-Defendant's Role in Attack," *Contra Costa (CA) Times*, June 13, 2013.

12.   Walter, "A Brutal Attack outside a School."

CHAPTER TEN: HERE'S A STORY, *ROLLING STONE!*

1.   James Yodice, "Does Privilege Breed Contempt at Duke?," *Albuquerque (NM) Journal*, April 25, 2006.

2.   Selena Roberts, "When Peer Pressure, Not a Conscience, Is Your Guide," *New York Times*, March 31, 2006, http://query.nytimes.com/gst/fullpage.html?res=9D04E0DC1230F932A05750C0A9609C8B63.

3.   Helen Benedict, "Why Soldiers Rape: Culture of Misogyny, Illegal Occupation, Fuel Sexual Violence in Military," *In These Times*, September 2008, http://inthesetimes.com/article/3848.

4.   In less than a year's time, between September 2013 and July 2014, there were four major articles on campus rape in the *Times*, each between 2,360 and 5,424 words long, two beginning on page A1 and one on the cover of the Sports Section. Walt Bogdanich, "Reporting a Rape, and Wishing She

Hadn't," *New York Times*, July 13, 2014, A1 (5,424 words) (available online at http://www.nytimes.com/2014/07/13/us/how-one-college-handled-a-sexual-assault-complaint.html); Richard Pérez-Peña and Kate Taylor, "Fight against Sex Assaults Holds Colleges to Account," *New York Times*, May 4, 2014, A1 (2,360 words) (available online at http://www.nytimes.com/2014/05/04/us/fight-against-sex-crimes-holds-colleges-to-account.html); Michael Winerip, "Stepping Up to Stop Sexual Assault," *New York Times*, February 9, 2014, ED14 (3,181 words) (available online at http://www.nytimes.com/2014/02/09/education/edlife/stepping-up-to-stop-sexual-assault.html); and Greg Bishop, "A New Low at Rising Vanderbilt," *New York Times*, September 7, 2013, D1 (2,853 words) (available online at http://www.nytimes.com/2013/09/07/sports/ncaafootball/new-heights-and-an-unsettling-low-for-vanderbilt-football.html).

5. Nexis search for "duke lacrosse and rape!" for 2006: sixty results, beginning on March 29, 2006.

6. Matt Carroll, "Men Accused of Assaulting Penn State Students in Vehicle," *Centre Daily Times* (State College, PA), March 26, 2013, http://www.centredaily.com/2013/03/26/3554443/men-accused-of-assaulting-penn.html.

7. Terri Sanginiti, "Student Charged with Rape," *News Journal* (Wilmington, DE), November 12, 2013, available online under the headline "Goldey-Beacom Student Charged with Rape," at http://www.delawareonline.com/story/news/crime/2013/11/11/goldey-beacom-student-charged-with-rape/3495161/.

8. "Man Sentenced for Attempted Rape at College of Idaho," *Idaho Statesman* (Boise), August 27, 2013.

9. *Daily Gazette* (Schenectady/Albany, NY), August 4, 2012.

10. James Carroll, "Sexual Assault and a Culture Unmoored," *Boston Globe*, July 21, 2014, http://www.bostonglobe.com/opinion/2014/07/21/sexual-assault-and-culture-unmoored/8U9vHHo4JbC7V0xEEd905O/story.html.

11. Ibid. ("When legions of endangered children arrive at America's southern border, officials look only to speed up their expulsion. Powerful voices think the solution to immigration reform is the restriction of admission to elites.")

12. See, e.g., "Alleged Ringleader Convicted in 2008 Gang Rape of Lesbian Woman in Richmond," CBS-San Francisco, December 18, 2013, http://sanfrancisco.cbslocal.com/2013/12/18/alleged-ringleader-convicted-in-2008-gang-rape-of-lesbian-woman-in-richmond/.

13. The few news stories that even acknowledged the jury's express finding that Salvador was a member of the Sureño gang failed to specify that it is a *Mexican* gang. See, e.g., ibid. ("In addition, jurors found true that he inflicted great bodily injury on the victim and committed the crimes in affiliation with the Sureño gang.")

14. Associated Press, "Mom, Grandma, Stepfather Accused of Beating, Tying Kids to Beds in Wheelersburg Home," May 7, 2014, http://raycomgroup. worldnow.com/story/24704847/email-for-help-leads-to-3-ohio-child-abuse-arrests; Holly Zachariah, "Ongoing Coverage; Neighbors Shocked to Learn of Abuse inside Scioto County Home," *Columbus (OH) Dispatch*, February 14, 2014, http://www.dispatch.com/content/stories/local/2014/02/14/neighbors-shocked-to-learn-of-abuse.html; and Frank Lewis, "Sex Abuse Trial Begins Monday," *Portsmouth (OH) Daily Times*, October 21, 2014, available online under the headline "Child Rape Trial Begins Monday," at http://portsmouth-dailytimes.com/news/news/152178593/Child-rape-trial-begins-Monday.

15. He was somehow at large two years later when he was accused of raping another girl the same way, prompting him to flee Colorado. "One of Colorado's Most Wanted Sex Offenders Arrested in Tucson by U.S. Marshals," press release, U.S. Marshal's Service, May 15, 2013, http://www.usmarshals.gov/news/chron/2013/051513f.htm.

16. "Man Charged with Statutory Rape," *News & Observer* (Raleigh, NC), August 14, 2007.

17. Police/Fire Log, *Sacramento (CA) Bee*, January 18, 2004.

18. "Tier Placements: Trafficking in Persons Report," U.S. Department of State, 2013, http://www.state.gov/j/tip/rls/tiprpt/2013/210548.htm. See also *Trafficking in Persons: Global Review; House International Relations Subcommittee on International Terrorism, Nonproliferation, and Human Rights*, 108th Cong. (2004) (statement of Holly Burkhalter, U.S. Policy Director, Physicians for Human Rights Committee, citing India, Thailand, Burma, and Nepal as examples of countries with "large commercial sex industries and a significant trafficking problem").

19. Michael Fumento, "AIDS—a Heterosexual Epidemic?," *Commentary* 2, no. 3 (Summer 1997), available online at http://www.haciendapub.com/medicalsentinel/aids-heterosexual-epidemic ("The reason HIV spreads more easily in places like Thailand…is because other sexually transmitted diseases that cause genital lesions run rampant there. These lesions have repeatedly been demonstrated to tremendously facilitate the transmission

of HIV. Intravenous drug abuse is also a serious problem in Thailand."); "World Population Profile," U.S. Census Bureau, 1994, p. 56, https://www. census.gov/population/international/files/WPP-1994.pdf (data from South Korea, the Philippines, and Taiwan show that less than 1 percent of sex workers are infected with AIDS). See generally Charles A. Thomas Jr., Kary B. Mullis, and Phillip E. Johnson, "What Causes AIDS? It's an Open Question," *Reason*, June 1994, www.reason.com/archives/1994/06/01/what-causes-aids.

20. Steven Erlanger, "A Plague Awaits," *New York Times*, July 14, 1991, http:// www.nytimes.com/1991/07/14/magazine/a-plague-awaits.html.

21. See Jason Richwine, "IQ and Immigration Policy" (PHD diss., Harvard University), ProQuest Dissertations and Theses, Appendix A (listing immigrant percentages from each country), available online at Scribd, http:// www.scribd.com/doc/140239668/IQ-and-Immigration-Policy-Jason-Richwine.

22. Gardiner Harris and Hari Kumar, "Clashes Break Out in India at a Protest over a Rape Case," *New York Times*, December 23, 2012, http://www. nytimes.com/2012/12/23/world/asia/in-india-demonstrators-and-police-clash-at-protest-over-rape.html.

23. Amarnath Tewary and Heather Timmons, "As Protests Sweep Delhi, Another Gang Rape in Bihar," *India Ink* (blog), *New York Times* blogs, December 19, 2012, http://india.blogs.nytimes.com/2012/12/19/as-protests-sweep-delhi-another-gang-rape-in-bihar/.

24. Anjani Trivedi, "Are Delhi's Buses Safe for Women?," *India Ink* (blog), *New York Times* blogs, December 17, 2012, http://india.blogs.nytimes. com/2012/12/17/after-another-gang-ape-in-north-india-questions-raised-about-delhis-buses/.

25. Mark Memmott, "Reports: American Woman Gang-Raped in India," NPR, June 4, 2013, http://www.npr.org/blogs/thetwo-way/2013/06/04/188593230/reports-american-woman-gang-raped-in-india.

26. Lauren Wolfe, "Women Alert to Travel's Darker Side," *New York Times*, May 25, 2014, http://www.nytimes.com/2014/05/25/travel/women-alert-to-travels-darker-side.html.

27. "Sexual Exploitation of Children in Latin America," Inter-American Children's Institute, 2002.

28. Maria Cecilia Espinosa, "Latin America: Women Murdered, Raped—and Ignored" Inter Press Service, November 11, 2004, http://www.ipsnews. net/2004/11/latin-america-women-murdered-raped-and-ignored/.

29. Ibid.
30. "Mexico City Rolls Out Sex-Segregated Buses," CBS News, January 24, 2008, http://www.cbsnews.com/news/mexico-city-rolls-out-sex-segregated-buses/.
31. Trivedi, "Are Delhi's Buses Safe For Women?"
32. Fjordman, "Oslo Rape Statistics Shock," *fjordman* (blog), July 24, 2005, http://fjordman.blogspot.com/2005/07/norwegian-government-covering-up.html. ("Two out of three charged with rape in Norway's capital are immigrants with a non-western background according to a police study.")
33. Jamie Glasov, "Muslim Rape, Feminist Silence," FrontPage Magazine, February 22, 2011, http://www.frontpagemag.com/2011/jamie-glazov/muslim-rape-feminist-silence/; and Fjordman, "Muslim Rape Wave in Sweden," FrontPage Magazine, December 15, 2005, http://archive.frontpagemag.com/readArticle.aspx?ARTID=6251.
34. Ibid.
35. Dalia Mattar, trans., "Edited Transcript of Sheik Hilali's Speech," October 27, 2006, *Australian*, October 27, 2006, http://www.theaustralian.com.au/news/nation/edited-transcript-of-sheik-hilalis-speech/story-e6frg6nf-1111112425808?nk=2631db060d5de73eeb994cf14e603933.
36. Benjamin Toff, "Lara Logan Interview Leads Sunday Ratings," *New York Times*, May 3, 2011, http://www.nytimes.com/2011/05/03/arts/television/lara-logan-interview-leads-sunday-ratings.html.
37. Wolfe, "Women Alert to Travel's Darker Side."
38. "Mexican Police Charged with Rape of Italian," BBC.com, February 21, 2013, http://www.bbc.com/news/world-latin-america-21543550.
39. Stephen Puddicombe, "Canadian Tourist Accuses Mexican Police of Raping Her," CBC News, January 17, 2011, http://www.cbc.ca/news/world/canadian-tourist-accuses-mexican-police-of-raping-her-1.989082.
40. "Six Arrested over Rape of Spanish Tourists in Acapulco," BBC.com, February 13, 2013, http://www.bbc.com/news/world-latin-america-21454647; Associated Press, "CNN: Mexican Official Says Rape Victims Knew Attackers," February 6, 2013, available online at *USA Today*, http://www.usatoday.com/story/news/world/2013/02/06/mexico-acapulco-tourist-rape/1895735/; and Associated Press, "Acapulco Gang Rape Case Overshadows Peak Tourist Season," CNN, February 7, 2013.

41. Nicola Goulding and Phil O'Sullivan, "Norwegian Woman: I Was Raped in Dubai, Now I Face Prison Sentence," CNN, July 21, 2013, http://www.cnn.com/2013/07/20/world/meast/uae-norway-rape-controversy/.

42. Nicola Goulding et al., "Dubai Ruler Pardons Norwegian Woman Convicted After She Reported Rape," CNN, July 22, 2013, http://www.cnn.com/2013/07/22/world/meast/uae-norway-rape-controversy/.

43. Associated Press, "India Arrests 6 over Swiss Tourist's Gang-Rape," CBS News, March 17, 2013, http://www.cbsnews.com/news/india-arrests-6-over-swiss-tourists-gang-rape/; Kumar and Timmons, "Tourist in India Is Gang Raped, Police Say," *India Ink* (blog), *New York Times* blogs, March 17, 2013, http://query.nytimes.com/gst/fullpage.html?res=9503E2D9173BF934A25750C0A9659D8B63.

44. Associated Press, "British Woman Jumps from Third-Floor Hotel Room in India to Avoid Attack as Government Introduces Tougher Rape Laws," *National Post* (Toronto), March 19, 2013, http://news.nationalpost.com/2013/03/19/british-woman-jumps-from-third-floor-hotel-room-in-india-to-avoid-attack-as-government-introduces-tougher-rape-laws/.

45. Associated Press, "Brazilian Authorities Detain 14-Year-Old Suspect in American Tourist Gang Rape Case: Report," April 8, 2013; Mac Margolis, "American Student Gang-Raped in Rio during Drive through Hell," Daily Beast, April 2, 2013, http://www.thedailybeast.com/witw/articles/2013/04/02/american-student-gang-raped-in-rio-during-drive-through-hell.html.

46. Hari Kumar and Ellen Barry, "Danish Tourist Says She Was Gang-Raped in India," *New York Times*, January 15, 2014, http://www.nytimes.com/2014/01/16/world/asia/danish-tourist-says-she-was-gang-raped-in-new-delhi.html.

47. "Polish Woman Raped, Search On for Cab Driver," *Hindu*, January 5, 2014, http://www.thehindu.com/news/national/polish-woman-raped-search-on-for-cab-driver/article5539224.ece.

48. Carol Kuruvilla, "Young German Charity Worker Raped While Traveling on Indian Train," *New York Daily News*, January 16, 2014, http://www.nydailynews.com/news/world/young-german-charity-worker-raped-indian-train-article-1.1581863.

49. Martin Beckford and Amanda Perthen, "British Holidaymaker 'Is Raped by Security Guard in Her Hotel Room at Red Sea Resort,'" *Daily Mail* (UK), March 22, 2014, http://www.dailymail.co.uk/news/article-2587083/British-holidaymaker-raped-security-guard-hotel-room-Red-Sea-resort.html.

50. Wolfe, "Women Alert to Travel's Darker Side."

51. Ibid.

52. Ibid.

53. "Cops: Fake N.Y. Cabbie Tries to Rape Woman in front of Kids," CBS News, August 28, 2014, http://www.cbsnews.com/news/cops-fake-cabbie-tries-to-rape-woman-in-front-of-kids-in-new-york-city/. ("According to investigators, the suspect is Hispanic and possibly in his 40s. The victim said he spoke Spanish and had an earring in his right ear and manicured eyebrows.")

54. Little information was revealed about the victims, except that they, like their attacker, did not speak English. Andrea F. Siegel, "Teen Sentenced to 12 Years for Attacks on Woman, Child," *Baltimore (MD) Sun*, November 9, 2010, http://articles.baltimoresun.com/2010-11-08/news/bs-md-ar-rape-stabbing-20101108_1_annapolis-police-crime-victims-attacks; and "In the Region," *Baltimore (MD) Sun*, February 18, 2009, http://articles.baltimoresun.com/2009-02-18/news/0902170075_1_flannery-chen-perry-hall.

SPOT THE IMMIGRANT! CASE NO. 3: DEATH SENTENCE CHAMPIONS

1. See Sam Howe Verhovek, "Houston Knows Murder, but This…" *New York Times*, July 9, 1993, http://www.nytimes.com/1993/07/09/us/houston-knows-murder-but-this.html; John Makeig, "Girls' Hour of Terror before Death Detailed," *Houston (TX) Chronicle*, February 1, 1994; "Office of the Clark County Prosecuting Attorney: Jose Ernesto Medellin," http://www.clarkprosecutor.org/html/death/US/medellin1116.htm; and "Office of the Clark County Prosecuting Attorney: Peter Anthony Cantu," http://www.clarkprosecutor.org/html/death/US/cantu1224.htm.

2. Mike Tolson, "Justices Reject Killer's Appeal; Execution Date Can Be Set for the 1993 Murders of Ertman, Peña," *Houston (TX) Chronicle*, April 20, 2010.

3. Makeig, "Girls' Hour of Terror."

4. Ibid.

5. Ibid.

6. "Office of the Clark County Prosecuting Attorney: Jose Ernesto Medellin."

7. Makeig, "Girls' Hour of Terror."

8. "Office of the Clark County Prosecuting Attorney: Peter Anthony Cantu."

9. Jeremy Peters, "In Raising Immigration, G.O.P. Risks Backlash after Election," *New York Times*, October 20, 2014, http://www.nytimes.

com/2014/10/21/us/in-raising-immigration-gop-risks-blowback-after-election.html.

10. Verhovek, "Houston Knows Murder."

11. Allan Turner, "In Case That Shook City, Controversial Execution Nears," *Houston (TX) Chronicle*, August 4, 2008.

12. Jennifer Liebrum, "O'Brien Gets Death Sentence," *Houston (TX) Chronicle*, April 10, 1994.

13. Turner, "In Case That Shook City."

14. "Office of the Clark County Prosecuting Attorney: Jose Ernesto Medellin."

15. *CBS This Morning*, October 12, 1994.

16. S. K. Bardwell, "Teenagers' Legacy: Double Murders Changed Texas Law," *Houston (TX) Chronicle*, June 25, 2003.

17. Ed Stoddard, "Texas Defies World Court with Execution," Reuters, August 6, 2008, http://www.reuters.com/article/2008/08/06/us-usa-mexico-execution-idUSN0531256220080806.

18. "Convicted Mexican-Born Killer Executed," *Brownsville (TX) Herald*, August 6, 2008.

19. Verhovek, "Houston Knows Murder," *New York Times*, July 9, 1993.

20. Bardwell, "'Animal-Like' Gang Initiation Snared 2 Girls," *Houston (TX) Chronicle*, July 1, 1993.

21. Nexis search: "All English Language News" in "All available dates" for: "jose medellin and mexic! and (houston or texas or ertman or pena or cantu or rape or gang)"; or "jose ernesto medellin and mexic! and (houston or texas or ertman or pena or cantu or rape or gang)."

22. Doug Cassel, "Bush Could Still Turn into a Champion of Oppressed," response to "Inhuman: In a Post-9/11 World, Does America Still Stand Tall on Rights?," *Chicago Tribune*, November 28, 2004, http://articles.chicago tribune.com/2004-11-28/news/0411280073_1_human-rights-torture-president-bush.

23. See, e.g., Makeig, "Judges Call for 5 Trials at One Time," *Houston (TX) Chronicle*, September 16, 1993; Terri Langford, "Six Suspects Held in Gang Rape, Slayings of Two Teen-Agers," Associated Press, July 1, 1993; News Services, Addenda, *Washington Post*, July 2, 1993; T. J. Milling and Bardwell, "Six Teens Held in Two Girls' Rape-Murders," *Houston (TX) Chronicle*, June 30, 1993.

24. "A Travel Advisory," editorial, *New York Times*, March 14, 2005, http://www.nytimes.com/2005/03/14/opinion/14mon2.html?_r=0.

25. Jose Ernesto Medellin v. Texas, 552 U.S. 491 March 25, 2008.

26.   Tolson, "Justices Reject Killer's Appeal."

CHAPTER ELEVEN: WHY DO HISPANIC VALEDICTORIANS MAKE THE NEWS, BUT CHILD RAPISTS DON'T?

1.   According to the Pew Research Center, in 2012 there were 33.7 million Hispanics of Mexican origin in the United States. Of those, "half (51%) are in the U.S. illegally while about a third are legal permanent residents (32%) and 16% are naturalized U.S. citizens." Ana Gonzalez-Barrera and Mark Hugo Lopez, "A Demographic Portrait of Mexican-Origin Hispanics in the United States," Pew Research Center Hispanic Trends Project, May 1, 2013, http://www.pewhispanic.org/2013/05/01/a-demographic-portrait-of-mexican-origin-hispanics-in-the-united-states/. But Pew uses the census's undercount of illegal aliens, as we saw in chapter 2. According to Pew, "More than half (55%) of the 11.1 million immigrants who are in the country illegally are from Mexico." So making that 55 percent of *30 million* illegal aliens, rather than 55 percent of 11.1 million, adds another 10 million Mexican illegal immigrants to Pew's estimate, bringing the total number of Mexicans in the United States to 43.7 million.

2.   Such as this one: J. Russell Mikkelsen, "What's Weird about Norway," Medium.com, September 29, 2013, https://medium.com/@jrmikkelsen/whats-weird-about-norway-b1a51c79a3d0.

3.   Associated Press, "Ohio: Life Sentence in Murders and Rapes," *New York Times*, December 31, 2013, http://www.nytimes.com/2013/12/31/us/ohio-life-sentence-in-murders-and-rapes.html.

4.   Guandique had already assaulted two other women jogging in the same area of Rock Creek Park. Terence P. Jeffrey, "Who Let Ingmar In?," Human Events Online, February 24, 2009, http://humanevents.com/2009/02/25/who-let-ingmar-in/ (originally printed in 2002, before Guandique's conviction, when the D.C. Police and media were still looking at Democratic Congressman Gary Condit).

5.   According to what Reyes told a fellow prison inmate in 1999, he was in the park when he heard the victim's screams, so he waited for the gang assaulting the woman to leave before raping her himself. Barbara Ross and Alice Mcquillan, "Inmate Says Reyes Raped Her After Teens Attacked," *New York Daily News*, December 5, 2002, http://www.nydailynews.com/archives/news/inmate-reyes-raped-teens-attacked-article-1.503689.

6.   Ross and Mcquillan, "Inmate Says Reyes Raped Her After Teens Attacked."

7.   See, e.g., Edward Conlon, "The Myth of the Central Park Five," October 19, 2014, http://www.thedailybeast.com/articles/2014/10/19/decoding-the-crime-of-the-century-the-real-story-of-the-central-park-five.html; Annaliese Griffin, "A Profile of Matias Reyes," *New York Daily News*, April 9, 2013, http://www.nydailynews.com/services/central-park-five/profile-matias-reyes-article-1.1308560.

8.   Lorena's battered-wife defense came later. See, e.g., David Margolick, "Witnesses Say Mutilated Man Often Hit Wife," *New York Times*, January 12, 1994, http://www.nytimes.com/1994/01/12/us/witnesses-say-mutilated-man-often-hit-wife.html.

9.   Larry Welborn and Vik Jolly, "Woman Who Sliced Off Husband's Penis Gets 7 to Life in Prison," *Orange County (CA) Register*, June 29, 2013, http://www.ocregister.com/articles/kieu-235704-ocprint-husband-penis.html.

10.   Ralph Blumenthal, "No Name, Few Clues: The Case of 'Baby Hope,'" *New York Times*, September 21, 1991, http://www.nytimes.com/1991/09/21/nyregion/no-name-few-clues-the-case-of-baby-hope.html.

11.   J. David Goodman, "As Police Chased Leads about 'Baby Hope,' Those Who Knew Her Kept Quiet," *New York Times*, October 14, 2013, despite-furor-over-baby-hope-many-family-members-remained-silent.

12.   See, e.g., James C. McKinley Jr., "Man Indicted in the Killing of 'Baby Hope,'" *New York Times*, November 21, 2013, http://www.nytimes.com/2013/11/22/nyregion/man-indicted-in-the-killing-of-baby-hope.html.

13.   Kevin Dolak, Aaron Katersky, and Mark Crudele, "Mother of 'Baby Hope' Identified after 22 Year NYPD Search," ABC News, October 8, 2013, http://abcnews.go.com/US/mother-baby-hope-identified-22-year-nypd-search/story?id=20506860.

14.   "Da Vance Announces Indictment of Conrado Juarez for 22-Year-Old Cold Case Murder of 'Baby Hope,'" press release, New York County District Attorney's Office, November 21, 2013, http://manhattanda.org/press-release/da-vance-announces-indictment-conrado-juarez-22-year-old-cold-case-murder-"baby-hope".

15.   Michael Schwirtz and William K. Rashbaum, "Cousin Arrested in 'Baby Hope' Killing after 22 Years," *New York Times*, October 12, 2013, http://www.nytimes.com/2013/10/13/nyregion/baby-hope.html.

16.   "Suspected 'Baby Hope' Killer Pleads Not Guilty: Lawyer Disputes Conrado Juarez's Confession to Police," CBS New York, November 21, 2013, http://newyork.cbslocal.com/2013/11/21/man-accused-in-baby-hope-case-due-in-court/.

17.   Dean Schabner, "Baby Hope Case: Cousin Arrested in 22-Year-Old Killing," ABC News, October 12, 2013, http://abcnews.go.com/US/baby-hope-case-cousin-arrested-22-year-killing/story?id=20554415.

18.   Matthew Chayes, "Conrado Juarez, Accused Killer of 'Baby Hope,' Remanded to Jail," *Newsday*, October 17, 2013, http://www.newsday.com/news/new-york/conrado-juarez-accused-killer-of-baby-hope-remanded-to-jail-1.6247875.

19.   Kristina Sgueglia, "'Baby Hope' Suspect's Attorney Challenges Alleged Confession," CNN, November 21, 2013, http://www.cnn.com/2013/11/21/justice/new-york-baby-hope-suspect-indictment/.

20.   Shayna Jacobs, "Conrado Juarez, Accused Killer of 'Baby Hope,' Indicted by Manhattan Grand Jury, Lawyer Says," *New York Daily News*, October 21, 2013, http://www.nydailynews.com/new-york/uptown/accused-killer-indicted-baby-hope-slay-article-1.1492284. See also Jacobs, "'Baby Hope' Slay Suspect Conrado Juarez Pleads Not Guilty," *New York Daily News*, November 21, 2013, http://www.nydailynews.com/new-york/nyc-crime/baby-hope-slay-suspect-pleads-not-guilty-article-1.1525280.

21.   Associated Press, "Conrado Juarez Confesses to Assaulting and Killing Anjelica Castillo," *People*, October 12, 2013.

22.   See, e.g., Schabner, "Baby Hope Case," Comments Section, http://abcnews.go.com/US/baby-hope-case-cousin-arrested-22-year-killing/story?id=20554415#disqus_thread.

Guest

I really don't get the mother or the older daughter who returned home eight years ago. I don't get the secrets…If the mother had always suspected that the dead child was her daughter, why didn't she come forward? Also, didn't understand that her husband disappeared with the child, but it was a cousin who confessed.… I don't understand the older daughter never discussing events with her mother. This story makes no sense.

Rick Rope Guest

I agree. I don't understand the mother's behavior whatsoever. The only thing that would explain it is if she was on drugs at the time.

Lynn Mann

Seems everything went wrong here…Mom doesn't at least visit girls? Dad doesn't know daughter is missing? Neighbors don't see anything wrong? Sister doesn't say anything?

23. Abigail Wilson, "Guerra-Garcia Enters Alford Plea in Child Sex Case," *Dodge City (KS) Daily Globe*, March 7, 2013, http://www.dodgeglobe.com/article/20130306/News/130309360; "Dodge City Woman Charged in 2 Year Old Child Abuse Case," KansasNews.com, April 5, 2013, http://www.westernkansasnews.com/2013/04/dodge-city-woman-charged-in-2-year-old-child-abuse-case/; Wilson, "Woman Sentenced for Helping Rapist Flee Dodge," *Dodge City (KS) Daily Globe*, May 9, 2013, http://www.dodgeglobe.com/article/20130508/News/130509257#ixzz3IKi9eWuU.

24. "Bloomington Men Plead Guilty to False Documents," *Peoria (IL) Journal Star*, February 28, 2014, http://www.pjstar.com/article/20140228/News/140228936. The same day Muhedano-Hernandez was indicted for making child pornography, the grand jury also handed up an indictment of Michael E. Ontiveros for possessing child pornography.

25. "California Woman, Abducted at 15, Is Found after 10 Years," *New York Times*, May 22, 2014, http://www.nytimes.com/2014/05/22/us/kidnapped-california-woman-found-safe-after-10-years.html.

26. Jose L. Medina, "Two Sent to Prison on Charges of Sexual Contact with Minors," *Las Cruces (NM) Sun-News*, June 14, 2007, http://www.lcsun-news.com/news/ci_6145011.

27. Alyssa Duranty, "Agency to Deport 31 L.A.-Area Sex Offenders," *Orange County (CA) Register*, June 7, 2014.

28. Stan Finger, "24 Wichita-Area Arrests Part of Six-State ICE Operation," *Wichita (KS) Eagle*, June 18, 2014, http://www.kansas.com/news/article1146477.html.

29. Nebraska v. Hector Medina-Liborio (S. Ct. Neb.), April 5, 2013, available online at https://supremecourt.nebraska.gov/sites/supremecourt.ne.gov/files/sc/opinions/s12-200.pdf.

30. New Jersey v. Fajardo-Santos, Supreme Court of New Jersey, July 8, 2009, available online at http://caselaw.findlaw.com/nj-supreme-court/1399310.html.

31. "2012 American Community Survey 1-Year Estimates, Hawaii: Hispanic or Latino Origin by Specific Origin," U.S. Census Bureau, http://factfinder2.census.gov/faces/tableservices/jsf/pages/productview.xhtml?pid=ACS_12_1YR_C03001&prodType=table.

32. Lila Fujimoto, "10-Year Term for Illegal Immigrant in Sex Abuse Case," MauiNews.com, April 19, 2012, http://mauinews.com/page/content.detail/id/560337/10-year-term-for-illegal-immigrant-in-sex-abuse-case.html?nav=10; Associated Press, "Illegal Immigrant Sentenced in Maui Molestation," April 19, 2012, available online at *Hawaii Tribune-Herald*, http://hawaiitribune-herald.com/sections/news/state/illegal-immigrant-sentenced-maui-molestation.html.

33. S. L. Wykes, "Life Plus 35 Years for Rapist Who Left Girl, 4, for Dead," *San Jose (CA) Mercury News*, June 25, 1994.

34. Paul Fiel Narvios: Naturalized: July 29, 1980; DOB: 5/25/1948, Residence: California, Civil Record: 1980. Available online at the U.S. Naturalization Record Indexes, 1791–1992 (Indexed in World Archives Project), Ancestry.com, http://search.ancestry.com/cgi-bin/sse.dll?gl=40&rank=1&new=1&so=3&MSAV=0&msT=1&gss=ms_f-40&gsln=Narvios&uidh=000.

35. See, e.g., "Girl, 10, Gave Birth—Abuser Sentenced," *San Francisco Gate*, September 9, 1999; and [Unnamed story], Associated Press State, September 9, 1999.

36. Matthew Sheffield, "Liberals Fall for Hoax 'Study' Claiming Fox News Viewers Are Mentally Deficient," Newsbusters, December 10, 2012, http://newsbusters.org/blogs/matthew-sheffield/2012/12/10/liberals-fall-hoax-study-claiming-fox-news-makes-people-stupid#sthash.L9GBdVZX.dpuf.

37. "Special Session on Children: A Response to the Needs of Children and Adolescents Worldwide," Latin American and Caribbean Youth Network for Sexual and Reproductive Rights, Women's Health Collection, January 1, 2003.

38. Ibid.

39. "Statistics on Teen Pregnancy," Teenshelter, November 11, 2006, http://www.teenshelter.org/Jims_Statistics_on_Teenage_Pregnancy_11-11-06.pdf. See also Joyce A. Martin et al., "National Vital Statistics Reports: Births; Final Data for 2010," Table A, U.S. Centers for Disease Control, August 28, 2012, http://www.cdc.gov/nchs/data/nvsr/nvsr61/nvsr61_01.pdf.

40. Fay Menacker et al., "Births to 10–14 Year-Old Mothers, 1990–2002: Trends and Health Outcomes," Table A, Centers for Disease Control: National Vital Statistics Reports, November 15, 2004, http://www.cdc.gov/nchs/data/nvsr/nvsr53/nvsr53_07.pdf.

41. Rafael Romo on *CNN Newsroom*, February 7, 2013, transcript available at http://www.cnn.com/TRANSCRIPTS/1302/07/cnr.07.html.

42. Daniel Bates, "Girl Aged Nine Who Gave Birth to Baby in Mexico Didn't Realize She Was Pregnant until Seven Months—and Her Mother Didn't Think It Was a Crime," *Daily Mail* (UK), February 7, 2013, http://www.dailymail.co.uk/news/article-2274988/Girl-aged-gave-birth-baby-Mexico-didnt-realize-pregnant-seven-months—mother-didnt-think-crime.html.

43. Gerard Couzens, "Argentine Schoolgirl, 12, Gives Birth to Twin Sons (On Same Day Mexican Nine-Year-Old Became a Mother)," *Daily Mail* (UK), February 7, 2013, http://www.dailymail.co.uk/news/article-2274916/Argentine-schoolgirl-12-gives-birth-twins-sons-day-Mexican-year-old-mother.html.

44. Simon Tomlinson, "Tribal Law Protects Boy, 15, Who Impregnated 10-Year-Old Colombian Girl from Under-Age Sex Charges," *Daily Mail* (UK), April 11, 2012, http://www.dailymail.co.uk/news/article-2128007/Tribal-law-protects-boy-15-impregnated-10-year-old-Colombian-girl.html.

45. See, e.g., Natalie Evans, "Babies Having Babies: A New Mum Aged Nine and the World's Youngest Mothers in Medical History," *Mirror* (UK), February 6, 2013, http://www.mirror.co.uk/news/weird-news/worlds-youngest-mum-top-10-1589383.

46. Kathleen Vaughn, "Pregnancy in Childhood: Letter," *British Medical Journal*, October 8, 1933, http://www.bmj.com/content/2/3798/759.2.

47. See, e.g., Evans, "Babies Having Babies."

48. "Shock for Family as Eight-Year-Old Girl Gives Birth to Twins: Girl Aged 8 Gives Birth to Twins," *The People*, June 12, 1994. (A top obstetrician in Little Rock, Arkansas, said: "In my 11 years of experience here, I have never heard of a case where the mother is so young," adding, "I would have thought it was a medical impossibility before Dr. Elders came across the fact.")

49. Working off of *Wikipedia*'s "Youngest Mothers" entry, and adding a few they missed, this is the list of specific, reported births to girls aged ten or younger since 1990:

    Bolivia—eleven cases (or twelve if you count the Bolivian immigrant who gave birth at age ten in Chile)
    Colombia—nine (or ten if you count the ten-year-old Colombian immigrant who gave birth in Spain). One was an eight-year-old girl forced into prostitution by her own mother ("Colombia: Girl Prostitute Pregnant at 8," ANSA English Media Service, September 10, 2004).

Brazil—nine

Mexico—six

Peru—six

Argentina—six

Honduras—two

Nicaragua—two (not including the nine-year-old Nicaraguan girl who got an abortion after being impregnated by a twenty-year-old, which is the only part of the story that got the undivided attention of the American media)

El Salvador—one

50. In 2013, the entire population of these nine countries was estimated to be 463 million, about 50 percent greater than America's population of 316 million.

51. Briefs, *Myrtle Beach (SC) Sun-News*, January 29, 2006.

52. Developed-country list of births to girls aged ten or younger:

- One child pregnancy in Switzerland to immigrants from Cameroon. "10-Year-Old Gives Birth to a Child," *Times of India*, September 20, 2005, http://timesofindia.indiatimes.com/world/rest-of-world/10-year-old-gives-birth-to-a-child/articleshow/1236732.cms.

- Two child pregnancies in Spain to immigrants from Colombia and gypsy immigrants from Romania. The ten-year-old gypsy girl, Elena Chiritescu, was impregnated by her thirteen-year-old cousin, who had been raised as her brother. See, e.g., Nick Fagge and Tamara Cohen, "Tragic Tale of Star-Crossed Lovers," *Sunday Times* (Australia), November 7, 2010. (Luckily for us, the *New York Times* is on a campaign to bring more gypsies to America!)

- One child pregnancy in Belgium to a ten-year-old girl and a thirteen-year-old father in 2005, about whom no ethnic information is available. Hints that the case did not involve Belgian nationals include the fact that the little girl's mother was delighted and that a Dutch medical journal's report on the pregnancy noted that birth control for ten-year-olds was being prescribed mostly to "ethnic girls." "Doctor Calls 10-Year-Old Belgian Girl's Birth 'Dangerous,'" FoxNews.com, October 3, 2007, http://www.foxnews.com/story/2007/10/03/doctor-calls-10-year-old-belgian-girlrsquos-birth-lsquodangerousrsquo/.

- Actual American, William Edward Ronca, struck in 2006.
- One child pregnancy in the United States when, in 2008, Guadalupe Gutierrez-Juarez, thirty-eight, an illegal immigrant from Mexico, was arrested in Idaho, along with his twenty-seven-year-old illegal alien girlfriend, Isabel Chasarez, after the girlfriend's ten-year-old daughter showed up at an Idaho hospital nine months pregnant and medical staff called the police. Nick Draper, "Child Rapist Sent to Prison," *Idaho Falls (ID) Post Register*, November 26, 2008.
- In California, fifty-year-old immigrant Paul Narvios repeatedly raped his girlfriend's nine-year-old daughter, getting her pregnant. See, e.g., "Girl, 10, Gave Birth—Abuser Sentenced," *San Francisco Gate*, September 9, 1999; and [Unnamed story] Associated Press State, September 9, 1999.
- In 2011, a thirty-three-year-old illegal immigrant from Haiti, Fede Datilus, became the fourth "American" child-impregnator after getting a nine-year-old girl in Florida pregnant. See, e.g., Wayne K. Roustan, "Lantana Man Gets Life in Prison for Impregnating Girl, 9," *Sun Sentinel* (Fort Lauderdale, FL), March 23, 2011.

53. Alexis De Tocqueville, *Democracy In America*, vol. 2, trans. Henry Reeve (1840), Kindle version, 3212.

54. The Latin American and Caribbean Youth Network for Sexual and Reproductive Rights, for example, issued a policy statement on adolescent girls' "rights" including, the "right to decide whether or not to have sex, free from coercion or violence." Latin American and Caribbean Women's Health Network, "Special Session on Children: A Response to the Needs of Children and Adolescents worldwide? (Sexual Rights and Reproductive Rights)," 2003, available online at http://www.thefreelibrary.com/Special+session+on+children%3A+a+response+to+the+needs+of+children+and...-a0105915326.

55. Christopher McDougall, "Slick Transit Gloria," *New York Times Magazine*, April 7, 2002, http://www.nytimes.com/2002/04/07/magazine/07TREVI.html.

56. "Mexico: Rape Victims Denied Legal Abortion," Human Rights Watch, March 7, 2006, http://www.hrw.org/en/news/2006/03/06/mexico-rape-victims-denied-legal-abortion.

57. McDougall, "Slick Transit Gloria."

58. Shana L. Maier, *Rape, Victims, and Investigations: Experiences and Perceptions of Law Enforcement Officers Responding to Reported Rapes*

(London: Routledge, 2014), 82, available online at https://books.google.com/
books?id=eZbOAwAAQBAJ&pg=PA103&dq=Violence+and+Victims+20
07+Reporting+to+the+Police+by+Hispanic+Victims+of+Violence+Renni
son&hl=en&sa=X&ei=QtSXVLf6OsKdNvLng5gK&ved=0CB8Q6AEwA
A#v=onepage&q=accepting&f=false.

59. Ibid., 82–83.

60. That was in 2005. Between 2000 and 2010, the Hispanic population in
     Mecklenburg County grew from 6.5 percent to 12.2 percent. Linda Shipley
     and Laura Simmons, "Demographic and Economic Changes in
     Mecklenburg County, N.C.," Slide 6, UNC Charlotte Urban Institute,
     October 2011, http://www.slideshare.net/uipublicaffairs/demographic-
     economic-changes-in-mecklenburg-county-nc.

61. "The Boys' Club: Victims of Statutory Rape Still Low Priority with County,"
     Creative Loafing (Charlotte, NC), August 3, 2005, http://clclt.com/charlotte/
     the-boys-club/Content?oid=2360018.

62. U.S. Department of Health and Human Services, *Child Maltreatment, 2006*
     (Washington, DC: Government Printing Office, 2008), http://archive.acf.
     hhs.gov/programs/cb/pubs/cm06/cm06.pdf.

CHAPTER TWELVE: KEEP AMERICA ~~BEAUTIFUL~~ MULTICULTURAL

1. CNN Wire Staff, "McCain Blames Some Arizona Wildfires on Illegal
    Immigrants," CNN, June 19, 2011, http://www.cnn.com/2011/US/06/19/
    arizona.mccain.wildfire.claim/.

2. "John McCain: Immigrants Caused Arizona Wildfires," Huffington Post,
    June 19, 2011, http://www.huffingtonpost.com/2011/06/19/john-mccain-
    illegal-immigration-arizona-wildfires_n_880145.html.

3. Lee Hockstader, "John McCain Fans the Fires of Immigration Intolerance
    in Arizona," *Washington Post*, June 20, 2011, http://www.washingtonpost.
    com/blogs/post-partisan/post/john-mccain-fans-the-fires-of-immigration-
    intolerance-in-arizona/2011/06/20/AGJV56cH_blog.html.

4. "Grijalva Condemns McCain Statement Accusing Undocumented
    Immigrants of Causing Arizona Forest Fires—Still No Evidence Offered,"
    press release, Office of Congressman Raul M. Grijalva, June 20, 2011, http://
    grijalva.house.gov/news-and-press-releases/grijalva-condemns-mccain-
    statement-accusing-undocumented-immigrants-of-causing-arizona-forest-
    fires-ndash-still-no-evidence-offered/.

5. E.g., sparks from all-terrain vehicles, welding machines, recreational shooting, or fireworks. U.S. Government Accountability Office, *Report to Congressional Requesters: Arizona Border Region: Federal Agencies Could Better Utilize Law Enforcement Resources in Support of Wildland Fire Management Activities* (Washington, DC: Government Accountability Office, November 2011), http://www.gao.gov/assets/590/586139.pdf.

6. See, e.g., Douglas Stanglin, "McCain Links Some of Arizona Fires to Illegal Immigrants," *USA Today*, June 20, 2011, http://content.usatoday.com/communities/ondeadline/post/2011/06/mccain-links-arizona-fires-to-illegal-immigrants-but-offers-scant-evidence/1#.VQsmXhDF_w8; and Frank James, "McCain: Forest Service Gave Info That Illegal Immigrants Started Wildfires," NPR, June 20, 2011, http://www.npr.org/blogs/itsallpolitics/2011/06/20/137307094/mccain-forest-service-gave-info-that-illegal-immigrants-started-wildfires ("Absolutely not, according to what I've been told.").

7. U.S. Government Accountability Office, *Report to Congressional Requesters.*

8. Ibid.

9. Ibid.

10. Associated Press, "News in Brief from the San Joaquin Valley," September 25, 2002.

11. Adam Burke, "The Public Lands' Big Cash Crop," *High Country News*, October 31, 2005, http://www.hcn.org/issues/309/15867.

12. Nick Madigan, "Marijuana Found Thriving in Forests," *New York Times*, November 16, 2002, http://www.nytimes.com/2002/11/16/us/marijuana-found-thriving-in-forests.html.

13. David Castellon, "Officials Get Aggressive to Rid Foothills of Pot," *Tulare (CA) Advance-Register,* September 21, 2005.

14. Associated Press, "News in Brief from the San Joaquin Valley," September 25, 2002; Julie Cart, "Park's Pot Problem Explodes," *Los Angeles Times*, May 14, 2003, http://articles.latimes.com/2003/may/14/local/me-pot14.

15. Ginger Thompson, "Mexico Leader Presses U.S. to Resolve Migrants' Issues," *New York Times*, November 27, 2002, http://www.nytimes.com/2002/11/27/world/mexico-leader-presses-us-to-resolve-migrants-issues.html.

16. Richard Stana, *Border Security: Additional Actions Needed to Better Ensure a Coordinated Federal Response to Illegal Activity on Federal Lands* (Washington, DC: Government Accountability Office, November 18, 2010), photos at 20–22, available online at http://books.google.com/books?id=Q

oddG13hCwQC&pg=PP2&lpg=PP2&dq=BORDER+SECURITY+Additio nal+Actions+Needed+to+Better+Ensure+a+Coordinated+Federal+Respo nse+to+Illegal+Activity+on+Federal+Lands+november+2010&source=bl &ots=bb2Nu1yHfI&sig=2GOQkuHTxHvqPzpXFHNR79W_8lU&hl=en &sa=X&ei=-G9mVPSTEIudgwSuyIOABw&ved=0CDQQ6AEwAw#v=on epage&q=monument&f=false. ("In our November 2010 report, we reported that BLM officials posted warning signs at 11 entrance locations of the Sonoran Desert National Monument to warn the public against travel on portions of the monument because of potential encounters with illegal border crossers.")

17. See Jodi Peterson, "After 11 Years, Organ Pipe Cactus National Monument Reopens," *High Country News*, September 17, 2014, http://www.hcn.org/ articles/after-12-years-organ-pipe-national-monument-reopens.

18. Stana, *Border Security*. ("In our November 2010 report, we reported that BLM officials posted warning signs at 11 entrance locations of the Sonoran Desert National Monument to warn the public against travel on portions of the monument because of potential encounters with illegal border crossers.")

19. See, e.g., ibid.; John Ritter, "Drug Agents Can't Keep Up with Pot Growers," *USA Today*, October 13, 2005, http://usatoday30.usatoday.com/news/ nation/2005-10-12-pot-growers-cover_x.htm; and Burke, "The Public Lands' Big Cash Crop."

20. See, e.g., Burke, "The Public Lands' Big Cash Crop."

21. Victor A. Patton, "High Times Ahead? Marijuana Number One Illegal Crop in Merced County," *Merced (CA) Sun-Star*, August 11, 2007, http://www. mercedsunstar.com/incoming/article3251353.html (quoting Neil Compston, task force commander of the Merced Multi-Agency Narcotics Task Force).

22. Ritter, "Drug Agents Can't Keep Up with Pot Growers."

23. Madigan, "Marijuana Found Thriving in Forests."

24. Julie Scelfo, "Five Beginners' Steps to a Greener Home," *New York Times*, March 11, 2009, http://www.nytimes.com/2009/03/12/garden/12greenhome. html?_r=0.

25. Zusha Elinson, "Budget Cuts Endanger State's Marijuana Eradication Program," *New York Times*, July 29, 2011, page A17, available online at http://www.nytimes.com/2011/07/29/us/29bccamp.html?pagewanted=all &gwh=F19F5AD64AC492D28C2BD1AEAFA1211D&gwt=pay. This was the only additional article that came up on the topic, in various Nexis

searches of the *New York Times*, such as: "national park and (marijuana or pot) w/s (grow! or garden! or farm! or plant!)"; and "(mexic! or cartel) and "national park and (pot or marijuana) w/s (grow! or garden!)" for the past twenty years.

26.   Sean Garmire, "Pot Farms Busted on State, Federal Land," *Eureka (CA) Times Standard*, September 13, 2008.

27.   Beth Greenfield, "Land of the Giants," *New York Times*, September 19, 2008, http://www.nytimes.com/2008/09/19/travel/escapes/19mile.html.

28.   Madigan, "Marijuana Found Thriving."

29.   Tim Bragg, "Shots Fired at National Park Rangers in Pot Raid," *Fresno (CA) Bee*, August 9, 2007

30.   Cart, "Park's Pot Problem."

31.   Ginger Thompson, "Where Butterflies Rest, Damage Runs Rampant," *New York Times*, June 2, 2004, http://www.nytimes.com/2004/06/02/international/americas/02butt.html.

32.   Ibid.

33.   Andres Castillo and Walyce Almeida, "Case Study: Eco-Journalism and Cleaning Up Sumidero's Canyon," Salzburg Academy on Media and Global Change, 2013, http://www.salzburg.umd.edu/print/lessons/eco-journalism.

34.   See, e.g., a few recent travel blogs—with photos: Rebecca Pokoro, "Exploring the Sumidero Canyon," *The Girl and Globe* (blog), June 29, 2014, http://thegirlandglobe.com/sumidero-canyon/ (with pictures); Monica Rodriguez, "2014 Sumidero Canyon, Mexico," *Monica in the World* (blog), April 14, 2012, http://monicaerodriguez.wordpress.com/2014/04/05/2014-sumidero-canyon-mexico/; Dany, "Sumidero Canyon: The Good, No bad, but Some Ugly," *Globetrotter Girls* (blog), September 7, 2010, http://globetrottergirls.com/2010/09/sumidero-canyon-good-no-bad-some-ugly/ (after detailing the garbage, this travel blogger added: "Anyway—I hope Mexico is on your list of countries to visit.... It's an amazing country, and so diverse.").

35.   Dudley Althaus, "Litter Choking Streets throughout Mexico," *Houston (TX) Chronicle*, June 25, 2007, http://www.chron.com/news/nation-world/article/Litter-choking-streets-throughout-Mexico-1824829.php.

36.   "Video: Tulum's Dirty Beaches," CoastalCare.org, January 25, 2011, http://coastalcare.org/2011/01/tulums-dirty-beaches/.

37.   Althaus, "Litter Choking Streets throughout Mexico."

38.   Ibid.

39.   Ibid.

40.   Ibid.

41. Ibid.
42. Seth Mydans, "U.S. and Mexico Take On a Joint Burden: Sewage," *New York Times*, August 22, 1990, http://www.nytimes.com/1990/08/22/us/us-and-mexico-take-on-a-joint-burden-sewage.html.
43. "South Bay International Wastewater Treatment Plant (SBIWTP)," Recovery.gov, http://www.ibwc.state.gov/mission_operations/sbiwtp.html.
44. "Angeles Trashed over Labor Day," *Modern Hiker* (blog), September 8, 2011, http://modernhiker.com/2011/09/08/angeles-trashed-over-labor-day/.
45. Brigid Schulte, "Wheaton Neighborhood Is the Face of Montgomery's Shift to Majority Minority," *Washington Post*, February 15, 2011, http://www.washingtonpost.com/wp-dyn/content/article/2011/02/14/AR2011021404044.html.
46. Ibid.
47. "Who Cleans Up after the Party?," letter to the editor, *Desert Sun* (Palm Springs, CA), September 30, 2010.
48. "Mapping L.A.: Vermont Square," Comments Section, *Los Angeles Times*, 2009–2012, available at http://maps.latimes.com/neighborhoods/neighborhood/vermont-square/comments/.
49. Ibid.
50. Victor Zuniga and Ruben Hernandez-Leon, eds., *New Destinations: Mexican Immigration in the United States* (New York: Russell Sage Foundation, 2005), 205.
51. Wcross, "Is Litter an Issue in Your Area?," Democratic Underground, February 6, 2005, http://www.democraticunderground.com/discuss/duboard.php?az=view_all&address=268x242.
52. Maria Cramer, "Mime Plan's Language Draws Offense," *Boston Globe*, May 3, 2005, http://www.boston.com/news/local/massachusetts/articles/2005/05/03/mime_plans_language_draws_offense?pg=full.
53. Jorge Trevino, who runs an anti-littering campaign in Mexico, said: "If you throw trash on the highway here in Mexico, no one says anything." Althaus, "Litter Choking Streets."
54. Alejandra Lopez, "Demographics of California Counties: A Comparison of 1980, 1990, and 2000 Census Data," Stanford University, Center for Comparative Studies in Race and Ethnicity, June 2002, http://web.stanford.edu/dept/csre/reports/report_9.pdf. (San Bernardino County in 1980: 82.4 percent white, 18.5 Hispanic; Riverside County in 1980: 82.1 percent white, 18.9 percent Hispanic).

55. "State andCounty QuickFacts: San Bernardino," U.S. Census Bureau, http://quickfacts.census.gov/qfd/states/06/06071.html.

56. "State and County QuickFacts: Riverside, CA," U.S. Census Bureau, http://quickfacts.census.gov/qfd/states/06/06065.html.

57. "Joshua Tree National Park Graffiti Prompts Closure of Rattlesnake Canyon Area," Huffington Post, April 12, 2013, http://www.huffingtonpost.com/2013/04/12/joshua-tree-national-park-graffiti_n_3070310.html.

58. "California—Race and Hispanic Origin for Selected Large Cities and Other Places: Earliest Census to 1990," U.S. Census Bureau, http://www.census.gov/population/www/documentation/twps0076/CAtab.pdf.

59. "Rancho Cucamonga (City), California," U.S. Census Bureau, http://quickfacts.census.gov/qfd/states/06/0659451.html

60. "Graffiti Vandals Deface California's Scenic Sapphire Falls," *USA Today*, June 23, 2013, http://www.usatoday.com/picture-gallery/news/2013/06/25/graffiti-vandals-deface-californias-scenic-sapphire-falls/2455089/?AID=10709313&PID=6147661&SID=11i8nm3i8urp1; see also "Bitches Love the Bees," Flickr, http://www.flickr.com/photos/60811444@N05/8538200224; and David McNew, "Vandals Target Los Angeles Area National Forests," Getty Images, June 24, 2013, http://www.gettyimages.com/detail/news-photo/rocks-and-cliffs-are-covered-with-graffiti-near-sapphire-news-photo/171415503.

61. Neil Nisperos, "U.S. Forest Service to Close Cucamonga Canyon," *Inland Valley Daily Bulletin*, August 22, 2013, http://www.dailybulletin.com/general-news/20130822/us-forest-service-to-close-cucamonga-canyon.

62. "Cucamonga Canyon Closure Update," City of Rancho Cucamonga, no date, http://www.cityofrc.com/news/displayarchive.asp?Type=1&targetID=5.

63. Ibid.

64. "Sapphire Falls Trail, Reviews," AllTrails.com, http://alltrails.com/trail/us/california/sapphire-falls.

65. "Official Sierra Club Population Policy," SUSPS.org, http://www.susps.org/history/scpolicy.html.

66. Ibid.

67. Kenneth R. Weiss, "The Man behind the Land," *Los Angeles Times*, October 27, 2004, http://articles.latimes.com/2004/oct/27/local/me-donor27.

68. See Matt Kettmann, "It's Not Easy Being Green," *Santa Barbara (CA) Independent*, March 11, 2004, http://media.independent.com/pdf/matt_k/sierracover.pdf.

69.   Darren Samuelsohn, "Greens Move to Heal Immigration Reform Rift,"
       Politico, June 2, 2013, http://www.politico.com/story/2013/06/immigration-
       reform-greens-environment-92099.html.

CHAPTER THIRTEEN: CARLOS SLIM: THE *NEW YORK TIMES'* SUGAR DADDY

1.   Editorial Board, "The Koch Party," *New York Times*, January 25, 2014,
       http://www.nytimes.com/2014/01/26/opinion/sunday/the-koch-party.html.
2.   Ralph Blumenthal, "New Strains and New Rules for Agents along Mexican
       Border," *New York Times*, August 12, 2004, http://www.nytimes.
       com/2004/08/12/us/new-strains-and-new-rules-for-agents-along-mexican-
       border.html.
3.   Editorial Board, "Mr. Obama, Go Big on Immigration," *New York Times*,
       July 3, 2014, http://www.nytimes.com/2014/07/04/opinion/mr-obama-go-
       big-on-immigration.html.
4.   See, e.g., Joe Hagan, "Bleeding 'Times' Blood," *New York*, October 5, 2008,
       http://nymag.com/news/media/51015/; Douglas McCollam, "Sulzberger at
       the Barricades," *Columbia Journalism Review*, July 15, 2008, http://www.
       cjr.org/cover_story/sulzberger_at_the_barricades.php?page=all; and
       Lawrence Wright, "Slim's Time," *New Yorker*, June 1, 2009, http://www.
       newyorker.com/reporting/2009/06/01/090601fa_fact_wright?current
       Page=al.
5.   See, e.g., McCollam, "Sulzberger at the Barricades."
6.   Wright, "Slim's Time."
7.   Hagan, "Bleeding 'Times' Blood."
8.   Wright, "Slim's Time."
9.   See, e.g., ibid.
10.   Eduardo Porter, "Mexico's Plutocracy Thrives on Robber-Baron
       Concessions," *New York Times*, August 27, 2007, http://www.nytimes.
       com/2007/08/27/opinion/27mon4.html?pagewanted=print. ("In 1990, the
       government of President Carlos Salinas de Gortari sold his friend Mr. Slim
       the Mexican national phone company, Telmex, along with a de facto
       commitment to maintain its monopoly for years. Then it awarded Telmex
       the only nationwide cellphone license.")
11.   Slim's Telmex had an earnings margin of 47 percent in 2008, nearly twice the
       28 percent average profit for major telecommunications operators in the United
       States, Canada, the UK, France, Spain, and Sweden. Slim's mobile service, Telcel,
       had an average profit margin of 64 percent, compared with an average of 37.6

percent in all other OECD countries. "The Telecommunication Sector in Mexico," in *OECD Review of Telecommunication Policy and Regulation in Mexico* (OECD Publishing, 2012), 37, http://www.keepeek.com/Digital-Asset-Management/oecd/science-and-technology/oecd-review-of-telecommunication-policy-and-regulation-in-mexico/the-telecommunication-sector-in-mexico_9789264060111-3-en#page24.

12. Porter, "Mexico's Plutocracy."

13. Wright, "Slim's Time."

14. Porter, "Mexico's Plutocracy."

15. Wright, "Slim's Time."

16. "The Telecommunication Sector in Mexico," 18–20.

17. Ibid. (Mexico cell phone penetration: 78 percent, compared with 93 percent in Colombia, 97 percent in Ecuador, and 98 percent in Communist Venezuela).

18. Ibid., 33.

19. Wright, "Slim's Time."

20. "Planet Plutocrat," *Economist*, March 15, 2014.

21. "The Telecommunication Sector in Mexico," 33.

22. Joseph Galante, "CompUSA, Falling to Competition, to Shut Down after Holidays," Bloomberg News, December 8, 2007, http://www.bloomberg.com/apps/news?pid=newsarchive&sid=aomuLvfkNzTY&.

23. Wright, "Slim's Time."

24. Ibid.

25. Wright, "Slim's Time." Such high interconnection rates are expressly outlawed in the United States in order to foster competition. See, e.g., MCI Telecommunications Corp v. Ohio Bell Telephone Company SBC 376 F.3d 539; 2004 FED App. 0232P (6th Cir.), July 20, 2004, available online at http://caselaw.findlaw.com/us-6th-circuit/1296128.html#sthash.QK2eJZ4W.dpuf. ("In order to promote competition in the telecommunications market, the [Telecommunications Act of 1996] requires incumbent providers to allow new market entrants, such as MCI in this case, to utilize the incumbent provider's network and buy the incumbent provider's telecommunication services for a fair price. See 47 U.S.C. §§ 251(a)(1) & (c). These arrangements were necessary to minimize the barriers to market entry erected during the period in which the incumbent provider functioned as a monopoly.")

26. "The Telecommunication Sector in Mexico," 33.

27. Ibid., 17–18.

28. According to the Pew Research Center, in 2012 there were 33.7 million Hispanics of Mexican origin in the United States. Of those, "half (51%) are in the U.S. illegally while about a third are legal permanent residents (32%) and 16% are naturalized U.S. citizens." Ana Gonzalez-Barrera and Mark Hugo Lopez, "A Demographic Portrait of Mexican-Origin Hispanics in the United States," Pew Research Center Hispanic Trends Project, May 1, 2013, http://www.pewhispanic.org/2013/05/01/a-demographic-portrait-of-mexican-origin-hispanics-in-the-united-states/. But Pew uses the census's undercount of illegal aliens, as we saw in chapter 2. According to Pew, "More than half (55%) of the 11.1 million immigrants who are in the country illegally are from Mexico." So making that 55 percent of 30 million illegal aliens, rather than 55 percent of 11.1 million, adds another 10 million Mexican illegal immigrants to Pew's estimate, bringing the total number of Mexicans in the United States to 43.7 million.

29. Congressional Budget Office, "Migrants' Remittances and Related Economic Flows," February 2011, p. 2, http://www.cbo.gov/sites/default/files/cbofiles/ftpdocs/120xx/doc12053/02-24-remittances_chartbook.pdf. According to the U.S. Department of Commerce's Bureau of Economic Analysis (BEA), it's $20 billion a year.

30. Ibid., 17 (relying on data from the International Monetary Fund and the World Bank).

31. Steven Camarota, "Welfare Use by Immigrant Households with Children," Center for Immigration Studies, April 2011, http://cis.org/immigrant-welfare-use-2011 (analyzing the census's 2009 and 2010 Current Population Survey questions about welfare use in immigrant-headed families, legal and illegal, with at least one child under the age of eighteen).

32. Congressional Budget Office, "Migrants' Remittances," 10.

33. In surveys, 70 percent of illegal immigrants from Mexico say the money they send home is used exclusively for consumption; 96 percent say it is used for both consumption and savings. Ibid.

34. Patricia Laya, "Mexico's Richest Man Urges Young U.S. Immigrants into Workforce," Bloomberg News, August 13, 2014, http://www.bloomberg.com/news/2014-08-13/mexico-s-richest-man-urges-young-u-s-immigrants-into-workforce.html.

35. Editorial Board, "Migrants and the Middlemen," *New York Times*, July 9, 2014, http://www.nytimes.com/2014/07/10/opinion/migrants-and-the-middlemen.html?_r=0.

36. Editorial Board, "Migrants and the Middlemen."

37. Editorial Board, "Mr. Obama, Go Big."

38. Charles Lane, "A National Immigration Scandal," *Washington Post*, July 9, 2014, http://www.washingtonpost.com/opinions/charles-lane-a-national-immigration-scandal/2014/07/09/26dd4384-077e-11e4-8a6a-19355 c7e870a_story.html.

39. "Flaws in Immigration Laws," editorial, *New York Times*, September 29, 1997, http://www.nytimes.com/1997/09/29/opinion/flaws-in-immigration-laws.html.

40. "Salvaging the I.N.S.," editorial, *New York Times*, August 10, 1997, http://www.nytimes.com/1997/08/10/opinion/salvaging-the-ins.html. The *Times* also praised Clinton's INS commissioner, saying the "border is tighter, and the I.N.S. is deporting record numbers of criminal aliens." Sam Dillon, "U.S. Tests Border Plan in Event of Mexico Crisis," *New York Times*, December 8, 1995, http://www.nytimes.com/1995/12/08/us/us-tests-border-plan-in-event-of-mexico-crisis.html.

41. Hal Salzman, Daniel Kuehn, and B. Lindsay Lowell, "Guestworkers in the High-Skill U.S. Labor Market," *Economic Policy Institute*, April 24, 2013, http://www.epi.org/publication/bp359-guestworkers-high-skill-labor-market-analysis/.

42. Deborah Sontag, "Increasingly, 2-Career Family Means Illegal Immigrant Help," *New York Times*, January 24, 1993, http://www.nytimes.com/1993/01/24/nyregion/increasingly-2-career-family-means-illegal-immigrant-help.html.

43. Ibid.

44. Stuart Taylor, "Inside the Whirlwind: How Zoë Baird Was Monstrously Caricatured for the Smallest of Sins, Pounded by the Press and Popular Righteousness, and Crucified by Prejudice and Hypocrisy," *American Lawyer*, March 1993.

45. Sontag, "Increasingly, 2-Career Family."

46. Taylor, "Inside the Whirlwind."

47. Richard Berke, "Judge Withdraws from Clinton List for Justice Post," *New York Times*, February 6, 1993, http://www.nytimes.com/1993/02/06/us/judge-withdraws-from-clinton-list-for-justice-post.html.

48. "The *News & Record*'s Eighth Annual Roundup of the Idiotic, the Ironic and the Just Plain Weird," *News & Record* (Greensboro, NC), December 31, 2001.

49. "Poverty Overview: Context," World Bank, April 7, 2014, http://www.worldbank.org/en/topic/poverty/overview.

SPOT THE IMMIGRANT! CASE NO. 4: INDIAN SEX SLAVES IN BERKELEY

1. See Anita Chabria, "His Own Private Berkeley," *Los Angeles Times*, November 25, 2001, http://articles.latimes.com/2001/nov/25/magazine/tm-7947; Nirshan Perera, "Eyewitness in Reddy Case Foiled 'Family Affair,'" *India Abroad* (NY), August 24, 2001; and Diana Russell and Marcia Poole, "The Lakireddy Bali Reddy Case," Women against Sexual Slavery, 2003, http://www.wassusa.com.

2. Chabria, "His Own Private Berkeley"; Perera, "Eyewitness in Reddy Case."

3. See Chabria, "His Own Private Berkeley"; Lisa Fernandez, "Judge Urged to Be Tough: Petitioners Ask Maximum Penalty for Landlord in Sex Slave Case," *San Jose (CA) Mercury News*, June 8, 2001; Fernandez, "8-Year Prison Term Set: Berkeley Entrepreneur Sentenced for Importing Minors for Sex," *San Jose (CA) Mercury News*, June 20, 2001; Perera, "Eyewitness in Reddy Case"; and Russell and Poole, "The Lakireddy Bali Reddy Case."

4. Fernandez, "8-Year Prison Term."

5. Kayitha Sreeharsha, "The Bystander Problem," *India Currents*, May 13, 2013, https://www.indiacurrents.com/articles/2013/05/13/bystander-problem.

6. Ibid.

7. Eric Konigsberg, "Couple's Downfall Is Culminating in Sentencing in Long Island Slavery Case," *New York Times*, June 23, 2008, http://www.nytimes.com/2008/06/23/nyregion/23slave.html.

8. The *Berkeley High Jacket*'s story ran on December 10, 1999. See, e.g., Alyse Nelson, *Vital Voices: The Power of Women Leading Change around the World* (San Francisco: Jossey-Bass, 2012), 216.

9. Leslie Wayne, "Workers, and Bosses, in a Visa Maze," *New York Times*, April 29, 2001, http://www.nytimes.com/2001/04/29/business/workers-and-bosses-in-a-visa-maze.html (3,464 words). "Fraud in obtaining visas has also been found, including one tragic case in Berkeley, Calif., in which three Indian girls were brought in on H-1B visas for sexual purposes. The case came to light in November 1999 after one of the three, a 17-year-old pregnant girl, died of carbon monoxide poisoning in the rented apartment the girls shared. Last month, the landlord, Lakireddy Reddy, 63, a native of India worth more than $50 million, pleaded guilty in federal court in Oakland, as did two of his relatives. His two sons have also been charged in the case, in which the group is accused of fraudulently bringing Indian nationals to the United States for cheap labor and sex."

10.   Russell and Poole, "The Lakireddy Bali Reddy Case."

11.   See Chabria, "His Own Private Berkeley"; Fernandez, "Judge Urged to Be Tough"; and Fernandez, "8-Year Prison Term Set."

12.   Josh Richman, "Judge Won't Alter Sentence of a Man Who Smuggled Girls," *Oakland (CA) Tribune*, May 23, 2006.

13.   See Chabria, "His Own Private Berkeley."

CHAPTER FOURTEEN: EVERY SINGLE IMMIGRATION CATEGORY IS A FRAUD

1.   Scott Russell, "Back to the Future: New Wave of Refugees Lacks Family Connections for Support," *Minneapolis (MN) Star Tribune*, August 9, 2008, http://www.startribune.com/local/minneapolis/281197521.html; and Mila Koumpilova, "New Somali Refugee Arrivals in Minnesota Are Increasing," *Minneapolis (MN) Star Tribune*, November 1, 2014, http://www.startribune.com/local/minneapolis/281197521.html.

2.   Jonathan J. Cooper, "Oregon Governor's Fiancee Admits to Sham Marriage," Associated Press on Yahoo! News, October 10, 2014, http://news.yahoo.com/oregon-governors-fiancee-admits-sham-marriage-233257798—politics.html.

3.   Jenifer Warren, "Growers Hail Parts on Search Warrants, Amnesty," *Los Angeles Times*, December 7, 1986, http://articles.latimes.com/1986-12-07/local/me-1296_1_search-warrant; and Robert Pear, "Congress; Whither the Immigration Bill?," *New York Times*, July 15, 1986, http://www.nytimes.com/1986/07/15/us/congress-whither-the-immigration-bill.html ("The farmers, who have for years employed illegal aliens, say they need a ready supply of labor, or else their crops would rot in the fields").

4.   David North, "Lessons Learned from the Legalization Programs of the 1980s," ILW.com, http://www.ilw.com/articles/2005,0302-north.shtm.

5.   Ibid.

6.   Richard Behar, "The Secret Life of Mahmud the Red," *Time*, June 24, 2001, http://content.time.com/time/magazine/article/0,9171,162453,00.html.

7.   Ibid. See also Julie Farnam, *U.S. Immigration Laws under the Threat of Terrorism* (New York: Algora Publishing, 2005), 13–17.

8.   Behar, "The Secret Life of Mahmud." See also Farnam, *U.S. Immigration Laws*, 13–17.

9.   Behar, "The Secret Life of Mahmud."

10.   Ibid.

11.   Ibid.

12. Ibid.
13. Mary B. Tabor, "Bombing Suspect's Wife Holds On as Her Husband Awaits Trial," *New York Times*, May 4, 1993, http://www.nytimes.com/1993/05/04/ nyregion/bombing-suspect-s-wife-holds-on-as-her-husband-awaits-trial. html.
14. See, e.g., Ron Scherer, "Bombing Probe Shines Spotlight on Amnesty Law," *Christian Science Monitor*, March 16, 1993, http://www.csmonitor.com/ layout/set/r14/1993/0316/16012.html.
15. See, e.g., ibid.
16. See United States v. Ramzi Yousef, 327 F.3d 56 (2003), 97, available at http:// law.justia.com/cases/federal/appellate-courts/F3/327/56/625679/.
17. Ibid., 105.
18. Weston Kosova, "The INS Mess," *New Republic*, April 13, 1992, http://www. newrepublic.com/article/politics/the-ins-mess.
19. Vivek Wadhwa, "Our Real Problem Is the Brain Drain," response to "Do We Need Foreign Technology Workers?" on *Room for Debate* (blog), *New York Times* blogs, April 8, 2009, http://roomfordebate.blogs.nytimes. com/2009/04/08/do-we-need-foreign-technology-workers/?_r=0#vivek.
20. Wadhwa, "Chinese and Indian Entrepreneurs Are Eating America's Lunch," *Foreign Policy*, December 28, 2010, http://www.foreignpolicy.com/ articles/2010/12/28/chinese_and_indian_entrepreneurs_are_eating_ americas_lunch.
21. In 2000, 32 percent of skilled workers in Silicon Valley were foreign born, mostly from Asia. Piero Scaruffi, "The Survivors (1999–2002)," in *A History of Silicon Valley* (2010), http://www.scaruffi.com/politics/sil15.html.
22. Ron Banerjee, "Worker Visas That Work," *Financial Post*, April 17, 2013, http://business.financialpost.com/2013/04/16/worker-visas-that-work/.
23. Harichandan Arakali, "India's Startup Scene: Will VC Dollars Create the Next Amazon?," *International Business Times*, October 7, 2014, http://www.ibtimes. com/indias-startup-scene-will-vc-dollars-create-next-amazon-1696876.
24. Vinod Dham, "What the United States Can Gain from Working Closer with India," *Innovations* (blog) *Washington Post* blogs, September 29, 2014. http://www.washingtonpost.com/blogs/innovations/wp/2014/09/29/what- the-united-states-can-gain-from-working-closer-with-india/.
25. Neesha Bapat, "How Indians Defied Gravity and Achieved Success in Silicon Valley," *Forbes*, October 15, 2012, http://www.forbes.com/sites/ singularity/2012/10/15/how-indians-defied-gravity-and-achieved-success- in-silicon-valley/.

26. Renew Our Economy (verified account @renewoureconomy) tweeted: "Jean-Luc Vaillant and @kgimvalley, 2 of the 5 founders of @LinkedIn, were born and raised in Europe #smwnyc #smw14 #immigration," https://twitter.com/renewoureconomy/status/436510787923116032.

27. Benjamin Franklin, *Observations concerning the Increase of Mankind, Peopling of Countries, etc.* (Boston: S. Kneeland, 1755), available online at at https://archive.org/stream/increasemankind00franrich/increaseman kind00franrich_djvu.tx.

28. David S. Broder, "For Gates, a Visa Charge," *Washington Post*, March 19, 2006, http://www.washingtonpost.com/wp-dyn/content/article/2006/03/17/AR2006031701798.html.

29. "Bill Gates Lies to Congress about Microsoft's H-1B Wages," Programmers Guild, http://programmersguild.org/docs/bill_gates_lies_about_h1b_wages.html.

30. Ibid., citing *Seattle Post-Intelligencer*.

31. Craig Barrett, "A Talent Contest We're Losing," *Washington Post*, December 23, 2007, http://www.washingtonpost.com/wp-dyn/content/article/2007/12/21/AR2007122101919.html.

32. Ron Hira and Jerry Luftman, "Is There a Tech Talent Shortage?," Information Week, January 7, 2008.

33. Marco Werman, "H-1B Skilled-Worker Visas under Fire," *The World*, Public Radio International, March 6, 2013, http://www.pri.org/stories/2013-03-06/h-1b-skilled-worker-visas-under-fire.

34. James Pope Gray, "Contract, Race, and Freedom of Labor in the Constitutional Law of 'Involuntary Servitude,'" *Yale Law Journal* 119 (2010).

35. Ibid.

36. Ibid.

CHAPTER FIFTEEN: SHUT IT DOWN

1. U.S. Government Accountability Office, *Report to Congressional Requesters: Criminal Alien Statistics* (Washington, DC: Government Accountability Office, March 2011), 7 and 10, http://www.gao.gov/new.items/d11187.pdf.

2. See, e.g., William Branigin, "INS Accused of Giving In to Politics; White House Pressure Tied to Citizen Push," *Washington Post*, March 4, 1997.

3. Jessica Vaughan, "ICE Document Details 36,000 Criminal Alien Releases in 2013," Center for Immigration Studies, May 2014, http://cis.org/ICE-Document-Details-36000-Criminal-Aliens-Release-in-2013.

4.   Adriana M. Chávez, "Border Patrol Agents Arrest Two Convicted Sex Offenders," *El Paso (TX) Times*, January 20, 2011, http://www.elpasotimes.com/ci_17148642?source=most_viewed.

5.   Of course, inasmuch as it is impossible to get any details about Antonio Batista from a media obsessed with the behavior of drunken athletes on college campuses, perhaps Batista's family has been here for generations. If so, it doesn't say much for citizenship altering the sexual habits of immigrants.

6.   Sam Dolnick, "Asylum Ploys Play Off News to Open Door," *New York Times*, July 12, 2011, available online under the headline "Immigrants May Be Fed False Stories to Bolster Asylum Pleas," at http://www.nytimes.com/2011/07/12/nyregion/immigrants-may-be-fed-false-stories-to-bolster-asylum-pleas.html.

7.   Ibid.

8.   Simon Marks, "Somaly Mam: The Holy Saint (and Sinner) of Sex Trafficking," *Newsweek*, May 21, 2014, http://www.newsweek.com/2014/05/30/somaly-mam-holy-saint-and-sinner-sex-trafficking-251642.html.

9.   *Asylum Abuse: Is It Overwhelming Our Borders? Hearing Before the Committee on the Judiciary, House of Representatives*, 113th Cong. 2 (2013) (statement of Judiciary Committee Chairman Bob Goodlatte), http://judiciary.house.gov/_cache/files/121ef25f-d824-448e-8259-cce4edc03856/113-56-85905.pdf. ("Currently, data provided by DHS shows that USCIS makes positive credible fear findings in 92% of all cases decided on the merits. Not surprisingly, credible fear claims have increased 586% from 2007 to 2013 as word has gotten out as to the virtual rubberstamping of applications.")

10.   See, e.g., Brad Hamilton, "Dominique Strauss-Kahn 'Refused to Pay' Hooker Maid for Sex," *New York Post*, July 3, 2011, http://nypost.com/2011/07/03/dominique-strauss-kahn-refused-to-pay-hooker-maid-for-sex/.

11.   Dolnick, "Asylum Ploys Play Off News."

12.   See Andrew Jacobs, "Bronx Suspect May Be Rapist of 51 Women," *New York Times*, April 8, 1999, http://www.nytimes.com/1999/04/08/nyregion/bronx-suspect-may-be-rapist-of-51-women.html; Juan Forero, "Serial Rapist Gets 155 Years; Judge Suggests His Crimes Contributed to Diallo Shooting," *New York Times*, August 2, 2000, http://www.nytimes.com/2000/08/02/nyregion/serial-rapist-gets-155-years-judge-suggests-his-crimes-contributed-diallo.html.

13. Alan Feuer, "$3 Million Deal in Police Killing of Diallo in '99," *New York Times*, January 7, 2004, http://www.nytimes.com/2004/01/07/nyregion/3-million-deal-in-police-killing-of-diallo-in-99.html.

14. See, e.g., Angelica Medaglia, "Diallo Cousin Still Fights for a Foothold," *New York Times*, July 31, 2007, http://www.nytimes.com/2007/07/31/nyregion/31diallo.html?pagewanted=all.

15. Dean Meminger, "NY1 Exclusive: Amadou Diallo's Family Thinking of Buying Property Where He Was Killed," NY1, May 22, 2014.

16. Medaglia, "Diallo Cousin Still Fights."

17. Bonnie Gunn, "Diallo's Mother on Race and Justice," *Student Life* (Washington University in St. Louis), April 6, 2001, http://www.studlife.com/archives/News/2001/04/06/DiallosMotherOnRaceandJustice/. ("'He was killed because he fit a stereotype,' [Diallo's mother] said.") See also "Parents of Amadou Diallo Mark Five Years Since Their Son's Shooting—Part Two," NY1 News, February 3, 2004. ("It's always the old story—a young black man.")

18. Celia W. Dugger, "After a 'Kafkaesque' Ordeal, Seeker of Asylum Presses Case," *New York Times*, April 1, 1997, http://www.nytimes.com/1997/04/01/nyregion/after-a-kafkaesque-ordeal-seeker-of-asylum-presses-case.html?pagewanted=print.

19. Ibid.

20. Ibid.

21. Ibid.

22. Ibid.; C. O. Awani, "Nigerian Asylum Seeker Claimed False Identity," letter to the editor, *New York Times*, http://www.nytimes.com/1997/05/12/opinion/l-nigerian-asylum-seeker-claimed-false-identity-034002.html; and Dugger, "Doubts Cast on Identity of Nigerian Who Says He's a Political Refugee," *New York Times*, May 24, 1997, http://www.nytimes.com/1997/05/24/nyregion/doubts-cast-on-identity-of-nigerian-who-says-he-s-a-political-refugee.html?src=pm&pagewanted=2&pagewanted=print.

23. Ibid.

24. Ibid.

25. Suketu Mehta, "The Asylum Seeker," *New Yorker*, August 1, 2011, http://www.newyorker.com/magazine/2011/08/01/the-asylum-seeker.

26. Dolnick, "Asylum Ploys Play Off News."

27. Gerry Harrington, "Studies: 70 Pct. of Immigrants Want to Cry," United Press International, May 29, 2012, http://www.upi.com/Top_News/World-News/2012/05/29/Studies-70-pct-of-immigrants-want-to-cry/42731338276600/.

28. Sarah Stuteville, "Hate Crimes Inflict Fear That May Never Fade," *Seattle (WA) Times*, February 27, 2015, http://www.seattletimes.com/seattle-news/crime/hate-crimes-inflict-fear-that-may-never-fade/.

29. "New SPLC Report Finds Growing Hostility, Discrimination against Latinos in Wake of Alabama's Anti-Immigrant Law," States News Service, February 27, 2012, available online at the Southern Poverty Law Center, http://www.splcenter.org/get-informed/news/southern-poverty-law-center-report-finds-growing-hostility-against-alabama-latinos.

CHAPTER SIXTEEN: I WROTE THIS CHAPTER AFTER NOTICING HOW STUPID RICH PEOPLE ARE

1. David S. Broder, "Carter Yields Early in Night," *Washington Post*, November 5, 1980.

2. "U.S. Elections: How Groups Voted in 1984," Roper Center, http://www.ropercenter.uconn.edu/elections/how_groups_voted/voted_84.html.

3. The only other Republican presidential candidate to win *as* small a percentage of the black vote as Reagan in 1984—9 percent—was Bush in 2000, presumably because of Bush's fixation on sucking up to Hispanics. "U.S. Elections: How Groups Voted in 2000," Roper Center, http://www.ropercenter.uconn.edu/elections/how_groups_voted/voted_00.html.

4. Richard Harwood, "Middle Class Gave Victory," *Washington Post*, November 7, 1984.

5. Peter Brimelow has noticed. Peter Brimelow and Edwin S. Rubenstein, "CA GOP's Problem: Not Hispanics, But Whites (and, Of Course, Idiot Leadership)," VDARE, July 31, 2012, http://www.vdare.com/articles/ca-gop-s-problem-not-hispanics-but-whites-and-of-course-idiot-leadership.

6. "California: Presidential Election Results," NBC News 2012 Decision Desk, http://elections.nbcnews.com/ns/politics/2012/California/president/#.VM1ja2TF8rP.

7. Nate Cohn, "Why the Numbers Say Texas Stays Red," *New Republic*, August 12, 2013, http://www.newrepublic.com/article/114280/dont-bet-blue-texas-methodology-addendum. ("Unfortunately, Texas was scrapped from the state exit polls in 2012, making it hard to say just how much worse Obama performed than he did four years ago. But the county results make it quite clear that Obama fared much worse among white voters than he did in 2008.... Depending on the exact increase in Latino turnout, there's an outside chance that Obama fell into the teens... with 75-plus percent of the

white vote, Republicans will be able to endure incremental increases in the Hispanic share of the electorate for a long, long time.").

8. Ibid. ("In fact, Obama's performance among Texas whites last November was historically bad: Probably the worst in the history of the party.")

9. Vlae Kershner and Susan Yoachum, "Wilson Gambles on Immigration Plan: Must Appeal to Moderates," *San Francisco Chronicle*, August 12, 1993.

10. See, e.g., Bill Stall, "Governor Is One of Few to Dismiss Wilson Presidency," *Los Angeles Times*, November 12, 1994, http://articles.latimes.com/1994-11-12/news/mn-61607_1_pete-wilson. And *USA Today* editor Al Neuharth, for example, wrote that Wilson "is far out front for the rejuvenated Republican Party's presidential nomination."

11. Barbara Boxer won a regular Senate election; Dianne Feinstein won a special Senate election; and Bill Clinton won a presidential election.

12. William Safire, "Self-Deportation?," *New York Times*, November 21, 1994, http://www.nytimes.com/1994/11/21/opinion/essay-self-deportation.html.

13. Tim Golden, "The 1994 Campaign: Mexico; Government Joins Attack on Ballot Idea," *New York Times*, November 3, 1994, http://www.nytimes.com/1994/11/03/us/the-1994-campaign-mexico-government-joins-attack-on-ballot-idea.html.

14. B. Drummond Ayres Jr., "The 1994 Campaign: California; Huffington Admits Hiring Illegal Alien," *New York Times*, November 1, 1994, http://www.nytimes.com/1994/10/27/us/the-1994-campaign-california-huffington-admits-hiring-illegal-alien.html.

15. "After Proposition 187, Heading North," *Economist*, November 19, 1994 (source: Voter News Service).

16. The legislature flipped from 47 to 33 Democrats to a 40–40 tie. See Mark Gladstone and Carl Ingram, "Brown Reign as Speaker in Jeopardy," *Los Angeles Times*, November 10, 1994, http://articles.latimes.com/1994-11-10/news/mn-61020_1_speaker-willie-brown.

17. Ibid.; and Gebe Martinez, "*Los Angeles Times* Poll: A Look at the Electorate," *Los Angeles Times*, November 10, 1994, http://articles.latimes.com/1994-11-10/local/me-61453_1_times-poll.

18. Ken McLaughlin and Mary Anne Ostrom, "Proposition 187 Drew from Wide Spectrum in Lopsided Victory," *San Jose (CA) Mercury News*, November 13, 1994.

19. John King, "In Defeat, Democrats See Even More Trouble Ahead," Associated Press, November 10, 1994, http://www.apnewsarchive.

com/1994/In-Defeat-Democrats-See-Even-More-Trouble-Ahead/id-f516aee4edf7c2f29e239c14bbf431cd.

20.   Robin Toner, "Bitter Tone of the '94 Campaign Elicits Worry on Public Debate," *New York Times*, November 13, 1994, http://www.nytimes.com/1994/11/13/us/1994-election-advertising-bitter-tone-94-campaign-elicits-worry-public-debate.html?pagewanted=1; and Philip J. Trounstine, "Why Are Voters So Angry?," *San Jose (CA) Mercury News*, November 13, 1994 (white men "abandoned the Democrats in droves," while "it was women who stood for sanity").

21.   Cathleen Decker and Amy Wallace, "Wilson and Brown Cap Long, Grueling Race," *Los Angeles Times*, November 8, 1994, http://articles.latimes.com/1994-11-08/news/mn-60401_1_governor-campaigns.

22.   Martinez, "*Los Angeles Times* Poll."

23.   Tod Robberson, "Mexicans Angered by Proposition 187 Approval," *Houston (TX) Chronicle*, November 10, 1994.

24.   "Enrollment by Ethnicity for 2011–12," Educational Demographics Unit, California Department of Education, http://dq.cde.ca.gov/dataquest/Enrollment/EthnicEnr.aspx?cChoice=DistEnrEth&cYear=2011-12&cSelect=1932276—CEA+LOS+ANGELES+CO&TheCounty=&cLevel=District&cTopic=Enrollment&myTimeFrame=S&cType=ALL&cGender=B.

25.   *This Week with David Brinkley*, ABC News, October 30, 1994.

26.   "After Proposition 187."

27.   Byron York, "Winning Hispanic Vote Would Not Be enough for GOP," *Washington (DC) Examiner*, May 2, 2013, http://www.washingtonexaminer.com/byron-york-winning-hispanic-vote-would-not-be-enough-for-gop/article/2528730.

28.   Chris Cillizza, "The Republican Problem with Hispanic Voters—in 7 Charts," March 18, 2013, http://www.washingtonpost.com/blogs/the-fix/wp/2013/03/18/the-republican-problem-with-hispanic-voters-in-7-charts/.

29.   Belinda I. Reyes, ed., *A Portrait of Race and Ethnicity in California* (San Francisco: Public Policy Institute of California, 1996), Figure 9.1, http://www.ppic.org/content/pubs/report/R_201BRR.pdf.

30.   "U.S. Elections: How Groups Voted in 2012," Roper Center, http://www.ropercenter.uconn.edu/elections/how_groups_voted/voted_12.html.

31.   Greg Pierce, "Inside Politics," *Washington Times*, July 5, 2004, http://www.washingtontimes.com/news/2004/jul/5/20040705-122634-4736r/?page=all. (John Kerry on Al Sharpton: "[T]here was one person who consistently was

always there, keeping the peace and the compass going in the right direction. And that was Rev. Al Sharpton.")

32.   See e.g., Frank Bruni, "Bush Seeks to Boost Image with Minorities," *New York Times*, July 6, 2000, http://www.nytimes.com/2000/07/06/us/bush-seeks-to-boost-image-with-minorities.html; Alex Kuczynski and Matthew Purdy, "The Props Talk Back: Young Performers Mix Bush's Message with Their Own," *New York Times*, August 4, 2000, http://www.nytimes.com/2000/08/04/us/philadelphia-diary-props-talk-back-young-performers-mix-bush-s-message-with.html; Eric Schmitt, "Two Amigos Visit Toledo and Court Its Mexicans," *New York Times*, September 7, 2001, http://www.nytimes.com/2001/09/07/world/two-amigos-visit-toledo-and-court-its-mexicans.html; Christopher Marquis, "Bush, and Democrats, Plan Speeches in Spanish," *New York Times*, May 5, 2001, http://www.nytimes.com/2001/05/05/us/bush-and-democrats-plan-speeches-in-spanish.html.

33.   Frank Newport et al., "Democrats' Election Strength Evident across Voter Segments," Gallup, November 9, 2006, http://www.gallup.com/poll/25399/democrats-election-strength-evident-across-voter-segments.aspx.

34.   "Centrists Deliver for Democrats," Pew Research Center, November 8, 2006, http://www.pewresearch.org/2006/"11/08/centrists-deliver-for-democrats/.

35.   Bush's proposal for the partial privatization of Social Security was dead by early 2005.

36.   "Iraq," Gallup, http://www.gallup.com/poll/1633/iraq.aspx.

37.   "Washington Post-ABC News Poll," *Washington Post*, April 10, 2006, http://www.washingtonpost.com/wp-srv/politics/polls/postpoll_immigration_041006.htm.

38.   "Fact Sheet: The State of American Public Opinion on Immigration in Spring 2006: A Review of Major Surveys," Pew Research Center Hispanic Trends Project, May 17, 2006, http://www.pewhispanic.org/2006/05/17/the-state-of-american-public-opinion-on-immigration-in-spring-2006-a-review-of-major-surveys/.

39.   Similarly, between March and April of 2006, Harris Research polls showed that Americans citing immigration as a problem soared from 4 percent to 19 percent. Fourteen percent of respondents volunteered "immigration" as the main problem facing America in an AP/IPSOS poll in April—four times the number as before the Senate took up comprehensive immigration in March. In a Pew Research poll in April 2006, 10 percent of all respondents cited immigration as the nation's biggest problem, including nearly 20

percent of Republicans. Almost all of these poll results were available by subscription only—and, needless to say, few news outlets reported the findings. The poll results were, however, recorded at "Salience of Immigration Rising," Mystery Pollster, April 20, 2006, http://www. mysterypollster.com/main/2006/04/salience_of_imm.html.

40. Lydia Saad, "Halting the Flow Is Americans' Illegal Immigration Priority," Gallup, April 13, 2006, http://www.gallup.com/poll/22408/halting-flow-americans-illegal-immigration-priority.aspx.

41. "Fact Sheet: The State of American Public Opinion."

42. "Washington Post-ABC News Poll."

43. From "Fact Sheet: The State of American Public Opinion":
New York Times/CBS News Poll
Immigration is a serious problem: 89%
Very serious: 59%
Somewhat serious: 30%

FOX News/Opinion Dynamics Poll
Immigration is a serious problem: 91%
Very serious: 63%
Somewhat serious: 28%

Time Magazine Poll
Immigration is a serious problem: 89%
Extremely serious: 32%
Very serious: 36%
Somewhat serious: 21%

Quinnipiac University Poll
Immigration is a serious problem: 88%
Very serious: 57%
Somewhat serious: 31%

44. "Salience of Immigration Rising."

45. Ibid.; and "Fact Sheet: The State of American Public Opinion."

46. Jeffrey M. Jones, "Majority Says Population Growth Is Major Problem for U.S. Future," Gallup, July 14, 2006, http://www.gallup.com/poll/23770/majority-says-population-growth-major-problem-us-future.aspx.

47. "Conservative Leadership Declaration Opposing Amnesty/'Guest Worker' Proposals," HowardPhillips.com, June 19, 2006, http://www.howardphillips.com/archive0606.htm.

48. Julian Aguilar, "A Young Bush Works to Nurture Hispanic Roots within the Republican Party," *New York Times*, March 4, 2012, http://www.nytimes.com/2012/03/04/us/george-p-bush-works-to-nurture-hispanic-roots.htm.

49. "Young Voters Supported Obama Less, but May Have Mattered More," Pew Research Center, November 26, 2012, http://www.people-press.org/2012/11/26/young-voters-supported-obama-less-but-may-have-mattered-more/. See the chart "Among Young Whites, Men Backed Romney, Women Were Divided." Among eighteen-to-twenty-nine-year-old black men, 19 percent voted for Romney, and somewhat contrary to the chart's title, more white women supported Romney than Obama, 49 percent to 48 percent.

50. Walt Harrington, "On the Road with the President of Black America," *Washington Post*, January 25, 1987. (Jesse Jackson: "Reagan's politics are racist.")

CHAPTER SEVENTEEN: MOST OF OUR CHAMPIONS ARE SELLOUTS—HALF OF THE REST ARE INCOMPETENT

1. "Florida Senate Debate," *State of the Union with Candy Crowley*, CNN, October 24, 2010. (Rubio: "First of all, earned path to citizenship is basically code for amnesty. It's what they call it. And the reality of it is this. This has to do with the bottom line that America cannot be the only country in the world that does not enforce its immigration laws.")

2. See "Video: Marco Rubio Immigration," YouTube video, uploaded by user "CONREPALLIANCE," March 25, 2009, starting at 2:19, https://www.youtube.com/watch?v=PfmLR2l4cR4&feature=youtu.be&t=1m29s; and "Rubio in 2010: I'll Never Support Amnesty," WND.com, April 9, 2013, http://www.wnd.com/2013/04/rubio-in-2010-ill-never-support-amnesty/#svp8IHvwAbLROHtV.99.

3. "North Korea Least Favorable Among Nations," Gallup, February 19, 2014, http://www.gallup.com/poll/167489/north-korea-least-favorable-among-nations.aspx.

4. David McCabe, "Poll: Americans Dissatisfied with Immigration Levels," *Hill*, January 29, 2015, http://thehill.com/blogs/blog-briefing-room/news/231107-poll-americans-dissatisfied-with-immigration-levels#.VMppa98SXrQ.twitter.

5.   Steve Bousquet and Alisa Ulferts, "Hijackers Got State IDs Legally," *St. Petersburg (FL) Times*, September 16, 2001, http://www.sptimes.com/News/091601/State/Hijackers_got_state_I.shtml.

6.   Jeff Zeleny, "A Florida Bush Stays Silent, and to Many, That Says a Lot," *New York Times*, January 30, 2012, http://www.nytimes.com/2012/01/30/us/politics/jeb-bush-remains-silent-on-endorsement.html.

7.   Michael Luo, "Walking a Tightrope on Immigration," *New York Times*, November 18, 2007, http://query.nytimes.com/gst/fullpage.html?res=9E04E1DD1530F93BA25752C1A9619C8B63.

8.   Peter Baker, "Jeb Bush Talks Approach If He Runs for President," *New York Times*, April 7, 2014, http://www.nytimes.com/2014/04/07/us/politics/jeb-bush-outlines-campaign-strategy-should-he-choose-to-run.html.

9.   Trip Gabriel, "Stance on Immigration May Hurt Perry Early On," *New York Times*, September 24, 2011, http://www.nytimes.com/2011/09/24/us/politics/rick-perrys-stance-on-immigration-may-hurt-his-chances.html.

10. Gabriel, "Stance on Immigration."

11. Peggy Fikac, "Perry's Border Fence Quip Rings a Bell," *Houston (TX) Chronicle*, October 3, 2011.

12. Robin Abcarian and Maeve Reston, "Perry's View on Border Issues Is Migrating Rightward," *Los Angeles Times*, August 21, 2011, available online under the title "Perry Moves Right on Immigration," at http://articles.latimes.com/2011/aug/20/nation/la-na-0821-perry-immigration-20110821.

13. Adam Nagourney et al., "Immigration: Complex Test for 2 Parties," *New York Times*, April 28, 2010, available online under the title "Immigration Poses Complex Test for Democrats and Republicans," at http://www.nytimes.com/2010/04/28/us/politics/28immig.html.

14. See, e.g., Ashley Parker, "Paul Spells Out His Plan for Immigration Overhaul," *The Caucus* (blog), *New York Times* blogs, March 19, 2013, http://thecaucus.blogs.nytimes.com/2013/03/19/speech-by-paul-expected-to-support-citizenship-path-for-illegal-immigrants/. (Paul said he wanted illegals to "join the workforce and pay taxes.")

15. Raul Reyes, "Running Out of Time," *Daily Record* (Morristown, NJ), April 13, 2014, http://www.dailyrecord.com/story/opinion/2014/04/13/gop-running-out-of-time-on-immigration-reform/7553743/.

16. Jeremy W. Peters, "G.O.P. Groups Offering Cover on Immigrants," *New York Times* July 2, 2013, http://www.nytimes.com/2013/07/02/us/politics/gop-groups-offering-cover-for-lawmakers-on-immigration.html.

17. Jonathan Martin, "Tea Party Aims at Incumbents, but Falls Short," *New York Times*, April 5, 2014, http://www.nytimes.com/2014/04/05/us/politics/tea-party-challenge-to-republican-incumbents-fizzles.html.

18. Dave Montgomery, "Senate Approves Immigration Overhaul," *Philadelphia Inquirer*, May 26, 2006, http://articles.philly.com/2006-05-26/news/25401366_1_illegal-immigrants-immigration-law-senate-plan.

19. James O'Toole, "Santorum Tries Immigration as a Key Issue," *Pittsburgh (PA) Post-Gazette*, July 9, 2006; and Brett Lieberman, "Immigration Surfaces in Senate Race," *Patriot News* (Harrisburg, PA), July 30, 2006.

20. See, for example, the transcript of the February 22, 2012, presidential debate. "Full transcript of CNN Arizona Republican Presidential Debate," CNN, February 22, 2012, http://www.cnn.com/TRANSCRIPTS/1202/22/se.05.html; and Jeremy Duda, "Romney, Santorum Battle, but Little Focus on Arizona Issues," *Arizona Capitol Times*, February 22, 2012, http://azcapitoltimes.com/news/2012/02/22/romney-santorum-battle-but-little-focus-on-arizona-issues/.

21. Jay Root and Julián Aguilar, "Cruz Tries to Claim the Middle Ground on Immigration," *New York Times*, September 12, 2013, http://www.nytimes.com/2013/09/13/us/cruz-tries-to-claim-the-middle-ground-on-immigration.html?pagewanted=all&_r=0.

22. "Sen. Cruz Opening Statement on Immigration Legislation," press release, Ted Cruz, U.S. Senator for Texas, May 9, 2013, http://www.cruz.senate.gov/?p=press_release&id=140.

23. "Sen. Ted Cruz, R-TX, Intvd on Bloomberg TV," Analyst Wire, January 30, 2014.

24. Ashley Parker and Julia Preston, "Immigration Bill Allies Aim for Added Support," *New York Times*, May 23, 2013, available online under the headline "Allies of Immigration Bill Aim for Added Support," at http://www.nytimes.com/2013/05/23/us/politics/allies-of-immigration-bill-aim-for-added-support.html.

25. Rebecca Fater, "Romney: State Troopers Should Have Power to Arrest Illegal Immigrants," *Lowell (MA) Sun*, June 22, 2006, http://www.lowellsun.com/front/ci_3967655; and Fater, "Feds Say State Can Bust Illegal Immigrants," *Lowell (MA) Sun*, December 6, 2006, http://www.lowellsun.com/front/ci_4788846.

26. Evan Lehmann, "Immigrant Rights Advocates Denounce Romney Order," *Lowell (MA) Sun*, December 15, 2006.

27. Steve Leblanc, "Reilly, Romney Spar over Immigrant Tuition Bill," Associated Press, November 1, 2005.

28. So you know that I'm not tricking you, his full statement on immigration the Sunday before the midterm elections was: "You're going to see a provision, first of all, to secure the border. Second of all, to deal with those who come here illegally. And third, to make sure our immigration policies are more open and transparent.... That's going to happen. You're going to see a bill actually reach the desk of the president if we finally have someone besides Harry Reid sitting in the Senate. So, we're going to get it done."

29. Tony Lee, "Exclusive: Sarah Palin: Romney in 'Never Never Land' on Amnesty," Breitbart.com, November 2, 2014, http://www.breitbart.com/big-government/2014/11/02/exclusive-sarah-palin-romney-in-never-never-land-on-amnesty/.

INDEX